METAMORPHOSES OF GLOBAL LAW

This book takes an interdisciplinary approach to the relationship between law, time, and new technologies to explain the emergence and transformation of global law, with a special focus on the platform economy.

It describes the metamorphoses of global law based on an experimental understanding of legal theory that moves beyond the systematisation of dogmatic categories and the reproduction of prefabricated theories. It offers a novel and sound theoretical approach to the formation of society within a highly digitalised and platform-oriented world, drawing on the work of several influential authors, such as Niklas Luhmann, Gunther Teubner, Carl Schmitt, Jürgen Habermas and Lawrence Lessig, among others.

The book addresses the myriad questions that the platform economy poses for law, shedding light on the possibility of hybrid regulation – ie, a combination of political-constitutional external regulation and self-regulation by digital code – in an effort to move beyond simplistic notions of platform governance. It provides a comprehensive exploratory analysis of the phenomena of digitalisation, platformisation, big data, algorithms, and their significance for law in global society.

European Academy of Legal Theory Monograph Series: Volume 19

EUROPEAN ACADEMY OF LEGAL THEORY MONOGRAPH SERIES

General Editors
Professor Mark Van Hoecke
Professor François Ost

Titles in this Series

The Harmonisation of European Private Law
Edited by Mark Van Hoecke & Francois Ost

On Law and Legal Reasoning
Fernando Atria

Law as Communication
Mark Van Hoecke

Legisprudence
Edited by Luc Wintgens

Epistemology and Methodology of Comparative Law
Edited by Mark van Hoecke

Making the Law Explicit.
The Normativity of Legal Argumentation
Matthias Klatt

The Policy of Law
A Legal Theoretical Framework
Mauro Zamboni

Methodologies of Legal Research
Which Kind of Method for What Kind of Discipline?
Edited by Mark van Hoecke

Objectivity in Law and Legal Reasoning
Edited by Jaakko Husa and Mark van Hoecke

An Introduction to Comparative Law Theory and Method
Geoffrey Samuel

The Tapestry of Reason
An Inquiry into the Nature of Coherence and its Role in Legal Argument
Amalia Amaya

Democracy and Ontology
Agonism between Political Liberalism, Foucault and Psychoanalysis
Irena Rosenthal

Global Constitutionalism and Its Challenges
to Westphalian Constitutional Law
Martin Belov

Legal Validity: The Fabric of Justice
Maris Köpcke Tinturé

Paradigms in Modern European Comparative Law: A History
Balázs Fekete

Agency, Morality and Law
Joshua Jowitt

The Nature and Impacts of Noncompliance
Edvaldo Moita

Metamorphoses of Global Law: On the Interaction of Law,
Time, and Technology
Ricardo Resende Campos

Metamorphoses of Global Law

On the Interaction of Law, Time, and Technology

Ricardo Resende Campos

·HART·
OXFORD · LONDON · NEW YORK · NEW DELHI · SYDNEY

HART PUBLISHING

Bloomsbury Publishing Plc

Kemp House, Chawley Park, Cumnor Hill, Oxford, OX2 9PH, UK

1385 Broadway, New York, NY 10018, USA

Bloomsbury Publishing Ireland Limited, 29 Earlsfort Terrace, Dublin 2, D02 AY28, Ireland

HART PUBLISHING, the Hart/Stag logo, BLOOMSBURY and the Diana logo are
trademarks of Bloomsbury Publishing Plc

First published in Great Britain 2025

Copyright © Ricardo Resende Campos, 2025

Ricardo Resende Campos has asserted his right under the Copyright, Designs and Patents
Act 1988 to be identified as Author of this work.

All rights reserved. No part of this publication may be: i) reproduced or transmitted in any form,
electronic or mechanical, including photocopying, recording or by means of any information storage
or retrieval system without prior permission in writing from the publishers; or ii) used or reproduced
in any way for the training, development or operation of artificial intelligence (AI) technologies, including
generative AI technologies. The rights holders expressly reserve this publication from the text and
data mining exception as per Article 4(3) of the Digital Single Market Directive (EU) 2019/790.

While every care has been taken to ensure the accuracy of this work, no responsibility for
loss or damage occasioned to any person acting or refraining from action as a result of any
statement in it can be accepted by the authors, editors or publishers.

All UK Government legislation and other public sector information used in the work is
Crown Copyright ©. All House of Lords and House of Commons information used in
the work is Parliamentary Copyright ©. This information is reused under the terms
of the Open Government Licence v3.0 (http://www.nationalarchives.gov.uk/doc/
open-government-licence/version/3) except where otherwise stated.

All Eur-lex material used in the work is © European Union,
http://eur-lex.europa.eu/, 1998–2025.

A catalogue record for this book is available from the British Library.

A catalogue record for this book is available from the Library of Congress.

Library of Congress Control Number: 2025943301

ISBN:	HB:	978-1-50996-345-4
	ePDF:	978-1-50996-347-8
	ePub:	978-1-50996-346-1

Typeset by Compuscript Ltd, Shannon

For product safety related questions contact productsafety@bloomsbury.com

To find out more about our authors and books visit www.hartpublishing.co.uk.
Here you will find extracts, author information, details of forthcoming events
and the option to sign up for our newsletters.

Metamorphoses of Global Law is a winner of the European Award for Legal Theory. Past winners include:

Michel Paroussis (1994), *Theorie des juristischen Diskurses*

Emilios Christodoulidis (1996), *Law and Reflexive Politics* (Kluwer 1998)

Scott Veitch (1998), *Moral Conflict and Legal Reasoning* (Hart 1999)

Fernando Atria (2000), *On Law and Legal Reasoning* (Hart 2001)

Matthias Klatt (2002), *Making the Law Explicit* (Hart 2008)

Mauro Zamboni (2005), *The Policy of Law* (Hart 2007)

Amalia Amaya (2008), *The Tapestry of Reason* (Hart 2015)

Maris Köpcke (2011), *Legal Validity* (Hart 2019)

Irena Rosenthal (2015), *Democracy and Ontology* (Hart 2018)

Andrej Kristan (2015), *Law & Other Enigmas*

General Editors

Professor Mark Van Hoecke and Professor François Ost

This book is dedicated to Bruna, Lola and Vincent.

Foreword

RICARDO CAMPOS RAISES the extremely ambitious question of an appropriate determination of the fundamental legal structures in the digitised global society by undertaking an innovative and consistently interdisciplinary approach. The author systematically and historically seeks to reconstruct the relations between law, time and technology to derive guidelines for the socially appropriate development of digital law from its transformations, testing this approach in practice on the example of digital platform regulation. At the same time, he draws on the general debate on transnationalisation to substantiate his profound theoretical considerations on the relationship between law, time and technology.

The aim of the work is to make tangible the dependence of the general context of law by translating it into an equation with three unknowns: postfunctional differentiation society – development of digital technologies – new forms of linking law to time. In these three complexes, new historical and social contexts are addressed that concretely determine the opportunities and limits of a future digital law of platforms. The work programme is outlined roughly as follows: a reorientation of law production processes itself, which permeates the production of law within the institutional contours of the nation-state in the transnational context of the organisational form to the current phase of law production from the self-regulation of algorithm-driven digital platforms, bringing a new form of legal observation.

Each of these three stages has its own value. The central challenge, naturally, lies in the third step: preparing a new legal model and its concept of time for the globalised digital society from the confrontation with interdisciplinary discussion. Campos's original contribution is then to work in a peculiar intermediate area – in the triangle of social sciences, general legal theory and legal dogmatics – about the new development of a global digital legality.

Ricardo Campos's main thesis is that future society would no longer be characterised by functional differentiation but by a peculiar 'dispersion', and that law would be subject to a corresponding change in its form. The 'hybridisation' of law would be the consequence, that is, its situational intersection with heterogeneous social practices: with technologies, with new forms of knowledge generation, with the transformation of subjectivity, with the constitution of decision-making centres, and with the emergence of new communication media.

Given the self-imposed difficulties of the work, the exploratory and experimental approach offered here should be considered a success because Campos manages to develop new perspectives from the confrontation of theoretical positions at first glance mutually incongruous and historical development trends on the one hand, and the dogmatic and political-legal premises of a complex legal material on the other, thus making plausible the main thesis presented based on the normative material and the ongoing discussion on the reform of global digitality.

The comprehensive examination in the first chapter of the functional differentiation of society and its possible successor formation, a dispersion society, especially with its connection to legal institutionalisations, should be judged as particularly successful. Equally positive are the original interpretations of post-colonial developments and their effects on the globalisation of society and law in the second chapter. There is great scientific significance in penetrating these widely branching and hardly manageable masses of material, selecting legally relevant elements, reinterpreting them in a theoretically sophisticated way, providing them with sensitive and at the same time realistic evaluations, and further developing them towards concrete legal structures. I find these two chapters, theoretically and historically informed, to be particularly impressive also in view of the extensive bibliographic references with a high degree of precision. And they are written with heart and soul, that is, with great passion. A large amount of autonomous, original and independent thoughts becomes clear in reading the work. Campos recurrently seeks to rethink the theoretical and social material on the problem of a law of dispersion and formulates a series of original thoughts.

The other chapters, which seek to define a new form of law for social dispersion in the digital age, naturally must face the difficulty that the development of law is still entirely unpredictable. Campos's evaluations are therefore excellent experiments without claiming absoluteness, which is obviously not his fault but rather the contingency of future legal developments. Both the organisation chapter and the digitality chapter contain meritorious analyses of the new situation and at the same time have a quite exploratory and experimental character on the question of the restructuring of law and its semantics of time. The most important innovation for a legal model of digitality may lie in Campos's ideas about hybrid regulation, that is, the mix of external political-constitutional regulation and self-regulation through digital code. In this idea of cooperation lies an important core and at the same time a resounding argument against overly simplistic notions of platform governance from whose development more can be expected. Against the usual criticisms of the factual dominance of economic interests, a counterweight is presented here with the help of a normative prioritisation so resolute of the rationality of digitalisation in relation to its environment. Campos thus positions himself at the forefront of the current state of the global debate. Besides informative comments on the details of liability for immunity, it is to his credit that he precisely names the open questions that future research will have to address, especially highlighted in his view.

In conclusion, Campos works through a catalogue of important issues that the platform economy poses for law. He initiates the search for a new semantics of time for law that would have to engage with the predictive and future behaviour modelling of human behaviour of the platform business models. The new moment lies in a different modelling of temporality normativity by law. Individual behaviour would no longer be primarily modelled in this context by the state's sanctioning possibilities externally, but by an infrastructure of network protocols, digital self-executing mechanisms, where the processing of personal data and the direction of decision would basically occur in the medium itself. The fact that even the temporal forms of law are now subject to digitalisation – with this Campos probably highlighted an interesting aspect of the changes in the legal concept of time.

In summary, Campos delves into deep and often distant debates, re-linking them and placing them at the state of the art on the subject and often advances clearly and positively the boundaries set by the state of the art. He formulates in a profound and consistent language extremely complex social contexts and developments. On the theme of his work, he undertakes several daring incursions into impassable terrains, formulating his positions and reconstructions in detail that offers the reader a special intellectual pleasure of appreciation. In these exploratory adventures, he manages to elaborate positions with an extremely original, structured, and complex argumentation of a law of the global society suitable for the current digitalisation.

Gunther Teubner
Professor Emeritus of Private Law, Sociology and
Philosophy of Law, Johann Wolfgang Goethe University,
Frankfurt am Main. Member of the world's leading scientific
academies, including the British Academy (London),
Accademia Nazionale dei Lincei (Rome),
and Academia Europaea (London).

Foreword

THE AIM OF Ricardo Campos's book is to describe the evolution of global law based on an experimental understanding of legal theory, a legal theory that 'does not limit itself to the systematisation of dogmatic categories, the reproduction of pre-fabricated theories, and a clear disciplinary framework'. The history of this evolution starts with international law mediated through the state. In a first evolutionary step, classical international law is replaced by a novel 'dominance of relationship', as new techno-social developments require society to adopt a new form of sectoral coordination of social knowledge. Organisations then play a crucial role in the creation and evolution of the normativity of global society. This step is also described as the metamorphosis 'from state-centric to organisation-mediated global society law'. The second evolutionary step, which we are currently witnessing, is again characterised by a change in the way social knowledge is generated: Today, the production of social knowledge is no longer primarily oriented towards the organisational form but is increasingly focused on digital platforms where law-formation processes intertwine with a transnational dynamic of data- and algorithm-driven processes.

A searching, experimental approach to legal theory is deemed necessary by Campos because the law of global society is a law 'driven by existential unease'. This unease is identified in the fact that the global society, in a state of constant change, makes 'secure observational standpoints from which modern society could observe itself increasingly rare and precarious'. Law, like modern art, becomes a phenomenon that eludes clear definition, takes on a hybrid character, and connects with society itself. The law of a society or even a law of society may no longer exist because law, in a certain sense, is society itself.

The experimental character of this book is crucial for its understanding. Campos is not interested in the reproduction, variation and further development of an existing theory, such as systems theory. While he uses certain pieces of systems theory for his own orientation, his legal theory can be described as one oriented towards everyday social and cultural processes. Therefore, Campos also integrates fundamental sociological elements and insights, but within an open, flexible theoretical framework designed for self-learning and further enrichment of knowledge.[1] This framework is based on a fundamental

---

[1] Niklas Luhmann also often emphasised the limit of explicit knowledge, for example, in *Die Gesellschaft der Gesellschaft*. vol. 1, 1997, 38: the use of meaning in social systems always entails references to the unknown, to the excluded, to the indeterminable, to information deficits, and to non-knowledge itself. However, Luhmann's theoretical project is clearly concerned with the

limitation of conceptual-theoretical knowledge. This corresponds to the object of study: 'The legal normativity developing in global society is, rather, characterised by complex processes of hybridisation, i.e., by the intersection with various social practices, technologies, institutional processes, and new forms of knowledge generation. Legal normativity is more complex than any reduction of complexity through description.' Therefore, legal theory should 'function as an "experimental sandbox" or "knowledge laboratory"', providing 'a flexible testing, revision, and reflection space for new legal-social visions, theories, and approaches from the new contexts of a constantly changing society'. Without a cultivation of this experimentalism at its core – Campos also refers to this form with Rudolf Wiethölter as a 'poietic non-system' (poetisches Un-System) – the discipline of legal theory is reduced to an echo chamber of its own past, 'with serious risks of isolation'.

A central legal-theoretical node of the experimental network of the 'poietic non-system' is that since the early modern period, society has begun to shift its 'foundations of orientation from experience to expectation'. With this shift from a past to a future orientation, 'a certain alienation of humans from their history' is produced, as the past can no longer serve as the unbroken authority of society and law. 'The novelty of the modern era lies above all in its temporality.' Society opens up to an open future that it and its technical realisations create themselves, thereby expanding the possibility space of modern society. The resulting uncertainty about the future must henceforth be managed through self-produced artefacts, through 'the constant generation of fictions and artificial preconditions such as new social conventions'. Since the seventeenth century, a 'language of self-organisation' has been developing, which gradually also becomes conceptually explicit. This is understood as a decentralised form of social knowledge production, such as the conversion of politi-cal obligation from divine right to a (social) contract. Modern law is involved in the process of producing 'artificial, aesthetic artefacts ... and visual strategies', which also has an implicit dimension, and with the help of which society 'builds itself mechanisms and structures of temporal reference'. Law must – 'starting from the temporal problem of orientation stability' – as a self-artificial product 'establish a somewhat stable order beyond tradition'.

This raises the question of what a functional description of law, oriented towards comprehensive structuring and ordering processes, could look like. Campos first seeks an answer to this question in an examination of theoretical pieces of Niklas Luhmann's systems theory. For him, Luhmann is the author who, unlike many others such as Habermas, Dworkin, or Kelsen, views the

'conceptuality of a social theory', with 'conceptual decisions', in which the non-conceptual and prefigurations lying before language/semantics struggle to find a place, mainly as 'structural couplings' that remain quite marginal. Yet, it is precisely this dimension of the becoming of the new that concerns Campos, with the non-concept of poiesis in the sense of Vico, especially with the non-concept of (digital) technologies.

law from a perspective appropriate to the (temporal) problems of modernity and especially anchors the function of law in temporal reference. Luhmann's legal function revolves around a 'generalised temporal binding through the stabilisation of expectations', with the legal system itself seen as a 'dynamic order of permanent change'. Consequently, the expectations that Luhmann's law protects are not timeless stable legal ideas or principles of justice, but a legal normativity anchored in temporal binding, whose 'essence' lies in 'already allowing a preview of how others should behave in future situations'. It is about expectations that are characterised by the fact that they cannot learn, because any form of learning would relativise the certainty of the stability of future behavioural requirements. Luhmann early on turned against the 'symbiotic relationship between law and politics' and assumed their functional separation. But even for Luhmann, national institutional conditions such as a dense positive (printed) statutory law, state courts and state law enforcement apparatuses remained obvious at least as a prerequisite for the effectiveness and efficiency of securing normative legal expectations, while the validity of law emerges from the temporised system itself.

From this binding of law (and legal function) to the societal-wide safeguarding of normative expectations, Campos posits an original thesis that a discomfort arises in Luhmann's theory: because modern society is constructed by Luhmann from the outset as a functionally differentiated world society, systems theory must be able to comprehend and theoretically represent adequately a society that not only leaves behind the territorial boundaries of the nation-state as a social order principle and its institutionalisations, such as a dense network of courts and law enforcement agencies, but has established rapidly changing adaptable structures in various global (functional) systems such as science and economy. These systems do not simply operate in a lawless space, but also not in a legal space comparable to that of the nation-state with its institutionalisations, that is, without 'basic elements of a centralised order by enforcement mechanisms'. Campos writes:

> Law as a form of time binding and its inherent function of stabilising normative expectations could only be developed within the institutional conditions that have grown in the nation-state, such as the positivity of law, state legislation, state courts, and so on. Law as a form of time binding presents itself as a product of the institutional conditions existing in the nation-state anyway. The inadequacy of the structures of expectations for global society on which law builds its social function reveals a deep unease of Luhmannian theory with itself. At the heart of the systems-theoretical conception of law and politics gapes a wound, which is nothing less than the anachronism of a reproduction of nation-state characteristics that cannot keep up with the progressive aspirations of a global society. At this point, Luhmann admits to himself that the processes of world society are faster than the reality of the subsystems of law and politics (state), which try to catch up with them but still fail miserably at it even with a thirty-year gap. Sometimes it is brought up ironically, sometimes directly and forcefully, but without ever making it particularly clear

that a permanent self-doubt remains immanent to the theory. Moreover, Luhmann has not succeeded in formulating clear contours of what the contribution of law in world society would be to the shaping of social freedoms, as was the case with the experience of nation-states.

Campos sees a way to articulate the contribution of law to the shaping of social freedoms in global society more precisely than Luhmann himself in the work of Gunther Teubner. For Campos, Teubner's pluralist legal theory has many advantages over Luhmann's legal theory. While Luhmann narrows the legal function to securing normative expectations and does not engage closely with the processes of ordering and legal formation in global society, Campos finds in Teubner an endeavour that opens up to processes of spontaneous societal legal formation, allowing them to emerge from 'highly specialized fragmented dynamics'. Unlike Luhmann, Teubner can demonstrate that the role of law in the process of globalisation is not diminishing but increasing, especially through private regimes that emerge from heterarchical contexts. For Teubner, it is no longer the state or constitutional state that represents the ultimate point of reference for the validity and legitimacy of law, the tight coupling of law and politics, but rather a global law without a state. Indeed, since the constitutional turn, the question of constitution has been at the centre of Teubner's thought, the idea of a global constitutional law. However, global constitutionalism is guided by the interest in institutionalising the strong cognitive dynamics of global systems such as science and economy, while at the same time containing their expansion dynamics by prescribing procedures for self-restraint.

Teubner arrives at these possibilities because he does not interpret the increase of cognitive elements in global law as a dissolution of all legal normativity, but sees the global growth of spontaneous law itself and its 'strong cognitivism' as a novel legal normativity beyond mere expectation security, and especially does not abandon the 'structuring role of law for the other functional systems'. Campos meets these (and other considerations of Teubner's) with much sympathy, but he repeatedly expresses reservations about linking the structuring and ordering achievements of the legal system with the idea of functional differentiation; this is often dressed in the formula of 'maintaining a "border hygiene" of social processes'. Although this objection does not make it entirely clear how the determination of the legal function and the structure of normative expectation security are related (nor whether Luhmann and Teubner have comparable or different legal concepts), Campos is of the opinion that Teubner ultimately remains too attached to the notion adopted from Luhmann of a 'primacy of functional differentiation at a global level' and a related notion of the fragmentation of global law and its self-constitutionalisation in these fragments. Thus, Teubner's transnational constitutional pluralism suffers from a 'weak correlationism' (in the sense of Quentin Meillassoux). 'To make the thesis of the fragmentation of transnational law and all practical examples theoretically plausible, the primacy of functional differentiation itself must be absolutised without exception: without functional differentiation at the global level, there is no fragmentation thesis and no self-constitutionalisation thesis.'

Without entirely abandoning the orientations and insights gained in the engagement with Luhmann and Teubner, Campos gives his thinking an independent experimental theoretical framework throughout the course of the book. With this, the author aims to escape the impasse of systems theory, 'the maintenance of "border hygiene" of social processes', avoid Luhmann's diagnosed unease, and 'direct the conceptual efforts towards the process of transformation of global law'.

These conceptual efforts essentially look like this: the metamorphoses of global law are described as a process interacting with the metamorphoses of society itself. This is linked to the assumption that the law of global society develops in complex hybridisation processes at the various levels of society's own metamorphoses in an almost opaque manner. Campos assumes a silent 'dimension of "poiesis" inherent in complex society'. With C.A. Bayly, he speaks of a 'multicentric nature of social change in global society', of a dispersed 'contact culture' which is primarily the result of a new 'culture of goods' in the sense of Frank Trentmann and new communication and transport technologies. In other words, Campos presupposes a supporting role for material and infrastructural conditions for the phenomenality of legal normativity and its change, such as the alteration of spatial management possibilities through media and telecommunication technologies or modern logistics. For his concept of global law, technological innovations in the fields of transport, information and communication technologies are constitutive. Campos particularly emphasises the role of the 'materiality of communication', for example in the form of 'devices' such as the 'rotary machine as a printing technique', the phonograph and its development into the gramophone, or, in the sixth chapter, the materiality of data structures, algorithms or machine learning.

Thus, the experimental project continues to take shape: Campos is concerned with a history of the evolution of global law through a dynamic originating from technology and things, as it has particularly early altered life forms in cities worldwide. This dynamic is crucial for Campos, and its provisional end is found in a novel digital platform economy. Therefore, the last part of the work is devoted to an attempt to classify this developmental step in terms of legal theory, supported by the flow of materiality of intelligent technology. Catherine Malabou vividly spoke of this as the fourth blow to our narcissism: after Copernicus, after Darwin, and after psychoanalysis. This is also accepted by Campos, and an important intuition guiding Campos in his endeavour is the question of whether the 'function of law – a comprehensive structuring of social horizons – can only be a property of domestic legal development that will disappear with the increasing processes of de-bordering in global society – not least through the internet and increasing digitalisation'.

Against this backdrop, Campos reconstructs the emergence of modern international law from the international system of sovereign territorial states. Campos sees international law simultaneously as the origin of modern global law, where the state and the political stand at the centre. For Campos, however, it is crucial that the modern state and its stabilisation in the model of liberal democracy are attributable to both domestic and global societal conditions – and cannot be explained purely endogenously or purely domestically, as in the case of Kelsen or Jellinek. 'State and state transformation are phenomena that converge and cannot be placed in a historical sequence. They are products of the self-transformation of global society, insofar as there is a constant process of coevolution between the state, regional, and transnational levels – right from the start.'

This original dependency of the modern liberal state and its international law on a global society is deepened in an interesting and engaging interpretation of Carl Schmitt by Campos. In Campos's view, Schmitt emerges as the first postcolonialist. Campos is particularly interested in Schmitt's fears, 'which led him to project his writings against certain social developments associated with a liberal tendency of modern society'. Schmitt's crucial contribution is seen in his early adoption of a global perspective in international law, leading to an 'emergence of international law from a global logic', whose founding myth dates back to 1492 and not to 1648 (Peace of Westphalia). His thought demonstrates that the practices of international law of civilised nations are based on a concept of culture that cannot be separated from European expansion into overseas territories and colonialism. For Schmitt, the unity of the *ius publicum europaeum* ultimately rests on a Eurocentric concept of culture, 'which gives substance to the necessary homogeneity of the concrete order of European international law', whereas those not civilised in the European sense were excluded from this international law. Schmitt's perspective thus largely corresponds to a widely accepted postcolonial view of the performative power of European culture and language, which, however, fails to recognise that the demise of the concrete order resulted precisely from 'the formation of impersonal processes that cannot be traced back to a center of power'; it was the result of an 'impersonal dynamics of (world) society', which for Campos leads back to the multicentric nature of social change, a heterarchical contact culture, the culture of goods, and the technologies of communication and transportation, to immigration, consumption, free personal development in large cities, etc. 'Not a world of power, not a world of reason, but a world of things – the new social dynamics of large cities shaped the new fractures in legal-political concepts.'

This decentralised order is also referred to as one of the 'dominance of relationships'. It supersedes the dominance of the political and leads to a dispersion of sovereignty in global society. For this transition, the shift from court to city, the increased significance of urban daily routines, liberal individualism, and much more are of great importance,[2] leading to the emergence of 'urban cultures worldwide that display an increasingly uniform and distinct pattern of life' throughout the nineteenth century; and not just in Europe. Against this background, Campos interprets the emergence of international law and the prominent role of legislative treaties, the construction of the sovereign legal entity as part of this contractual relational form, which could now also be transferred to other states beyond the European domestic sphere, thus creating a whole new dimension of international legal actions beyond dynasties and marital and family networks. While the legal technique of legal fictions thus offers a new level of complexity for global relationships and allows the establishment of a legal order beyond tradition, in a further step, the development of a new *lex mercatoria* or private ordering within international law becomes possible, establishing itself as a basis for a system of private property and commercial exchange beyond the reach of the state. As consumption in large cities gains in importance, freer trade agreements, networks of trade consulates, and other international economic agreements emerge. This 'decentralized dynamics of contacts' is also referred to as the 'inner uncontrollable new dynamic of world society'.

The decay of the old order, the first evolutionary step in the development of global law after the *ius publicum europaeum*, is the movement 'from statecentered to organization-mediated global society law'. Campos now develops the view that the decentralised dynamics of contacts are associated with the breakthrough to the society of organisations in the second half of the nineteenth century and the rise of a novel, organisation-based knowledge generation. Their social and legal structures could no longer be depicted in political theories and demanded an opening to the inherent structures of industrial society. This is first discussed through the analysis of a correspondence between Carl Schmitt and Ernst Forsthoff: while Schmitt's partisan appears in it as a catechontic figure, as a retarder of the 'depoliticization of global society' and agent for creating 'culturally substantial large spaces', for Forsthoff it is clear that the partisan would 'remain a marginal phenomenon in the state of industrial society'. According to Forsthoff, this is largely due to the transformation of the state itself into an organisation-based technical state of public welfare, withdrawing the cultivation of power from the political to operationalise it 'increasingly through decentralized, organization-based structures'. This observation finds a theoretical counterpart in Foucault's theory of governmentality and also underlies his analyses of discipline and normalisation, which are asserted in an '(organization-based) biopolitics'.

---

[2] As shown by Gilberto Freyre, who developed a cultural theory of dense description before Clifford Geertz, this process in Brazil has its counterpart in the emergence of an urban bourgeoisie that only gradually manages to distance itself from the country's model and its culture of 'mansions', which is connected to Portuguese aristocratic culture.

While Schmitt, Forsthoff, and Foucault deal with the occurrence of all these phenomena in a political-power theoretical paradigm, Campos is concerned with the decentralised (dispersed) self-organisation processes of global society, now in the form of 'knowledge generation through organizations'. While the society of organisations is usually associated with issues of economic constitution, with labour relations, the working relationships of large groups organised around capital and labour, or the emergence of special organisations in international law, Campos initially focuses more generally on the exponential increase in mass-produced goods and technical devices traded and exchanged globally, on the functionality of various technologies such as telegraphy, power supply and rail transport, the necessity of standardising screws and threads due to the global spread of different machine types, etc, to emphasise the importance of organisations beyond war resolution. The legal-theoretical core thesis that unfolds here might be summarised as follows: in the organisation-mediated global society law, the normativity of global law is determined by private organisations and their sectoral knowledge regimes, which are reflected, among other things, in 'multilateral open-access treaties tailored to a subject area'. These generate new knowledge and technologies, whose goods shape the lifeworld of (urban) people and lead to a global interweaving of technical, economic, and legal structures, in particular a 'cognitive basis, dispersed process of global knowledge generation through technical standardization procedures within organizations'. Thus, global law contributes to initiating a process of creating conditions for the construction of a world culture. This chapter also leads to a focus on the juridification of cultural goods, thereby touching on a subject that might not seem to be of particular relevance to the processes of global law formation at first glance.

In the process of globalisation, intelligent information and communication networks play a central role. In particular, globally standardised knowledge technologies have gained enormous importance. Therefore, it seems consistent to refer to examples from the cultural sector when describing a novel capacity of the organisation to produce legal-technical knowledge management that has determined and changed global law since the late nineteenth century. Because the beginnings of the most recent constellation of global law, the transition to a 'new order of knowledge in the digital context', can already be observed earlier in the cultural area. Only through such historical retrospections can the plausibility of current assumptions be tested; otherwise, they risk remaining mere speculation. Moreover, copyright laws, which Campos addresses, form an important condition enabling global trade on online platforms in music, books, etc. Another important point is added: the dynamics of global society result not only from processes of meaning and success media like money but especially from the dynamics of technological knowledge first realised in England, understood as a cipher for material things and artifacts usable in everyday practice, which drive and enhance the impersonal dynamics of poiesis and remain to some extent opaque and ungraspable for subjects, even increasingly distancing themselves from the 'human sensory apparatus' with the rise of societal complexity. Therefore, Campos particularly focuses on the change in copyright law and the development of the protection of the 'shapeless voice', induced by a media 'pivot' (Friedrich Kittler). 'In this context, the media conditions are factors of cultural differentiation with serious implications for the conditions of juridification. Media become cultural techniques, especially as they constitutively produce new chains of action and connection.'

Digital media and the associated pivot now determine the global conditions of juridification. The digital, through artificial intelligence, big data, and algorithmisation, brings about a new order of knowledge with far-reaching impacts on people's life-worlds, which cannot yet be fully perceived semantically and thus must be experimentally grasped with certain 'threshold experiences' (or exploratory probes). This movement also devalues the close link in Luhmann's work between the concept of law and the category of expectation. A new temporal horizon emerges, no longer congruent with the culture of printing, referred to as a new era of 'uninfluenceability of simultaneous events', 'in which neither experience nor expectation provides a standard for the formation and stabilization of institutions and orientation for the actors' anymore. Luhmann's cognitive mechanisms have found a new embodiment in the digital technologies of the platform economy, giving clear and current contours to the prophecy of law as a European anomaly.

The concept of the network represents a threshold experience. With the network concept, 'a relational logic of social structure formation moves to the center of attention', which also affects the describability of law and articulates a crisis of demarcation that undermines the legal epistemology of the system; in its place comes the notion of an impurity of law or phenomena of blurring. This particularly results in an opening of the legal system to the production of social knowledge, so that the prevailing view is that legal normativity is produced in a structure of factors that are legal and extralegal in a strict sense. Campos views these manoeuvres, leading to the absurdity of a hybrid legal concept with a 'ghostly schematic openness', as productive, but he believes that the transformation of the internet into a digital platform economy, emerging over recent years, exhibits a mix of heterarchical and hierarchical elements that the semantics of the network concept no longer captures; the platform is not just a network. 'The success of platforms as a business model arises precisely from this duality, from this ambivalence inherent in the concept, integrating claims of totality and freedom, heterarchy, and hierarchy in one model.'

The institutional framework of platforms, 'data structures, algorithms, or machine learning', is a farreaching phenomenon that not only changes knowledge generation but also potentially our understanding of political economy and commercial markets. The challenges arising from this would structurally overburden a work on the metamorphoses of global law. Therefore, Campos limits his focus to a small segment of changes and their legal consequences, specifically the depiction of changes in the public sphere where social networks become producers of everyday knowledge. Here the author outlines in a dense but extremely stimulating manner how the public sphere initially transforms from a decentralised impersonal culture based on the exchange of opinions and information among individuals to an organisation-based form. 'Regardless of Jürgen Habermas's idealization of the public sphere of a society of individuals, over the course of the 20th century, the public sphere began to structure itself around the symbiotic relationship between new technologies – radio, print, television, etc – and organizational forms. The "loss of publicness within large organizations" is compensated for on one hand by the much greater reach of new information dissemination technologies, which democratize access to information, and on the other hand by the competition between organizations and the media.' While the public sphere of organisations could still be constituted at the nation-state level, Campos sees in the new regimes of the digital economy a global technological infrastructure to which legal normativity is also linked. This does not create a vacuum of legal normativity itself, but the combination of verticalising elements with hierarchical elements produces novel opportunities for freedom, but also clear dangers of rights violations. An example of this is the early regulatory history of the platform economy in the United States, the creation of Section 230 of the Communications Decency Act (CDA). According to Campos, this has gone hand in hand with court reactions too tied to the organisational paradigm, ultimately shifting legal protection to self-regulation by the platforms (and the guarantee of their immunity in case of third-party rights violations), which can only be addressed through a kind of proceduralisation of fundamental communication and media rights.

What a piece of work! On one hand, there is a connection of ever-new aspects, materials and insights that occasionally leave the reader dizzy and do not always make it easy to find the red thread in a sea of intelligent and guiding references, also because some thoughts oscillate in different formulations and are elusive here and there. On the other hand, there is indeed a wealth of ideas and associations, a continually reconfiguring network of surplus meaning that would suffice for ten more books. All this coupled with a clear analytical vision, a sense for nuances and subtle distinctions that demonstrate the excellence of this author on every page and the impressive level at which his work argues.

The greatest merit of this work, in my opinion, is that it demonstrates that the concept of globalisation is one of the most problematic ever formed. There is not 'the' globalisation, but at best repeated new impulses of globalisation and global legal formation processes since the discovery of the New World, which Campos convincingly differentiates – statehood, large organisations, networks, and platforms. However, these three evolutionary steps or metamorphoses in the process of global legal formation, as this book also shows, cannot in turn be separated from nation-state developments or, thinking of Silicon Valley, from regional developments and the social practices that emerge from them, to which the law must connect if it wants to be part of a way of life and not just a political project. By insisting, like the Scottish Enlightenment, on a coevolution of the national and transnational as a condition of statehood and also as a condition of transnationality, and by highlighting the significant importance of knowledge and technology paradigms for global legal formation, Campos contributes significantly to a sober assessment of 'globalisation' and its law. Rather than further polarising the intellectual discourse with scenarios of 'power shifts' in favour of 'large corporations' and the end of law in 'surveillance capitalism', Campos concentrates his intellectual energy on describing how global law has changed over the last hundred years and in which direction questions of platform regulation can be discussed and led to balanced solutions in the future.

To conclude with a critical remark, perhaps what changes in the digital world is not so much the future orientation itself, but rather 'the modeling of forms of society's temporal binding', the modelling of expectation, and not so much the relationship between security and uncertainty, as sometimes suggested by Campos. It would then be important to describe this transformation history more precisely, and at this point, it might be helpful not to separate the temporal dimension too strongly from the factual dimension. The metamorphoses of global law themselves repeatedly refer – in a pleasantly productive and original manner – to the absurdity of a 'hybrid legal concept' that thinks of the law more like an assemblage or structure without permanently stable boundaries with strong non-conceptual components.

Thomas Vesting
Professor of Public Law, Legal Theory and
Media Theory at Johann Wolfgang
Goethe University in Frankfurt am Main.

Preface

THIS BOOK IS the result of the doctoral work presented at Goethe Universität Frankfurt am Main, Germany, at the turn of the year 2020/2021. It was supervised by Prof. Dr. Dr. hc. mult Gunther Teubner, with Prof. Dr. Dr. hc. Thomas Vesting as co-supervisor, and the chairman of the defence panel was the director of the Max Planck Institute for Legal History and Legal Theory, Prof. Dr. Thomas Duve. The original work received the highest distinction *summa cum laude*, having been written and presented in German, which is why the English text may exhibit cadence and linguistic structure characteristic of the German language. The German version won the Werner Pünder Award in 2021 as the best work in the humanities related to the theme of freedom in contemporary times at Goethe Universität Frankfurt am Main. The English version won the award from the European Academy of Legal Theory/Académie Européenne de Théorie du Droit (EALT) in 2022.

The work reflects the intellectual environment of the *Frankfurter rechtstheoretisches Kolloquium*, a traditional weekly seminar on Legal Theory at the Goethe Universität Frankfurt am Main Law School, deeply rooted since the post-war period under Franz Böhm – creator of ordoliberalism together with the economist Walter Eucken – and from the early 1960s under his chair successor Rudolf Wiethölter, and at the end of the 1990s, Gunther Teubner. Since 2013, with Gunther Teubner's retirement, Thomas Vesting, Rudolf Wiethölter, and I – and occasionally Gunther Teubner – have been maintaining this tradition, which has always included participation by leading figures in law and related sciences such as Jürgen Habermas, Jan Assmann, then president of the German Constitutional Court Andreas Voßkuhle, Marietta Auer, Axel Honneth, Michael Stolleis, and many others. Being able to teach alongside great names in law and, above all, to humanise various theoretical frameworks through personal contact and interaction, also provided a distinct perspective on theories, thoughts and authors, especially a keen eye on their most intimate theoretical vulnerabilities. The interdisciplinary hallmark of the *Frankfurter rechtstheoretisches Kolloquium*, the understanding of law as a constantly transforming social phenomenon, and the recognition of the inherent incompleteness of any grand theory deeply marked this work.

In this sense, viewed today, the work is much more a 'second-order observation' of transforming social processes, and of how authors and thought traditions have observed these transformations, especially aiming to identify and address the blind spots in these authors' and traditions' readings of said processes. Besides the product of observing blind spots, the book also reflects the attentive gaze of three people who supported, accompanied and fostered it with much love and patience: Bruna, Lola and Vincent. The first, my wife, always believed in this work, even when I myself doubted it. The second, Lola, born at the beginning of this journey, awakened me to a world of affection hitherto unknown. The third, Vincent, born almost at the end of the work, brought the completeness of my family core and the essential energy for its completion.

Ricardo Campos
Frankfurt am Main, 21 September 2022.

Contents

Foreword .... *xi*
Foreword .... *xv*
Preface .... *xvii*

Introduction 1
    A. The Referencelessness of Modern Law 1
    B. Book Approach and Clarification 3

1. **Anomaly as Legal Development** 8
    A. Niklas Luhmann's (World-)Society: The Discomfort in
        Systems Theory 8
        I.   Introduction: From Misspecification to Anomaly 8
        II. The Self-Evidence of a Theory: The Fact of the World
            Society 10
        III. The World (Society) of Systems Theory 13
    B. Teubner's Rescue of Systems Theory? Differentiation Theory
        Beyond the State 17
        I.   Introduction 17
        II. The Reinvention of the Systems Theory (of Law) for the
            World Society 18
        III. Law without Authority? Validity without Third Parties? 20
        IV. The Paradox of Validity and the Validity of Paradox:
            The Law of the World Society 22
        V. Thinking in Terms of Correlates/Correlations 26

2. **Law as a Form of Time Binding** 29
    A. Introduction 29
    B. The Change in the Semantics of Time: The Crisis of
        Political Obligation 30
    C. The Invention of the Contingent Future 32
    D. Time and Law: The Change in the Semantics of Law 34
    E. Outlook: A New Attempt at the Metamorphosis of Law in
        Global Society 38

3. **The Disintegration of the Old Order** 40
    A. Introduction 40
    B. Dominance of the Political 42
        I.   Reading Carl Schmitt: The First Postcolonialist? 42

       II. Taking Names, Giving Names, Taking Land: The Linguistic
           Dimension of the Law of World Society 44
       III. The Fragmentation of the Ius Publicum Europaeum:
            World Society Beyond Westphalia...47
       IV. The New Productivity of the Individual and the
           Disintegration of the Old Order..50

4. **The Birth of the New World from the Culture of Dispersion** 55
   A. Dominance of the Relationship...55
      I. Introduction 55
      II. The Dispersion of the Global Society 56
      III. The Birth of a Discipline: International Law............................57
      IV. The Sovereign Legal Person and the New Form of Relation
          of Global Society 58
      V. The Disintegration of the Old Order and the Transformation
         of Trust in the World Society...60
      VI. Coevolution of the National and Transnational......................62
   B. World without Unity..63

5. **The Law of Organisations** 65
   A. Introduction 65
   B. The Anachronistic in the Political: The Structures Inherent in
      Industrial Society..66
   C. The Emergence of Organisations Beyond War Management............71
   D. The Legalisation of Cultural Goods...72
      I. New Media, New Laws? 74
      II. The Management of Legal Normativity by Organisations 75
      III. Transnationalisation of Authors' Rights 78

6. **The Law of Platforms**..82
   A. Introduction: What does the Digital Mean?......................................82
   B. On the Threshold after the Threshold: Knowledge, Networks,
      Data and Platforms..85
      I. On the Threshold: Networks..85
      II. After the Threshold: Platforms...89
      III. A New Political Economy of Platforms?...................................91
   C. The Public in Transition: From Organisation to Platform 94
      I. The Founding Myth of a New Economy: § 230 CDA................97
      II. The Consequences of the New Immunity Liability for the
          Collective Dimension of Communication 99

D. A New Regulation for the (Transnational) Collective Dimension of Communication?..101
E. The Time of the Platforms..102

Outlook..107

Notes *109*
Bibliography *161*
Index *187*

Introduction

A. THE REFERENCELESSNESS OF MODERN LAW

THE LOGIC OF modern legal thought is in crisis. The tradition of formalism – which feeds on its own internal conceptual contexts of an egocentric discourse, in which the mere description of institutes, concepts, and judicial decisions is sufficient to describe law and distinguish it from other social practices – is no longer sufficient for the apperception of the central role of law in shaping modern society. Not only does law influence social processes and practices, but society itself acts on law as a driving force for its transformation. In this sense, law is never a product of egological self-referentiality. Nor is law merely a product of national legislation, as the sociologist Eugen Ehrlich implied in his writings on the patchwork region of Bukovina in the early twentieth century.[1] Neither is it a mere resonance chamber of economic relations – a view widely present in Marxist legal theory and in the modern frameworks of economic analysis of law.[2] Nevertheless, moving away from an economic determinism of law does not mean that law is detached from society.

Just as law is not reducible to economic determinism, neither is it reducible to a democratic determinism. Counterintuitive as it may seem, law interacts co-constitutively with various social dimensions that are not exclusively related to the production of social bonds through collective decisions. Several (fundamental) rights aim at promoting the production of social knowledge and communicative diversity,[3] and this is where an indispensable function of modern law lies, in which it also cultivates decoupling from the will of the sovereign majority or the will of a sovereign. In this respect, favouring a collective dimension through emergent effects of the exercise of rights, in which law is also involved, cannot be reduced to the construction of a *volonté générale*.[4] One could even recall here modern institutions, such as that of constitutional jurisdiction, which present themselves as a form of demarcation of an 'authoritarianism of will or democracy' in the safeguarding and preservation of an individual dimension that is not at the disposal of will-forming processes. In other words, law is also not a pure product of the determinism of a will, be it tyrannical or democratic.

The impracticalities that arise from an unambiguous determination of the legal phenomenon, regardless of whether it derives from law itself or from an extrinsic origin, reveal its thoroughly hybrid character.[5] And it is precisely this hybrid character of law, distanced from normative causal determinism, that makes it modern. Law feeds on contentious and fragile foundations, which law itself contributes to create and is influenced by.

This book deals with such a modern legal phenomenon, which distances itself from any determinism, be it God, nature, reason, state or itself. Modern law does not struggle constantly only against intra-social colonisation processes that arise from deterministic or colonising tendencies.[6] The underlying function of modern law is to both deal with and relate two normative (legal) layers, such as the more evident layer of norms – commands, decisions and institutes – and the more latent, opaque and difficult-to-access infrastructure of trans-subjective social processes and new technologies.[7] Thus, there would also be no law of *one* or even *of* society: law is, in a sense, society itself.

The title of this book, *Metamorphoses of Global Law*, is meant to suggest that the metamorphoses of law are at the same time metamorphoses of the society in which law has been developed, without having any teleological determination of meaning in both temporal and social sense. As repeatedly emphasised by Rudolf Wiethölter: it can be, but it does not necessarily have to be. Law entangles itself in numerous social practices without necessarily completely identifying itself with them and without giving any guarantee of the temporal duration of such entanglement. The lack of determinacy of law is not seen here as in the semantic sense given by Herbert Hart in the discussion of analytic theory of law,[8] but as in a normative-social determinism of law as a social institution enmeshed in complex and hybrid social processes, that does not allow itself to be appropriated by potentially totalitarian formulations (or totalitarian visions).

Metamorphosis or transformation is also associated with a tendential course of detachment from one's own being or nature. In his Lectures on Aesthetics, Hegel, describing transformations, contrasts the meaning of the spiritual with that of the natural, and metamorphosis or transformation appears as a process of degradation of the spiritual.[9] In a sense, the long process of secularisation of law and its lack of a unified and solid foundation, fed by a deterministic origin, present themselves as processes of degradation of the static and perennial normative foundations of law. This semantics of degradation is also used by sociologist Niklas Luhmann to explain the evolution of law in global society. According to Luhmann's view, law as we know it is a European anomaly or an aberration of a space-time progression that is unlikely to be repeated in the further development of global society. Degradation, anomaly, or misspecification of human development are descriptions of a law that is in constant movement and at the same time contains no external guarantee of its own inherent nature, validity, or normativity.[10]

The law of global society or the law of new technologies is a law driven by an existential unease. In this respect, law exhibits the same contours of crisis as contemporary art. What makes an object a work of art today? Arthur Danto, when validating a particular object as a work of art based on the observation of Andy Warhol's Brillo Boxes, distances himself from the authoritative figure of an empowered person or elite that would give an object the official status of a work of art.[11] Rather, according to Danto, it is crucial that the field of art, which has also undergone a long process of 'degradation' characterised by a renunciation of any external determinism of its essence, belongs to an institutionalised discourse that defines whether or not an object is a work of art.[12]

The law of global society faces similar challenges. The existential uneasiness resulting from the process of 'degradation' or metamorphosis deprives law of a deterministic guarantee of essence. No external authority can guarantee law, be it reason, the state, or God. This also applies to law's own self-reference and to any notion of its uniqueness and irreplaceability. Therein lies the modern character of law: dealing with an indeterminate complexity and also being an engine for the construction of new complexities and relations. The existential uneasiness that arises from an origin crisis poses new challenges to law insofar as it becomes increasingly hybridised and embedded in (extra-legal) social practices. The transnationality of law is a consequence of such development, for it emerges from the fate or entanglements between law, society, new technologies and new economic models, rather than a law that simply emerges outside states.

Who would authorise themselves to call a particular social practice 'law' in this context? Particularly with the advent of new computer technologies, normative structures that shape, influence, or even make possible the exercise of (fundamental) rights, no longer have their legal provenance from reason or from the state. On the contrary, these new normative structures tend to structure the individual's field of action – and that of the state – resting upon modelling of the technological medium and the designing the business model of the digital platforms themselves. Cross-border effects are part of everyday operations of the medium or technology. A law that is epistemologically constituted from state-oriented semantic models finds its greatest existential crisis in the development of these new technologies and the transnationality inherent in these technologies. Was the 'old' law merely a historical anomaly? Or does this lead to rediscovering the importance of the legal structures of the nation-state? Can current developments be reduced to the *transnational vs. national* polarisation? These are some of the issues that will be addressed in the course of this book.

B. BOOK APPROACH AND CLARIFICATION

This book attempts to trace the new evolution of law, which during its development tended to lose its own roots and fixed references, regardless of whether they were linked to the nation-state institutional frameworks or to the figure of a third party outside law that ensured its legitimacy and validity. In this regard, the book has a clear initial point of reference: it starts from the theoretical self-doubt of the sociologist Niklas Luhmann about the further development of law in global society. His anxieties and uncertainties project onto the realisation of a society increasingly focused on new technologies and cross-border effects, for which the traditional mechanisms of law and politics, centred on the nation-state, find it increasingly difficult to play the same role they played up to the time when he was writing his major works of the mature phase. The 'Luhmannian malaise' or 'Luhmannian uneasiness' described here serves as a fulcrum for the argument of this book, for it is accompanied by a theory that succeeds in describing the modern conditions of law with great precision.

Beyond the Luhmannian malaise or uneasiness mentioned here, this book is concerned with the development of law in global society and its preconditions. Although the book starts from a systems-theoretical question, it also points out unobservable elements of systems theory, i.e., the hybridisation and order-forming processes that emerge within global society. Communication alone does not define what constitutes a global society; rather, it is the order-formation processes and practices that form society and shape the contours for individual and institutional action. Although in principle they have certain concrete characteristics, such social structures are often latent and elude an overarching description. At this point, the experimental character of this book becomes clear, as it seeks to distance itself from template-like paradigms that only lack application. A logic of experimental contacts between different disciplines should be cultivated and then tested.[13] The boundaries of these disciplines, which have become contingently institutionalised in the course of history, also do not prove to be a firm and substantial guarantee of eternal stability – in a similar way to the phenomenon of law. Under present conditions, no discipline can claim to have privileged access to reality on its own. Nor can any discipline claim to be able to fix its current disciplinary boundary marker for eternity.

From the chosen starting point, the dilemma of global society is not primarily a normative concern. It is not a matter of outlining a normative, institutional design so that global society can develop a 'healthy' legal-political integration. Nor is it a matter of replicating a form of social differentiation developed within the framework of a few nation-states in global society. Rather, the legal normativity that develops in global society is characterised by complex processes of hybridisation, i.e., intersections with different social practices, technologies, institutional processes, and new forms of knowledge generation. Any description of legal normativity reduces its complexity. Sometimes legal normativity permeates issues of the constitution and transformation of subjectivity. Sometimes it permeates the constitution of decision-making centres – and their decay. Sometimes it permeates knowledge-generation structures. Sometimes it permeates the emergence of new media, or it permeates the process of migration into technology.

This book aims to take one – among several – possible points of observation and description for the conditions and processes that can structure the law of world society. Thus, it does not intend to be a work *in a paradigm*, but to put forth a work on paradigm – as always pointed out by the German jurist Rudolf Wiethölter – in which the effects resulting from the correlations of authors and disciplines are placed higher than the authors and disciplines themselves. The central role of legal theory for legal thought is also evident here. After the long process of degradation of the essence of law – in the sense described above – legal theory can no longer fulfil the function of restoring a lost, nostalgic integrity of law.[14] Rather, legal theory should function as an 'experimental sandbox' or 'knowledge laboratory'[15] by providing a flexible testing, revision, and reflection forum for new socio-legal visions, theories, and approaches in the new contexts of an ever-changing society. Certainly, addressing legal dogmatics is one of the important reflection materials for legal theory, but nevertheless it cannot be reduced to a systematisation of dogmatic institutions. Both law and legal dogmatics are part of broader social processes and social constraints that they themselves cannot guarantee, much less determine. A neighbourhood-informed theory of law must seek precisely to stimulate experimental contacts between descriptions of social processes, authors, disciplines and legal dogmatics in order to connect and locate the legal phenomenon within a broader perspective and its inherent conditioning factors, which we call society. Meanwhile, this book attempts to show a possible reconstruction of the relationship between law and society, or law and technology, using the example of global society.

Chapter 1 addresses the theme of Luhmannian unease expressed in the concluding sentence of his project on the law of society. When the book in question was published in the 1990s, Luhmann, faced with the development of a society that clearly diverged from the development of law in the institutional context of the nation-state, puzzlingly questioned his own project of law. The question of whether law could also play the role of a 'katechon of de-differentiation' in world society, as it used to do within the institutional frameworks and contours of the nation-state, is exemplified by the new developments in systems theory on the subject of the fragmentation of law in world society. However, before embarking on a possible replication of the social function of law's structuring role in global society, it is necessary to delineate the meaning of the function of law in modern society as a form of time-binding in which law structures the invention of a contingent future of society by creating mechanisms for coping with an increasingly uncertain future – which is done in Chapter 2. Against the background of the importance of law for the construction of the temporal dimension of society, it becomes clear that modern law increasingly loses fixed social references and becomes a fluid law that poses problems for the question of its validity as a social practice. In this context, it is more important to trace order-building processes within this global society than to assert the existence of a global society resulting from the communicability of new technological media.

Chapter 3 deals with the order-forming processes of global society. From the methodological point of view, the objective of the chapter centres on seeking the cultural conditioning factors and immanent structures of global society, thus distancing itself from the typical and recurrent derivation of the existence of a global society as a product of the communicability resulting from the new technologies. To this end, it is crucial to examine which social and structural elements have led to the disintegration of the old order, that was centred on the so-called *ius publicum europaeum*. The process referred to in Chapter 4 as the 'birth of the new world from the culture of dispersion' attempts to draw attention to the complex process of co-evolution between national and transnational levels of law, a process that cannot be reduced to the control of a sovereign will or power. Reading this change as a shift from a period of dominance of the political in the Schmittian sense to a period of tendential hegemony of relations draws attention to a process of dispersion of legal normativity that was previously centralised in what Carl Schmitt called 'concrete order'. At this point, reading Carl Schmitt against the grain offers a great advantage. Though stigmatised for his involvement in the political developments of Third Reich, the author had a good sense of the impersonal social processes then still *in status nascendi*, against which he mostly directed his conceptual-theoretical contributions.[16] In this sense, the disintegration of the *ius publicum europaeum* is not a process that takes place exclusively outside nation-states. Rather, it is shaped by many internal, i.e., nation-state, conditions, such as the productivity of a new form of subjectivity within metropolitan areas, and consequently a product of increased contacts between the newly recognised states within the global society. Global society and its interconnections gradually became too complex to be handled from a perspective based on the normativity of a *ius publicum europaeum*.

Given the increase in social complexity following the disintegration of the old order, even dealing with the complexity of global society by dissolving the concrete order of the *ius publicum europaeum* was not sufficient to deal with the new situation of global society's complexity. Chapter 5 therefore deals with the transformation of legal structures as a correlation of the increasing social complexity of global society, which was consolidated in the generation and management of both technical and legal sector knowledge by organisations. Social problems could no longer be managed exclusively in the 'law of states' but are now also transmitted in the form of organisations, both at the national and transnational levels. This gives rise to new contours of global law in the transition from a state-mediated society to a global society, in which the role of organisations in the juridification process is becoming increasingly important. This process takes place through the intertwining of legal, technical and economic issues in an increasingly global society.

Finally, Chapter 6 addresses the current state of development of law in global society, where the organisational form and its inherent form of knowledge generation and legal normativity are increasingly forfeiting space in a society that focuses more and more on digital platforms. In the transition from one social structure to another, it is not only law that encounters difficult circumstances. There is also a moment of incongruity in the relationship between semantics and social structures, as the platform society combines two moments in its structuring axis that have so far been described separately at the semantic level: heterarchy and hierarchy. The combination of the verticalising factor with the horizontalising factor gives rise to the new digital society, and the same combination also gives rise to the current challenge for law to ensure the generation of the new (innovation) on the one hand and to create new mechanisms to prevent massive infringements of rights on the other. The final chapter concludes by analysing the current transformation of the public sphere through digital platforms, including possible directives for a legal framework which may be more adequate for the social platform structures of the new society.

1

Anomaly as Legal Development

A. NIKLAS LUHMANN'S (WORLD-)SOCIETY: THE DISCOMFORT IN SYSTEMS THEORY

I. Introduction: From Misspecification to Anomaly

'Therefore it may well be that the current prominence of the legal system and the dependence of society itself and most of its functional systems on a functioning legal coding are nothing but a European anomaly, which might well level off with the evolution of world society.'[17]

This sentence enigmatically concludes Niklas Luhmann's 1992 monograph on law, and reveals – according to the present book – a deep discomfort with systems theory insofar as it raises the question of whether functional differentiation as the primacy of modern society can be replicated in the global context the way it has developed in the nation-state – that is, in a few nation-states. In particular, with respect to the role of law, the so-called anomaly thesis raises the question of whether the centrality – or, in Luhmann's words, 'current prominence of the legal system' – that law had within the nation-state, on the one hand as a guarantor or structurer of independent social spheres, such as science, art, economics, education, etc, and, on the other hand, as a facilitator of a minimum of congruent temporal and social orientation, would be replicated in global society along the lines of the nation-state. For Niklas Luhmann, this social and societal dependence on law, as demonstrated in the legal development of the nation-state, clearly presented itself as a European anomaly. Whether the subjunctive used by Luhmann in this last sentence of the book *Law as a Social System* should be changed to the indicative with the historical distance of almost thirty years is the question I will attempt to answer in this chapter.

With the concept of the European anomaly, Luhmann wants to draw attention to a central aspect of functional differentiation and to anticipate in a speculative way that, with the evolution of the world society – due to the particularities of its (expectations) structures – in the near future, the legal form as we know it will no longer be the form with which law will develop. Such discrepancy between the forms of law that have developed within the institutional framework of the national state and those that have developed without the preconditions of the nation-state institutional framework has significant implications, especially for the possibility of containing infringements of rights, but also for the structure of society and thus for its form of differentiation.

Already in the early 1970s – in his essay on the world society – these clear outlines and discrepancies in the development of national law, global law and the form of social differentiation had become apparent.[18] Even then, Luhmann viewed with certain reservations the almost symbiotic relationship between law and politics that had emerged with the advent and consolidation of nation-states as the ideal type of any democratic constitutional state. In Luhmann's view, this peculiar combination of law and politics, which had tended to develop in a standardised way worldwide in the nation-states as a pattern formation, was nothing more than a 'misspecification of human development'.[19] A year later, in his famous *A Sociological Theory of Law* (1972), Luhmann reinforced these observations, related to the relationship between politics and law in global society.[20] The positivity and function of law, as they had strongly characterised the legal system of the national state, would be reshaped by an incorporation of cognitive mechanisms, due to the peculiar dynamism of global society: overall human expectation specifications, given by the norm fidelity of positive law, would be replaced by the problem-solving capacity of learning structures, and coercive enforcement in terms of the nation-state pattern would be replaced by flexible adaptation.[21,22] Twenty years later, after the publication of his essay on world society and the book *A Sociological Theory of Law*, he calls this 'misspecification of the development of mankind' a 'European anomaly', and ends his project on modern law and its development in society with that sentence.[23]

According to Luhmann, the tendency to cognitivise social structures has inevitably changed the conventional role of law with the rise of the global society – even before the emergence of the Internet. But law also plays a central role in systems theory: both in creating a minimum of common orientation for social action in a society that no longer rests on universal foundations of tradition,[24] and, in Gunther Teubner's interpretation in particular, in further developments of the theory in structuring modern social differentiation – even if there is no centrality of a system, in the sense that society would be determined by a system alone. In this sense, fundamental rights in particular would indeed hold a unique function insofar as they ensure the safeguarding of the functional differentiation of society[25] or, in Luhmann's words, as they 'serve to preserve a social differentiation potential and insofar to stabilise a differentiated social structure'.[26] The anomaly thesis does not necessarily need to be interpreted as a direct questioning of the functional differentiation scheme and its spread in world society itself. Rather, it is concerned with thematising the shift in meaning from the predominance of normative mechanisms to cognitive mechanisms, which alters the weights of differentiation within world society, and at the same time, and not least, the role of law within this shift. In other words, the anomaly thesis is primarily concerned with questioning the role of law within the theoretical pattern of a society that is functionally differentiated globally when the institutional preconditions of law – such as the positivity of law, a constitutional jurisdiction, parliament, and all the connections and interdependencies between these institutions – are no longer present in world society. It is precisely at this point that Niklas Luhmann casts doubt on whether the 'dependence of society itself and most of its functional systems on a functioning legal coding' – as under nation-state conditions – would take on a central role in world society.

The primacy of the cognitive over the normative structures in world society, as described by Luhmann, shifts the weights of the functional systems in that sense and raises two essential questions: on the one hand, whether law – and fundamental rights – would assume the same role as a 'guardian' of a balanced differentiation in world society and, on the other hand, whether law can continue to assume the function of a 'guardian of time'. Taking up a biblical metaphor used by Carl Schmitt, can modern law continue to play the role of a *katechon*, i.e., an 'adversary' or 'stopper' of the de-differentiation of society on the one hand, and as a temporal stabiliser of an open future, on the other, in the development of world society?[27] Or is the use of the katechon figure for world society an anomaly itself?

II. The Self-Evidence of a Theory: The Fact of the World Society

'No one, I think, will dispute the fact of a global system.'[28] With this declaration, Luhmann repeatedly takes the self-evidence of a world society as the starting point of his reflections.[29] What was still considered counterintuitive within the social sciences in the post-war period is nowadays quite self-evident: there is a world society in which there is a global and networked communication infrastructure to which access is made possible by computers or smartphones. For new generations, the perception of an unprecedentedly accelerated world is something that is part of everyday life and therefore does not require complex and abstract theoretical constructions.[30] However, this perception has not always been common in social sciences.[31] Although the apodictic assertion of a world society sounds almost banal to everyday life, the assertion of global simultaneity has profound consequences for Luhmann's theory as a whole. One of the main consequences of taking this form of global society for granted is that the nation-state space is no longer the primary differentiating schema of reality. This point first raises the question: how does the transition from a society that was characterised by its organisation within a state framework to a society with a world-society horizon take place? In other words: if the formation of processes of order relied (up to a certain point) on institutions associated with the nation-state (such as state courts, central banks, universities, parliaments etc) in order to reproduce the horizon of meaning in everyday life, how can one figure in the theoretical-conceptual apparatus the notion of a society that is increasingly constituted and mediated by a global horizon of communication?

Niklas Luhmann's (World-)Society: The Discomfort in Systems Theory 11

The key lies in the notions of medium and communication, both of which turn out to be central concepts of the theoretical architecture.

When it comes to the relationship between the national and the world-society levels, the first figure to appear in the discussion is the constitutive role of the spatial boundaries. It is part of the theoretical *common sense* in jurisprudence – and also in other disciplines – that the world is territorially divided into countries and the relations *between* these states are regarded as subjects of attribution that constitute the concept of an international society. This is also how the territoriality of a country is constituted: sometimes one is in Brazil, sometimes in the United States, sometimes in Germany, sometimes in Afghanistan. Traditional international law, for example, is based on ways of structuring connections between clearly demarcated territories. Borders – especially territorial ones – are usually artificial and not necessarily physical demarcations that separate the inside from the outside.[32] Systems theory is also based on this artificiality of exclusion as belonging or not belonging, but on a more abstract level. This artificiality of exclusion mechanisms goes back to the increase of structure formation in the face of increased social complexity, and does not refer, for instance, solely to the delimitation of territories. If one starts from this complexity and not from demarcation or ground marking, a view of the modern complex society that would start from the demarcation of territories alone is inadequate precisely because modern societies are no longer[33] characterised only by the production of social knowledge through the interaction of individuals within a given and demarcated space.[34] The accessible spaces of experience in society expand from communication among those present to communication among those absent; this is precisely what constitutes a modern theory of society. Above all, through the use of 'strategies of managing space' such as telecommunication technologies and modern logistics, new kinds of 'own spaces' are emerging below, within, and beyond state borders.[35]

What the formation of 'own spaces' in world society means is directly related to the form of constitution of one's own boundaries by functional systems, which can no longer be limited to the territorial logic of states. Social systems 'are not limited in space at all, but have a completely different, namely purely internal, form of boundaries'.[36] Law is distinguished from economics, politics, art, and so on by its specific binary coding. Primarily, therefore, it is a matter of delimiting contexts of meaning within society rather than spatial boundaries.[37]

Boundaries in functionally differentiated society are, according to systems theory, procedures that are connected to expectation structures and communication processes and are internally mediated by meaning. At the latest since the publication of *Social Systems* (1984), Luhmann has attached importance to the statement that the boundary does not form a third realm between system and environment, but is modelled from the system.[38] Sometimes one participates in legal communication, sometimes in economic communication, sometimes in political communication.[39] And it is in this context that the relationship between border constitution and global society faces the question of whether, with the strengthening of global society, the form of segmentation into territories, and thus the phenomenon of territorial borders, would disappear. Within this framework, Rudolf Stichweh points out that the theory of global society 'do[es] not exhibit any built-in prejudice in favor of the disappearance of classical boundaries of, for example, the nation-state. Its thesis is only that a macro-order is emerging for which it is true that, among many other things, the function of national borders is being redefined from the system-building level of world society.'[40]

This conceptual discrepancy between what is accepted as a boundary in everyday language and in some sciences and the systems theoretical concept has become a supporting pillar of the systems theory of world society, especially with regard to the relationship between world society, functional differentiation and the functional systems. Thus, Luhmann emphasises that it is precisely the uniqueness of spatial boundaries that makes it clear 'that they are respected neither by truths nor by diseases, neither by education nor by television, neither by money (if one includes credit needs) nor by love'.[41] These media – truth, love, money, writing, printing, electronic communication media, etc[42] – are not oriented to, and cannot be limited by, territorial boundaries. They enable the formation of meaning of different communication contexts, which in turn can be generalised and made expectable – even beyond the state.

In his manuscript from the 1970s, published in 2017 under the title 'Systems Theory of Society', the topic of world society is treated in an interesting way with reference to growth, evolution and self-limitation (of the media). In Luhmann's view, growth is not related to population growth, but to the increase of the communication potential of systems through their media, on the one hand inward (increase of their own complexity) and on the other hand outward through the 'inclusion of communications outside traditional territorial boundaries of the social system'.[43]

This central theme touches on the point of the disproportionate nature of the growth of and between systems – especially in their transition to global society – and its impact on other systems and their environment. The primacy of the functional boundary has always distorted the territorial boundaries conceived 'in everyday life', thus transgressing them. Wanting to nevertheless maintain them, contrary to the apodictically asserted functional differentiation of politics and law, is then viewed, in this way, always as an artificial and regressive reconnection whose effectiveness depends on the nation-state border regime or nation-state institutional conditions. Therefore, it becomes clear that there is a diachrony in the growth of systems among themselves, and that functional differentiation is not linear.[44] The main point, however, is the question that arises after media-induced growth, namely 'whether there are structural limits to possible relations of complexity for society itself that act as opportunities for growth'.[45] Luhmann's answer to this problem of expansion or growth by systems in world society, however, is a self-limitation by its own medium, such as the economy by its medium of money,[46] without introducing law as a '*katechon of de-differentiation*' into world society.[47]

And here is the point where the anomaly thesis again becomes relevant to the whole theoretical architecture. As mentioned above, there is a certain incontestability of world society and the associated functional differentiation as a form of social differentiation. Thus, the equation of world society and the concept of society inevitably leads to the primacy of functional differentiation in global society. The anomaly thesis seems to state that the growth tendencies of the media of functional systems within the nation-state would somehow be modulated or at least tempered by the proper functioning of the legal code – hence the reference to the 'current prominence of the legal system'.[48] From this perspective, the anomaly thesis also makes clear that there is indeed a 'dependence of society itself and most of its functional systems on a functioning legal coding' for structuring social freedoms within the state, and that this reliance of society on law would not take the same form in the further development of world society. Or, as Luhmann puts it (not without a certain scepticism), it would tend to simply disappear or weaken. In order to better understand the significance of the consequences of the transformation of the form of modern law in global society, first it is necessary to clarify what the concept of world society means within systems theory, apart from the mere indication of its factuality.

III. The World (Society) of Systems Theory

Linking the concept of society with the concept of world society is a recurring process in the twentieth century that does not only occur with the writings of Niklas Luhmann. Lawyers, political scientists and other sociologists have repeatedly pointed out that processes of socialisation beyond nation-state borders gradually increased over the course of the twentieth century. Georg Schwarzenberger, for example, spoke of a 'world society' in which power relations alone existed as constitutive units of this form of society.[49] Philip C. Jessup, in his 'Storrs Lectures' at Yale in 1956, put the accent on *transnational law* and the new '*transnational situations*' arising from modern means of communication and new models of contract.[50] Following general systems theory, Morton Kaplan has distinguished national and supranational systems.[51] Talcott Parsons also developed a conflict sociological perspective on the problem of international order formation in the few texts he wrote on the subject.[52] Nonetheless, Immanuel Wallerstein was the most consistent in making the shift from the national to the global level: for him, the feature of the formation the world society's structure lies not alone in the differentiation of states, but in the world economy that has been forming since the sixteenth century and its capitalist logic, which is characterised by unequal exchange. Despite the narrowing of the description to a purely economic context, Immanuel Wallerstein works out the global context most clearly as an independent object of investigation.[53]

Although the common methodological starting point of all these authors is the world society, Luhmann can nevertheless be seen as an antipode to the concepts developed by Talcott Parsons, Immanuel Wallerstein and Georg Schwarzenberger. Luhmann distinguishes himself from Parsons' normative functionalism by deciding, as early as in the 1970s, to rely on a model that differs conceptually from Parsons' notion of integration. Behind this conceptual decision, the concrete starting point is the affirmation of the hypothesis of the existence of a global society independent of any normative foundation. Moreover, unlike Wallerstein, Luhmann does not long to equate the concept of society with the concept of a capitalist world economy, just as, unlike Schwarzenberger, he wants to avoid the concept of society being overlaid by a concept of power. Luhmann understands the concept of society, from a differentiation-theoretical perspective, as a social system encompassing the world society, which exists in polycontextual communication contexts of differentiated subsystems.[54]

In a pre-autopoietic style, Luhmann takes up the idea of world society in 1971 by conceiving the world society no longer as hypothetical, but as becoming world horizon. In doing so, Luhmann accentuates knowledge- and communication-based dimensions of world society, which he presents as 'knowledge of the accessibility of knowledge as a demand trap' and as a 'worldwide communication network'. From this knowledge-based approach, described by himself as a speculative hypothesis,[55] he concludes with a 'change of leadership' leading to a strong increase of the cognitive component of the structures of world society in contrast to the normative one. In other words, Luhmann points out that world society will not evolve in the form of a stabilisation of given expectations, but rather through learning adaptation to the structural conditions and changes of this form of society.[56]

In his later studies, Luhmann further supported the concept of communication and described the concept of world society as 'the appropriation of the world in communication'.[57] This means that world society is implied in every communication, regardless of spatial distances and the presence of the participants.[58] Following the concept of communication, systems theory can trace macro-structures back to micro-properties and make the transition of the concept of society from the national to the global level.

In this sense, Luhmann advocates a double version of the concept of world society: first, on the basis of a social systems theory, world society denotes the unity of the totality of the social, and conversely, on the level of social theory, the concept becomes a specific type of system among others. In other words: world society is a social system that includes itself.[59] According to the perspective of systems theory, the condition for the emergence of world-social structures lies principally in the global communicative accessibility,[60] which brings about the interconnectedness of the global and the local in communicative acts. In this sense, world society is the unity of all communications that are accessible to each other.[61]

Indeed, in his late book *The Society of Society* (1997), Niklas Luhmann diagnoses 'epistemological blockages' in social theory where a persistent tradition of identifying society and the nation-state has prevailed.[62] This tradition, he argues, has led to the concept of society being characterised by two fundamental assumptions: normative integration and territorially bounded units along the lines of nation-states.[63] It is precisely against this tradition that Luhmann interprets society as meaningful communication that is related neither to territories nor to groups of people. Nation-state boundaries are no obstacle to communication, but become, like all other social structures, only its internal differentiations.[64] Society, according to this view, is a single global communication system, understood as an ultimately all-encompassing social system.[65]

If one questions what is 'social' in the concept of society in this differentiation theory, one will inevitably come across the system-theoretical specificationof functional differentiation, which Luhmann himself also emphasised in the controversy with Jürgen Habermas.[66] This also applies to the case of the further development of world society: the socio-structural primacy of the particular form of differentiation of functional differentiation can be reconciled with world society in such a way that the genesis of world society[67] and the enforcement of functional differentiation in this sense are 'one and the same process',[68] which drives communications with the help of the dissemination media in global space.[69]

It is particularly noteworthy that the listed facts argue for the 'fact' of a world society beyond a normatively integrated world. Although this already begins to form slowly with the intensification of communication relations from the sixteenth century on, the essential changes, however, only take place with the further development of technology or with the emergence of new communication media and, in particular, the development of modern communication technologies.[70] At this point, Luhmann repeatedly falls back on concrete examples: printing, television[71] and computers,[72] which caused the breakthrough in this respect. With the development of such technologies, the boundaries that were previously given by the things themselves were overcome by new communication media. No physical barriers could stop world communication anymore. With these media, 'all space-related centralisms were transcended' and thus the plausibility of the accessibility of all communications related to the concept of the world society was created.

What seems obvious at first glance, namely that we live in a world society, leads conceptually to a visible loss of precision in the hasty equation of the terms world society and society, mediated by the concept of communication.[73] As Thomas Schwinn rightly points out, a conceptual and categorical difference must be stated between the possibility of global communication and the resulting formation of social structures. One phenomenon of communication is the possibility of global communication beyond nation-state borders. The formation of order-building processes, conversely, is a different matter altogether: 'Communication is a very simple form of sociality that does not bind the actors mutually; order, on the other hand, is a higher level. To subsume all these different qualities of the social under the world society concept is not very helpful and is accompanied by a loss of analytical precision.'[74]

In addition, other important questions, which have already been addressed on the occasion of the anomaly thesis, gain relevance again: how would the form and shape of the functional differentiation of a global society develop if law in the nation-state fulfilled the function of a 'katechon of de-differentiation' but could possibly no longer perform the same role in the further development of world society? In the last chapter of his book on law, Luhmann also hints at possible legal developments outside the nation-state. Although he vehemently asserts that one could 'hardly speak of a world-unified legal system as a functional system of world society',[75] Luhmann at the same time states that one can 'hardly deny' that 'world society has a legal order even without central legislation and jurisdiction'.[76]

At this point, Luhmann leaves concrete indications of a law that develops beyond the nation-state, but without functionally differentiating itself in the global realm: law in global society could evolve through traditional private international law and human rights. Following this intuitive approach of Luhmann, some authors rely on a driving force of human rights violations that induced scandals regarding the development of a new form of positivity of law.[77] These views, however, seem to involve the same conceptual incoherence and theoretical imprecision that Thomas Schwinn pointed out in the case of the social theory of a global society centred on communication, in which order-forming processes are confused with communication. While the positivity of law is associated with an infrastructure of institutional preconditions (such as courts, parliament, the public sphere) and a cultural prestige as an achievement of freedom, the scandal of 'evidence of violations of law' (Luhmann) would be further removed from order formation and closer to the speed and dissemination possibilities of communication mechanisms.[78] Would such transformations be a functional equivalent of the stable institution-based developments within nation-states? Or would they be merely provisional and lacking in institution-building power for the constitution of stable social structures? One could speculatively formulate one thing in this regard: law derived from scandals may admittedly be (momentary) law, but without any prospect of ground-level structure formation.[79]

It is becoming increasingly clear that in the interrelationships of social structure and semantics there is indeed a crisis of the changing social structures of world society, which ultimately leads to a 'decay' of the semantics of modern law. Niklas Luhmann described this transformation well, but could only speculate about its future. Especially as far as the role of law in world society is concerned, he did not forecast any concrete development. However, his indications of a semantic rupture of law and the contradictions inherent in his concept of global society offer the possibility of using this observation to search for new ways of framing the phenomenon of law that depart from the forms given by the experience of nation-states.[80]

The theme of the development of global society and, in particular, Luhmann's speculation on the extent to which law can no longer guarantee a minimum of common temporal orientation, later advances to become the guiding principle of the theoretical construction of world society in the works of authors such as Gunther Teubner, for whom the legal function of structuring spheres of freedom and containing excesses is projected onto the world level. Although Gunther Teubner is primarily credited with incorporating other theoretical and practical lines into the basic conception of systems theory, he starts from some central presuppositions already found in Niklas Luhmann. Nevertheless, Teubner avoids deriving the self-evidence of the theory of functional differentiation solely from the accessibility of communication. Thus, he is already able to fend off Thomas Schwinn's criticism of equating communication with order-building structures in advance. Teubner's view is rather directed at the processes of order formation of legal structures within the world society and their institutionalisations and containments by law.[81]

The next sections discuss how this theoretical construct has found support on the debate about the development of rights in global society. In a sense, Teubner is able to explore social phenomena beyond the conceptual archipelago of systems theory that have not been previously observed by Niklas Luhmann. This not only makes the theoretical development more complex, but also creates the possibility of observing a new phenomenon: a right without 'authority' that articulates itself beyond the state. Although Teubner's theory advances within the inherent limits of the concept of law, which depends on the institutional bonds of the nation-state, it also does not occur without some ambivalences. They will be addressed in the next section.

B. TEUBNER'S RESCUE OF SYSTEMS THEORY? DIFFERENTIATION THEORY BEYOND THE STATE

I. Introduction

The fact that globalisation, according to Luhmann, leads to a weakening of law is mainly due to the fact that he has strongly oriented himself to the distinction between cognitive and normative expectations for the description of law as a form of time-binding.[82] This narrowing of (systems) theory makes the functioning law of modernity, once it begins to articulate itself beyond the state, an exceptional case in human history. For this reason, the Luhmannian form of law can only be thought for the nation-state with its institutional framework. The frame of reference for the systems theory account of the legal phenomenon remains the nation-state and its institutional preconditions and conditions, even though the central concept of systems theory, communication, is not actually oriented to territorial boundaries. In this sense, the concept of law in Luhmann's theory of law points to ineluctable state-centred elements. The anomaly thesis is a central starting point in this context, because here Niklas Luhmann himself questions the plausibility of his conceptual apparatus, developed over three decades, so as to be able to interpret the process of legal development in such a way that the assumed form of law, which had emerged within the institutional and social bonds of the national state, could not be repeated in the same form at the world level.

The anomaly thesis, however, not only addresses the possible inadequacy of modern law in its temporal dimension to form or stabilise a secure horizon within global society for the projection of individual and institutional action in a society that no longer finds a certain future determined by tradition. In Luhmann's words, it also draws attention to a possible decline in the 'dependence of society itself and most of its functional systems on a functioning legal coding'. Until then, the functioning of the legal code represented, especially under the institutional conditions of the nation-state, a determining feature for guaranteeing individual and institutional spheres of freedom, and thus reflected to a large extent the degree of social differentiation of a society. Luhmann had first introduced this interpretation of the central role of law and, in particular, of fundamental rights as guarantors of social differentiation or as 'barriers to de-differentiation' in his book on *Fundamental Rights as Institutions* (*Grundrechte als Institution*) (1965), but had not clearly taken it up again in the following decades. For the field of law of world society and in the context of systems theory conceptualisation, this role of orchestrating social differentiation through fundamental rights is taken up centrally by Gunther Teubner.[83] In this context, the following question arises: can law continue to play the role of a 'katechon of de-differentiation' under the institutional conditions of world society?

II. The Reinvention of the Systems Theory (of Law) for the World Society

In the 1990s, Gunther Teubner revisited the concerns of systems theory, reified in the thesis of the anomaly, and further developed this paradox. His formula for the development of law in world society is, in clear allusion to Grotius, '*ubi societas, ibi ius*'.[84] Teubner thus suggests that the Luhmannian appraisal of the 'degradation' or lesser importance of law with regard to the further development of a world society is an incorrect assessment of the complexity of the legal phenomenon beyond the state. Regardless of the criticism, he insisted at the same time that the basic conceptual apparatus of systems theory, with further refinements and variations, can still be used for an interpretation of the development of law in the world society. This sounds paradoxical, and indeed it is.

Inspired by Eugen Ehrlich, Teubner distances himself from Luhmann's concept of law with regard to state-centredness in the conventional systems-theoretical sense by detaching the dependence of the reproduction of law from state legislation and jurisprudence and seeking a new legal pluralist theory of 'spontaneous processes of law formation'.[85] Unlike Eugen Ehrlich, however, Gunther Teubner postulates that the law-creating character of the new globalised processes does not arise from customs, traditions, and rural practices as in Ehrlich's Bukovina, but rather that the 'new Bukovina' emerges from highly specialised, fragmented dynamics, which he attempts to set forth within the framework of a new theory of legal pluralism.[86] The role of law in the globalisation process is increasing, not decreasing.

Teubner's new legal pluralism, inspired by systems theory, even gained practical plausibility: against a background of extensive fragmentation of international law, the International Law Commission (ILC) addressed the issue in 2000.[87] The final report is based on a draft proposed by Martti Koskenniemi in 2006.[88] From the development noted, the report's basic line of argument concludes that the practice of international law has moved away from a 'general international law', that is, distanced itself from a semantics of universality and generality of international law, and has become more specialised and sectoral. Koskenniemi shows in the report that the problem of fragmentation of international law is not a purely academic-theoretical issue, but a development based on a profound change in the structure of world society. This phenomenon poses a serious challenge to practitioners of international law.[89] The introduction of the fragmentation thesis[90] into the discussion of international law by the United Nations International Law Commission has, on the one hand, led to discomfort within the discipline itself[91] and, on the other hand, allowed for new contact zones between jurisprudence (international law) and neighbouring disciplines (such as sociology). As a result, the semantics of fragmentation and the theory of functional differentiation linked to it made a career within the globalisation debate and international law.[92]

Teubner's global revitalisation of systems theory is oriented towards the legal phenomena of global society that Luhmann did not consider. With his interest in global legal processes, Teubner directs his conception to the blind spots of Luhmann's conceptual decision regarding the development of law in global society. In contrast to the anomaly thesis, however, Teubner does not start only at the level of global socialisation through communicative networks, but establishes another level of transnational orders in the form of processes of socialisation whose development goes back to *private regimes*.[93] And he goes one step further with the basic thesis that these transnational legal processes would ultimately not increase and be limited to the mere need for norms – due to the lack of centralised global legislation – but would be developments that were at the same time on a constitutional path. *Private regimes* are not simply juridifications,[94] but undergo constitutionalisation processes, which in many respects resemble those of the nation-states.

'Regime thinking' is part of a new, broader way of looking at law that has emerged in the last twenty years,[95] which, under the term *pluralist jurisprudence*,[96] broke with a strong 'epistemological blockade' that until then had dominated several areas of law. According to the approach that had prevailed until then, law was necessarily to be derived from an authoritative instance, with authority in this context always emanating from something hierarchically superior, the state. Teubner breaks almost counterintuitively with this tradition by situating law in global society as an indirect product of globalised processes of social differentiation. In his case, law is not derived, but inferred from heterarchical contexts. This conceptual and theoretical choice has profound consequences for the concept of the validity of law, one of the central pillars of traditional theories of law.

III. Law without Authority? Validity without Third Parties?

The question of the validity of law is one of the central themes of legal theory. The starting point is to justify why law is different from other social sets of rules and conventions, so that an attempt can be made to solve the puzzle of the origin of the validity of law.[97] The answer, commonly used in this discipline, combines two important aspects of the discussion. The doctrine of the source of law, previously decoupled from the state,[98] acquired a hierarchical component linked to the state with the emergence and strengthening of the nation-state from the nineteenth century onwards. According to this influential tradition, which remains weighty to the present, law acquires validity from the moment when a norm established by the state can refer to another, higher norm. The problem of validity becomes one of tracing norms back to norms set by the state.[99] In an ideal-typical way – within the framework of a democratic (re-)reading of this centralist model of the chain of legitimation thought – the legitimation and at the same time the validity of the law – and of the state decision – is present when it has been derived from successive hierarchical levels up to its summit at the democratic legislator.[100]

Within this state-centred tradition, the problem of the validity of law has always led to a recourse to the final, ultimate ground of law. Especially in legal theory and legal philosophy, many scholars have had to obscure or justify this theoretical question. H. L. A. Hart thought he could eliminate the problem by introducing a second layer of law – the so-called 'secondary rules'.[101] Jürgen Habermas tried to channel the problem by embedding a discursive justification of law.[102] Hans Kelsen consistently tried to eliminate the paradox of the ultimate justification of law with a prohibition of recourse in the form of a veto norm (basic norm), which is actually a figure standing outside of law.[103] The paradox of the foundation of law or the validity of law became clearer and clearer over time, and at the same time more and more in need of unfolding.[104] Even when the modern *vis ac potestas* is clothed in democratic terms, the problem of validity can never be neatly remedied. As Marie Theres Fögen rightly pointed out, the problem of the validity of law always needs new companions or substitutes – sometimes spirit, sometimes purpose, sometimes meaning, sometimes history, sometimes system, sometimes nature, sometimes reasons, sometimes interest, sometimes values – and in the end one tries it with good reasons.[105] Law, and the autonomy of law therein, has never justified the sanctioning power of the state without having a companion with it.[106]

Michael Stolleis, for example, shows, from a legal-historical perspective, how the justification of the legitimacy of law passed from concept to concept in the course of the centuries and depending on the respective material circumstances of the time.[107] In this context, the concept of legitimacy becomes a fugitive in terms of legal history. As soon as the concept could no longer be a *master in its own house*, it had to flee. For Michael Stolleis, the last station of escape remains the modern constitution. Before the last station, however, there were other stations of flight for the concept of legitimation of law, such as God, tradition, will, nature and reason. For the explanation of future stations, however, (legal) history as a discipline does not consider itself entitled. This reflexive task is handed over to theory.

Within this semantics of escape, Niklas Luhmann argues that law in modernity should no longer be understood from within itself, but as something that wanders within itself. The way in which the legal system constantly reproduces its own unity is what Luhmann calls a 'circulating symbol'.[108] In this way, Luhmann does not refer validity to an ultimate norm, such as a veto norm, as is the case with Hans Kelsen. He establishes the validity of law by referring to the process of recursivity of the operations of law itself. The temporalisation of law thereby becomes validity itself.[109] Even if Niklas Luhmann shifts the problem of validity to the temporal structures of law, the framework conditions of the reproduction of unity and of the validity of law in the systems-theoretical sense remain very much oriented to the close linkage of the state legislative and judicial apparatuses.[110] Within the nation-state framework of legal validity, therefore, the normative consistency of law has always been a decisive factor for the concept of law as a form of time-binding. Under the institutional framework of the nation-state, law must produce redundancy in its decisions.[111] In this respect, law produces itself through itself, even if only within the framework of the nation-state. If the problem of validity can no longer remain merely latent, hidden or invisibilised, law must externalise its own foundational paradox to other systems – either with the help of a twelfth camel[112] or through structural couplings as it is the case of the constitution of law and politics.[113]

Against all attempts to solve the problem of the validity of law through this migration of legal legitimacy, Gunther Teubner postulates an idiosyncratic middle way for its solution. As will be discussed in more detail in the next chapter, Teubner claims, on the one hand, that Stolleis's position of adopting the state constitution as the last stop in the migration of the concept of legitimacy and, at the same time, validity, is (in)compatible with the social structures that

22 Anomaly as Legal Development

have been developed in globalisation. On the other hand, he tries to resurrect the spirit of modern constitutionalism by affirming that the concept of constitution is, under certain circumstances, quite relevant for understanding the phenomenon of law after globalisation.

In fact, it is repeatedly confirmed that the modern constitution finds no equivalent in world society, since the production and reproduction of law in world society takes place 'far from politics', given that there is no such strong connection between law and politics in world society as was still ideal in the tradition of the positivity of law within nation-states.[114] If the production of law does not necessarily derive from a state authority (whether democratic or not), if the fundamental paradox of law can no longer be externalised into democratic politics, if the model anchored in the national state-law tradition of the positivity of law can no longer explain the production and reproduction of law in global society, would not this very new law be the true anomaly? Or, to put it another way, how does Gunther Teubner deal with the validity and legitimacy of a law that no longer emerges through its close connection to a democratically legitimised political system? How and where is the fundamental paradox of law externalised or veiled?

IV. The Paradox of Validity and the Validity of Paradox: The Law of the World Society

According to Teubner, the resulting 'ruin' of traditional law and the shattering of the conventional hierarchy of law is not the responsibility of the 'great theories': the main culprits are neither Jacques Derrida nor Jürgen Habermas or even Niklas Luhmann.[115] Instead, he says, it is largely globalisation itself as a social phenomenon that is shaping the deconstruction of the unitary and hierarchical tradition of the nation-state.[116] In this respect, there is a strong similarity between Teubner's and Luhmann's diagnosis of world society. Both see globalisation as an inescapable phenomenon that overturns the foundations of a society centred on the nation-state.[117] However, this shared diagnosis ends in contradiction when attention is focused on the role of law and the way law evolves in global society. Niklas Luhmann views with suspicion and even scepticism the development of law in global society as completely different from the way it had developed in nation-states. For this development of law in the global society provides a provocative description of the national development of law as an exceptional case or even the much-named 'European anomaly', which is not to be repeated in the evolution of a world society.

It is precisely at this point that Gunther Teubner distances himself from Niklas Luhmann. For the latter, there would be no qualitative discrepancy[118] between the development of law within and outside the nation-state,[119] especially as far as the structuring role of law for other functional systems is concerned. In Teubner's view, however, the same structuring role of law – or in the vocabulary of systems theory, the 'support of medial reflexivity of social systems by law' – continues to exist in world society. Luhmann, if anything, questions precisely this structuring role of law in several passages, especially vehemently in the concluding sentence of his book *Law as a Social System*.[120] It is not enough to return again and again to the central thesis according to which, he argues, the 'current prominence of the legal system and the dependence of society itself and most of its functional systems on a functioning legal coding are nothing but a European anomaly, which might well level off with the evolution of world society'.[121]

The reading of Luhmann proposed here differs from Teubner's interpretation in that all essays and passages dealing with world society, not least when it comes to law, are precisely borne by the already described unease and the insistence on an inadequacy of the legal model of the nation-state in the further development of world society. Teubner's view, on the other hand, points to a Luhmann reading according to which the system-theoretical legal model is overstrained.[122] The social and technological conditions of global society, which constitute the problem of the learning adaptation of subsystems to the structural primacy of the new society, assign to law (global society) a role that differs from that exercised within the institutional framework of the nation-state. Whereas within the nation-state law would be concerned to perform its function – especially in the face of uncertainty generated by an increasingly uncertain future – by stabilising generalisable minimum parameters of action, especially in the form of conditional programmes, law in global society would instead move to support structural conditions of the learning capacity of all subsystems through standardisation.[123]

In this context, the standardisation of conditions, which can only take place in a decentralised way in world society, points to a law that functions more as a generator of new possibilities or new variations than to a law that gives away or limits social horizons of action through the institutionalisation of medial reflexivity.[124] A function of the law of world society as a promoter of medial reflexivity of all social systems connotes precisely, in Luhmann's words, a 'dependence of society itself and most of its functional systems on a functioning legal coding', and would crystallise this form of law into an anomaly par excellence in the sense conceded by Niklas Luhmann. Rather, the standardisation of structural conditions in the sense of a law of world society would be more closely tied to the contours of a specific form of hybrid legal normativity that produces and drives the production of sectoral standardisation processes of world society – often of a technical-legal nature. In this context, law appears primarily as an accompanying phenomenon of various social practices, and therefore it emerges as an enabler of a common, technical, flexible horizon for third-party action within certain specialised sectors of world society.[125] In lieu of being tied to conditional programmes and to the stabilisation of normative expectations, this thoroughly cognitive, learning law would instead be tied to procedural forms and to the creation of forums that enable the interaction of different rationalities, which not least serve the exercise of sectoral, hybrid knowledge generation within global society.[126]

Only when one recognises that there is no qualitative discrepancy between the legal form in the nation-state and that in the global society,[127] can one understand why the use of the constitutional concept for the law of the global society is insisted upon.[128] It is precisely based on this semantic-conceptual linearity between transnational and national legal tradition[129] that the fundamental paradox of law in global society is further unfolded. However, the support of medial reflexivity (of social systems) by law is only possible if law is qualitatively different from simple juridification[130] and is on the way of constitutionalisation.[131] 'It is about constitution and not only about regulation',[132] as Teubner repeatedly emphasises. Put into a formula: without the constitutionalisation thesis, there is no unfolding of the legal paradox in world society. But it is not about a totalitarian constitutionalisation in the sense of a constitution for the whole global society, as a product of normative constructions or even only good intentions,[133] but about a certain form of constitutionalisation of different media of other functional systems within the world society.

The semantic-conceptual linearity of the legal tradition in the transition to a global society is made clear particularly by applying the sociological method of generalisation and respecification to the transnational constitutional contexts.[134] The aim is to identify in the transnational subfields the specific tests of quality developed in the tradition of constitutionalism of the nation-state, with the important difference[135] that the concept of constitution, although essentially reflecting the concept of constitution of the nation-state, no longer has a state reference structuring the relationship between law and politics. Teubner multiplies the application of the constitutional concept to cases where sectorial parallelism of law and different social systems occurs in global society. The motto is: constitution as double reflexivity of social and legal processes.[136] There are similarities between Luhmann's and Teubner's concept of constitution in the sense that both authors are concerned with double phenomena and their linkage.

Here, the similarities and discrepancies between Gunther Teubner's version of system theory and Niklas Luhmann's starting point can be seen clearly. The central similarities touch on two points: (a) the structuring role of the constitution for other social spheres, in that fundamental rights protect other social spheres from a complete politicisation or totalisation of society;[137] (b) the central question of the validity and legitimacy of law in terms of how law and other social systems resolve the 'paradox of their own self-reference'.[138] At this point, Luhmann repeatedly makes the case, with respect to the constitution of the nation-state, that one of the central roles of the modern constitution would be to solve the problem of legitimation of the legal system and the political system by enabling both to externalise their foundational paradoxes to each other.[139] The constitution would be a kind of 'structuring indifference zone' between law and politics, channelling communication between the two spheres without allowing them to merge into each other at the expense of freedom. However, this structuring and at the same time legitimising role of the constitution in both systems could only take place within the institutional framework of the nation-state, as it required several institutional preconditions, such as positivisation of law, legislation, administrative regulation, and adjudication, including constitutional courts. However, Niklas Luhmann rules out a transfer of these (nation-state) evolutionary achievements to the world society.[140,141]

It is precisely at this point that the question arises whether Teubner's understanding could in some way represent a salvation of systems theory with regard to the role of law in global society or – conversely – whether Teubner's view would rather lead to an overcharge of law in global society, since the associated increasingly cognitive social structures of global society could no longer provide the institutional conditions of the nation-state.

Transnational constitutional pluralism is understood as a generalisation and respecification of the ideal-typical structuring function of the constitution as it has taken place in the nation-state between law and politics, going beyond the institutional context of the nation-state.[142] The concept of constitutionalisation in social constitutionalism is based on the assumption that globalisation leads to an autonomisation of communication media such as money, knowledge, law and power, thus setting their autonomy against the institutional and territorial boundaries of the nation-state as the product of a particular form of social differentiation. In this context, the law of world society is not posited as following the (nation-state) pattern of positivisation, but is seen as a correlate of a particular form of social differentiation: law, in the further development of world society, always remains related to large functional systems and regimes through co-evolutionary processes. The legal regimes and subsystems emerged parallel to fragmentation phenomena of other social spheres.[143] These generated a 'global law without the state', which was the foundation of the multidimensionality of global legal pluralism in the first place.[144]

In this scenario of social fragmentation and an associated fragmentation of law, the problem of the validity of law shifts from a conflict of norms or principles to an orthogonal collision situation. Without resorting to a third instance as a possible solution, the legal form would perform its role in an entirely different way: instead of the conventional role of preserver of legal consistency and unity, it would assume the role of preserver of the heterarchical structuring of mutual permeability and reflexive sensitivity of transnational regimes.[145]

Even if Teubner distances himself from Luhmann's systems theory in many respects – as, for example, with the concept of constitution – he nevertheless has to accept implicit theoretical assumptions of Luhmann's systems theory: a central one of them is the primacy of functional differentiation at the world level. Teubner unites with Luhmann the view that the primary form of differentiation of world society is the functional one.[146] Contrary to Luhmann, however, Teubner believes that the legal system cannot be seen as only territorially differentiated, as is the case with the political system. In a sense, he succeeds – with

26 *Anomaly as Legal Development*

respect to law – in leading systems theory out of the impasse of a methodological nationalism. Nor is the law of world society reduced exclusively to human rights development and private international law. 'Regime thinking' also attempts to avoid the Luhmannian equation of communication and order formation by not deriving the concept of society from communicative global interconnections,[147] but rather by pointing primarily to order-forming processes, such as *lex financiaria, lex constructionis, transnational criminal law*, or *transnational internet law*. Law itself fragments within the global society parallel to the regimes whose functional desideratum is fulfilled by the primacy of functional differentiation.

V. Thinking in Terms of Correlates/Correlations

Law and its metamorphoses often prevent the replication of models developed within a particular time frame and on the basis of particular social experiences in different contexts. This also contributes to the fact that any reconstruction of a particular social complexity is limited by the impossibility of a complete description of society itself. As Hegel astutely points out, one cannot expect to 'get behind' what the object *itself* is.[148] Although there is no special access to the 'object', the social sciences develop their own forms of access to the social object through internal plausibility tests of conceptual constructions. In this context, the French philosopher Quentin Meillassoux has pointed out that this plausibility test in the humanities often necessarily – in order to be able to confirm something as plausible – lives on a (conceptual) positing of correlations. According to Meillassoux, many philosophical traditions of the West are based on certain forms of conceptualisation that might prevent the perception of the increase of contingency. Meillassoux has called these forms 'thinking of correlations'.

One of many examples is Kant's philosophy and its normative basis. It is based on correlations, which build a primary correlation circle, which is mutually stimulated.[149] This is correlationism, characterised as follows: 'in disqualifying the claim that it is possible to consider the realm of subjectivity and objectivity independently of one another'.[150] There would be first a basic assumption, and thus a necessary correlation, and then, in the second moment, a clarifying opening to the world made possible by the correlation. According to Meillassoux, correlationism 'in fact includes us irrevocably in our relation to the world, without giving us any means to say that this relation itself contains the basis of a true absolute'.[151]

In this sense, post-Kantian authors such as Niklas Luhmann and Jürgen Habermas would also be examples of a form of thinking in terms of correlations. For example, Jürgen Habermas, in order to operationalise the basic concept of communicative action for further purposes, must presuppose a universal pragmatics: without universal pragmatics, (there may be) no communicative action, no consensus.[152] Niklas Luhmann's conceptual architecture is also afflicted by thinking in terms of correlations. Luhmann himself postulates: 'there are systems'.[153] System and environment stand for the same epistemic function as the old European pair subject/object. Only after correlation is enacted can systems theory operationalise itself. There can be no system independent of its environment, and there can be no system theory independent of this correlationism.

In a certain sense, Teubner's transnational constitutional pluralism suffers from a 'weak correlationism' if it inevitably has to presuppose that, on the world-societal level, a polycentric globalisation and the functional differentiation it implies have prevailed as a form of differentiation of society.[154] The suspicion of a 'weak correlationism' is based above all on the fact that the primacy of functional differentiation is hypostasised as the new absolute within the theory building. In order to make the fragmentation thesis of transnational law and all practical examples theoretically plausible, the primacy of functional differentiation itself must be made absolute without exception: without functional differentiation at the world level, there is no fragmentation thesis, no self-constitutionalisation thesis, and ultimately no social constitutionalism.[155]

For the present book, given its intrinsically experimental character, it is necessary to distance oneself from a placed correlationism, since the current technological society has as intrinsic features the rapid change and an inevitable process of constant conceptual fraying. In this sense, an experimentalism that gives way to legal theory in this society presents itself as an indispensable task of this discipline. In this sense, it must experiment, test, try out, and establish links with later developments. The departure from functional differentiation and its form of conceptual operationalisation of reality means at the same time an opening for the observation of a set of other possibilities and – at the same time – inherent social constraints, whose observation was made impossible by a previously set conceptual correlationism. One must make the unobservable of theory observable again through such openings.

Quentin Meillassoux's speculative materialism has opened up a very interesting perspective for this reason. Illustrated by the example of philosophy, he has shown above all how thinking in terms of correlations has not only narrowed the contact zones of the various disciplines, but has also inevitably carried with it a plethora of blind spots. According to Meillassoux, philosophy has become entangled in epistemological blockages, making it impossible for it to build bridges between the various sciences.[156] Epistemologies have subscribed to the correlations diagnosed by Meillassoux and have thus fostered a kind of 'religionization of reason'. The question for the present work now remains: how can one get out of this vicious circle of correlationism in order to interpret the further development of law within the world society?

Such stance of distancing oneself from conceptual correlationism, however, presupposes for the present chapter a deepening of the role of law within the conceptual correlation of systems theory. Inevitably, this involves clarifying the role that the temporal dimension plays in relation to modern law, because according to this theory, law is precisely solving a problem that has arisen from the transformation of this social dimension. The opening of society to a future that can no longer be determined by the clear determinations of past experience first becomes a problem that society itself must solve by creating structures to deal with a temporal dimension of this increasingly uncertain future. At this point, law has a primary function that has to do with a certain assurance of an expectable common horizon of action. This function will be the subject of the next chapter, and as such, for the purposes of this chapter, one must always keep in mind that the anomaly thesis aims to do just that: to question whether this function, performed by law within the frameworks and institutional conditions that exist in the nation-state, can persist within the institutional and technological conditions that began to emerge in the early 1990s with the advent of the global society described by Niklas Luhmann.[157]

2
Law as a Form of Time Binding

A. INTRODUCTION

TIME IS A regime that is not only connected with the cultural dimension of any society, but is an essential condition of it. In this context, the time regime cannot be reduced to a physical event of universal time measurement.[158] Rather, time means a relationship in which past, present and future relate to each other. These relational relationships sediment themselves in particular ways of life and social practices and become observable in this way. 'Many cultures assume that the future lying at one's back can be inferred from the "past = present" lying before one's eyes …'[159] The main difference between modern and older time regimes is that the latter gives more weight to the past as a normative basis for both present and future action.[160] The time regime of modernity breaks with this traditional form of time order to the extent that there is a radical change of orientation from the past to the future.[161] This temporal reorientation not only affects everyday human action but also forces society at the institutional level to create mechanisms that can deal with a more open future that is less structured by the past.[162]

In this setting, Luhmann and Koselleck, despite numerous differences in detail, locate the last major transformation of modern society in an identical time period. Koselleck's saddle time ('Sattelzeit') theory takes place within the framework of what Luhmann described in his model of the transition from stratificational to functional (or modern) societies.[163] Both explicitly assume that a profound transformation of the temporal dimension took place between about 1750 and 1850. Luhmann in particular attributes to this development a relevance for the organisation of modern society as a whole that can hardly be overestimated in its effect on his theory. The conversion of the semantics of time to the past/future schema, 'from the shift of primary orientation from the past (identity) to the future (contingency)',[164] is central to both modern law and the theory of world society.[165] With regard to law and its development in global society, the anomaly thesis probably expresses this sensitive aspect more accurately and explicitly takes up this very temporal dimension of society. Can law, as a form of time binding, perform the same role and function in global society as it does in the nation-state? Before answering this question, it is necessary to elaborate how the semantics of time has changed and also how the semantics of time simultaneously part of the social-political semantics.

B. THE CHANGE IN THE SEMANTICS OF TIME: THE CRISIS OF *POLITICAL OBLIGATION*

The modern semantics of time has numerous antecedents in history. In general, it could be said that time gradually becomes a social problem only when everyday experience and tradition increasingly cease to provide a stable framework for the orientation of action. Only when the impact of the change in the semantics of time is posed more comprehensively within the context of the orientation of everyday action and social institutions is it possible to grasp the problems of reorganising a society at the individual, institutional, and collective levels. An analysis of the change of the time regime that starts solely from the technical advances that made the universalisation of time possible[166] prevents the observation of the cultural and, at the same time, sociological dimension of the phenomena stemming from the transformation of the temporal structure of society.[167]

Modern contract theories also had to solve the modern problem of time as far back as the seventeenth century. On a non-materialist level, the Hobbesian dilemma already shows how, after the break with the Christian-Aristotelian tradition, neither ancient certainty nor nature itself was 'timely appropriate' enough for the contouring or creation of a stable social order. Orientation to something abstract, fictional (the contract), rather than to what was mediated through the self-evidence of established tradition posed new challenges to social order.[168] In this direction, Hegel as well was later guided by the distinction between nature and freedom, and in the end he recognised that both the time-honoured idea of nature and the modern idea of freedom were concepts that had gradually moved away from the 'idea of tradition' or 'the concept of tradition' – as a stable founder of social meaning – since about the eighteenth century.[169]

But the emergence of the figure of contract is an important indication of a silent and constant change in the production of social normativity, be it in the implicit or explicit dimensions of society. In this sense, the crisis of *political obligation* in the mid-seventeenth century, through the emergence of the figure and language of the contract, points to a 'linguistic turn' that became increasingly important in the context of cultural, political, and – above all – social life in the modern era.[170] Within this framework, (modern) governance was increasingly[171] dependent on a 'poetic power', i.e., on an incessant production of artificial, aesthetic artifacts, or, as Horst Bredekamp puts it, 'visual strategies' that first had to be staged.[172] Thus, the then explicit dimension of society – based on violence, positing of an authority, etc – gradually began to distance itself from the implicit dimension of society – shaped by conventions, social norms, etc – in that the cohesion and stability of society were from now on constantly dependent on the elective relationship of authority and its (artificial) preconditions.[173]

A person's personal and individual experiences are also affected by this change, which is not least the social construction of a new social consciousness of the subject who agrees to be bound. As Terry Eagleton and Victoria

Kahn show, this was not so much a product of liberalism in *statu nascendi*, now known for its widespread features of autonomy and formal equality. Rather, it was the gradual emergence of a lateral consciousness, articulated in disavowal of the state and the sovereign, and formed in neighbourly, heterarchical relationships.[174] Thus, Kahn notes, 'the seventeenth-century subject of contract was not this modern subject of formal equality but rather, at one and the same time, richly imagined "aesthetic" subject of passion and interest, and an artifact of the creative powers of language'.[175] Pure violence was supplemented by a 'poetic violence' and the social role of nature-given sociality and virtue was thereby weakened,[176] so that the foundation of modern *political obligation* became more fragile and depended on the constant generation of fictions and artificial preconditions such as new social conventions.

With regard to the temporal dimension, it can be said that the language of the contract and the contract itself were the space of an incalculable obligation that attempted to locate the horizon of previous political obligations beyond nature-given sociality and virtue. Victoria Kahn makes this forcefully clear: 'Leviathan opened up ways of looking at human contracts, history, and nature as contingent constructs, that is, as merely probable fictions or narratives rather than universal facts.'[177] However, it is not only the *political obligation* itself that should be emphasised, but also the form in which the changes occur: new linguistic conventions – articulated in books, characters, and writings – take the place of innate obligations, notions of virtue, and moral-ethical justifications.

In this sense, the crisis of *political obligation* in the seventeenth century affected both the relationship between sovereign and subject and the relationships among subjects. In this perspective, the language of self-organisation also spread – in the eighteenth century in England and in the nineteenth century in continental Europe – across various spheres of the social – for example, in economics, politics, law, biology, and cognition – where the patterns of mechanical explanation and tradition reached their limits. Probability predictions increased and causal explanations declined. Sheehan and Wahrman interpret the language of self-organisation in some ways also as a form of dealing with a 'blind spot' of the Enlightenment legacy, which had operated with hard distinctions such as rational/irrational, order/chaos, reason/force, etc, in social self-description. In this context, the language of self-organisation offers a different way of imagining society, so that an ordered world increasingly seemed possible only on the basis of a fragile, temporary, and unfenced foundation.[178]

This development suggests that the problem of time, or even the concept of time itself, is strongly linked to a shift in orientation, and thus does not start only from the technical aspects of time. To the extent that society no longer reproduces itself in terms of the repetition of customs and traditions, the question arises at the level of both individual and institutional action as to how to socially coordinate or give rise to parameters of behaviour. Contract and self-organisation were two decentralised, God-given forms of coordinating action that enabled society to deal with a future that was increasingly open and thus increasingly uncertain.

At the level of global society, the central theme of this book, there is a clear connection between the transformation of the temporal dimension and the level of individual and institutional action. The structuring of the form of action coordination and the related shaping of expectations through a strong attachment to tradition is particularly present in the semantics of the *ius publicum europaeum*, as discussed in Chapter 3. As here in the *crisis of political obligation*, where a clear switch from past to future takes place, with crucial consequences for both the semantic and structural levels of society, at the level of world society this temporal change of guidance also occurs through the insertion of the figure of the contract, which now plays a crucial role as a driving force that dissolves the centralised power of the concrete order of the *ius publicum europaeum* and opens up more space for a decentralised dynamic of society's self-organisation. The orientation of action to a past that is less and less able to provide clear foundations for concrete action in the present is the consequence of a society increasingly built on provisional and artificial foundations as a condition of modernity itself.

C. THE INVENTION OF THE CONTINGENT FUTURE

Focusing on an understanding of the world as one that is gradually losing its secure foundations of self-description, the issue of time and the temporalisation of semantics becomes one of the most important points in understanding the transformation that is taking place precisely in the modern era. The novelty of the modern era is, above all, its time. This refers to the 'processuality of the modern era' as a gradual acceleration of the empirical substrate, that is, a change in experience in the sense that, from about the eighteenth century, new events changed the temporal structure of experience itself. According to Koselleck, 'the temporalization of semantics increases the difference between experience and expectation, because expectations have become more and more distant from all experiences made'.[179] Expectations only became possible as a category juxtaposed to experiences when the present began to mark a cut that, as past *and* future, thwarts any notion of a linear continuum. In this sense, the temporalisation of the eighteenth century is to be understood against the background of the 'immobilisation' ('detemporalisation') of nature that preceded it in the sixteenth century.[180]

In contrast to the historical process of pre-modern history, which was strongly influenced by the old European continuum of experience, modern times are co-determined by a new temporal category: that of expectation.[181] The deterioration of expectation and experience, or, in other words, the shift of the basis of orientation from experience to expectation, i.e. from the past to the future, also shows, as J. G. A. Pocock puts it, a certain alienation of man from his history,[182] in that experience and tradition themselves are no longer able to determine action oriented toward the future. The future is no longer seen as salvation, but as something uncertain. In contrast to a traditional fisherman, an entrepreneur or an inventor perceives a different relationship between the horizon of expectation and the horizon of experience, because for the entrepreneur or inventor the future takes place in the mode of contingency, which he tries to reflect and process. Variability is a constant for him.

With reference to modern times, it can thus be stated not only that man has a changeable reference to time, but also and principally that society itself builds mechanisms and structures of reference to time. Michael Foucault, for example, took up the motif of temporalisation in his early book, *The Order of Things: An Archaeology of the Human Sciences*, where he attempted to show the 'episteme' behind the connection between words and things in the Western history of knowledge from the sixteenth to the twentieth centuries. His critique of the anthropological horizon of modernity is introduced in parallel with the replacement of a spatially oriented order of knowledge with a temporal one.[183] In this context, Foucault speaks of spatial representation, which 'changes completely from the nineteenth century on. The theory of representation disappears as the general basis of all possible orders ...' Foucault also dates – like Koselleck and Luhmann – the inception of the disciplinary subject and the emergence of complex information stocks to the period between 1775 and 1825.[184] Indeed, time becomes a signifier of modernity,[185] even if many thinkers want to leave it in the shadows.[186] Nevertheless, natural physical time and its forms of counting differ from historical times[187] in that the constitution of time and history is socially – and not just natural-technically – conditioned.[188]

Traditional or archaic cultures, which had a traditional time order, put much emphasis on the past as a normative basis for the present time and its future orientation, which follows from the fact that these societies lived in very concrete and simultaneous interaction.[189] For this reason, that is, interaction as a constitutive form of sociality, the formation of short and mobile time horizons takes place. The time regime of modernity, on the other hand, breaks with this form of orientation to the past by changing the orientation from the past to the future.[190] However, this does not happen unconditionally; on the contrary, the modernity of modern time consists in the fact that it 'culturalises' the physical time order,[191] or, in our sense, that it advances temporalisation and makes the pluralisation of time semantics part of the changed framework of Western – and worldly – cultural development. Present is no longer the notion of a linear continuum, but a difference of past and future. This becomes the new semantics of time in modernity.[192] Naturally, law participates in this self-transformation process of society and becomes one of the most important sources of mediation between an increasingly uncertain future and a past that can no longer be secured. In other words, the challenge of law in modernity, starting from the temporal problem of orientation instability, is how law can establish a somewhat stable order beyond tradition.

The anomaly thesis picks up precisely this point. While today's science, technology and economy increasingly endow a flexible horizon of experiences and demand more learning ability and adaptations, modern law in the European-traditional – particularly in the nation-state – sense was rather oriented towards structuring the needs of the different social spheres and their horizons of possibility in such a way that a certain limitation of this space of possibility, i.e. of the future, took place through an institutional anchoring of the orientation of action. The question is whether this function of law – to be a comprehensive structuring of social horizons – can only be a property of domestic legal development that will disappear with increasing processes of dissolution of boundaries in world society – not least through the Internet and increasing digitalisation. In order to answer this question, it is necessary first to take a closer look at what the role of law as a social form of time binding – among others – actually means for society.

D. TIME AND LAW: THE CHANGE IN THE SEMANTICS OF LAW

In 1955, Gerhart Husserl wrote a treatise on the subject of law and time. His writing, however, was still characterised by an existential-philosophical consideration of the 'historicity' of *Dasein*. The time references of law, according to Husserl, consequently turn out as expected. The three known time dimensions occur in detail in the following form: past-oriented jurisprudence, future-oriented legislation, and present-oriented administration. In this theoretical construct, the concept of law is endowed with *a priori* and thus supra-temporal kernels of meaning, in which the time reference of legal structures is more in the background than in the foreground.[193]

Niklas Luhmann, on the other hand, looks at law from the perspective of time.[194] In his view, what distinguishes modern society from other forms of society lies precisely in the fact that modern society can design its own future, or rather, put it up for disposition. For this, however, society must invent forms and strategies to deal with this openness to the future. In this context, law appears as a consolidated form of dealing with it, in which law structures the horizon of action through legal norms or minimises the abundance of possibilities. Only when one has such temporal dimension of modern society in mind can one adequately address the question of the anomaly thesis that precedes this point, by asking whether the temporal references of law are at all adequate for the form of world society.

Time binding means that dealing with the realisability of the future is limited. In this sense, time binding is not about the determination of the future – because time itself cannot be bound – but about the realisation of the future in the present. The future, present only as a horizon in the present, is limited or expanded by irreversibilities in the present itself, without possibly affected parties being able to participate. The social costs – including inequality, disadvantage or preference, which arise from the non-reversible indifference to third parties – require society to establish evolutionary mechanisms for the 'management' of the open disposition of the future.

These available complex open time horizons depend on certain social (cultural) techniques and evolutionary achievements that provide more possibilities for the social. Formulated in the terminology of systems theory, this means that when social complexity puts a system under selection pressure, the concept of meaning plays the role of guardian of this selection, i.e., it serves as a kind of guarantor for the connectivity of further operations that[195] are subject to a selection constraint. The time dimension appears as the most important level of meaning systems, which are primarily time systems,[196] i.e., machines for coping with complexity or complexity machines. The *Dasein*, the existence of a meaning system, subsists only within its temporal existence. There is no compelling instance that ensures that the next operation will continue.[197] It can be, but it does not have to be. It follows that meaning systems are never in an ontological state.[198]

The fact that the future is up for grabs in modern society says nothing about the form of dealing with it. Time itself cannot be fixed, but society for its part creates structures or forms of (expectation) structures for dealing with an open future. In the economy, the regulative handling of scarcity is also a social form of time binding. One can think of the daily orientation of our lives toward (property) prices that are not bound to any place.[199] Although the prices of the future cannot be set in stone, we make daily decisions that are projected into the future as a possible horizon. The scarcity controlled by the money mechanism increases the abstractness of the relation between future and past in a special way.[200]

There are similar structures for the analysis of law. However, to look at law from the perspective of time is is, to say the least, unusual within legal theory. Jürgen Habermas, for example, focuses predominantly on the social dimension at the expense of the temporal dimension – and therefore focuses almost exclusively on consensus.[201] Ronald Dworkin, on the other hand, attaches importance to (moral) integrity without considering that the factual and the temporal are themselves constitutive for the normativity of law.[202] Hans Kelsen, in turn, emphasises the connectivity of norms (factual dimension) as the basis of the validity of law[203] and therefore neglects, for instance, the construction of subjective rights, which exert a strong influence on the constitution of modern society through both the temporal and social dimensions.[204] The list could be extended accordingly.[205]

The increase of the space of possibility (*Möglichkeitsraum*) in modern society generates the problem of dealing with uncertain certainties or certain uncertainties. One can no longer expect that accumulated experience will provide secure clues for decisions and their consequences in the future. This uncertainty requires more and more structures to deal with it, but without the need to abolish it completely. Especially for modern law, the formation of structures of expectation is of central importance in this context. Within this framework, the categories of time, structure and expectation exhibit profound historical and technical dependencies on the one hand, and show an extreme openness to the future on the other.

The key to Luhmann's understanding of law therefore lies in the future reference of the legal function[206] or in the time dimension itself.[207] The function of law is thus generalised time binding by stabilising expectations – whereby law can stabilise expectations only in a time-dependent way, namely 'in such a way that law makes its own mutability available for regulatory tasks'.[208] Law guarantees time stability through standardisation and simultaneously produces sociality by enabling behaviour. However, law cannot guarantee social stability through its function. This is due to the nature of the modern form of law in contrast to the legal form of a simple, non-complex society whose law is assumed to be given by the environment, as in the unchanging concept of natural law, for example.

The function of modern law lies precisely in providing a stable structure for a society that is becoming more complex, while at the same time guaranteeing its flexible changeability through the positivity of law. 'Law thus legitimately enters into flux, it adjusts itself to a more rapidly flowing time.'[209] The rupture in the social time dimension of the modern era requires law to form a dynamic 'order of permanent change',[210] in which the autonomy of law becomes very closely linked to its function.[211] The functional specification of law is therefore related to a specific function, which can only take place through its own coding.[212] At this point, the famous distinction between cognitive and normative expectation becomes central. Legal norm from the perspective of time-binding dimension, through which expectations are projected into the future. The persistence of expectations takes place by invoking norms. Conforming or deviant behaviour is counterfactually condensed through a recursive operationalisation of dogmatic differences, or, in short, operations within the legal system with reference to the legal code. The point of the concept of norm as a form of time binding is precisely that it already makes it possible to visualise how others should behave in future situations.[213] In this way, law, in a counterfactual manoeuvre, creates the restriction and the structuring of the horizons of possibility of other social spheres – not only of people – and performs a fundamental function for society. Law makes it possible 'to (be) certain about the future in the face of its inherent uncertainty'.[214] In this sense, modern law assumes a social role as guardian of society's time,[215] in that legal normativity is based in large part on 'indifference to unpredictable future events'.[216]

The important role that law plays in modern societies as a guarantor of a minimum of communal orientation when tradition no longer provides a sufficient standard for social action is questioned by Luhmann himself at various moments from the 1970s onward, especially when he returns to the problem of the configuration of world society. The anomaly thesis is above all the expression of a theory that doubts itself, a genuine Luhmannian unease, because it clearly opposes two different legal developments: on the one hand, the development that takes place within the institutional limits and possibilities of the experience of the nation-state, and on the other hand the development that takes place outside the institutional constraints of the nation-state and presents a difficulty in adapting to the old legal form.

Law as a form of time binding and its inherent function of stabilising normative expectations could only be developed within the institutional conditions that have grown in the nation-state, such as the positivity of law, state legislation, state courts, and so on. Law as a form of time binding presents itself as a product of the institutional conditions existing in the nation-state anyway. The inadequacy of the structures of expectations for global society on which law builds its social function reveals a deep unease of Luhmannian theory with itself. At the heart of the systems-theoretical conception of law and politics gapes a wound, which is nothing less than the anachronism of a reproduction of nation-state characteristics that cannot keep up with the progressive aspirations of a global society. At this point, Luhmann admits to himself that the processes of world society are faster than the reality of the subsystems of law and politics (state), which try to catch up with them but still fail miserably at it even with a thirty-year gap. Sometimes it is brought up ironically, sometimes directly and forcefully, but without ever making it particularly clear that a permanent self-doubt remains immanent to the theory. Moreover, Luhmann has not succeeded in formulating clear contours of what the contribution of law in world society would be to the shaping of social freedoms, as was the case with the experience of nation-states.

In a sense, the anomaly thesis suggests that, on the one hand, the degree of structuring of various social spheres with significant effects on the exercise of individual freedoms is a role conferred upon law that depends on certain conditions in which it cannot guarantee itself. These social preconditions, now closely linked to the new technologies with cross-border effects, create new conditions and conditioning for the relationship between law and social knowledge (society) within the world society. On the other hand, the anomaly thesis indicates that the fixation of the legal function on the prior performance of conditional programmes[217] – the level of programming in the Luhmannian construction that is used 'to reintegrate law into society'[218] – is reaching its limits within world society. The consistent specification of the level of programming to conditional programmes as opposed to purpose programmes reveals a certain preference for a form of law that always and necessarily operates retrospectively and downstream,[219] and in this context it also reveals a certain inseparability from the norm-setting and decision-making structures typical of the nation-state, such as the institutions of parliament and the state courts.[220]

And here is an important point to reinforce and clarify the thesis established in this chapter: it is not a matter of denying social differentiations that transcend the territorial boundaries of the nation-state. This seems almost self-evident when one observes recent developments in science, economics, and the current digitisation of society. In a sense, this book is precisely concerned with a possible form of social differentiation of global society, but one that does not conform to the primacy of functional differentiation. What we question in the context of this chapter, following the anomaly thesis, is whether law would play the same role with the emergence of technological and global society that it had in the institutional framework of the nation-state. And, following on from this, what the consequences of answering this question would be for the limits and opportunities of law in contemporary society. In this respect, the inherent facticity of technological and global society, which would require time binding through cognitivity, is precisely in tension with the Luhmannian concept of law, which is fixed in the classical conditional programme and also remains largely dependent on the institutional conditions in the nation-state. This not only limits the access of law to social knowledge stocks, thus limiting the reference of law to an infrastructure of social conventions and technologies, but at the same time also dictates the adaptability or the inability to adapt through learning limits of law within a society increasingly operationalised by new media and business models of new technologies.

E. OUTLOOK: A NEW ATTEMPT AT THE METAMORPHOSIS OF LAW IN GLOBAL SOCIETY

A productive way out of the 'vicious circle of correlationism' is to look for new contact zones between neighbouring disciplines, authors and law, and to 'test' the effects arising from the contacts and reflections for an observation of dimensions and practices that until then were in a blind spot of conceptual reproduction or in the hard disciplinary demarcation of certain descriptions or observations on the process of transformation of law and modern society. At this point, the experimental character of legal theory – which is not limited solely to the systematisation of dogmatic categories, to the reproduction of prefabricated theories, and to a clear disciplinary framework – has an enormous advantage in dealing with a society that is in constant flux. In a society increasingly co-determined by new digital technologies, safe vantage points from which to observe modern society are becoming increasingly rare and precarious. In this scenario, opening legal theory to new challenges and experiments beyond the discipline's canon has become a condition for the discipline of legal theory itself. Like all other fields in today's society, it has no external guarantee that ensures its permanent legitimacy. On the contrary, the dynamic and innovative character of providing a space for an internal discovery process to generate knowledge about the idiosyncrasies of modern society becomes one of the primary functions of legal theory. Without this, the discipline is reduced to a resonance box of its own past – with serious foreclosure risks.

In the context of the present work, the metamorphoses of world law are understood as a process interacting with the metamorphoses of society itself in several dimensions. Among other things, these metamorphoses of society take place sometimes in the development of a new technology, sometimes at the level of the transformation of subjectivity, sometimes in the creation of new forms of generating social knowledge. Within this framework, the law of global society is a law that evolves within complex hybridisation processes at the different levels of metamorphoses of society itself in an almost opaque way. In this scenario, the cultivation of a 'border hygiene' (A. Koschorke) of social processes is opposed to a dynamic that is rather expressed in a 'poetic un-system' (R. Wiethölter). The procedure of a poetic un-system starts from a dimension of '*poiesis*' inherent to complex society[221] and at the same time distances itself from the logic of functional differentiation of clear markings of borders or the control of society from a regulative perspective.

The aim of the present work is to trace this dynamic of a 'poetic un-system' and to focus on both moments, i.e. on a first moment of the creation of social and legal normativity and on a second moment to describe how a dynamic is created that can no longer be described with old European terms such as system, reason, morality, spirit, values, and so on. Therefore, the work focuses on the supporting role of the material and infrastructural conditions of legal normativity and on how the changes in these conditions challenge law. The disintegration of the old order, which is analysed in the next chapter, has cultural conditioning factors that are reflected in a correlation between the national and transnational plans. A novel logic of relations between state legal subjects begins to emerge, as current techno-social problems demand from society new forms of sectoral coordination of social knowledge. Organisations then play an important role in creating the normativity of global society. The current scenario is marked by a change in the way social knowledge is generated, which is no longer primarily oriented toward organisational form, but increasingly focused on digital platforms. This not only changes the conditions of possibility for law, but also its own function.

3

The Disintegration of the Old Order

A. INTRODUCTION

THE NEXT CHAPTERS will take up and elaborate Niklas Luhmann's troubling question about the further development of law in global society. As shown, the anomaly thesis grounds a theoretical unease peculiar to systems theory in its analysis of the evolution of global society and its law.[222] The decision to place a strong cognitivism at the centre of explaining the development of law in global society[223] undermines Spaemann's hypostasised comparison with Hegel[224] in that it clearly shows how the operational weakening of systems theory's economy of the boundary, in terms of boundary hygiene,[225] entails a sustained inconsistency in the theory for understanding this phenomenon of law beyond the nation-state. Based on the outcome of the previous chapter, the next three chapters attempt to break out of this impasse in systems theory, avoid the diagnosed malaise, and put conceptual efforts into the process of transforming global law.

Philip C. Jessup made the concept of transnational law well known through his 'Storrs Lectures' at Yale in 1956.[226] With this neologism, Jessup pointed to a social development that had not been captured by previous traditional legal semantics. For Jessup, '[p]art of the difficulty in analyzing the problems of the world community and the law regulating them is the lack of an appropriate word or term for the rules we are discussing'.[227] Since then, and for the last sixty years, an almost unmanageable literature on the field of transnational law has emerged.[228] However, although the concept had been elaborated in several studies, it remains current and challenging to traditional international law mainly because of the significant message it has shaped. The new *'transnational situations'* (Jessup) are constellations that can no longer be necessarily subsumed under the state-centered dichotomy of *public* and *private international law*.[229] *'Transnational situations'* are those relationships that simultaneously transcend national borders and presuppose the multilateral participation of national jurisdictions and transnational institutions.[230]

Following this semantic opening to a new possibility of observation, which founded a new experimental subject (*'global law'*),[231] several new fields of research emerged from practice-based research, including *lex mercatoria*,[232] consumer protection,[233] *corporate governance*,[234] *corporate responsibility*[235] and *transnational litigation*.[236] Even within legal theory, a new field of research is emerging through the discovery of the transnational. The so-called legal pluralist approach can now emancipate itself from its fixation on an anthropological point of view and enter a new terrain.[237] Partly since then, the discussion about the transnational has already been associated with a pluralist approach.[238]

It is not just new fields of research and practice that are being invented for the new *'transnational situations'* (Jessup). Even the tradition of state theory is undergoing a change of mindset through the 'discovery of the transnational'. A prominent recent case in this point is the 'transformation of the state' approach.[239] Some research approaches that emerged after the discovery of the transnational, including this one in particular, trace in some sense a historical genesis that follows a seemingly clear and consistent sequence: first, the state exists, but it suffers a loss of meaning as a result of the discovery of the transnational. The state, understood as a historical phenomenon, is stylised by the semantic construct of a 'Golden Age' (Leibfried/Zürn), so that in a second step a 'dethronement of the state' diagnosed by Carl Schmitt suggests itself.[240] According to this approach, however, the relevant conditions for a dethronement of the state are conditions that arise from the new transnational constellations and not from domestic conditions, as in Carl Schmitt's view.[241] At the beginning of sovereignty is its loss.

The 'transformation of the state' approach follows this genealogy, and it is reasonable to suspect that such approach may be the product of an important traditional lineage in German state theory. This tradition, whose most prominent representatives are Georg Jellinek and Hans Kelsen, has a peculiar way of understanding the phenomenon of statehood. Jellinek's and Kelsen's two-sided doctrine – despite the separation of the social entity from legal institutions and the partial inclusion of the social side of law in the legal debate – has as a consequence that only the legal side of this distinction remains relevant for the description of the legal object.[242] This tradition of state-law debate, which tends to foreground the engodenous features of statehood, has obscured a thoroughly important component of the conditions of emergence and change of statehood, which – due to factors such as new technologies, new institutional ambitions favouring the transformation of modern subjectivity, new forms of social knowledge generation, and others – are precisely in a complex co-evolution between the national and the transnational level. Even with the three-element doctrine (namely state territory, permanent population, and government-state power), only endogenous elements that lead to the formation of statehood are reflected. All external impulses and cultural conditioning are not included in this internal reflection.

For Hans Kelsen, on the other hand, there is a clearer separation between the social substrate and the conceptual normative legal substrate, despite the proximity to the two-sided doctrine of his master Jellinek. Focusing on a 'pure theory of law' that allegedly also serves as an 'explanation of the state', Kelsen points to an almost absolute identification of law and the state.[243] This not only confirms Hermann Heller's criticism that Kelsen's theory of the state is nothing more than a 'theory of the state without the state'[244] to be an important observation, but above all it shows for the present study that an important tradition of state theory, especially in Germany, has neglected cultural conditioning factors of the formation of the modern state and its transformation. If Jellinek's approach obscures the conditions of formation and transformation of statehood, the equation of law and state in Kelsen's sense seems to make any interdisciplinary approach between law and its social preconditions an impossible task, mainly because of its epistemological approach.[245]

Above all, insights such as 'we are in an age of transformation (of state) that began in the 1970s'[246] testify to a theoretical anachronism or even the complete absence of an interdisciplinary conception of law. The state and its transformation cannot be separated from its cultural and social conditioning, especially not from the emergence of the state and its stabilisation in the model of liberal democracy. Only when the internal and external conditions are taken into account can one properly understand the phenomenon of statehood and its transformation. The state and its transformation are phenomena that converge and cannot be placed in a historical order. They are products of the self-transformation of world society – insofar as there is a constant process of co-evolution between the state, regional and transnational levels – from the very beginning.

B. DOMINANCE OF THE POLITICAL

I. Reading Carl Schmitt: The First Postcolonialist?

Carl Schmitt is considered the most discussed German jurist of the twentieth century[247] and, as Hannah Arendt asserted, Schmitt is 'undoubtedly the most important intellectual in Germany in the field of constitutional and international law'.[248] Within the debate on legal theory and the history of ideas, Schmitt's writings are also repeatedly taken up in discussion.[249] In international law, his oeuvre has found more and more echo through the interpretation of its contemporary impact.[250] Especially since 11 September 2001, Schmitt's central concepts for the global conjuncture offer critical-analytical tools with '*astonishing contemporaneity*'.[251] Schmitt's account of the limitless character of a discriminatory concept of war, which restricts war to no framework to be observed, interprets those new 'humanitarian wars' as the return of a 'just war' in the sense of medieval theology. The morally inspired wars place the intensification of antagonisms between friend and enemy at the centre of the political arena, viewing the enemy not simply as an adversary but as an absolute opponent to be destroyed. In this context, both the universalist and the international concepts of law are turned into weapons on the side of interventionism in the form of moral war.[252]

In addition to this specific, conceptual application, to the updating of Carl Schmitt in the international law debate as well as to the rediscovery of his work,[253] there is another important dimension to his oeuvre. This is not necessarily related to a possible practical application of Schmitt's theory and writings. Nor is it connected with the path that led him to political positions in the historical context of his existence. This interesting dimension lies on a different level, connecting, on the one hand, Schmitt's ability to describe social phenomena and paradigms from a conceptual and historical reconstruction, and, on the other hand, with his own anxieties that led him to project his writings against certain social developments related to a liberal tendency of modern society. For the present book, it is essential to reconstruct these two described levels using the example of the transition from a global society articulated on the basis of a dominance of the political to a society increasingly mediatised by more decentralised relations. While Carl Schmitt describes this development as the demise of a legal form, other authors – such as Chris Bayly – describe it as the birth of the modern world, and so does the present book.

At this point, Martti Koskenniemi offers an interesting reading of Carl Schmitt. He starts from the thesis that Schmitt's writings on international law provide a fruitful basis for postcolonial theory, since Schmitt succeeded in establishing conventional 'legal realism' as a more advanced approach.[254] Koskenniemi is not alone in this interpretation. In recent years, it has become a theoretical self-understanding in the literature to construe this form and reading of international law as its true historical structural formation, which ultimately makes Carl Schmitt the 'first' postcolonialist of international law and at the same time makes it possible to treat him as a profound elucidator of the colonial roots of international law.[255] Indeed, Schmitt assigns a special significance to overseas colonies in shaping the history and structure of modern international law with respect to land status in international law. Schmitt has thus come close to a method of quasi-materialist reconstruction of the foundations of international law, thereby distancing himself from a vision of international law as *ius naturale et gentium* as well as from strict positivism.[256]

The modern international system of sovereign territorial states, i.e., the emergence of modern international law, is directly related to the 'Age of Discoveries' and the colonial encounter between Europe and the non-European world. Originating in the second half of the sixteenth century, its decline begins at the end of the nineteenth century, and its final decline in the twenieth century with the process of decolonisation and the formal abolition in international law of the colonial difference between European soil and overseas territories, state and colonies – the 'civilised' and the 'uncivilised' peoples.[257] Schmitt's important contribution to this narrative is that he attempts to trace the history of the modern state system beyond a single continent and to take an explicit global perspective.[258] His approach thus attacks the view that international law emerged solely from the endogenous practices of European states, as in the myth of Westphalia.²⁵⁹ Moreover, he clearly questions the working methods of international law scholars and, in particular, the methodology that separates the conceptual framework of the discipline from the social substrate that correlates with these concepts.

The so-called *ius publicum europaeum* is based on such system, which began with the European expansion. In this context, the territorial status of the colony was placed at the centre of the conditions of the formation of international law, contrary to the founding myth of Westphalia.²⁶⁰ The *ius publicum europaeum* is based on a distinction between European sovereign countries – where the norms and standards of modern liberal rights applied – and overseas colonies – where these standards of modern liberal rights did not apply. However, this distinction is based on a fundamental paradox that can be described as a kind of 'exclusionary inclusion'. Thus, wars could be fought between European countries in colonies with relative peace on European territory.²⁶¹ A parallel to this is the duality of the English *common law* system, where a difference prevailed between English law for English soil and other areas where the power of the Crown donned a different garb. The unique position of the colonies – which were included in modern world politics but excluded from the norms and legal standards applicable to European sovereign countries – occupies an exceptional and at the same time decisive position for the consolidation of the structure of the Eurocentric order at that time. Thus, a zone of peace was created in the European centre by outsourcing conflicts to overseas territories.²⁶²

II. Taking Names, Giving Names, Taking Land: The Linguistic Dimension of the Law of World Society

In this context of inclusion through exclusion and, above all, in the context of an approach to the emergence of international law from a global logic, the central role of the taking of land must also be reconstructed, since this procedure represents one of the central pillars of the *ius publicum europaeum* in the Schmittian sense. The process of (land) taking has a constituting effect only if the taker succeeds in giving a name to it.²⁶³ The relation of *nomos*, taking, and name can also be seen as an etymological relation, which, concealed by a certain invisibilisation technique, is inherent in the relation of power and naming. When one speaks, one speaks in the name of something: in the name of the constitution, in the name of God, in the name of justice, in the name of law. In this way, the modern form of legitimation of any kind of power is constructed, be it political power, legal power, economic power, etc.²⁶⁴ This constellation, however, is not about laying claim to the gift of a name by speaking in the name of another, but about being allowed to speak in the name of the name itself.²⁶⁵ In other words – as will be shown – in this approach, language itself is perceived as an important dimension of the law of world society, so that land-grabbing and naming become one on the linguistic level.

Thomas J. Lawrence addresses precisely this problem with regard to the emergence of international law. In his essay 'Is there a True International Law?' he addresses the question of whether modern international law, lacking the basic elements of a centralised order by enforcement mechanisms, should nevertheless be called law. As a result, he affirms the view that modern international law should not be presented as '*law as force*' and – since the positivist description of law is historically contingent – it therefore cannot be applied to all orders in all times. Modern international law should rather deal with the subject of order. The form of concretisation of this order should not be regulated by force or by the formation of enforcement mechanisms in international law, but by a regulated flow of communication of European nations:[266] 'the rules which determine the conduct of the general body of civilised states in their mutual dealings'.[267]

The challenge of international law, from this point of view, is not to dominate the world directly by force, as all other empires in history have already done, but to generate a mechanism to replace particular European contexts by establishing a common language of Europeans: not an exclusive physical force, but a linguistic one. Lawrence exemplifies the '*ordering functions of international law*' through conceptual constructions in the context of the *Conférence de la Haya de droit international privé* (HCCH 1893). In this context, Lawrence approaches Carl Schmitt's argumentation and especially his theory of names. Schmitt is also not concerned with placing the founding paradox of international law in the self-binding of a sovereign – due to the lack of central enforcement mechanisms – but externalising it in a common belonging to a circumscribed space as a concrete order.[268]

On the semantic level, this social structure of a few states, princely houses and dynasties as bearers of a European domestic cooperative reflects the dimension of concrete order thinking by making a constitutive distinction between civilised, semi-civilised and uncivilised within the dogmatic terms of international law. The unity of the *ius publicum europaeum* is based on this distinction, which itself is based on a diversity of land status as a central category of international law at that time.[269]

The Eurocentric concept of culture is important for Carl Schmitt because it gives substance to the necessary homogeneity of the concrete order of European international law. Internal homogeneity was until then based on a socially plausible distinction between 'civilised', semi-civilised 'barbarians' and savage peoples.[270] However, the juridification of this particular concept of culture has practical consequences: by it, the 'non-civilised' – as tribes and pirates – would not fall under any scope of protection derived from the legal framework of concepts and institutions of international law, such as hosting a permanent diplomatic mission or diplomatic protection. They are excluded from the infrastructure of rules of international law or participation in world society.[271]

This dimension of power, articulated primarily at the level of language and having performative effects on the constitution of law and the structuring of social expectations within a society, has been particularly emphasised by the postcolonialist critical movement, as Annelise Riles shows: 'the project of international law rests on an essentialisation of culture that privileges the role of international law as a mechanism of bridging the void between cultural boundaries'.[272] In the same vein, but within the postcolonialist movement of international law, Antony Anghie focuses his argument on the constitutive role of cultural difference in the emergence, rise and preservation of modern international law. 'Given that the civilised-non-civilised distinction expelled the non-European world from the realm of law and society ... cultural difference was translated into legal difference.'[273]

While the emergence and maintenance of the *ius publicum europaeum* was due to a culturalisation of the concept of law, its demise resulted precisely from the operationalisation of legal concepts, legal fictions, and a dynamic of contacts and interconnections beyond the concrete order of the European national community that gradually took root.[274] Postcolonial thinkers, however, tend not to perceive the dimension of the formation of impersonal processes that are not traceable to a centre of power, as will be shown in the next chapter. For such tradition of thought, the cultural difference on which international law is founded is the same cultural difference that continues to be co-reproduced in the current system of rights of global society.[275] In a sense, it constitutes the element of a permanent state of exception that excludes the possibility of an impersonal dynamic of (world) society. In light of this, postcolonialists approach poststructuralists, and it is not unreasonable that Carl Schmitt is considered both a postcolonialist and one of the first poststructuralists – or at least the author who planted the first seeds of this with his study on the state of exception.[276]

On the one hand, global law as an anomaly in the Luhmannian sense offers few conceptual contours for the developmental structures of global law. On the other hand, Gunther Teubner's option is that of limiting the performance of law to the role of a structural provider against a kind of 'tyranny of the (expansive) media' that have become functionally – and also destructively – institutionalised within global society[277] (which Luhmann, at best, reserved for the scenario of institutional conditions prevailing in the nation-state).[278] Thus, it is left to the present book to address the blind spot of both readings of global society, which relates primarily to the ways in which the veiling of socio-legal normativity and cognitivity emerge, decay and are supplemented by other forms of generating social knowledge and legal normativity through processes of hybridisation. What Niklas Luhmann's anomaly thesis calls into question – bringing forth a true malaise within the perfection of conceptual symmetry of systems theory, expressed just as well as, in his words, 'the current prominence of the legal system and the reliance of society itself and most of its functional systems on a functioning of the legal code'[279] – is precisely the questioning of a legal model that contrasts exclusively with the intrinsic social conditions of global society.

In the context of this chapter, the aim is not only to trace unobservable features of the conditions and possibilities of law in global society associated with the two versions of systems theory discussed in the first chapter of this thesis. Equally emerging within the debate on the law of global society is an alternative reading of global society that, through the lens of the postcolonialist movement, does not locate the production and reproduction of the law of global society in the collision of different rationalities that have emancipated themselves from the territorial boundaries of nation-states. Rather, it is based on a moment of original impurity of law – and of society itself – that is subsequently perpetuated in this world society through a substantialisation of the concept of culture in the social fabric of all legal operations.

Both this chapter and this book as a whole also distance themselves from this substantive culturalism that is inherent in the postcolonialist debate on global society as a strong motif. This does not consist of a positing of a beginning (of culture). Conversely, it is a product of the gradual consolidation of a lateral rationality that is decentralised and largely unpredictable because it is realised primarily through the emergence of new contacts brought about by new techniques and technologies. In this sense, the world society is a culture of contact that was above all the result of a new 'culture of goods' (Frank Trentmann) and new communication and transport technologies that made the centrality of the *ius publicum europaeum* untenable. Not a world of power, not a world of reason, not a world of systems, but a world of things. The new social dynamics of big cities and their connections shaped the new ruptures of legal-political concepts.[280]

The linguistic dimension of the law of global society in the sense given by this concretisation of the concept of culture, both in the first postcolonialist and in his successors, stands in contrast to a global society that cannot be reduced to a concept of power and its further cultural reproduction within legal and social operations. For the purposes of this chapter – particularly the next section on dominance in relations – we will refrain from positing a beginning of culture in terms of postcolonial studies and instead focus more on considerations of the multicentric nature of social change in global society as described by the British historian of South Asia, C. A. Bayly.[281]

III. The Fragmentation of the Ius Publicum Europaeum: World Society Beyond Westphalia

Martti Koskenniemi and Anne Orford have recently pointed out the unproductivity or epistemological blockage that results from a fixation of the gaze of international law, both as a legal discipline and as a historical discipline, on 'Westphalia' as the founding myth of international law. In a striking way, both say 'we don't always have to look at Westphalia ...'[282] In this sense, they seek to turn the gaze of international law away from its self-reference, and towards a global gaze that emerges from the recent current of global history.[283] In this context, much earlier Carl Schmitt also detached the emergence of international law from its self-referential description by categorically affirming that the founding myth of international law goes back to 1492 and not to 1648.[284] In other words, the 'era of discoveries' marked the beginning of the modern world and the global rise of international law, defining it as a law between states, that is, between European rulers.[285] This European core determined the *nomos* of the earth.[286] In this respect, both in Carl Schmitt's and in the postcolonialist tradition, modern international law is an effect or product of imperial expansion, of colonialism,[287] which was then further operationalised through cultural distinctions, thereby shaping the whole system from the beginning.

The existence of the *ius publicum europaeum* depended on a free colonial soil outside Europe. The modern interstate system of international law emerged with the inclusion of geographical external borders of Europe during colonial expansion into America.[288] In other words, Schmitt rejects the myth of Westphalia, according to which the state system and modern international law are said to have emerged from an almost rational agreement among European countries to avoid war and mutual violence.[289] Instead, he argues, the idea of violence and war remains central to the formation of the law of a Eurocentric global society, not in the sense that the problem of war must be abolished, but in the sense that this concern is constitutive of international law insofar as a hedging of war is made possible by the interstate European spatial order.[290] Here it becomes clear that for Schmitt the appropriation of a new world, its colonisation, is the global event in the history of European international law which, with seemingly endless free spaces, made the internal law of an interstate European order possible and feasible.[291]

The *ius publicum europaeum* is not only a historical statement or construction, but not least also a theoretical (re)construction of a specific, cultural dimension of global relations.[292] In this context, Carl Schmitt uses the relationship of two central concepts, namely '*nomos*' and 'concrete order', to conceptually clarify the historical events of the emergence of modern international law. 'Concrete order' in this context connotes not only one of Schmitt's opinions in the constitutional law discussion of the Weimar period.[293] *Konkrete Ordnung* belongs to institutional legal thought and is characterised by a peculiar intermediate position between abstract normativism and a groundless decisionism.[294] It focuses on a supra-personal or trans-subjective moment of law and society and shows that the normative force of law depends on this supra-personal dimension of the social – i.e., a moment that cannot be reduced to the legal relations between single individuals standing on their own.[295]

'*Nomos*' is the 'original word' of law, and Cicero's translation as '*lex*' is, according to Schmitt, 'among the heaviest burdens of our occidental conceptual and linguistic culture'.[296] In attempting to purge *nomos* of the meaning of *lex*, Schmitt distances himself from the structuring of impersonal relations by abstract concepts of the Roman legal tradition and brings law closer to an original first division associated in international law with land seizure, where the spatial origin is emphasised.[297] Law does not serve to enable impersonal relations but, in an 'original spatial sense', to bind them to place and tradition.[298]

In this sense, the *nahme* (as a word derivative of *nomos*) becomes the *nomos* for the Schmittian understanding of law as the central figure of an original act and thus the basis of all further concrete orders and all further law.

This conceptual connection of *nomos* and concrete order as a form of conceptual constitution of the *ius publicum europaeum* wants to point in particular to the dimension of the symbolic order of civilisation constitutive of the formation of law, which is at the same time a theory of foundation and preservation. It cannot be understood as a normative programme, but rather as a particular social process. Accordingly, it points to a regularity that precedes law. Carl Schmitt's *nomos* of global society was expressed in the real formation of a concrete order that gained its homogeneity from the concept of civilisation.[299] This concrete order was a real domestic cooperative of European peoples, principalities, states and nations, which structured the system of European equilibrium, whereby it cannot be reduced to a simple inter-state order and only subsequently acquires its meaning and logic within the framework of this concrete order.[300] This trans-subjective moment of tradition has held together (up to a certain point), the social world-societal substrate of the global order.

Koskenniemi follows a current tendency to extract a positive dimension for postcolonial studies from Carl Schmitt's studies of international law and transform them into productive material beyond the 'polemical debunking literature'[301] that followed Schmitt. For the present work, however, it is crucial to clarify, in addition to the position explained above, when and under what conditions the system of *ius publicum europaeum* breaks down.[302] In contrast to Koskenniemi, who situates the collapse in the interwar period,[303] the present work links the decay of the *ius publicum europaeum* to the emergence of increasingly impersonal social dynamics, decentralised from various factors such as increased contacts between world regions, immigration, consumption, free personality development in major cities, the growth of non-European cities, and, above all, a cultural dimension to the transformation of the subjective level. The *ius publicum europaeum* could no longer cope internally with these increasing, new impersonal social dynamics.

Indeed, there are a number of events that determined the world order in the interwar period or caused the old order of the *ius publicum europaeum* to decisively perish. The Versailles Peace Treaty, the League of Nations,[304] and the special treatment of the Rhineland as a historical, political and legal abnormality[305] are undoubtedly events that point to a shift in the order of the power structure in world society. The submission of the Geneva League of Nations to the Monroe Doctrine, which entailed the renunciation of any possibility of intervention vis-à-vis the American states,[306] the intervention possibilities of the Geneva League of Nations, and the Kellogg Pact[307] were the last events that finally dissolved the old European order.

In addition to these important events, however, the decline of the *ius publicum europaeum* or, as Schmitt called it, 'the dissolution of the European order in "international law"' had already taken place from about 1890, and finally ended in 1939 with the beginning of World War II. The concrete order of the *ius publicum europaeum*, which based the European order on a few sovereign countries, families, and dynasties and allowed for coordination for 'common deliberation' (C. Schmitt)[308] and the European system of equilibrium, began to crumble, especially with the policy of recognising non-European states. A long process that began with the Monroe Doctrine of 1823 cut a deep and spreading crack in the concrete order of the '*Droit public de l'Europe*'[309] and even in Africa some countries began to acquire statehood, although fewer in number than in Latin America.[310] The concrete order was undercomplex for the new world of relations.

This practice of recognition – or, according to Carl Schmitt, the 'extension of European international law' due to the increased complexity of contacts between countries and the resulting lack of control of access to global society by the concrete European order – contributed decisively to an irreversible rupture with the structure of global society at that time.[311] Gradually, a constellation of more than fifty heterogeneous countries (such as Persia, China, Korea, Brazil, Siam, Turkey, etc) and their contractual relations with each other developed on the margins of the Eurocentric concept of civilisation, so that the homogeneity and the undercomplexity of the *ius publicum europaeum* led to its implosion.[312] The logic of the rise of organisations – which will be the subject of the next chapter – as a result of the increasing complexity and the need to provide answers to practical problems arising from the intensification of contacts between countries and peoples, also accelerated the process of recognition of new countries within the international law community, as was the case with Japan (1886) and Siam (1885) when they entered the Universal Postal Union.[313] Gradually, a dominance of relations emerges: a new type of sociality that moves away from the world determined by the dominance of the political.

IV. The New Productivity of the Individual and the Disintegration of the Old Order

The disintegration of the *ius publicum europaeum* is only the tip of the iceberg of a profound social self-transformation that the world underwent in the nineteenth century. With his concepts of the concrete order and the nomos, Carl Schmitt had described a process of law formation that was confronted by the newly emerging global society. The new society underwent an impersonal and decentralised creative process of dispersion in various social spheres, which pointed to a different attitude of society toward the new. The disintegration of the old nomos of the earth was now a legal and (at the same time) social process that, through the creation and experimentation of the new at the national level, produced a new international order. Such order, through a high degree of diffusion and contact thanks to modern means of communication and transportation, approached not only an economic system. In this context, a certain concrete order, namely that of tradition, was by no means timely for the new, primarily impersonal social dynamic, which gradually no longer carried with it any semantic safeguarding by a theory of name.[314]

What is methodologically pursued here as the coevolution of national and global social processes is also articulated above and below the deformation of legal institutions at the national and international levels. Other dimensions of the social also play an important role in this kind of coevolution. Especially in contexts of cultural change – which are meant here with reference to the 'law of states' – it becomes clear how legal normativity goes hand in hand with social upheaval, be it in terms of modern subjectivity formation, in terms of representation, in view of the transformation of existing or the invention of new techniques, or in view of the now central role of large cities. Jürgen Osterhammel emphasises the central role of cities, which as generators of connections and relationships between individuals also act globally as 'gateways to the world'.[315]

The discussion about political romanticism (1919) and the concept of occasionalism that followed it[316] offer a special occasion to brush Schmitt against the grain and to orientate oneself on the psychoanalytic methodology of Freudian negation.[317] In other words, it is not a matter of going through the lessons of Carl Schmitt, but of tracing his deepest fears. Political Romanticism provides us with the opportunity to observe a particular new form of legitimation, coordination and generation of human action beyond ultimate instances of social control – be it God, tradition, nature, reason or constitution.[318]

For Tim Blanning, the Romantic Revolution had the same profound effect on social structure as the fall of the Bastille in 1789 and the industrialisation that began in England.[319] However, the Romantic movement was decentralised in nature and dependent on numerous social factors. According to Blanning, historical determinants were necessary to achieve social capillarity, perhaps the most serious of which was the transition from court to city.[320] The growing population of cities, the publication of books, literacy,[321] and communication itself created new cultural frameworks in which an experimental 'logic of trial' transcended traditional boundaries. The creation of new common places such as cafés in cities is an example of the emergence of the 'oxygen of the public sphere' (J. Brewer), understood as authentically operating nodes of a network of diverse social institutions and customs. These were new places where a practising cultivation of the exchange of opinions could take place beyond the centrality of the court.[322]

Culture before the Romantic movement was a culture of re-presentation in the sense of *making present*, i.e., a realised design of the superiority of courtly and royal honour.[323] Even in philosophy, this semantics of the centrality of representation left its mark. Hegel's pejorative attitude toward the Romantic art form as 'absolute inwardness,' as the highest expression of an 'absolute subjectivity,' was already a sign of discomfort with the modern form of centralisation. The thesis of the end of art was related to the fact that the new productivity of the individual could not be a real representation of the true and therefore appeared only 'grimace-like'.[324]

This is exactly the point Carl Schmitt takes up with his thesis of Occasionalism. The Romantic movement or the 'structure of the Romantic spirit' is the expression of Occasionalism, which indicates an expansion or extension of the aesthetic, leading to the dissolution of the hierarchy of the spiritual sphere. Schmittian political romanticism, that is, subjective occasionalism, embodies the 'recasting' of important social positions. In romanticism, the individual subject takes the place of God as the new and highest instance of the absolute.[325] God can be represented by the institution of the church, but the subject is not capable of representation and its form of relation no longer follows a hierarchical but a heterarchical form.

(Romantic) art is considered a prime example of profound changes in social structures. Schmitt interprets romantic art as 'an art without publicity and without representation'.[326] For Schmitt, however, publicity and representation are two core components of political form. In his work 'Roman Catholicism and Political Form', ecclesiastical representation serves as a prime example of modern political form.[327] According to it, there is an elective affinity between the (Catholic) Church and the state, Catholicism and political thought. Against the Protestant interpretation of the formal as the expression of an increasingly invisible, inwardly exercising quality of the subject, Schmitt emphasises the value of representation.[328] According to Schmitt, an anti-Roman affect does not exist because of the simple historical fact that the Catholic Church represents a power continuum – the political heir of the Roman Empire. Rather, the anti-Roman affect comes from the political effect of the Catholic Church as a *complexio oppositorum* and the principle of representation tied into it.[329]

On the institutional level, Schmitt aims to accommodate the political potential of the Catholic Church for such developments, especially by anchoring its political dimension associated with representation.[330] In the Catholic Church's form of representation, 'through the representative Christ himself, *in persona*, lies its superiority over an age of economic thought'.[331] Occasionalism is a social dynamic which finds its strongest expression only in the art form and is extended by other dimensions of the social. Occasionalism implodes the logic of representation as a personal concrete institution. Or better: occasionalism itself represents the impossibility of representation in modernity.

The transition from the court to the city (J. Brewer) is crucial as a structural condition of emergence for the modern (romantic) subject. This transition represents a historical anchor for the Romantic movement, which Schmitt locates in the new bourgeoisie as the bearer of the Romantic movement, and thus the rule of the liberal middle class.[332,333] The latter asserts itself against the ruling aristocratic educated class. The subject of the Romantic movement and its bearer, the liberal middle class, is the role model of a society that is designed to produce and generate the new beyond that centrality. This is particularly evident in the dynamics of the flourishing cities of the nineteenth century, where the centrality of court culture was diminished by the need to produce, create, and generate trust within anonymous and impersonal relationships or networks.

Schmitt himself names a series of reoccupations (*Umbesetzung*) that occurs as a result of the Romantic movement: the church is replaced by the theatre, the religious by drama or opera material, the house of God by the museum. New factors emerge as an absolute or objective instance.[334] Indeed, as Tim Blanning notes, the secularisation of religious power in turn leads to a sacralisation of art. Art gains autonomy, which is why a network of different museums is founded almost simultaneously in many places – especially in large cities.[335] Not only the king is revered, but also the medium itself, art. At the same time, as Schmitt notes, art is no longer capable of representation,[336] but only of (re)production. This secular reoccupation of art, which at the same time entails a new 'sacral' occupation, opens up the social for the production and testing of new social transgressions beyond tradition on an individual and on a social level.

The 'discovery' or 'invention of inwardness'[337] presents itself rather as an epiphenomenon of the self-transformation of society, which increasingly in the course of the nineteenth century and the emergence of state formation described here led to determining, but was not determined by it, constitutive influences in sociality. However, at the same time, many events from the most diverse areas of society were taking place. In Germany, the humanistic Gymnasium became a standardised institution after its invention in the 1830s. The European university became a cultural export, and the mobility of knowledge was also a mobility made possible by technology. In 1838, Friedrich List designed a railroad network. In 1835, the length of the line was no more than six kilometres; by 1875, it was already over 27,930 kilometres. Consumption becomes global and culinary diversity ubiquitous.[338] The transition from market to store – with the emergence of department stores[339] and restaurants – was a necessary concomitant of the industrialisation and internationalisation of food production.[340]

A world that could not be shaped by oneself and that could no longer be represented as a whole was dispersed into many fragments of history and put to the test anew. In this scenario, the novel became the supporting figure of this time, taking its place in the fabrication of fictions and fictional experiences through the invention of the indirect or experienced speech of the bourgeois novel.[341] Balzac's extraordinary invention lay in the novel's focus on urban conditions, meaning that a young man's life could be exciting without being shipwrecked on a desert island or signing a pact with the devil.[342] 'To arouse the protagonist and the reader it is no longer necessary to embark on a journey: much better to stay in town.'[343] With the advent of modernity, the apology of the 'exception' gradually loses its suggestive power in various social spheres. Instead, the routine of everyday urban life moves to the centre.

The passivity of the Romantic, lamented by Schmitt, who 'perceive[s] an abundance of associative possibility[s]',[344] becomes the form of relation of the emerging new sociality. The form of occasionalism, which evades participation in the constitution of modern subjectivity and, above all, in the definition of a normative hierarchical instance of coordination of society, is also expressed in the relational form of world society after the disintegration of the *ius publicum europaeum*. Occasionalism, through the absence of a *causa*, of a necessary constraint, of a compelling causation, of a commitment to a final and definitive norm, presents itself[345] as the antipode of the centralisation of a concrete order of the *ius publicum europaeum*.

The 'lack of any relation to a *causa*' successively becomes the guiding form of modernity. The cultural spaces for subject invention are expanded in many states in the course of the nineteenth century up to World War I. In contrast, the symbolism of the political — whether represented within nation-states or on the world level[346] — suggests the possibility of an 'activity intervening in the real contexts of the visible world',[347] i.e., the possibility of a domination of society by an external and representative authority.[348] The concrete order of the *ius publicum europaeum* embodied such an instance by creating a place of 'common deliberation, common points of view, common ordering actions of a European land seizure on non-European soil'.[349]

The system of *ius publicum europaeum*, based on two fundamental semantic distinctions — civilised and uncivilised peoples and the diversity of land status — which will be referred to here as the period of dominance of the political, is increasingly losing its suggestive power with the onset of the new cultural framework of modernity. The Eurocentric nomos of the earth, which existed until World War I and was based first on a dual equilibrium between land and sea, then afterward on a concrete order, is undermined by the dispersion of sovereignty described here. The dominance of the political is slowly being supplemented or replaced by the dominance of the relational.

4

The Birth of the New World from the Culture of Dispersion

A. DOMINANCE OF THE RELATIONSHIP

I. Introduction

THE DISINTEGRATION OF the old order was intertwined in large-scale transformational contexts that cannot be exhaustively explained in causal terms. One important dimension, to which Benedict Anderson draws attention, is that of the rise and spread of the state form.[350,351] The medium of printing played a central role as a 'cultural factory' of new (national) fictions: the emerging reading public thus shared a narrative cosmos and soon imagined itself as a national community of shared origins and future destinies. This performativity of political imagination (Y. Ezrahi) and its dependence on an increasingly impersonal process designed to intersect different institutions in major cities, admittedly, point to an important condition of the disintegration of that centrality. The transition from the dominance of the political to the dominance of the relational connotes the scenario of the birth of a new (modern) world made up of fluid connections and contacts rather than a firm substantive foundation.

The rise and spread of the form of state that no longer fit within the limited framework of a few European sovereign states of the *ius publicum europaeum*, the generalisation of concepts of nation, and the steady expansion of the capitalist economy may have given the world at the turn of the century an outward appearance of greater uniformity,[352] but on the other hand, societies within these broad boundaries have become more complex and diverse.[353]

For the present chapter, 'transition from the dominance of the political to a dominance of the relational' is meant to state that with the disintegration of that centrality – here the concrete order of the *ius publicum europaeum* through the tracing back of problems to a central point as well as the search for solutions – society itself must invent new mechanisms of conflict and complexity management. That modernisation developments are unequally distributed on the planet is obvious. But the great challenge after this disintegration is that societies must increasingly imagine new orders based more and more on fragmented foundations.[354] Such provisionality and the constant need to re-vary their foundations become the condition of modern society, not only due to the lack of a clear goal-determining centre. First and foremost, the constant need to maintain the fragmented foundations of the social by opening them to the new also becomes a condition of modern liberal society.

II. The Dispersion of the Global Society

Martti Koskenniemi, in his famous report on the fragmentation of international law, based on Wilfred Jenk's descriptions, interprets this phenomenon of fragmentation as the product of a deficiency: '[the] international world lacked a general legislative body'.[355] The narratives of the fragmentation of world law that have dominated the legal debate on global society since the last decades follow the logic of projecting the national experience onto the global level, but without considering the historical facets and constraints of its own development. Both the narrative of fragmentation and the conceptualisations of the fragment itself possess this malformation.[356]

One way to escape this heavy affliction or upstream conceptual burden of unity semantics and its desiderata is to try out new concepts that denote dynamics that are not necessarily reducible to the conceptual correlationism of whole/part or unit/fragment. The concept of dispersion would be a possible candidate for such an enterprise.[357] Contrary to fragmentation, dispersion is to be thought of as a medium that does not necessarily dismantle something unified, but rather produces conditions in favour of new contacts, relationships, or ratios. Dispersion as a medium does not start from a figure of originality in order to explain transformations as upheavals. Nor is it about a deeper break with the 'institutional program' of modernity, but about certain social and technological conditions present in imagination or fiction that add more variations and complexity to the social. Dispersion is about the relationship between anonymous and unconscious masses of possible relations to the medium itself.[358]

The Weimar period turned the word 'dispersion' into a fighting term.[359] In the present book, dispersion of sovereignty does not mean the dismantling of the old sovereignty, nor decomposition of the concrete order (C. Schmitt), nor fragmentation of the *ius publicum europaeum*, and not even fragmentation of international law. Rather, what is meant here by dispersion as opposed to original decentralisation is that the emphasis on the fiction of sovereignty as a pattern of attribution itself becomes a medium which, through its transmission to different nations, peoples, or territories, generates a plethora of effects from which new social structures emerge. The dispersion of sovereignty as a medium instigates new relations without taking an unconditional recourse to a centre, which is here designated as an important dimension of the dominance of the relation.[360]

The dispersion of sovereignty as a medium means in this sense a certain open texture of (modern) law, which is not *primarily* designed to generate 'binding rules', or to construct rights and duties, but which evokes social conditions for the generation of new bonds beyond tradition. The transfer of the fiction of 'sovereignty' to non-European nations and peoples has led to new 'webs of signification', a new kind of imagination of the real,[361] which has contributed significantly to the demise of the *ius publicum europaeum*.

III. The Birth of a Discipline: International Law

The transformation and especially the increased complexity of the global society not only accelerated the relations and contacts in the world society, but also led to the birth of two important disciplines, formed to understand the new social dynamics: International Law and Sociology. Under the influence of the terminological innovation of Jeremy Bentham (1748–1832), the description of 'international law' first gained prominence over the established tradition of the 'law of nations' that had treated this field of law in the pre-modern era, usually in noticeable proximity to natural law.[362] The presence of international law in university curricula as a part of the 'law of nature',[363] and its gradual emancipation as a discipline in its own right, is itself a nineteenth-century phenomenon, a side effect of the transition from the dominance of the political to the dominance of relations.[364]

The process of scientification and professionalisation within the field of international law could no longer be reflected as philosophy or as pure diplomacy because of the increase in social complexity.[365] In the course of the nineteenth century, the institutes and legal matter of international law gradually began to distinguish themselves from other disciplines such as natural law, philosophy, theology and civil law.[366] The internal increase in complexity of the legal matter was a reaction to the increase in complexity of the relations of the world society.[367] The emergence of new problems required greater conceptual differentiation in the field of international law. Especially in the second half of the nineteenth century, there was an explosion of book publications, collections, and scholarly journals[368] resulting from scientific practice and systematisation.[369] Organisations such as the *Institut de Droit international* and the *International Legal Association*[370] were founded. A progressive autonomisation or 'scientificity' of the discipline took shape. Recourse to the concrete order of the *ius publicum europaeum* as a place of consultation (Carl Schmitt) for conflict resolution was no longer compatible with the complexity of the dominance of the relationship.

Due to the lack of codification, the treaty became the main figure of international law.[371] Certain types of (international) treaties functionally compensated at the same time for the lack of codification of international law and the disintegration of the *ius publicum europaeum*. They were therefore called 'legislative treaties', which led to the juridification of international relations as the 'treaty-making revolution of the 19th century'.[372] These treaties between states or quasi-states led to a decentralised possibility of recognition with the consequence of the admission of new states into the international law community. From a treaty-making practice between already consolidated states, non-consolidated states, and non-states among themselves, a decentralised push to recognise international law emerged within the international law community, with no centralised basis for whom would be received by it. The logic of treaty manifests itself in this context as an expression of a heterarchical network logic in which admission to the network did not occur via a multilateral treaty or as a phenomenon controlled from a centre, but rather quite possibly via the generation of new ties and trust beyond the found centre or tradition of European principalities.[373]

The precedents of international legal recognitions within the spatial determination of the old concrete order led not only to the emergence of international law as a discipline in its own right, but also to the emergence, through the dispersion of sovereignty, of a new form of relations in world society located beyond the *ius publicum europaeum*. The absence or weakening of a centre – expressed by Schmitt's concrete order – for the ordering and processing of conflicts within world society creates, on the one hand, great uncertainty about the succession of a model of society in decline. On the other hand, it inescapably opens up new possibilities for the articulation of a decentralised social dynamic – detached from the fiction of the legal person and the creation of new objects of attribution different from those present in the *ius publicum europaeum* – without which the birth of the modern world could not have taken place.

IV. The Sovereign Legal Person and the New Form of Relation of Global Society

The question of the attribution of legal personality and the various forms of justification for this attribution has always been a recurring theme in legal doctrine and has arisen in questions of either the scope of national law and the scope of international law.[374] From a temporal perspective, both the global and local levels reflected the need to personify nonhuman beings, and much of the discussion was therefore based on the use of metaphors from biology.[375] Otto von Gierke and Paul Laband wrote at the same time as Lassa Oppenheim, Hersch Lauterpach, and Emer de Vattel in this regard. The place of unconditional subjective explanatory consciousness as the social substrate for the attribution of juridical personal characteristics was gradually reoccupied by non-biological social realities or organised collectives, be they states or associations.[376]

At the transnational and national levels, new abstract relations that had a greater distance from traditional networks demanded a conceptual architecture from law that was better suited to a world increasingly articulated in heterarchical relations, rather than the hierarchical relations resulting from the remnants of a court culture. On a global scale, the creation of a new conceptual architecture through personification and its transmission to newly recognised states and territories has been emerging as a new way of encoding access to world society. There has been little reflection on the impact and consequences of the creation and transmission of legal personhood in the nineteenth century in global society. Without addressing structural change through the attribution of legal personality, Janne Nijman shows that this development of international law through the personification of states alongside emperors and popes meant the inclusion of new participants in the diplomatic community of Europe.[377] Leibniz already talked about international personhood (*persona jure gentium*) in technical terms.[378] But personification was a Janus-faced construction from the beginning, because when talking about personification of states or nations in *ius gentes*, the relations of emperor, pope, princes and nations had to be reassigned.[379] The problem here, however, lies primarily in justifying the answer to the question of which nations were to be considered sovereign and which were not.[380]

A kind of 'obsession with sovereignty'[381] accompanied the nineteenth century thanks to the newly introduced concepts of formalism, positivism and coexistence in international law. David Kennedy argues that what is seen here as the demise of the *ius publicum europaeum* and the 'birth of modernity' (Bayly) is actually only a rhetorical device – namely, primarily the invention of a progressive narrative – of the nineteenth century.[382] The reduction of this movement to a mere 'rhetorical device' prevents Bayly from observing the effects of this development of 'obsession with sovereignty' on changing the way trust was generated and produced in global society. With the standardisation through semantic artifacts such as 'states as legal subjects', and in particular the expressive increase in the transfer to other states beyond the European housing cooperative (*Hausgenossenschaft*), a new social dimension of possibilities for action, trust, and the formation of expectations opened up beyond concrete orders that were consolidated within a dense, manageable network of a few European states and principalities within the framework of the *ius publicum europaeum*. Legal fiction, in this sense, offers a new level of complexity for global relations and thereby enables the construction of decentralised relations beyond a concrete order in Carl Schmitt's sense.

Carl Schmitt recognises, among other things, the central role of the legal person in shaping global corporate law or European international law. However, he has an ambivalent relationship to the concept of legal personhood: Schmitt does not view the central role of the legal person as a legal fiction that enables the productive generation and dissemination of social knowledge or impersonal legal relations. Instead, his understanding of the legal person comes close to the idea of representation, using the example of the representation of Christ by the Catholic Church.[383] The question of the legal personality of states in the context of the *ius publicum europaeum* does not take on the dimension of the role of legal fiction in enabling new relations beyond tradition or even in being a medium of dispersion in the sense outlined here. Rather, in the Schmittian sense, it is the combination of spatial power complex and power of representation.[384] In these circumstances, publicity in the sense of a *publici juris* results from the constitution of a real spatial order that contains the meaning of a concrete order.

As a counterpoint to the Schmittian sense, the spread of the fiction of the juridical person on the globe presents itself as a legal technique in which a right is reproduced, articulated and transmitted. In the plan of self-description, i.e., the theory of the state, Niklas Luhmann points out an important change brought about in this context by the juridification of this concept of the person, i.e., the legal person. In Luhmann's view, it would have occurred as a consequence of the introduction of the abstract person, a switch from *virtus* to *ius*, and thus the opening of a range of social possibilities for new relationships within the newly emerging social context.[385] Instead of *virtus* (virtue) or concrete order in Schmitt's sense, in the course of the nineteenth century the normativity of law increasingly becomes an effect of the operationalisation of fictions, with profound social consequences for a society in which the artificial increasingly becomes part of the constitution of the real. This development accentuates the role of law as a mechanism of reality production that borrows from culture.[386] With Lawrence Rosen, one could say that 'the legal creation of facts thus summarises and stimulates our sense of reality',[387] and this is precisely the case with the performative effects of the so-called dispersion of sovereignty on global society.

V. The Disintegration of the Old Order and the Transformation of Trust in the World Society

Yan Thomas, in his studies of Roman law, makes it plausible that the legal fiction of Roman law brings forth the possibility of a new order beyond the arbitrariness of noble families and their inherent traditions and rites.[388] In this sense, law generates – or at least makes possible – a worldview that no longer remains tied to the centrality of the religious or to the order of tradition. A law that proceeds from decentralised particularities without the primacy of a unified knowledge emerges.[389] The birth of modernity (Bayly) with the demise of the *ius publicum europaeum* through the dispersion of sovereignty signifies precisely this development: the enabling of multiple horizontal relationalities beyond a concrete order (C. Schmitt),[390] which became possible only by attributing the legal fiction of a personality to states.[391]

One of the immediate consequences of the collapse of the *ius publicum europaeum* and the dispersion of sovereignty is the transformation of the generation and reproduction of trust in global society. The postcolonial approach, for example, fails to adequately observe this important change resulting from the shift from the dominance of the political to the dominance of the relational.

Trust in the period of dominance of the political was something that developed within a concrete order, that is, within the network of royal families, dynasties, and some European states. In such network, the legitimacy and justification for participation in global society was based on membership. In other words, participation in global society was coded by affiliation with this social network. The creation and structuring of trust within this society and the alignment of social expectations were directly related to membership in this European social network. Participation in global society was coded by affiliation with this social network. In other words, the creation and structuring of trust within this society and the alignment of social expectations were directly related to membership in this European social network.

The conversion of a society based on the concrete order of the *ius publicum europaeum* to one that tends to be based on the dispersion of sovereignties becomes a problem of reference in the generation of trust or for the question of what form of orientation of action is structurally enabled. If the taking of land no longer tends to be the constituent process of international law, being replaced by the relationship, the question becomes how to generate an infrastructure of formal and informal norms to support a new global order that is decentralised. If the focus is no longer on the connection between location and order (C. Schmitt), but on their lateral and horizontal linkage, it is necessary to ask under what conditions one can engage in this.[392]

The work of Spanish scholasticism on *ius gentium*, already presented in the sixteenth and seventeenth centuries, was able to unleash the semantic path of decentering the generation of trust in world society.[393] Even the emergence of treaty networks, only conditionally constituted by interstate relations, is an effect of this shift to the formation of decentralised trust. This symbiosis of legal conceptualisation, the conversion of the order of trust, and a society that no longer organises itself through the political but increasingly through relationships also set the stage for the development of a new *lex mercatoria* or private ordering, as 'the basis for a system of private property and commercial exchanges that operate beyond the reach of statehood'[394] can slowly establish itself.[395]

The point here, however, is to emphasise how the dispersion of sovereignty affected not just the matter of the *ius publicum europaeum*, but also the ways in which trust was generated and expectations structured in world society. As illustrated by Bayly, with the transition from the dominance of politics to the dominance of relations referred to here, there was a profound change in the old system of honorary consuls or consultation under local rules with the leaders of 'host' trading communities. They were replaced by networks of trade consulates and international economic agreements.[396] In this context, Frank Trentmann points to the emergence of a new *civic persona*: the consumer. The citizen-consumer gave (and still gives) a democratic appeal to free trade in the age of the emergence of mass politics.[397]

VI. Coevolution of the National and Transnational

Philosophy itself already has means of reflection on the subject of political economy on the dynamic relationship between the national and international levels. This is particularly evident in the writings of István Hont, in which, from a dual perspective of history and philosophy, the dependence of the nation-state on the internal sphere is brought into a necessary correlation with the external sphere.[398] This is especially the case in David Hume's essay 'Jealousy of Trade',[399] which was a product of the English eighteenth century, when the economy and its reflections gradually gained political weight for the internal constitution of the state. 'Jealousy', according to Hont, at that time connoted something between 'vigilance' and 'security', and was a clear allusion to Thomas Hobbes, who had placed the accent strongly on the constitution of internal sovereignty. 'Jealousy of Kings and Persons of Soveraigne Authority'[400] demonstrated in *Leviathan* this intuitive need for the formation of a cohesive and sovereign inner unity.

A 'political economy'[401] that focused not only on the political but also on its entanglement with the economic hinted at a new form of interdependence between politics and economics and, even more, the fundamental conditions of sovereignty. It situated itself in a hybrid space between realism and liberalism, ancient and modern republicanism, theory and political practice,[402] and in this sense also embodied a 'post-Machiavellian movement', when not only an authoritative sovereignty was central, but also a calculative sovereignty.[403] This same perception spreads to continental philosophy, such that Hegel in the nineteenth century, in his fundamental distinction between state and society, does not limit the social side of the distinction to the nation-state framework, but extends its reference to an external sphere of statehood toward world society.[404] In this sense, political economy becomes the essential feature of statehood and points to a moment of incompleteness and unpredictability of modern theories of sovereignty, namely a realm that is itself constitutive of sovereignty but eludes comprehensive rule or sovereignty.[405] This also makes clear that it hardly makes sense to talk about erosions or an end of sovereignty in the sense posed by Carl Schmitt, because modern sovereignty always presupposed erosions and fissures.[406] Or, in the sense of the present book: a co-evolution of the national and the transnational was part of the condition of statehood.

The change in the relationship between the national and the transnational within this process of co-evolution of global society is not only a deterministic result of what has been called the dispersion of sovereignty here in this chapter. Nor could this relationship be contained for long within the contours provided by the internal dynamics of the centralisation of the concrete order of the *ius publicum europaeum*. Coevolution as an interaction of both levels is the result of a multitude of conditionings and interconnections of factors that cannot be read from the perspective of searching for causal connections. Because it is an evolutionary process, not bound to a logic of progress, but to the procedure of providing more possibilities and variations that are established and transformed over time (i.e., with no guarantee of permanence or even eternity), an institution that certainly plays the role of a catalyst of complexity in this exposed sense would be the institution of the Zollverein. Not only did it play a central role within the borders of the national territory, but it was also a driving force for connections, relationships and contacts between territories and between individuals and companies from different territories.

This central position of Zollverein in the German modernisation process has not been overlooked by the exponent of research on the theory of the capitalist mode of production: Friedrich Engels, in his critical review of Karl Marx's 'Zur Kritik der Politischen Ökonomie' (1859), argued that the emergence of bourgeois society in Germany had come about only with the founding of the (German) Zollverein.[407] Prior to that, the conditions of bourgeois society and industrial development had been reduced from the 'outset to the most petty relations'.[408] The German Zollverein provides a remarkable example of the multiple effects of an institution that not only has an effect internally – or on the constitution of new internal structures and modern conditions – but also externally by, influencing the constitution and recognition of several states outside the concrete order of the *ius publicum europaeum*.[409]

This 'discovery of society'[410] was a great change from a holistic point of view, guided by a social body (state) or a comprehensive idea (religion), to which was added an openness to the new.[411] The discovery of society, however, must not be thought in terms of the nation-state, in the sense of a juxtaposition of state and society.[412] It was from the outset an opening to world society and, as the example of the German Zollverein shows, a driving force for the birth of bourgeois society and conceivable only in very close connection with this opening to world society. A second important dimension of the Zollverein concerns what is understood here as the dispersion of sovereignty and the associated demise of the *ius publicum europaeum*. The Zollverein had concluded[413] several treaties under international law with, among others, the Río-de-la-Plata states in Latin America.[414] A kind of exchange of free trade agreements for political recognition[415] took place, but ultimately led to a replacement of the old (European) 'community of states'.[416] To Carl Schmitt's regret, the dispersion of sovereignty through this 'law treaty-making revolution'[417] and recognition under international law finally led to a dissolution of the European order in 'international law'.[418] The expansion of European international law produced a more or less dense network of treaties and recognitions and thereby enabled the establishment of new forms of trust – beyond the tradition of the European concrete order.[419]

B. WORLD WITHOUT UNITY

As shown in this chapter, the new social dynamic had an important dimension in subjectivity as a means of releasing internal forces to test the new. To this end, cities, unlike the court, became the site of transformations. As Christopher Bayly points out, over the course of the nineteenth century, urban cultures emerged around the world, displaying an increasingly uniform and distinctive pattern of life.[420] And this is not unique to Europe. In non-European countries, in particular, a profound tension emerges between old royal and religious centres and the need for the state to prove its modernity.[421] New communication and transport technologies have accelerated contacts between different parts of the world, and thus central control by the normativity of a *ius publicum europaeum has* become increasingly precarious.

The transition from the dominance of the political to the dominance of the relational was therefore at the same time, in epochal terms, a right of ambivalences and, above all, of the factual necessity to deal with them. On the one hand, liberalism existed in its highest form, on the other hand, nationalism glowed; on the one hand there was rationalism and a science with amazing new inventions, on the other hand there was the re-mystification of the world by the romantic movement. Jürgen Osterhammel speaks methodologically in this context of a simultaneity of nation-building and globalisation processes. In the present work, instead of simultaneity, we speak of a co-evolution of national and transnational social processes that influenced each other. With the structural change of the relational form of law from a 'concrete order' to a dispersion of states, a new form of coordination of law was produced. In jurisprudence, this upheaval gave birth to a new discipline for the legal treatment of 'contacts'. The birth of international law therefore represented the emergence of a new form of relationality, which displaced the old relationality of the *ius publicum europaeum*.[422]

The transition from the dominance of the political to the dominance of the relational is also the product of precisely this indifference zone of modern paradoxes. However, these ambivalences are not abolished, rather they are further unfolded and shifted. In addition, with the increased challenge of inventing and trying new ways of dealing with uncertainty comes an increase in societal complexity that continues to evolve into a society of organisations (Chapter 3) and platforms (Chapter 4). Moreover, society no longer has a central place, a concrete order, into which problems can be projected. Instead, society has only itself and its self-description. It alone must come to terms with its problems and solutions – or not.

5

The Law of Organisations

A. INTRODUCTION

ONE OF THE central consequences pointed out in the last chapter is that with the increase of contacts, the emergence of new technologies and population growth in big cities, the apologia of both the 'exception' in the Schmittian sense and the cultivation of social normativity through the logic of centralisation, have gradually lost their suggestive power in different social spheres. And thus the central consequence of the last chapter ties in directly with the thesis of Chapter 1 about the increase of the cognitive dimension of society and the conditions of possibility of legal normativity in global society. Niklas Luhmann addressed this issue in what he called the anomaly thesis, in which he affirmed a clear scepticism of the 'reliance of society and its functional systems on a functioning of the legal code' as they have arisen in the law of the nation-state.[423] However, this does not simply mean that law disappears in the further development of global society. Instead, it takes on different, new forms and contours. This book attempts to show how global law, conditioned by the increasing complexity of society, is reproduced through the relations between states after the disintegration of the *ius publicum europaeum*.[424] However, with the increase in social complexity of global society, problems can no longer be solved exclusively within the 'law of states', but are now also handled in the form of organisations. This gives rise to new contours of global law in the transition from a state-mediated global society to a global society in which the role of organisations in the juridification process is becoming increasingly important. This process takes place in particular through the intertwining of legal, technical and economic issues in an increasingly global society.[425]

The relationship between law and technology is not one that emerges only with the digital age, as will be seen in the next chapter. This relationship intensified to a particular extent with the increase in contacts between different parts of the world and the population growth of cities compared to the countryside. All this happened in an increasing way from the second half of the nineteenth century.[426] In this context, technology and its standardisation processes became essential for almost all social spheres. An important feature that specifically distinguishes such moment from other moments for which technological progress was particularly formative is the fact that the organisational form, whether private or public, became central to the processing and generation of new techno-legal knowledge. The increasing presence of knowledge generation through organisations became crucial for coping with the growing complexity of world society, whether at the national level or at the transnational level.

This is not simply a matter of affirming that there is a causal relationship between technology and law. Technical parameters are not merely juridified. Rather, they are entanglements that can be described as overlapping semantics, hybrid normativities, or multinormativity.[427] This chapter will focus in particular on the gradual spread of the organisational form to manage a techno-legal knowledge, which another form of knowledge management, such as the interaction between individuals or states, could not handle. To this end, we will first address the letters exchanged between Carl Schmitt and Ernst Forsthoff, which reveals an inherent tension between a theory of sovereignty by Schmitt and the actual social structure of the industrial society. For the administrative scientist and Schmitt's student, it becomes increasingly obvious that a theory of the political – in this case, its further development into a partisan theory – has become more and more anachronistic and unlikely due to the inherent structures of industrial society.

The second part of this chapter, in turn, deals once again with the consequences of the lack of a normative centre of global society – as already described in Chapter 2 above when discussing the concept of the disintegration of the *ius publicum europaeum*. Indeed, the deficit of a 'concrete order' in Carl Schmitt's sense means that society itself must develop mechanisms to deal with the increasing complexity resulting from increasing interactions, relationships, and inventions. On a global scale, the production of sectoral knowledge, associated with productive capacity and the generation of legal and technical normativity based on technology and organisational form, becomes one of the central features of what is here called the 'society of organisations'. This leaning toward sectoral self-organisation through sectoral standardisation has significant implications both for the thematic framing within nation-states and for the constitution of the legal normativity of particular sectors themselves. The form of organisation and its capacity to produce legal-technical knowledge management will be decisive for the further development of law in the global society.

B. THE ANACHRONISTIC IN THE POLITICAL: THE STRUCTURES INHERENT IN INDUSTRIAL SOCIETY

The culture of correspondence of the bourgeoisie of the past decades is a common source for the study of political and ideological contexts. This applies not only to the famous correspondence of Marx and Engels,[428] but also to correspondence from completely opposite political camps. Goethe already attested that the 'correspondence of two or more persons who continue their education through activity in a common circle' is an invaluable historical source.[429] This can also be observed in the correspondence between Schmitt and Forsthoff.

Above all, theoretical incompatibilities between student and master can also be discerned, especially in those passages from which Forsthoff's perception becomes clear in the sense that there is an inherent incompatibility between the establishment of a new social structure and theories such as that of the political in Schmitt's sense. Even among legal scholars who are politically categorised on the same ideological spectrum, the difficulty of developing theories of sovereignty is becoming increasingly apparent as modern social processes become progressively intertwined with enabling more complexity and variation – and its consequences.

A letter from Forsthoff to Schmitt dated 20 May 1970, focuses on two topics: the commemorative issue for Hans Barion – a German Catholic canon lawyer who was stripped of his professorship after World War II – and the relationship between the partisan, i.e., the central figure of a new theory of the political, and his ability to adapt in industrial society. The first theme addressed in the letter is not relevant to the present book.[430] The second theme, on the other hand, is relevant; namely, the relationship between the partisan and industrial society that concurrently reveals new latent conditions in modern society with which Forsthoff is concerned regarding the development of law and state in industrial society.[431]

It is no coincidence that Schmitt dedicated the book 'Theory of the Partisan', syndicated in 1963, to Forsthoff on the occasion of his sixtieth birthday.[432] The letter mentioned above, conversely, is from 1970.[433] Schmitt's theory of the partisan is to be understood in the context of his comprehensive writings and essays on the concept of the political in the continuation of the Nomos and *Großraum* doctrine.[434] The partisan presents itself as an attempt to reintegrate the concept of the political into the debate on global society; that is, in the Schmittian vocabulary of a new nomos of the earth that, since the demise of the *ius publicum europaeum*, no longer exists in this form. For this reason, Schmitt's turn to a theory of the partisan can be seen in two respects as a search for the desideratum of a political (spatial) order that cannot be found and, at the same time, as an escape from the new kinds of social structures that take shape especially in the postwar period.[435] The partisan would be, in this sense, a theoretical figure that could stop the tendency of depoliticisation of the world society. The very partisanship inherent in the 'partisan' prevented any unification. At the same time, the partisan struggle brings to mind the polarising violence of the political.[436]

Accordingly, understanding the partisan as the last truly political being of the present fits extraordinarily well into the model coined in 'political theology' of the human opposites that have a constructive effect in the sphere of the political.[437] The partisan constitutes the political anew, serves a territorially limited place, and thus leads to the construction of spatially closed spaces that were decidedly separated from the outside by the struggle. In this respect, according to Schmitt, there was the possibility that the partisan struggle would lead to those large spaces that he had in mind as an ideal.[438] At the same time, it was precisely this characteristic of the partisan to be the last bastion of a global theory of the political that contrasted with the increasingly complex technical and impersonal infrastructure of society, which was constituted by the construction of long-term (but at the same time technically conditioned) contexts of expectation.[439]

It is specifically at this point that Forsthoff, with the due reservation of the seven-year gap after the publication of the book on the partisan, clearly expresses his scepticism about the persistence of a theory of the political in the new guise of the partisan. Forsthoff makes it clear that the partisan in the Schmittian sense 'will remain a marginal phenomenon in the highly industrialised affluent society', primarily because of the structures inherent in industrial society that, according to Forsthoff, guarantee 'the stability of the public sector'. At this point, he refers to his work *The State in Industrial Society* to testify that the stability of public conditions (at that time) did not derive solely from the actions of a state, but from the practical constraints of what he calls 'industrial society'.[440] The preconditions on which the state lived, and which it could not guarantee itself, were of a technical and organisational nature in the industrial context.[441]

Forsthoff's trivialisation of the political phenomenon in the Schmittian sense is directly related to the rise of a society of organisations, i.e., a society that is increasingly dependent on the advanced performance of organisations and the generation of knowledge in the organisational form.[442] Even the state, according to Forsthoff, takes on new contours in this context: the bourgeois state becomes a technical state.[443] The 'age of realisation' aims at the fact that the depoliticisation triggered by the technical industrial society deprives the state of the preservation of a political in the Schmittian sense as a function.[444] In other words, the political could no longer be monopolised internally by the state on account of a society of organisations.[445] Instead, the provision of services of general interest and social redistribution would become the main functions of the state. This would be accompanied by a logic of the pluralistic state, in which the 'interest-based expertise' of the associations and their power-political thrust would prove superior even to the political parties.[446] Here, considering the associations' growing importance, it becomes particularly clear how the dimension of organisation gains an increasing role within the national political framework.[447]

Nevertheless, as a child of his time, Ernst Forsthoff had an ambivalent relationship regarding the subject of technology. On the one hand, he followed his generation in a pessimistic view of people's growing dependence on technology; on the other hand, he turned this observation into his greatest contribution to constitutional and administrative law: the concept of *Daseinsvorsorge*.[448] It simultaneously crystallises the dependence of people, or as Forsthoff calls it, the 'social sensitivity of modern mass existence',[449] and the legal management of this dependence by organisation-based and technology-oriented public institutions.[450] *Daseinsvorsorge* is the semantic construction that best describes the crisis of bourgeois law centred on the generality and abstraction of liberties and the separation of the individual from the state.[451] According to Forsthoff,

Daseinsvorsorge is 'the field in which the liberal concern for liberty, with its tendency to disempower the state, ran itself dead'.[452]

The arguments, with which Forsthoff coined the term *Daseinsvorsorge*, are worth noting.[453] His construct is based above all on a sociological theory of modernisation, which he justifies explicitly with the increase in social differentiation, more specifically in the form of industrial society based on the division of labour, as a new form of allocation of social goods.[454] With the transition from rural to urban areas and the densification of living conditions, socialised living spaces increased in contrast to communalised spaces.[455] According to Forsthoff, the dependence of human existence on a plethora of (public) organisations, such as transportation and communication facilities, gas and energy supply, etc, allowed the state new 'possibilities for shaping and reshaping *Dasein* through this form of supply of technical infrastructure'.[456] This was also accompanied by a clear shift in the significance of state authority as a central ruling authority in the conventional sense.[457]

With this statement of new 'possibilities of shaping and reshaping *Dasein*' through the state, Forsthoff also, surprisingly, approaches Foucault's analysis on the intrusion of the new form of government, which the latter himself describes as governmentality.[458] The composition of the words government and mentality (*gouverne – mentalité*) aptly describes the crucial role of the state, which introduces practices of subjectivation into the social through its possibilities of shaping and reshaping *Dasein*.[459] In this sense, both Forsthoff and Foucault distance themselves from a modern concept of sovereignty in the Schmittian tradition of the state of exception and, for their part, focus on the widespread phenomenon of the penetration of (state) administration into the social sphere and its effects on subject constitution. In Forsthoff's work, technology has decisively 'broken free from its ties to the relations of production'.[460] His distance from Marx, however, turns into an approximation to Foucault's concept of discipline. The derivation of technology and power is then consistent. According to Forsthoff, the technical process, which is aimless in itself, is characterised by its special 'affinity to power'.[461] Power is no longer cultivated centrally via the 'degree of intensification of the political' (C. Schmitt), but is increasingly operationalised via decentralised organisation-based structures.[462]

These two moments are also taken up by Foucault: first of all, Foucault accentuates the inadequacy of the Marxist dialectical interpretive capacity, since for him 'the emergence of sexuality as a basic problem marks the slide from a philosophy of working man to a philosophy of speaking being'.[463] Then, he emphasises the moment of a society of organisations, or an industrial society, in which industrial normalisation or standardisation itself penetrates the semantic core of the choice of terms.[464] In French, *normalisation* means 'standardisation' in the prevailing everyday usage[465] and is very closely associated with the performance of organisations in Foucault's work.[466] The organisation of the modern prison serves as an ideal type for the nationwide disciplinary institutions of modernity.

The generation of knowledge by organisations is an important prerequisite for the exercise of social institutional power as a form of discipline in the Foucaultian sense. For the case of the prison, Foucault is troubled by the effective use of technical media, such as the technique of index cards,[467] which is crucial for the 'organisation of a system of documentation' that 'makes it easy to incorporate new data and information belonging to each individual sought'.[468] At the same time, he wonders why the role of index cards had been so little researched up to that point.[469] It was only through the form of organisation that slips of paper, and thus systematic databases, could generate effective knowledge that was essential to managing disciplinary action.[470] The Foucaultian normative *dispositif* thrives on organisation-based and technical presuppositions.[471]

Normalisation and standardisation as an organisation-based production, which Foucault traces back to the example of various institutions, such as the factory, the school and its predecessor, the monastery, to a standardised classification of bodies and lives into standardised times and spaces, are the basic structure of a disciplinary[472] or normalisation society.[473] In *La Volonté de Savoir*, Foucault returns to the triad 'norme/normalisation/*normalité*' through which, as in the book *Surveillance and Punishment*, the practical *dispositifs* and, above all, the emergence of 'bio-power' is analysed through *normalisation/standardisation*. In this sense, according to Foucault, a normalisation society presents itself as a historical 'effect of a technology of power directed at life'.[474] Forsthoff describes the birth of normality, which in Foucault's view asserts itself in (organisation-based) bio-politics, with the concept of the technical state and services of general interest, which would be equally unthinkable without an organisation-based infrastructure.

Finally, the birth of normality is the growth of society's reliance on standardisation processes, driven by the form of organisations, and it occurs long before the theoretical formulations of Foucault and Forsthoff. In particular, the increase in the importance of technology from the second half of the nineteenth century onwards inevitably leads to the opposite effect of an 'intensification of the political' (C. Schmitt). This phenomenon is particularly noticeable in the metamorphosis of global law in the transition from a law of states, which was dominated by contacts and relations between states, to a law reproduced through organisations.

The following sections will look at how new kinds of processes of normalisation and, above all, standardisation processes, were set in motion in world society in the form of organisations from the mid-nineteenth century. The increase in contacts between the newly established states, colonies and older states, which was composed of the greater movement of people and goods and the increase in the population of the major world cities, brought new challenges for the standardisation of diverse areas of society, which, due to the increasingly global dimension, were not to be fragmented into different state regimes with different centres of standardisation.

Not only the reduction of cross-border transaction costs, but above all the functionality of various technologies (such as telegraphy, energy supply and railroad transport, the need for standardisation of screws and threads due to the worldwide spread of machine types, etc) depended on the establishment of new forms of societal self-normalisation or self-regulation, which ultimately had to be handled in organisational forms. One organisational form that provided standardisation processes for the cross-border linkages of world society was the so-called administrative unions that advanced the role of self-organisation in world society. The nationality and internationality of this process of generation and setting of standards then went hand in hand with a form of co-evolution of the national and the transnational.[475] This can be illustrated by the example of the standardisation of electricity[476] and other infrastructure modernisations, which also form part of the later concept of 'services of general interest'.[477]

C. THE EMERGENCE OF ORGANISATIONS BEYOND WAR MANAGEMENT

In the literature on international law and political science, the question of the emergence and necessity of the organisational form to deal with concrete state affairs is often traced back to the issue of warfare. An example of this is David Kennedy's important essay 'The Move to Institutions', in which, drawing in particular on the founding of the League of Nations, he describes the added value of a transition from a global society focused on contacts between states to one increasingly based on organisations as a product of the post-World War I instrument of peacekeeping and dispute settlement between states.[478] In the same context, Gerard Mangone deals with the shift from state-centred to organisation-mediated world society law, seeing the Hague System in particular as one of the precursors of the new way of producing legal normativity.[479] The two are by no means alone in this assessment.[480]

Such reductionism when it comes to the role played by organising in configuring the legal normativity of global society, which, in the words of Henry Brailsford, ends in a certain manichaeism,[481] is being challenged by a new generation of studies.[482] They focus particularly on the softening of this understanding of the function of organisations, which is primarily focused on government action, and direct the focus instead to the inherently dynamic emergent self-organisations in global society. They thus focus primarily on observing the formative unfolding of the power of the social through organisations that, out of their sectoral expertise, enable multidimensional networking with governmental as well as non-governmental, i.e., private actors and scholars.

One of the most vivid examples of the production of legal normativity in the transition from a state-centred to an organisation-centred global society is the development of copyright law. In this context, institutionalisation through so-called administrative unions plays a crucial role in the global expansion of author protection.[483] It enabled a 'novel involvement of civil society actors, transnational networks, and international officials'. In this context, world law took on new features that were no longer purely intergovernmental, but neither should it be understood in terms of a world republic or a world state. Given the increased complexity and the impossibility of guiding the new (world) society by an ultimate foundation or centre, or in Schmittian terminology, the concrete order of a *ius publicum europaeum*, world society tends to be fragmented into technical sectors based on organisations.[484]

D. THE LEGALISATION OF CULTURAL GOODS

A given case can be reconstructed in different ways. Of course, (good) lawyers know this. Or rather: reconstructing facts differently is a knowledge that lawyers generally possess. If we take the relationship between technology and law as a starting point, this art of reconstruction by lawyers is particularly evident in the area of copyright and patent law. A common procedure is offered by the conventional practice of traditional legal dogmatics, which searches for an element of state law in order to then assume or describe the origin of law from norms from a piece of legislation. A second approach, alternatively, offers the legal-theoretical foundation of factual reconstruction, in which various elements neighbouring law are used to interpret the subject matter.[485] In an approach based on lateral contacts between disciplines, both a new view of the facts themselves is presented and a dogmatic boundary of the discipline is crossed.[486] Especially in areas of law where technological innovations play an important role in the transformation of social relations, contacts that are both cross-disciplinary and lateral offer a surplus of interpretive possibilities instead of a narrowing of the interpretive capacity.[487]

This is also the case with copyright law. In order to incorporate new elements of neighbouring disciplines and to avoid a narrowing to a purely dogmatic-methodological, nationalistic view, one can understand the driving force of the transformation of rights as a media-theoretical conflict between authors or creators and apparatuses and their legal stabilisation. Long before it was possible to quickly and easily detach texts, music and graphics or images from their material carriers, the conceptual language formation of intellectual property pointed to the duality of body and mind and challenged the classical dynamics of ownership.[488] The immaterial state of this form of property equates its mobility, transferability, and not least its reproducibility with the rise of publishing and media markets in industrialisation.[489]

This development, however, presupposes something that in the present work – following John Brewer – is called 'the social achievement of the transition from the court to the city'. This social precondition was crucial for the release of a new productivity of the individual, which is actually at the heart of the production of cultural goods protected by intellectual property.[490] Only through the gradual weakening of courtly relations with their centralist orientation could an awakening of modern book and art markets advance, and thus a plural professionalisation of writers, scholars, artists, composers and musicians could take hold in the second half of the nineteenth century, beyond courtly or ecclesiastical culture. The shift from courtly patronage to an increasingly broad, urban, impersonal public contributed to the demise of the old regime of early modern privileges, in which sovereigns, kings and emperors granted publishing or printing privileges in order[491] to channel the flow of information in a centralised manner through an instrument of political control and censorship.[492]

Intellectual property not only marks the difference between the creator and the created, as well as their institutionalised rebound through legal norms, but it also presents itself at the same time as an effect of the reproduction techniques that impacted practices of juridification from the nineteenth century onward. In this sense, Heinrich Bosse emphasises that 'work domination', i.e., the relationship between author and work, which then led to legal reforms in the nineteenth century, can only be understood as a printing technique from the introduction of the rotary press.[493] In other words, it is only when a new technical possibility of reproduction emerges that new forms of control over usage become inevitable.

Legalisation practices and reproduction techniques are phenomena that enrich each other. With the diversification of products and the invention of new techniques, it became necessary to stabilise more long-term expectations through law. In some areas, as in the case of authors' rights, this stabilisation was not achieved exclusively through national law because of the immateriality and easy mobility of the subject matter. In order to bring about a certain stable infrastructure as a horizon of expectation beyond nation-state borders, and thereby promote a broader circulation and production of cultural products, parallel forms of juridification emerged within the nation-state legal model. Beginning in the second half of the nineteenth century, they drove the legal stabilisation of social processes through institutions, associations, corporations, and organisations at the international level, primarily ensuring that an infrastructure of rules emerged within the global, sectoral expectation space.[494]

Accordingly, if we want to understand how these transnational structures emerged, and how they became irreplaceable for the modern development of copyright, the transformation of copyright is less traceable in the tradition of textual hermeneutics, which searches for the right meaning and better interpretation of legal texts, international treaties, and public debates.[495] Rather, it is concerned with changing social contexts, which places the emphasis on the materiality of communication[496] and its legal and social structural stabilisation. In this way, it is possible to observe the phenomenon of the configuration and reconfiguration of property rights as 'materialless law' beyond a nation-state conditioned legal dogmatic demarcation. It is primarily a matter of looking at the constitutional conditions of a modern copyright, at the co-evolutionary relationship between the transnational and the national level, and at the way society itself deals with the increase in its own social complexity. Without authors' rights, without an infrastructure of legal and technical rules, the global trade of music, books and other forms of cultural content products on online platforms would barely have been conceivable without a legal and technical infrastructure of rules.

I. New Media, New Laws?

From 1850 on, the emergence of ever new kinds of recording media posed an unprecedented challenge in legal discourse. How does legal normativity relate to the contingency of circumstances? For law, the change in media also means the necessity of new contingency management. The beginning of mass production of music boxes and new possibilities of transmitting musical works caused an upheaval from about the mid-1800s. In Germany and in France, different court decisions were made on this around 1865. The French court considered them to be unauthorised reproductions, while the German Imperial Court for the first time outlined a new concept of reproduction that differed from the reprinting privilege.[497] A new culture of reproduction in the music industry was already emerging, drawing attention to new distribution media and the adaptation of legal concepts to new means.[498]

The new technical apparatuses slowly became part of the population's lifestyle, exerting strong influence not only as furniture in hotel lobbies and in homes, but also as mere home entertainment apparatuses.[499] The new media and audiovisual apparatuses made a career in this sense. The invention of the 'Speaking Machine' by Thomas Alva Edison (1847–1931) in 1877 quickly led to the commercial production of the phonograph, beginning in 1878. The further development of the phonograph, the gramophone by electrical engineer Emil Berliner (1851–1929), who emigrated from Hanover to the USA, greatly improved the sound quality of Edison's 'Speaking Machine' and became the basis of the modern sound industry. Berliner founded the United States Gramophone Company and at the same time commissioned the Kämmerer & Reinhard doll factory in Germany to mass-produce gramophones starting in 1890.[500] To establish the gramophone, a series of ten titles by the singer Enrico Caruso (1873–1921) was recorded, which contributed to the gramophone's career. Slowly the gramophone became the new mass medium and at the same time established itself as a serious musical device. Devices for magnetic sound, the electric microphone, recording and reproduction, the electrodynamic loudspeaker, followed in 1898 and 1925, respectively.[501]

All of these new recording media, but especially the phonograph as a new medium, made recordings possible and at the same time favoured the individuality of the voice and the improvisational power of the artist, challenged the existing copyright law. The previous regime of copyright protected only musical notation, i.e., it used to take into account only the fixation of musical language on written notes; in short, it protected the music composer but not the formless voice. The transformation of the work from writing to voice was accompanied by the increase in the possibilities of dissemination through the technical invention of the cylinder. The phonograph did not have the glamour of a concert, but made possible a greater popularisation of music.[502] The novelty was not the written notes, but the individualised voice and the conditions of its technical reproducibility. Slowly, the feeling became established that the phonograph was not merely reproducing a mechanical rendition of the music engraver, but that it was actually the recording artist who was in the foreground.[503]

Regarding this change in media, Friedrich Kittler coined the term 'pivot' for a transformation through which the transition of media – in this case from writing to voice – is strongly emphasised.[504] The 'pivot', so understood, was accompanied by a shift in the meaning of leadership roles, in that the new technology meant that it was the tone-setter, rather than the note-setter, who gained the primary role in the growing new industry. Media conditions are, in this context, factors of cultural differentiation with serious implications for the conditions of juridification. New media become cultural techniques, especially insofar as they constitutively produce new chains of action and connection.[505] Law reacts to these cultural-technical media by providing new forms of coping with complexity. In this context, the emergence of new technologies and new apparatuses challenge precisely the limits of the claims to legal normativity hitherto conferred by the copyright regime. And furthermore, the 'battle of rationalities' between apparatuses and legal norms also challenges the limits of the form of generating legal normativity according to the nation-state oriented model. In this context, the new forms of complexity management provided by law to society do not remain bound solely to the traditional form of juridification through legislation. Rather, they call into being – especially in the case of copyright – a new, transnational, organisation-based generation of knowledge. Legal normativity is no longer the monopoly of nation-state legislation.

II. The Management of Legal Normativity by Organisations

The rise of knowledge and information as a central, cultural, social and economic resource of modern societies is a typical phenomenon of the second half of the twentieth century.[506] Although it is a later phenomenon (at least in terms of its semantic reflection), the immateriality inherent in the concepts of knowledge and information has driven structural developments prior to the semantic crystallisation of postindustrial society in the second half of the twentieth century. In particular, the process of organisation-based standardisation of various sectors of society set the course for the new postindustrial society to the extent that it enabled the creation of a flexible and dynamic techno-legal horizon of expectations within a process of multiple organisations. Such creation of a global infrastructure has been crucial for the communication and movement of people and cultural goods.[507]

The concept of governance offers a possible semantic description for this change in social structure, which entails advantages as well as disadvantages. The emergence of governance structures is historically situated from the 1990s onward, when a process of continuous migration of national decision-making competencies toward governance structures and institutions beyond the state becomes apparent.[508] However, this process does not take the form of a linear chronology, as implied by the 'transformation of the state'[509] approach of Michael Zürn and Stephan Leibfried. It is not the case that there was first the state or the 'state in its golden age', which was then buttressed by globalisation processes. The advantage of this approach lies in the clarification that many social processes cannot be traced back to the state alone. In this respect, the governance concept allows for a more complex description of transnational phenomena. The disadvantages lie in the historical specificity of the phenomenon. As already indicated, co-evolutionary processes between the national and the transnational are concomitants of a phenomenon of modern statehood that produces an intertwined regulatory structure between the national level and the transnational level. These processes intensify with the law of organisations mentioned here, which already gains in importance and intensity in the second half of the nineteenth century.

What is meant by the 'administration of legal normativity by organisations' is that both law and the form of organisation have taken on a central role in the process of international spread of technology, communication, transport and markets from the second half of the nineteenth century onwards. Without law and without the form of organisation as a transnational form of knowledge generation, such a development would have been unthinkable. As Arthur Nussbaum notes, the process of juridification of international relations has led to a structural change in international law in which the establishment of substantive administrative unions through multilateral treaties has replaced the international law treaties previously geared toward military and peacekeeping purposes.[510] A new type of treaty with law-making, open-accession, multilateral characteristics and, above all, with factual, organisational goals established itself as a compensatory mechanism for the lack of centralised, norm-setting authority in international law,[511] in that the regulatory proliferation and condensation of normative issues regulated many areas of world society across borders.[512] And the issues covered by it were not few in number: measurement and coinage systems, patent, trademark and design protection, river navigation, energy supply, railroads, postal (1874) and telegraph (1865) systems, the Sugar Convention (1902), the Occupational Safety and Health Convention (1906), and others.

From the perspective of legal source theory, in fact, all these organisations found their origin in a state act: the interstate international law treaties.[513] But these interstate international law treaties were different from the treaties that were commonly signed between states at that time. Namely, they were no longer purely interstate treaties of friendship, commerce, and navigation, but multilateral and open-accession treaties tailored to a substantive area. From a functional point of view, they went beyond the pursuit of the interests of states by establishing, on a contractual basis, an institutional permanence for an indefinite period of time, partly independent, subject-related structure. Miloš Vec emphasises the following elements: 'autonomy, norm-setting powers, rights of control, and even the beginnings of a jurisdiction of one's own – in this, a very cautious surrender of sovereign rights of the nation-states to the unions could be seen'.[514]

In particular, the dynamics of the sectoral division of the organisations' affairs, as well as the technical nature of the issues at stake, required dynamic forms of dispute resolution that differed from the traditional institute of diplomatic protection under international law.[515] Within this system of dispute resolution, mediated by a certain 'melting pot' of rationalities, a new dynamic emerged among diplomats, lawyers and technicians that could not be reduced to the interests of member states alone. Expert adjudication in international administrative unions[516] was, in this sense, a new way of dealing with the increasing social complexity of global society and, at the same time, with the need to establish minimum guidelines or minimum standards in technical areas of great global capillarity.

In this sense, administrative unions also created objective law and contributed to a cross-border, cognitively open set of instruments that did not just serve to reduce transaction costs by continually adding more private and public actors to the standard setting of various organisations. Last but not least, the logic of standardisation in trade, transport and communication through organisation-based alliances institutionalised the management of technical and legal uncertainties worldwide.[517]

The establishment of bureaus, conferences and commissions also proved to be a gain in autonomy vis-à-vis the signatory states, in that comprehensive cooperation came about in technical and different, (mostly) non-political factual contexts.[518] In this sense, the dogma of state sovereignty, according to which states are established as bearers of international law within a law of worldwide coexistence, was subliminally mutated by the 'technical-administrative' character of the administrative unions. Koskenniemi correctly emphasises at this point: 'if any generalization can be made in this regard, it is rather that the men were centrists who tried to balance their moderate nationalism with their liberal internationalism'.[519]

On the semantic level, it was only a matter of time before this structural change found resonance. Lorenz von Stein's coining of the term 'international administrative law' as early as 1866 drew attention to the transformation from coexistence to fact-based cooperation. Although Stein's position gained little reception in his time,[520] the notion of an international administrative law lives on to this day.[521] Notwithstanding, the self-description of legal facts by the ordinary formalistic processing of the material led to the suppression of transnational legal phenomena from the representations of administrative law or public law in general. The classical dogmatic foundation of the dualism of national and international law by Carl Heinrich Triepel was then the consistent epistemic closure of legal self-description to all these new developments.[522]

This development of the administrative union was admittedly far removed from the idea of an international community guided by solidarity in the sense of a '*bonum commune humanitatis*',[523] or common cultural values – even the provocative tone of Carl Schmitt: 'he who says "humanity" wants to deceive'.[524] However, cooperation is not meant here as the uniform, agreement-oriented action of the international community, but as a highly dynamic, cognitively based, dispersed process of worldwide knowledge generation through technical standardisation procedures within organisations.[525]

III. Transnationalisation of Authors' Rights

Among the various areas that have been shaped by legal normativity through organisations is the development of the transnational legal infrastructure for the protection of cultural goods. The growing economic, social and cultural interdependence in global society required a new mechanism that could juridify cultural goods, knowledge, and information beyond the borders of national states. The founding of the Berne Union in 1886, under Swiss supervision, filled precisely this gap by establishing a new scope for action beyond both purely interstate relations and state legislation to coordinate the interests of diverse groups of professionals, government officials, legal experts and economists. Something similar happened through the initiative of non-state actors such as writers, scientists, artists, musicians, publishers and lawyers, who, starting in the 1950s, promoted the cross-border recognition of authors' rights among the national and global public at international literary congresses and with the help of nationally and internationally organised interest and professional associations.[526]

Admittedly, there are differences between the national regulations for the protection of cultural property. To mention just a few of the most obvious of these: there are significant differences between the legal traditions of copyright in Great Britain and the United States, German copyright law, and the French *droit d'auteur*. Monika Dommann, however, aptly calls the 'copyright versus *droit d'auteur* versus *Urheberrecht* debate' that dominated legal discourse in the nineteenth and twentieth centuries' no more than 'a myth cultivated in the age of nationalism'[527] from which one should finally free oneself. The narrowing of a methodological nationalism in the matter of intellectual property rights should, nonetheless, be remedied by recent research with its emphasis on the importance of transnational coordination of development.[528] Dynamic coordination with the creation of a transnational structure to mediate the interests of various private and public actors, ensuring the stabilisation of expectations of intellectual property law on certain issues, has emerged especially in the media transition with the emergence of various new products that no longer fit into the previous legal categories.[529] Copyright, *Uhrheberrecht* or *droit d'auteur* are a consequence of the constant change of the medium and the emergence of constantly new products and business models. Their crisis is an ongoing movement and is not solely related to the profound change that accompanies the emergence of the new medium of the Internet and its new business models.

According to Miloš Vec and Karl-Heinz Ziegler, the creation of a new legal infrastructure for this purpose took place in connection with the intensification and restructuring of interstate relations as a process of juridification of international relations,[530] which also showed a very large participation of private actors.[531] In this sense, the founding of the Berne Union in 1886 was considered a 'world treaty'[532] for the protection of literary and artistic property.[533] As Isabella Löhr pointedly indicates, the Berne Union's effectiveness was based on its ability to coordinate interconnectedness between different players and, with the transfer of information and knowledge from one national territory to another, to institutionalise an essential feature of the unfolding modern world.[534]

Standardisation processes become prerequisite of other standardisation processes in the sense that one becomes a condition of the other. For example, the standardisation of time measurement was required by the intensification of long-distance travel and increasing intercontinental communication that began in the mid-nineteenth century.[535] Traditionally, time was measured locally and based on the position of the sun (solar time). On this basis, different places tended to have different local times, so people lived in multiple times at the same time, because each degree of difference in longitude meant four minutes of time difference. Only with the spread of new transportation and communication technologies (such as the railroad or the telegraph) did time synchronisation become essential. The invention of an abstract and standardised time in contrast to natural and biophysical rhythms of time perception bound to nature played a fundamental role in the globalisation of the nineteenth century.[536]

The development of transnational juridification would not have been possible without the creation of a transnational structure with a certain independence from the internal affairs of the confederated states. In the specific case of copyright law, this was done through the establishment of an office in Bern.[537] The bureau was not a supranational entity claiming legislative powers or similar sovereign rights, but rather had an executive character. Legislation was nevertheless carried out through the ratification of convention rules among member states and concluded in conferences and meetings. In this sense, the Berne Union was not an international organisation with legal personality under international law. It was not until the advent of World Intellectual Property Organization (WIPO), founded in 1967, that appropriate organisational arrangements were inserted into the treaty texts.[538] However, over time, the offices evolved from subject-centred institutions into organisations that achieved a certain degree of independence from the community of states that founded them and institutionalised the establishment of a transnational traffic of information and cultural goods in cooperation with nationally and internationally organised professional associations.[539]

The members of the treaty pact included a wide range of countries, as well as former colonies and protectorates: Switzerland, Tunisia, Great Britain (including the British colonies, protectorates and Ireland), Spain (including colonies), Belgium, the German Empire, France (including Algeria and the French colonies), Haiti and Liberia – nine states, all of which except Liberia ratified the treaty by 1887. Subsequently, Denmark, Japan, Luxembourg, Monaco, the Netherlands and its colonies, Norway, Portugal and its colonies, and Sweden signed, bringing the total number of countries that had signed the convention to seventeen by the start of World War I.

This multilaterally guaranteed recognition of authors' rights brought about a legal equality of domestic authors with foreign authors in the territory of the association. This exerted international harmonisation pressure on national legal systems. Principles such as the comparative protection period and national treatment,[540] which were enshrined in the founding treaty, guaranteed authors and users binding equal treatment and property protection across national borders. Minimum rights were also established so that any foreign author could be guaranteed a minimum level of protection of translations, performances, and reproductions, regardless of the applicable national law in the territory of the Union.[541] The Berne Union was therefore a novelty in international law, since this organisation-based form of juridification no longer focused on national interests, but on the individual, the author.[542] In this sense, an interaction or co-evolution between the national and transnational levels took place in the field of intellectual property, in that the Berne Union contributed to 'norm-building, standardization and information transfer'[543] of intellectual property.[544]

However, this development was not limited to the juridification of intellectual property. Trade, transport and communication were at the forefront of this process of internationalisation through a fixed framework of juridification and institutionalisation.[545] Other administrative unions were also established at the same time: the Telegraph Union in 1865 and the Universal Postal Union in 1874, both organisations with an office in Bern; the International Metre Convention in 1875 with an office in Paris; the International Association for Labor Legislation in 1900 with an office in Basel; the International Community for the Purpose of Hydrographic and Biological Exploration of the Seas, based in Copenhagen in 1901; and the International Association for the Regulation of Sugar Production in 1902, with headquarters in Brussels, the Seismological Union with an office in Strasbourg and the International Association for Public Hygiene 1907 with an office in Paris, the International Agricultural Association with the International Agricultural Institute 1905 with an office in Rome, etc.

The activity of the administrative unions in the second half of the nineteenth century was, as Armin von Bogdandy and Ingo Venzke note, 'entirely focused on the functioning of specific legal regimes'.[546] Transnational juridification in the field of copyright presented itself as one case among several. In this sense, the administrative unions were institutions of risk distribution and standardisation and, not in the least, constructors of sectoral stable horizons for a global society that lacked a centre radiating normativity. In short, they were 'part of a management of incipient interdependence in the industrial age'.[547] From this perspective, it also becomes clear how the previous semantic construction of the *ius publicum europaeum* as a centralised 'deliberative locus of a concrete order' (Carl Schmitt), as shown in Chapter 2 above, was too undercomplex when it comes to the management of the new cross-border interdependencies.

6

The Law of Platforms

A. INTRODUCTION: WHAT DOES THE DIGITAL MEAN?

In 1996, Niklas Luhmann assessed the changed possibilities of perception of social events that accompany the increase in complexity due to new technologies with the following sentence: 'the more complex the society, the firmer the simultaneity and thus the uninfluenceability of what is factually happening at any given moment'.[548] A more precise interpretation of the increasing uninfluenceability of simultaneous events in the digital world based on cases and practices was not yet possible for him in the 1990s. Nevertheless, he could already see that law in the form it had developed under the institutional framework within the nation-state – strongly linked to the stabilisation of normative expectations – would take on different epistemic contours in this technological and transnational context. It was only with the popularisation of the Internet, set in motion in the last two decades, that it became obvious how much all social institutions that had hitherto ensured the dynamic stability of orders, such as politics, economics, science, the press, the labour market, etc, are facing new challenges. Law, too, cannot avoid reacting to or adapting to this evolutionary self-transformation of modern societies.[549]

As shown in the previous chapter, since the nineteenth century the activity and generation of knowledge and legal normativity within organisations increased more and more, not only within nation-states but also in transnational settings. With the increasing complexity of regulations – often of a technical nature – which in turn required coordination that went beyond the logic of contact between nation-states, an organisational form of knowledge architecture solidified that not only enabled sectoral and thematically specific technical work, but also created a new, transnational legal infrastructure.[550] This generation of sectoral knowledge supplemented the generation of knowledge through interstate contact and not only dominated the way social knowledge was generated, but also shaped the culture of society in this period; in other words, an epistemology of mass culture.[551]

However, this organisation-based social order has undergone another profound transformation with the advent of new electronic means of communication: the new order of the digital, which restructures the old order of knowledge-based organisations, is characterised in particular by artificial intelligence, big data, and algorithmisation,[552] and has produced the forms and

Introduction: What does the Digital Mean?   83

design of the new order of knowledge in the digitised context, as emphasised by cultural theorist Jan Assmann. Digitised practices and media create 'productive instruments of world-making and world-production, [are] constructors of reality and thus also of the human being who lives in this reality'.[553] In this way, they generate a new artificial basis for human life or a new basis for the design of human life and personality development. The digital transforms the generation of social knowledge. Moreover, it also transforms the most intimate interactions and experiences of individuals and institutions with one another, which decisively influence their social trajectories.[554]

In this context of transformation, the American technology historian Michael S. Mahoney clearly expressed the change affecting today's society: in his view, there is no duplicity of worlds, i.e., the analogue and real world on the one hand and the digital and virtual world on the other. Rather, there is an actual transposition of the offline world into the computer, into the new technological devices and their networks, or into the online world. The digital therefore not only marks a fundamental change in the reality of life, but also deeply intervenes in the cultural dimensions of the social and its (re)structuring.[555]

With the emergence of digital realities, society's conception of its relationship to time is changing too. This, in particular, constitutes one of the central concerns of this thesis: to present the relationship between law and the temporal dimension. A crisis in the temporal dimension has been elaborated, as already shown in Chapter 1, especially by Reinhart Koselleck and Niklas Luhmann. Briefly returning to this point, it should be noted that for Koselleck the temporalisation of semantics in saddle time is to be understood as an enlargement of the difference between the space of experience and the horizon of expectation. He locates it where 'expectations have become more and more distant from all experiences that have been made'.[556] The experiences made (*gemachte Erfahrungen*), which were stored as generalised knowledge in society and used as a basis for references of new actions and interactions by both individuals and institutions, became fragile from the saddle period on. The orienting power of experience could no longer stabilise the common horizon of living together. In order to socially establish abstract mechanisms of societal coordination, the category of expectation came to the fore instead. Niklas Luhmann couples this 'disruptive moment' in experience with the spread of new media, in this case printing, and links his concept of law very closely to the category of expectation.

Assuming that there is an intrinsic relationship between the media and society – especially the media and law – one could almost intuitively say that the digital presents itself as an epochal caesura in comparison to the printed book.[557] This new epoch occupies an important place, especially in terms of the temporal and social dimensions – and thus also for law. A completely different temporal horizon emerges, which is no longer congruent with the time horizon of the printing culture.[558] This also has implications for the form of social differentiation, which in this book is considered as functional differentiation: if the social differentiation of systems theory is inseparable from the printing culture, what would be the consequences of the digital for the form of social differentiation? Therefore, in this book, the dimension of the organisation is particularly associated with the printing culture, resulting in a cultural environment in which the generation of new patterns of action repeatedly emerges from the traditional orientation to experience. The automation and digitalisation of various areas of life and society, conversely, form their own new time world(s), which in turn create new complex social relations based on the provision of artificial intelligence and adaptive algorithms in the computer and apparatus networks.[559]

The new 'culture of digitality'[560] also puts the relationship between knowledge and non-knowledge in a new light. With the advent of the digital, a profound change in the relationship between temporality and cognition can be experienced, which is comparably strong or at least stronger than the 'temporalization of the modern age' (R. Koselleck). The semantics of time, which for Luhmann and Koselleck is located in the difference between experience and expectation, already marks a first cognitive crisis of human knowledge. Before the popularisation of printing, everyday human perception was still strongly oriented towards tradition, belief and forms of estate-based orders.[561] The increasing decoupling of human experience from tradition fostered both human and social knowledge.[562] According to the systems theory pattern, from about the second half of the eighteenth century, not only did the individual produce knowledge, but society also produced knowledge about itself.[563] With the increase of social complexity, (social) knowledge became more distant from the human perceptual apparatus.[564] This growing distance between the knowledge produced by society and the knowledge stored by the subject can be experienced as a transition to the new era of the digital without a major theoretical construct. The separation of individual and society, which in the nineteenth century became primarily the subject of sociology, is marked by a new tension between the social and the temporal dimension.[565] The (saddle) time of the book-printing culture, as a 'peculiar symbiosis of future and society',[566] is confronted by a new form of the (dispersion of) order, no longer oriented only to organisation and book-printing. A new era of the 'uninfluenceability of simultaneous events' (N. Luhmann) is reached – the era of the digital, in which neither experience nor expectation any longer provide a yardstick for the formation and stabilisation of institutions and orientation for those taking action.[567]

All these developments undoubtedly have both positive and negative effects.[568] In this book, the focus is on which structural change is being made by a society that is increasingly mediated by digital platforms rather than organisations, and whose change requires an adequate reconstruction of legal categories. In particular, this shift from an organisation-centred society to one increasingly mediated by digital platforms has profound implications for shaping the constitution and transformation of global law. As noted earlier, the role of law in stabilising normative expectations in the manner prescribed by systems theory is being challenged by Niklas Luhmann. The increase in the involvement of cognitive mechanisms of rapid adaptation and learning as typical elements of new technologies to the everyday life of society presents itself as a major challenge to the classical law of the nation-state in its typical European forms. The platform society is the greatest exponent of this development of the increasing cognitive dimension of modern society. It has given clear and current contours to the descriptive prophecy of law as a 'European anomaly'.

At this point, the fundamental question of the role of law arises. Such question revolves primarily around whether law will dissolve into cognitive mechanisms or whether, in this new transnational technological society in which digital platforms combine two important elements (technology and transnationality), law will have to fulfil the other functions or tasks inherent in business models. Before addressing the concretisation of this question, it is first necessary to address concepts and theories that also state a constant dissolution of the society of organisations. Network theory in particular offers an important conceptual arsenal for dealing with this post-organisational society. Nevertheless, we must also address whether the metaphor and notion of network are appropriate concepts to describe the specifics of the rise of the platform society.

B. ON THE THRESHOLD AFTER THE THRESHOLD: KNOWLEDGE, NETWORKS, DATA AND PLATFORMS

I. On the Threshold: Networks

Hans Blumenberg uses a methodology called 'epochal thresholds' to identify ephemeral phenomena that belong to neither the previous nor the later era. According to Blumenberg, epochal thresholds represent an 'imperceptible limit' that only becomes clear in a differential analysis *ex post*.[569] The epochal threshold as a functional method thus stands in contrast to approaches that conceive of historical change as the reception and adoption of content into new forms or contexts. This approach is not intended to focus on identifying morphological continuity or discontinuity, but rather to capture the differences across which the reception of what has gone before has taken place.[570] In this sense, the notion of threshold links continuity with discontinuity. According to this method, there is no founder (of an epoch) that leaves the past behind. Thresholds are the zones of indifference, congruent places of frames for their reality,[571] which stand on two different sides of the epochal threshold.[572]

This expression of *transience* can also be observed at the conceptual level, that is, in concepts that express a certain 'that no longer' but at the same time a 'that not yet'. In the context of the discussion, terms are used that attempt to articulate the break with a certain social structure – a social structure that depended on organisations – to show that there are new social elements and structures that can no longer be thematised in the form of the organisation. Because these terms are articulated in a field of transience, of the transitory, they cannot yet capture the real structures of a new social complexity. This in-between space among organisations and what is here called 'digital' alone has led to a profound social transformation that affects not only law but also society as a whole. However, this in-between space remains as a threshold and the terms on the threshold, and thus they cannot adequately synthesise and make semantically perceptible something that emerges as a structural phenomenon after the threshold.

The threshold or in-between space mentioned here is co-reflected especially on the semantic level as a reaction to the gradual structural upheaval that has already been tested in new conceptualisations since the 1970s. For example, information society, knowledge[573] society, and network society were central conceptual forms that were consistently applied to describe the new knowledge order for the space in between.[574] Of course, the network concept is particularly prominent.[575] 'Network' is not, however, a concept used exclusively for the information society or knowledge society:[576] even for phenomena that predate the Internet, it shows great interpretive power, especially within cultural theory.[577] The added value of looking at certain social phenomena with the network concept is that the concept contains an interpretive capacity, which allows one to attentively approach and understand properties of non-hierarchical human organisational form that have concrete potential to shape social structures in newly emerging heterarchical ways.[578] In this context, the malleability of the network concept is particularly suited to the particularities of some current forms of society, which are increasingly characterised by knowledge and information and are not controlled by a sovereign centre (of power). For this reason, the network concept brings a relational logic of social structure formation to the centre of attention.[579]

For legal scholars, the notion of network is often associated with the identification of two distinct crises in recent decades: (a) a supposed crisis of the unity and hierarchy of law (and of society itself); (b) a 'crisis of boundary drawing' articulated within certain theoretical designs. Although the two phenomena can be treated analytically as independent features, both the crisis of boundary-drawing and the declared inadequacy of hierarchical social formation as a consequence of the social transformation of recent years mutually relate to each other.

The crisis of boundary-making diagnosed in network research can be seen in two ways: first, as an attempt to cope with the inherent insurmountability of (system) boundaries in classical systems theory, which consisted in dividing society into different segments and controlling one's own boundary as a form of decentralised 'boundary hygiene'.[580] However, the crisis of boundary-making manifests itself not only as a rebellion of Luhmannian succession articulated at the conceptual level. It also has weighty implications and repercussions for the framing of the concept of law, especially in terms of how hybrid phenomena or hybrid forms of normativity that do not meet the imperative of functional differentiation can be conceptually explained.[581] At this point, rebellion aims to interpret the dysfunctionality of law, which is not oriented toward stabilising normative expectations, as a central feature in explaining new social practices and, on the basis of this dysfunctionality or a certain impurity of law, to consider new phenomena that are intertwined with legal normativity.[582]

The notion of network in law also shows how the long process of the loss of ultimate landmarks of social certainty has had a profound effect on jurisprudential epistemology as well. Traditional legal epistemology focuses on hierarchy with terms such as 'system' or 'overall idea' (Gerber). Particularly in relation to the German variant of legal positivism, in which legal epistemology revolves around the hierarchical-deductive problem horizon, the concept of networks addresses how the formation of legal normativity currently has other presuppositions that no longer consist of the logic of state centralisation and the hierarchical cohesion of norms. Instead, reference is often made to the changing role of subjective law (and of the subject in general) and, not least, to the opening of modern legal systems to the production of social knowledge and legal normativity from a more heterarchical logic oriented towards self-organisation.[583] It is not without reason that the cases of 'relational contracts' and the form of emergence of business and legal relations in the 'garage logic' of Silicon Valley are repeatedly seen as the main phenomena of this development.[584] In this context, dominated by a logic of networks, legal normativity is understood as a normativity not simply derived from a centre, be it the state or not, but generated in a context of lateral and horizontal connection between state, organisations and society with serious consequences for the modelling of legal subjectivity involved in this context.

In recent decades, the crisis of the unity and hierarchy of law has been linked to the debate on the emergence of spontaneous law outside the institutional parameters of constitutional law and traditional international law.[585] The reliance of the concept of law on a conceptual framework fed by a hierarchy of rules, the political constitution, territoriality, the difference between legislation and courts, or national identity, is afflicted by a declining interpretive capacity to understand social practices from private transnational contexts, that is, outside institutional frameworks of the public sphere.[586] As a result, it is identified with the supposed crisis of boundary demarcation that results from growing social fragmentation and the associated hybridisation of social phenomena.[587] For this reason, fundamentally hybrid phenomena, which the previous concepts of law interpret as extra-legal phenomena, are captured by the concept of network. The added value of the network concept therefore lies precisely in what Ino Augsberg calls its 'ghostly, schematic openness'.[588]

Thus, not least because of its conceptual plasticity, the concept of network does not lack dogmatic application. The hope for a legal articulation of the concept of network lies above all in the attempt to lend a normative character to the concept, which focuses in particular on decentralised coordination or observation of the nodes of networks.[589,590] In administrative law, the concept of network can be used to articulate new constellations in the zone of indifference between private and public, formal and informal, cooperative and hierarchical. In civil law, Gunther Teubner has emphasised the added value of the term for new kinds of contractual constellations and has asked, principally, for an appropriate legal standardisation of corporate networks, such as virtual companies, just-in-time systems, and franchising chains, which usually conclude conventional bilateral contracts but at the same time generate multilateral or network-like legal effects in the sense of a network contract. The concept of network has also made a place for the educational constellation of a transnational law.[591,592] However, the introduction of the network concept has also met with headwind and criticism.[593]

In fact, it is undeniable that the concept of network, due to its plasticity, offers a way to illuminate properties also inherent to the new, knowledge-based, social practices resulting from the crisis of a social model based on the normative hierarchy. This network model, for example, was exceptionally well suited to the first phase of the establishment of the world wide web based on a creation of the network infrastructure through technical protocols (initially referred to as 'transmission control program' – TCP).[594] Enabling heterarchical linking of computers with data transmissions has gradually led to destabilisation of hierarchical relationships and to increasing heterarchisation.[595]

In this context, Tim Berners-Lee, one of the creators of the world wide web, makes an interesting analogy between infrastructure and service devices to explain how the separation of different layers distinguishes the construction of the web from that of the Internet. The web is an application that runs on the Internet, which in turn is an electronic network that transmits packets of information between millions of computers according to some open protocols. The analogy is that the web is like a household appliance that runs using the electrical grid. A refrigerator or a printer can function as long as they apply a few standard protocols – by operating at 120 volts or 60 hertz, for example. Similarly, any application – such as the web, email, or instant messaging – can run on the Internet as long as it uses some standard Internet protocols, such as TCP and IP.[596]

This first phase, in which technical protocols allowed an opening for the experimentation of new social experiences beyond the structural framework of a formal organisation, more or less marked the first two decades of the popularisation of the Internet. However, in this new scenario, an increasing trend of social dynamics occurs that differs from the earlier phase of consolidation of the Internet's technical standards, and which can no longer be captured by the semantics of the network concept.[597]

The construction of a cross-border universal grammar using protocols, through which a technical infrastructure of heterarchical relations has been produced, is characterised in the course of the last two decades by a new structure that can be designated as a new 'moment of the network'. This new 'moment of the Net', which has recently gained strength, is based on an unusual combination of the horizontality of relationships (heterarchical moment) with a verticalisation of these relationships (hierarchical moment), which in recent years has been referred to as the tendency towards the platformisation of the Internet.[598] In this context, Julie Cohen aptly specifies: 'a platform is not (just) a network'.[599]

The concept of the digital discussed in this book refers here precisely to this development of the platformisation of the Internet. The 'digital' refers to the material mediatisation of the social through electronic communication platforms. One of the pillars of this current development is 'datafication', from which an increasing embedding of social structures in algorithm-based 'ecologies of measurement and counting' is[600] achieved, which then shapes the new business model of digital platforms. First and foremost, the transition from the organisation as a form of knowledge production and social normativity to a society increasingly oriented toward digital platforms requires that the changes in the material and infrastructural conditions of the social be placed at the centre of the debate. Just as with organisations, digital platforms do not simply reflect the social: they co-produce the social structures in which we live.[601]

For this reason, as Gießmann emphasises, networks mark 'the spatial in-between',[602] and this in a double sense: on the one hand, they capture patterns of action or social practices that are located in the gray area of sovereign/private, controlled/evolutionary, hierarchical/cooperative, and formal/informal. On the other hand, networks also mark 'the spatial in-between' in the Blumenbergian sense as an epochal threshold, which presents itself as a transitory semantics and expresses the moment between the certain '*no more*' and the simultaneous '*not yet*'. This becomes particularly clear when the development of the Internet leaves behind an initial phase of consolidation of protocols that enable peer-to-peer communication and moves in the direction of a platformisation of the complete digital world.

II. After the Threshold: Platforms

The digital is not on the threshold, like the network concept, but follows it. It generates not only a new knowledge order, but at the same time a new cultural order, by decentering and at the same time reshaping the old form of knowledge and culture, which was oriented to organisations. Such upheaval affects the organisational form of information production by replacing the old industrial information economy that had prevailed from the second half of the nineteenth century to the twentieth century with a new form of platform-based data economy. This process of transition to a new digital order of knowledge and culture, in which the existing 'non-conceptuality' of the new (H. Blumenberg) challenges the old organisation-based order, simultaneously undercuts, on the one hand, simple notions of a restoration of 'community' that can always take on authoritarian, non-liberal features, and, on the other hand, libertarian solutions that prefer an 'anything goes' approach.

Inspired by media studies, Tarleton Gillespie offers a concise typology for platforms that goes beyond a purely computational definition, i.e., a system in which computer programs can run. He distinguishes between three levels: (a) the architectural (a surface or structure on which actions can take place), (b) the figurative (a [metaphysical] basis for opportunities, actions, and insights), and (c) the political (a set of principles on which a social actor takes a stand in order to address the public).[603] From this perspective, he is able to take a multifocal view on the phenomenon of platforms, distancing himself from the approach that reduces them to the concept of power or to 'platform imperialism'.[604] Thus, Gillespie combines negative aspects or negative externalities of the moment of verticalisation of platforms with positive externalities of horizontalisation inherent in the platform model. The success of platforms as a business model derives precisely from this duality, from this ambivalence inherent in the concept of integrating claims to totality and freedom, heterarchy and hierarchy in one model.[605]

At this point in particular, the platform concept can semantically cover phenomena that the network concept cannot. Similarly, the concept of the system, in the sense of systems theory, cannot capture the social structures that have emerged with the advent of the digital, since it is not just a matter of compartmentalising and reconnecting social sectors, but a complex process of hybridising social practices in the ambivalent form of combining a verticalising moment with a horizontalising moment. While the concept of the network has gained ground – especially after globalisation – by focusing on the horizontal aspects of the constitution of normativity, it has lost sight of the fact that recently, in the increasing virtual world, there is a strong tendency towards a combination of verticalisation and horizontalisation.

In this context, David Gugerli rightly emphasises that a move of the world into digital reality can be observed in recent decades.[606,607] However, this move has not only led to more horizontal relationships, but also to the aforementioned strange combination of verticality and horizontality, which was not recognisable before. There is a certain inseparable relationship between online platforms and social structures, in which online platforms do not simply mirror the offline world, but constantly co-produce new social structures. This performativity through mediation is an important aspect of the platformisation of the entire Internet. Platformisation in this sense means that a continuous encoding of human and institutional integrations is no longer based on traditional market or state protection mechanisms, but on new structures and business models focused on network effects of accumulation and data processing through algorithms. In this context, technology encodes sociability in a comprehensive way.[608]

Here, central questions arise about the consequences of restructuring when the form of cultural production and knowledge is determined by online platforms. Essentially, platforms are creating a new balance between private and public interests, that is gradually becoming clearer. The fact is that the new ecosystem has immediate implications at the local, national, and global levels, not least because of the technological possibilities. And thus the platform society is also changing the conditional framework of transnationality. In terms of global law, this is no longer a consequence of relations between nation states, the treatment of transnational technical issues by organisations, or the practice of transnational arbitration. However, the society of platforms is changing the conditions of transnationality, as well as the conditions of effectiveness of the evolutionary achievement of the constitution of the nation-state and the role of law in society in general.

At this point I return to the starting point of this book. Niklas Luhmann's self-doubt or discomfort – hypostasised in the anomaly thesis in the final sentence of his book *Das Recht der Gesellschaft* (The Law of Society) (1993) – tries to contrast two types of society. The first type is characterised by the degree of freedom, social differentiation, and its dependence on a functioning legal code that structures spheres of freedom in order to avoid a hypertrophy of one rationality over the other. Alternatively, Luhmann sketches another kind of society that had few clear contours at the beginning of the 1990s – the time of the book's publication. Despite these few clear outlines, however, he was already aware that this development of global society, including new technologies, had an inherent unadaptability or incompatibility with the Western legal tradition. In Luhmann's view, the first form of society, extremely dependent on law, would become weaker as a result of the development of global society. However, he does not answer the key question: in a global and technological society, what function will law play?[609]

The new society (of platforms) and its law, on the contrary, can presumably no longer be described with sufficient precision by the terms of knowledge society or network society, since new elements are emerging in the form of the social that were not previously present. For this reason, the concept of the platform society no longer lies on the threshold in the Blumenbergian sense as a kind of transitory semantics, but has long since left it behind.[610]

III. A New Political Economy of Platforms?

In view of the profound change brought about by what is referred to here as 'the digital', the main question remains whether the new platform society is also changing the current contours of political economy. Political economy as a concept only became popular from the second half of the eighteenth century. In this context, it was increasingly regarded as a description of modern economics committed to liberalism (which was still in its nascent stages), in contrast to the constitution of the 'whole house' of the old European tradition.[611] Different authors, such as Jean-Jacques Rousseau,[612] Joseph A. Schumpeter,[613] Max Weber[614] and Karl Marx,[615] had declared political economy to be their research focus. István Hont points out in this context of philosophy that the emergence of the concept of political economy marks a dividing line in Western thought that leads to a post-Machiavellian moment.⁶¹⁶ Machiavelli's theory and political teaching was guided by the concepts of *virtù* and *fortuna*. While *virtù* is directly related to judgement, that is, as individual qualities of rulers, *fortuna* refers to the dimension of the favour of fate and chance in the historical-social constellation of a state.⁶¹⁷ The balance between virtue and fated fortune was the magic formula for ensuring the stability of a government. The emphasis on a 'post-Machiavellian moment' with the introduction of political economy from the eighteenth century onward as a central theme of state affairs⁶¹⁸ suggests that the basis on which a government guaranteed its stability was no longer to be reduced to the fate and personal virtue of the ruler alone, but was also to encompass a broader dimension: the opening of society to the production of the new beyond tradition and destiny. Political economy became the form of reflection of this new development of society.

The emergence of political economy as a form of reflection on dynamic social processes also finds a relevant relation to the subject of this book. Political economy is then simultaneously a form of reflection on the metamorphoses of society, and similarly, on the metamorphoses of law. In fact, the emergence of political economy and the growing importance of the economic as a subject of the state, beyond attributes such as virtue and fortune of the person of the sovereign, are directly linked to what has been called here the disintegration of the old order, the dissolution of the *ius publicum europaeum*. With the transition from the age of the political to the age of relations, in which more and more nation-states have been created in a decentralised global politics of recognition of new states, the absence of a centre for the generation and administration of the normativity of global law, in the Schmittian sense of a concrete order of the few European sovereigns and princely houses endowed with virtue, has led to a dispersion of sovereignty and an increasingly decentralised interaction between the different local parts of the world.⁶¹⁹ Virtue and fortune of the person of the sovereign, still determining in the framework of the *ius publicum europaeum*, lose their central value in a world increasingly constituted by decentralised relations.

The newly released dynamic not only increased immigration between continents and countries,⁶²⁰ but also brought about a strong mutual influence of previously different cultural traditions. As Frank Trentmann showed, until the end of the nineteenth century, Japanese people drank mostly tea. At the beginning of the twentieth century, due to migrants returning from Brazil, a new culture of coffee was introduced to Japan. The first Brazilian café opened in Tokyo in 1908.⁶²¹ The idea of 'commercial sociability'⁶²² was not possible without the transnational dimension of these linkages. The production and distribution of new goods not only generated new contacts between regions and states, but also profoundly influenced the categories of everyday life.⁶²³ Even modern concepts such as civil society would be almost inconceivable without this development.⁶²⁴ The release of a new productivity of the individual beyond courtly culture, as described in the second chapter, points to an important social change with profound implications for social formation.

With the emergence of a society of organisations articulated not only in the internal structures of nation-states, but also as a form of generating legal-technical knowledge in the global society, the old order of political economy attached to traditional goods (land, capital, labour) is supplemented by new knowledge-based and professional goods.[625] This requires a new mode of generating social knowledge and thus also the specific emergence of a common horizon of expectations anchored in the central role of organisations and their form of knowledge generation.[626] A new post-capitalist knowledge-based form of production then takes on significance.[627]

However, the political economy is currently experiencing an equally drastic change with the intervention of the digital in the form of the platform economy. In particular, new technologies in the form of data structures, algorithms, or AI are producing a new kind of institutional framework that impacts the social order. 'Datafication' takes the place of knowledge in the society of organisations and classical commodities, presenting data and its relationalities as an unlimited resource of the digital world.[628] Platforms are the new 'refineries of the digital',[629] which, through the technology of collecting and processing personal and social information according to industrial standards, create a new economic order that allows new possibilities of action and new freedoms for individuals, but at the same time brings new constraints and conditioning for them.

In this sense, the economy of the platform replaces the analogue market and the political economy of the society of organisations. Whereas in the economy of the industrial age the market was the ordering ideal of a space in which the price of goods and services was regulated by the law of supply and demand, in the information economy this space is increasingly occupied by platforms, which mediate interactions both materially and algorithmically. In doing so, they are in a sense socially all-encompassing, as all lifeworlds are influenced by them. The world is becoming a digital reality, and platforms are becoming the infrastructures for all spheres of life: intimate relationships (Tinder), social interactions (social networks), family (WhatsApp groups), industry (industrial platforms),[630] government (e-government), education (K12 education), and so on. They refine and link personal data of consumers, companies and public institutions, creating new virtual representations of society. Above all, they create – in the words of Aleida Assmann – 'productive instruments for shaping and producing the world, [are] constructors of reality and thus also of the human being who lives in this reality'.[631] Not least, they create a world of new kinds of relations that would not be possible without the digital. Not only are new business models of various kinds emerging, but also many areas of society, such as medicine, culture, education, science, political preferences, etc, are being executed and processed throughout by the new political economy of the platform society.[632] The growing centrality of platforms and algorithms as modes of organisation and governance is thus changing not only the conditions of economic exchange, but also of society itself.

An inevitably new political economy brings with it many new opportunities, as well as new risks. As argued above, the central feature of the platform economy is that it combines in its operation two features that were previously considered antagonistic: hierarchy and heterarchy, although not necessarily in that order. If one were to treat the platform society as if it were merely perpetuating one aspect of the aforementioned symbiosis, one would be ignoring the fact that its own intrinsic value derives precisely from the inseparable combination of these two features.[633,634] The combination of claims to totality and claims to freedom of the new economy places the assertiveness of law or states to model the new economy under new conditions that are more opaque and sensitive than the conventional conditions of other social paradigms. A good example is the difficulty that competition law has in dealing conceptually with the new society. The shift of preemptive regulation into the realm of predictive modelling has become more difficult under the conditions of the platform society. In a market where information is massively mediated, path dependencies between companies and business models inevitably arise constantly, bringing problems to the conceptual framework of competition law through indifference between different types of markets.[635]

The next section discusses how the development of the platform society is transforming the contemporary modern public sphere in the transition from a public sphere previously focused on organisations and their inherent form of knowledge generation to one increasingly oriented toward transnational digital platforms. In this context, the collective dimension of communication is being recast by a new form of management of this collective dimension. As such, the detachment of the collective dimension of communication from national legal systems is more than a product of technological disruption, for it also relies on the construction of a legal infrastructure that poses new challenges for democratic nation-states.

C. THE PUBLIC IN TRANSITION: FROM ORGANISATION TO PLATFORM

'What we know about our society, indeed about the world in which we live, we know through the mass media.'[636] With this sentence, Luhmann succeeded in expressing the reality-structuring role of the mass media and the large journalistic organisations, where the shaping of social knowledge is condensed. Since the publication of his book *The Reality of the Mass Media* in 1993, however, the environment in which public information is produced and disseminated has changed considerably. Without recourse to in-depth theoretical grounding, the new 'fact of world society' (N. Luhmann) can be established simply in the everyday way in which individuals communicate and inform themselves. There is a clear migration of the communicative channels of society away from the large mass-media organisations to the new business models of digital platforms. Today, Luhmann's sentence could be paraphrased quite naturally as follows: what we know about our society, indeed about the world we live in, we know through social networks.

Another theorist of the effects of public communication on social (democratic) processes is Jürgen Habermas. The public sphere he describes as 'bourgeois' found its historical shape in what was described in Chapter 2 above as a process conditioned by the transition from the court to the city.[637] This change, following the notion advanced here, acted in accordance with a restlessness inherent in the system of *ius publicum europaeum*, as a new dynamic of contacts, decentralisation and dispersion emerged, affecting the social structure of the concrete order in the Schmittian sense.[638] The construction of a new urban public sphere, based on the increasingly important impersonal relationships, at the same time accomplished a new 'logic of experimentation'[639] beyond the centrality of the court.[640] It helped to shape the establishment of a spontaneous sphere of society that exerted social pressure on organised state power.[641]

Only the less centralised and tendentially impersonal culture created by the worldwide growth of cities in the second half of the nineteenth century,[642] combined with prerequisites such as literacy and the technology of printing, could lead to the emergence of a public-private communication network that was not limited to political issues.[643] Already in this society of individuals, the first contours of a society of organisations began to gain clarity, as the association system and its organisation gave new impetus to the emerging reading culture in the cities, especially in Germany.[644]

This public sphere of a society of individuals, which Habermas describes as the apogee of the form of the public sphere, disintegrated as society increasingly moved away from the pattern of individual-based debate culture of salons and cafés and toward the professional-editorial production and circulation of information by large journalistic organisations. Coffee houses and parlours were replaced in the twentieth century by the large organisations of welfare-state mass democracy.[645] Regardless of Habermas's idealisation of the public sphere of a society of individuals, the public sphere began to be structured around the symbiotic relationship between new technologies – radio, press, television – and organisational forms during the twentieth century. The 'loss of publicity within large organizations'[646] is compensated on the one hand by the much wider reach of new information dissemination technologies, which democratise access to information, and on the other hand by competition between organisations and the media.

The increasing importance of organisations and their way of generating knowledge for society is a clear characteristic of the rise of mass culture. The idea of mass culture, in contrast, does not imply a complete unification in the formation of individuality or the subject, as the term 'mass' already intuitively suggests. On the contrary, mass culture – closely linked to the growth of cities – opens up a new process of social pluralisation of interests, conventions, and ultimately individualities, which is to be located in the crisis of bourgeois consciousness. For the present section, however, the connection of the dimension of new knowledge producers as corporate actors and legal entities with the emergence of new media is of extreme importance. As Georg Christoph Tholen points out, the caesura or mediality of media consists in the fact that it eludes or shifts teleological directions of meaning.[647,648] With the emergence of mass culture and the advance of the symbiotic relationship between organisational form and new media, will-forming processes undermine an increasingly complex context of decentering and pluralising the public sphere without any teleological direction of meaning.[649]

This model of a public sphere oriented toward and configured by large organisations was accompanied by a nation-state regulatory regime focused densely on administrative law institutions.[650] A legal regime for linking technologies and organisational forms was justified, insofar as the type of communication disseminated by the media differs from intimate and private communication. Thus, the legal regime takes the form of public communication that can strongly shape collective opinion-forming processes. The collective dimension of communication that emerged from this combination of organisational form and technological media – the printing press, radio and television – has become a central aspect of contemporary public formation in modern democracies as a direct result of this ability to influence public opinion-forming processes.

This collective dimension of communication, previously configured and shaped within a nation-state system of administrative-law regulatory frameworks, has undergone a profound transformation in recent years, migrating from large organisations – and their media – to the new digital services with their business models. While the old technological forms were subject to the administrative-legal regime of nation-states, the new technologies of digital platforms are not subject to this national legal regime and have therefore been able to emancipate themselves from nation-state regulatory frameworks and take on a transnational communications character. However, this new fact of world society is not solely due to the technology inherent in the business model of the new economy, but depends to a large extent on its combination with the creation of a legal infrastructure that has been able to facilitate the emancipation of the collective communication dimension of large organisations and thus the emergence of a (world) society increasingly oriented toward digital platforms.

It is precisely this immanent relationship between law and technology that took up the initial topic of this book discussed in Chapter 1 above. By postulating that the law of the world society is a law that deviates from the tradition developed in the nation-state or, in Luhmann's words, a 'European anomaly', since it distances itself from normative mechanisms and approaches cognitive mechanisms, Luhmann indicates the preconditions of the emerging technological world or emerging world society.[651] Almost thirty years later, Lawrence Lessig drew attention to the importance of cognitive mechanisms for the formation of legal normativity with his famous thesis 'code is Law'. According to

Lessig, software and hardware form a plethora of social (and legal) conditioning that carries with it significant implications for the exercise and, at the same time, the violation of fundamental rights.[652] In short, legal normativity is very closely linked to changing technological conditions in an increasingly technological world.

The dissolution of law into cognitive mechanisms may nevertheless point to the danger of a tendency toward the economic colonisation of law in the deterministic sense of the word. The inability of the development of the law of global society to structure zones or spheres of freedom through a 'functioning legal code', as has happened in the institutional experience of the nation-state, does not mean that law is not part of the complex process of construction in the new transnational digital economy. This position is taken by authors who, like Shoshana Zuboff, argue that the new digital economy is emerging in a vacuum of legal normativity itself.[653]

The role of law was crucial to the shift or transformation of the collective dimension of communication from a public sphere of the society of organisations to one increasingly oriented toward digital platforms, which paved the way for the emergence of the new economy by creating a new liability regime for new intermediaries that differed from the liability regime of the intermediaries of the society of organisations. The semantic shift that resulted from the structural change of society[654] can be reconstructed in the American context of the debate in the 1990s and its dispersion into other jurisdictions. The rise of the platform society can only be inadequately or fuzzily read as the emergence of a 'surveillance capitalism' that emerged in a global legal vacuum. The non-state architecture of the Internet and its current development of platformisation simultaneously and necessarily combines verticalising elements with hierarchical elements, which are a paradoxical product of the symbiosis between totalising tendencies: clear dangers for violations of rights, area-wide rights of access and participation, with clear opportunities for freedom for the individual.[655]

I. The Founding Myth of a New Economy: § 230 CDA

The success of this new economic sector or platform society cannot be located solely in the moment of technological disruption or technological innovation.[656] Likewise, it would be inappropriate to derive it from a possible legal vacuum at the global level, as Shoshana Zuboff does. Certainly, the technological factor is an indispensable driving force for any process of building a new economy on a global scale. However, the technological factor alone would not be sufficient for such a global transformation. Law, meanwhile, plays a central role in creating a solid infrastructure for the institutional construction of long-term expectations that enables the production of a legally protected experimental field of action. Without this stabilising and behavioural dimension, which has created a new and open discovery process for a new economy, it would be difficult to achieve such a profound structural change as the transition from industrial to data capitalism.[657]

For the case of the transformation of the public sphere discussed here and the resulting transformation of the collective dimension of communication, the first major laboratory was undoubtedly the American scenario of the 1990s. The discourse surrounding the creation of Section 230 of the CDA[658] is still the subject of a great debate on the responsibility of Internet intermediaries.[659] In turn, what is crucial for the emergence of the new economy is that the present statute succeeds in excluding the application of the legal liability regime of the former intermediaries of the society of organisations, by creating a new legal regime for the new scenario of the economy *in status nascendi*. Jeff Kosseff makes clear the formative effect of the addressed Section 230 of the CDA for the emergence of the new economy, noting in this context that Section 230 represents the twenty-six words that created the Internet as we know it today.[660]

In the context of the emerging debate on a new form of regulation, which culminated in Section 230 of the CDA in 1996, the *quaestio iuris* was essentially concerned with the question of whether or not the new digital services would be legally responsible for illegal content generated by third parties on their platforms or electronic sites. Prior to the enactment of the CDA in 1996, this legal question related to the regulatory area of freedom of expression, which was the subject of the First Amendment of the US Constitution and, in its dogmatic jurisprudential construction, usually referred to the relationship between the protection of honour and freedom of expression.[661] It was precisely here that the central problem of the scope and limits of the First Amendment arose in the context of the emerging new economy.

With the First Amendment, the scope of regulation focused on the contours of a society in which the individual and, above all, organisations played a decisive role in building and shaping the collective dimension of information in society. Therefore, the First Amendment's scope of protection referred, on the one hand, to the relationship between the state and the individual[662] and, on the other hand, to journalistic organisations as the main vehicles of mass communication that gave contours to liability regimes.[663] Consequently, the First Amendment classically aimed at protecting the individual from state interference in his or her political right to express and disseminate thoughts and expressions,[664] and at the same time also at structuring the responsibility for information production in its collective dimension, which until then had been tied to the epistemic contours conferred by the society of organisations.[665]

In this context, the internal dogmatic structure of the First Amendment distinguishes between speakers, publishers, broadcasters, and pure intermediaries. The category of spokesperson focuses first and foremost on the relationship between the individual and the state, with the goal of ensuring a sphere of non-interference by the state in the free expression of the individual.[666] The categories of publishers and broadcasters, conversely, focus on the collective dimension of the production of social information and its conditioning factors within journalistic enterprises with editorial control of information – this category is particularly suited to the contours given to the collective dimension of information by the organisational society described here – and the category of distributors, which focuses in particular on the logistical infrastructure for the dissemination of information, but is not involved in the organisational editorial control of information production. In this last category, the scope of protection of the First Amendment was opened, resulting in the responsibility – within the scope of regulation imposed by the First Amendment – of intermediaries, like booksellers, libraries, and kiosks, when they had knowledge illegal content distributed through their infrastructure.[667]

The clear limits of the First Amendment of the US Constitution on the new society centred on digital services were particularly evident in the adjudication of two important cases on the liability of new digital services for content generated by third parties on their digital websites.[668] The semantic contours of such judicial disputes moved within the conceptual framework created by the First Amendment; namely, that of the collective dimension of information in the so-called society of organisations. In this sense, the courts raised, on the one hand, the question of whether digital services should have an analogous responsibility to that of journalistic organisations as publishers. On the other hand, they wondered whether the new digital services should be treated as distributors or as intermediaries, that is, as part of the infrastructure of pure content distribution. And here lies a peculiarity relevant to the context of the debate: if the new digital services were treated within the category of distributors, they would not be able to exercise moderation of content produced by third parties on their websites, otherwise they could be held responsible for illegal third-party content.[669]

At this point, the inadequacy of the First Amendment – which referred to the epistemic contours of the society of organisations and their associated infrastructure and focused on journalistic organisations with editorial control or distributors with their logistical infrastructure – became apparent.[670] The discussions of a new set of rules that culminated in Section 230 of the CDA sought precisely to distance themselves from this model, which inevitably involved the creation of immunity liability in order to create an environment of incentives for the new economy *in status nascendi* that differed from the contours conferred by the First Amendment.[671]

II. The Consequences of the New Immunity Liability for the Collective Dimension of Communication

The success of Section 230 of the CDA lies in the fact that it creates a new regulatory environment in two senses. On the one hand, Section 230 makes it possible to break away from prevailing legal accountability structures because Section 230 succeeded in departing from the dogmatic application of the US First

Amendment,[672] which moderation of third-party content was considered.[673] In this context, Jeff Kosseff declares Section 230 of the CDA to be a 'super-First Amendment',[674] which at the same time succeeded in creating a new legal responsibility for the new intermediaries that is completely different from the intermediary liability of a society of organisations.[675] The central intent in moving away from the application of the First Amendment was to promote the scope of self-regulation in a way that would allow companies to moderate content themselves,[676] but would not subject them to liability for content generated by third parties – analogous to the liability of publishers in the Society of Organizations.[677]

In this context, the implementation of Section 230 of the CDA had two important consequences for the reconfiguration and transformation of the collective dimension of information. First, there was a rapid rejection from the copyright and intellectual property field, which successfully positioned itself against the model of broad immunity for new intermediaries. The Digital Millennium Copyright Act (DMCA) of 1998 set the stage for an internal distinction in the 'marketplace of ideas' by limiting freedom of expression in the digital environment in property rights.[678] In this case, the (digital) medium or services were given greater responsibility for stopping copyright and property rights infringement in the distribution of protected content within their digital services. To the extent, the 'marketplace of ideas' which content dissemination touched upon issues not related to the property rights of copyright and intellectual property, such as aspects and issues related to honour protection, personality protection, and others, received less legal protection as they fell under the liability regime of broader immunity. Therefore, the protection of these individual rights became more oriented towards the self-regulation of companies according to their market preferences.[679]

The second important consequence is the definitive emancipation of the collective dimension of communication from the regime of administrative law tied to the nation-state and from the semantic contours, which until then had been guided by the social epistemology of the society of organisations. Although there has been, through the algorithms that perform content moderation,[680] a clear 'recasting' – in Hans Blumenberg's sense – of the place previously occupied by the editorial control of journalistic organisations and broadcasters for the collective dimension of communication, in the context of the change in the collective dimension of communication, the process of recasting of the collective dimension of communication has been a process of change. The process of recasting the collective dimension of communication has shifted, due to the semantic and structural changes described here, to a self-regulation of digital platforms in which private 'content moderation' is mediated by human and algorithm-based computer technology with cross-border effects.[681] As Tarleton Gillespie indicates, 'content moderation' is the commodity that platforms offer users.[682] Above all, they offer private transnational management of the collective dimension of communication, with clear consequences for the formation of public opinion in nation-states.

To be successful as a legal institution, however, the new liability regime required a process of global dissemination and thus its adaptation to the various national legal systems.[683] This complex process of 'translation', i.e. the transfer of legal institutions and their modified adaptation to different legal systems, has meanwhile made a decisive contribution to the promotion of the new digital economy, with the added economic value coming not only from the knowledge generation of the organisational form, but also from the active participation of third parties.

The dual system of structuring the global 'marketplace of ideas' or, to put it another way, the structuring of the transnational public sphere through digital platforms, ultimately found great receptivity in the legal systems of several nation states. Both the European Union's e-Commerce Directive 2000/31/EC and Sections 7–10 of the Telecommunications Act, with their concept of an upstream liability privilege, also followed an idea of promoting technology by strengthening self-regulation among companies.[684] As Aleksandra Kuczerawy rightly notes, the e-Commerce Directive is the European response to the US development, deviating with small variations from the parameters set by the American debate of the 1990s.[685] A special liability regime for intermediaries was also created in countries like Brazil to promote the self-regulatory dimension of businesses.

D. A NEW REGULATION FOR THE (TRANSNATIONAL) COLLECTIVE DIMENSION OF COMMUNICATION?

Renationalisation of the new collective dimension of communication does not seem to be an option even for systems like Germany's, which is oriented toward public curation of the collective dimension of communication (at least for public broadcasting) with an emphasis on maintaining diversity. Konrad Hesse's influential model of public opinion formation,[686] to be understood under the conditions of modern mass communication, is under scrutiny insofar as his functionalist interpretation of freedom of expression, focused on its impact on public opinion formation,[687] is currently being contrasted with the new conditions of private models of transnational digital platforms.[688] The debate around the issue of a possible narrowing of multiplicity in the new digital contexts,[689] contrasts with the multiplicity of channels, services, and communication possibilities for individuals in the platform society, and only shows that maintaining a semantics of the society of organisations, in which both channels and possibilities were conditioned by the very design of the medium (printing press, radio, and television), is incompatible with the social epistemology of the digital itself.[690] This would be like making the broadcasting councils of public broadcasters the curators of the transnational diversity of opinion-forming dynamics of social networks.[691]

102 *The Law of Platforms*

This does not mean, on the other hand, that it is not crucial for the new forms that the new platform society has given to the collective dimension of communication to adapt the law to the new conditions of this platform society, and also, conversely, to adapt the platform society to certain legal conditions in order to ensure the maintenance of standards of legal protection and an institutional underpinning of the public sphere in the digital world. This is especially important in the current scenario, where the new medium, which is an amplifier of opportunities,[692] largely coincides with the business model of a few companies.[693] This is also fundamentally due to the inherent characteristic of the platform society, in which there is an inseparable symbiosis between vertical and horizontal tendencies. In this context, the new intermediaries that take advantage of the new technologies have extensive *de facto* control over access to the new collective dimension of communication and can thus largely decide on the effective perceptibility of the liberties of third parties[694] and, ultimately, on the shaping of the new collective dimension of communication. Consequently, a legal methodology appropriate to the platform must necessarily take this new facticity of the platform society as its starting point.

While traditional information providers – publishers, broadcasters, telecommunications companies, and others – had statutory and constitutional obligations with respect to the discourse and flow of information they enabled and generated, the imposition of comparable legal and constitutional obligations on the new digital medium to ensure minimum standards of rights protection in the digital world seems largely futile.[695,696,697] In this context, there is a current tendency to modulate the responsibility of new intermediaries in an experimental context of greater liability of their own medium, while moving away from the model of immunity that originally aimed exclusively at promoting innovation in the context of the emergence of the digital economy.[698] One opportunity for modelling liability for the new intermediaries beyond the freedom of expression based on the (nation-state) political process lies in a kind of proceduralisation of basic communication and media rights that places a strong emphasis on protecting an impersonal process of opinion formation. A proceduralisation of legal protection in the platform society should take into account the dynamics of current computer networks and business models, in order to equate the protection of rights within the medium itself with a constant duty of observation on the part of the state courts.[699]

E. THE TIME OF THE PLATFORMS

In this book, the theme of time and its influence within the construction of modern society has been a topic of utmost importance. In the first chapter, this was evident in the approach to the theme of the crisis of political obligation in the seventeenth century and how, from that event on, society opened itself, especially through the figure of the contract, to the new possibility of imagining itself more artificially and contingently than was possible only and solely from tradition or God-given bonds. The strong tendency of modern society to create abstract mechanisms to deal with increasing complexity, pluralisation and an uncertain future is also present in the works of Ernst Kantorowicz. His important work, *The King's Two Bodies*, is not, as is commonly believed, primarily concerned with merely creating a mechanism to distinguish between official and individual personhood. The main focus of this work lies precisely in the problem of the temporality of all rules, which is expressed in the temporal depth structure present in the book. Accordingly, the figure of the incumbent is conceived as a reflex of a supra-individually valid continuum of office that guaranteed temporal stability to politics, i.e., in the words of Horst Bredekamp, that created a 'political time' distinct from religious or secular time.[700] In this context, Victoria Kahn points out that this simultaneous stabilisation and perpetuation of political time through an abstract artificial layer (of law) would have functioned as a form of prefiguration of the modern constitutional state, in which the inadequacy of a total correspondence between the body (including the concrete person) of the sovereign and sovereignty (as an abstract artificial construct) itself becomes the inevitable condition of the modern liberal state.[701] The (modern) state is not a precondition of sociality, but its product.

The very construction of the new modern political temporality that anticipates the modern constitutional state is a product of the profound transformation of the temporal dimension of society, in which the uncertain future within the political form of rule itself becomes a constitutive element of socialisation that can no longer be determined by the socially shared knowledge of tradition or given by God. In this context, the social dimension of time in society is inseparable from a guiding orientation of both individual and institutional action. Society's discovery of an open and contingent time, a time that cannot be clearly determined by tradition, makes modern law and its function, as also observed and analysed by Luhmann, an almost indispensable institution for social cohesion.[702] According to Luhmann, in this context, modern law would play a central role in modern society by ensuring a minimum of generalised orientation in a world where a common projection-horizon of action is becoming increasingly precarious. In other words, law would be a contemporary form of regulating the disposition of the future and its limitation within modern societies. The unease in systems theory discussed in Chapter 1 above, exemplified by the anomaly thesis, touches on this central aspect insofar as Luhmann himself questions his concept of law before the advent of a global and technological society in which common orientation within a legally stabilised horizon of expectation presents itself as a nearly, if not completely, impossible function to perform, and does so in a thoroughly puzzling manner. The legitimate *Gretchenfrage* to be asked at this point is: if law can no longer fulfil this function, what function would it have to assume in today's technological and global society?

While for Luhmann the problem of time in law is solved by inserting conditional programmes at the level of programming 'in order to reintegrate law into society',[703] i.e., through legal norms (conditional programmes) within the institutional conditions of the nation-state, the problem of time of the platform society does not primarily arise as a form of creating a common and stable horizon through legal norms or legal programmes and their effect and regulatory capacity on society. Rather, the new time bonds are increasingly produced by emergent trans-subjective and technological effects arising from legal relations within the institutional and technological conditions of the global digital society that go beyond the regulatory conditions of traditional law. According to Luhmann, the if-then form of conditional programmes offers the possibility of 'imagining order in the form of fixed couplings', and it would thus be in clear contrast to the dynamics and processes of hybridisation that characterise today's transnational digital environment on a large scale.[704] At this point, the anomaly thesis discussed in the first chapter not only becomes an uneasiness within the theoretical construct, but the theory itself becomes an anomaly in the further development of the digital global society, at least as far as the function of law within this society is concerned.

This tension is reflected precisely by the current question of the (in)avoidability of law enforcement or legal protection in the digital global world, which is inevitably related to the (in)compatibility of the semantics of modern law with the new social epistemology of the digital world. Vilém Flusser describes this discrepancy between semantics and social structure as the product of a long process of emigration of 'theorists from the cathedral and the monastery to the workshop', especially to today's 'industrial laboratories', where 'theory' can no longer be understood as 'the passive contemplation of ideals', but as the 'progressive elaboration of models' committed to 'practice, that is, observation and experimentation'. Above all, Flusser, a media theorist who emigrated to Brazil, emphasises that this discrepancy between semantics and social structure happens due to a tension shaped by the social modelling of two different media that express different rationalities, namely, the printing press and the digital. These two media produce two different ways of thinking: a 'letter thinking' and a 'number thinking'. According to Flusser, with the advent of computer technology, a distinct 'recoding of theoretical thinking from letters into numbers' would be characterised by the emergence of possibilities to design realities from the inherent ability of the new technologies.[705]

Currently, this duality between a 'letter thinking' and a 'number thinking', described by Flusser[706] as an incompatibility between the semantics of modern law and the inherent conditions of the digital world, is also taken up again and again – even if unconsciously – by other authors. This is especially true because the semantics of modern law is based on defining the orientation of human and institutional behaviour via programming through general, abstract norms and principles, while the social epistemology of the digital world has inherent dispersed dynamics characterised by its ad hoc personalised, experimental, and pattern-based approach.[707] Testifying to this incompatibility, however, says nothing about the possibilities of how to design a platform-adequate law for technological conditions. Without law, they do not work; with (old) law, it does not work either.

In this context, the time of platforms or orientation form and horizons of the society of platforms show themselves to be incompatible with the time of a 'letter thinking' or printing-press culture,[708] which could be modelled in a certain way by conditional programmes[709] or other forms of legal knowledge storage via norms and programmes so far. The time of platforms relinquishes the central problem of the temporal dimension and the current precariousness of the foundation of a common minimum horizon of action in a digital society. This makes itself perceptible not only at the individual level. At the institutional level as well, for example at the level of state action in the digital world, this withdrawal of the problem of action from the lack of clear parameters that could orient state action becomes quite evident. In the above example of the emancipation of the collective dimension of communication, this becomes particularly clear when reflecting on the question of the limits within which the state's ability to generate knowledge has so far helped to shape the contours of the collective dimension of communication in a model such as the German broadcasting model. This model was significantly reliant on both specific technologies – radio and television – and a regulatory model tied to the nation-state. From this, results the extreme difficulty of dealing with the new emancipation of the collective dimension of communication from mass-media, organisation-based conditions in the sense of regulation.

The dynamics of the new digital society require a law that does not operate merely 'as an afterthought, as a downstream system'.[710] And this is precisely because of the peculiarities of a new temporal dimension that the platform society brings with it, for, as Hartmut Rosa rightly indicates, one of the central features of the current 'temporalization of time' lies precisely in the fact that social bonds – as well as temporal bonds, are increasingly generated only in the process of execution.[711] Ino Augsberg argues that in this context of a technological, eventful society there is a need for a 'conversion of the perspective from time to temporality qua *Zeitigung*'.[712] This differentiation, which follows on from Martin Heidegger, expresses a stronger modelling of temporalised normativity of law.

From the perspective of this work, the necessary incorporation of time into law turns out to be particularly crucial for the relationship between law and new technologies. The time of platforms and the new forms of time-binding that have emerged from them start from the realisation that, at present, a large part of social practices – and their horizons of action – are currently technologically mediatised.[713] At the level of individual action, starting from the theme of the collective dimension of communication as given by digital platforms, this means that the behaviour of the user is not modelled in the foreground by an external state sanctioning possibility. Instead, this modelling of action – including its horizon – takes place primarily through an infrastructure of network protocols, digital self-enforcing mechanisms, and the lifting and processing of personal data that fundamentally takes place in the medium itself.[714]

At this point, the production of negative externalities is something almost inevitable, as is the simultaneous production of positive externalities. In the regulatory sphere, the first important point to be attested is not only the almost intuitive knowledge asymmetry between state and new digital business models. Regulation that intends to be effective in the context of network communication must therefore also develop as 'network regulation', whereby the regulatory structure necessarily opens up space for the construction and inclusion of multiple points of view beyond the state and the business model itself.[715] As the construction of the new public spaces in the digital world first emerges from private bilateral relationships and then takes the form of the Internet platform scenario described above, the resulting dependence of the exercise of communication-related fundamental rights on the mediation services of the new intermediaries shows that the traditional forms of communities standards control by state courts seem incompatible with the dynamics of network communication. This is accompanied by the need to shift legal protection to the medium itself and to establish a dynamic and procedural mechanism of relationship between state courts and conflict resolution within platforms through digital arbitration courts themselves. This presents itself as an opportunity to use law not only as an action 'in time' but also 'with the help of time', and thus also to bring about new institutions for platform-based law as a hybrid legal order model.[716]

Outlook

METAMORPHOSES OF GLOBAL law are metamorphoses of society itself, as has been described throughout this book. What distinguishes modern law from other forms of law is that it does not feed its normative conditions from a higher authority or instance.[717] Yan Thomas showed that a social dynamic was already emerging in Roman law – primarily through the formation of the city (*polis*) – which makes it plausible that Roman law developed a dynamic that was largely distinct from the arbitrariness of noble families and their tradition and rites.[718] Such potential, which was still in its infancy in Roman law, experienced a gradual increase in the nineteenth century, especially with a dynamisation of the impersonal dimension or a distribution of knowledge of society that culminated in the disintegration of the *ius publicum europaeum* described here. A tendency to detach the normative layers of law from the body of the sovereign ('displacement of the body') and its replacement by fictions[719,720] complicates the social conditions of locating power in a particular body or in a particular concrete place, as exemplified by the concrete order in the Schmittian sense for the contours of world law. Any attempt to give society a body in recent history, and thus to counter modern logic, the operationalisation of legal fictions and the associated support of a socially distributed knowledge for the emergence and maintenance of the democratic rule of law, has inevitably led to the suppression of individual freedoms.[721]

This elective affinity between modern law and legal fiction, and especially its positive externality that enables the construction of social relations beyond tradition, gains new contours in the current migration of the analogue world to computer networks and their devices. Although there is an inherent tension between the rule of code and the instrumental conditions of the rule of law, there are also opportunities to maintain a complementary relationship between the two processes of law formation. The emergence of new forms of dispute resolution that are inconsistent with the traditional forms of bureaucratic organisations of traditional justice[722] opens up new opportunities for modern mechanisms to protect the rights of third parties. Nevertheless, this cannot be read as an example of the functional anachronism of the judicial system of mass democracy. On the contrary, its crucial re-reading in the context of information capitalism involves the insertion of procedural mechanisms, in which state courts would play an important role in monitoring the formation of norms in semi-automated decision-making systems within digital platforms. The promotion of the self-organisation dimension must be accompanied by a duty of observation on the part of state courts, otherwise there is a risk of a complete emancipation of the 'rule of code' from the consolidated standards of the 'rule of law'.

The relationship between law and time, which was the starting point of this work, finds its greatest challenge in today's platform society. The structuring axis of this relationship has as its central parameter the transformation of social forms and structures that determine the orientation of human action. In this context, Reinhart Koselleck and Niklas Luhmann drew attention to a new category called 'expectation', which in modernity became increasingly determinant in shaping the horizon against which society aligns its actions. This category is characterised above all by its detachment from the temporal forms of orientation of human action that were based on experience or tradition.[723] New technologies, the growth of cities, and new laboratories of subjectivity made the future more uncertain, and it was at this point that law, as a form of time-binding, played the role of articulating the common ground of human action and of institutionally shaping the form of the relationship between society and the future. In this context, modern society and law in particular – due to the lack of stable criteria and parameters for the social orientation of individuals and institutions in an increasingly complex society – have created complex mechanisms that give rise to an increasingly uncertain future, which carries with it a central role in the construction of a common minimum horizon of social action. The hallmark of this future of modernity was its contingency and openness but, at the same time, the possibility of modelling a minimum horizon produced by the legal form.

Meanwhile, the platform society starts a new chapter of possible conditions in the relationship between law and the future – especially through the development of new technologies. And this new relationship is now characterised by the presence of new actors and technologies in the shaping of future of society. Whereas the relationship between the future and society was previously characterised by an indirect form of creating greater possibilities for action through an open future, the new scenario takes on different contours, in which the future itself and the orientation of human action guided by it become the scarce resource of new business models. The platform society is characterised by a broader participation of multiple actors in modelling forms of time-binding society. In this, time is no longer bound exclusively by law to an expectable common horizon of action, but rather by business models that bind the future itself and are thus capable of reinventing and even predicting it. Participation in this dimension of society, hitherto reserved for prophets, emperors,[724] reason, modern politics, is now also occupied by forecasting models and future modelling of human behaviour by business models which, based on new technologies and the accumulation and processing of data, achieve an even greater objectifying effect than the previous categories. The future of modernity as an uncertain one, characterised by its contingency structured in abstract mechanisms, is becoming an increasingly certain future that brings opportunities for human freedom, and dangers as well.[725] But where the danger is, does not the saving power also grow?

Notes

INTRODUCTION

[1] Eugen Ehrlich, *Grundlegung der Soziologie des Rechts*, reprint 1967. 4th ed., Berlin 1989, p. 390.
[2] Richard Posner, *Economic Analysis of Law*, 8th ed., Aspen 2011.
[3] Karl-Heinz Ladeur, *Negative Freiheitsrechte und gesellschaftliche Selbstorganisation*, Tübingen 2000, p. 165 ff.
[4] Jean-Jacques Rousseau, *Vom Gesellschaftsvertrag*, in: *Politische Schriften I*, Paderborn 1977, ch. 1.6.
[5] Christoph Möllers, *Die Möglichkeit der Normen. Über eine Praxis jenseits von Moralität und Kausalität*. Berlin 2015, p. 440 ff.
[6] Gunther Teubner, *Verfassungsfragmente*, Frankfurt am Main 2012, p. 214 ff.
[7] Vincent Descombes, Die Rätsel der Identität, Berlin 2013, p. 226 ff; Thomas Vesting, *Gentleman, Manager, Homo Digitalis. Der Wandel der Rechtssubjektivität in der Moderne*, Weilerswist 2021 i. E., manuscript p. 92.
[8] Herbert L. A. Hart, *The Concept of Law* (1966), Oxford/New York 1994, p. 128.
[9] G. W. F. Hegel, *Lecture on Aesthetics I*, Werke 13, Frankfurt am Main 1986, p. 270 ff. Martin Seel, *Das Naturschöne und das Kunstschöne*, in: Birgit Sandkaulen (Ed.), G. W. F. Hegel: *Vorlesungen über die Aesthetik*, Berlin 2018, p. 37 ff.
[10] Niklas Luhmann, *Das Recht der Gesellschaft*, Frankfurt am Main 1993, p. 585 f.
[11] George Dickie, *Introduction to Aesthetics. An Analytic Approach*, New York 1997; Georgie Dickie, *Art and Value*, Malden (Mass.) 2001.
[12] Arthur C. Danto, *What Art Is*, New Haven (Conn.) 2013, p. 135 ff; ed., Wiedersehen mit der Kunstwelt. Komödien der Ähnlichkeit, in: Arthur C. Danto, *Kunst nach dem Ende der Kunst*, Munich 1996, pp. 53, 57, 62.
[13] Thomas Vesting, *Staatstheorie. Ein Studienbuch*, Munich 2018, p. 19 ff.
[14] Ronald Dworkin, *Law's Empire*, Cambridge (Mass.)/London 1986, pp. 178–184.
[15] Hans-Jörg Rheinberger, *Historische Epistemologie zur Einführung*, Hamburg 2007, p. 52.
[16] Weigel rightly claims that Carl Schmitt provided the caricature of a modernity without a genealogy; on this see Sigrid Weigel, *Walter Benjamin. Die Kreatur, das Heilige, die Bilder*, Frankfurt am Main 2008, p. 71 ff. Even more precisely, one could go beyond this and say that Schmitt not only presents a 'caricature of modernity without a genealogy', but intends to caricature a counter-genealogy of modernity.

CHAPTER 1
ANOMALY AS LEGAL DEVELOPMENT

[17] Luhmann, *Das Recht der Gesellschaft* (fn. 10), p. 490.
[18] Niklas Luhmann, Die Weltgesellschaft, in: Niklas Luhmann, *Soziologische Aufklärung*, vol. 2: *Aufsätze zur Theorie der Gesellschaft* 5th ed., Wiesbaden 2005, p. 63 ff. Thomas Vesting sees the growing enthusiasm for world society in the postwar period, first in literature (Auerbach) and philosophy (Ritter) and later sociology (Luhmann), as a form of tacit 'revolt' in the face of the role nationalism had taken in World War II. See Vesting, *Staatstheorie* (fn. 13), p. 8 f.
[19] Thus, in the 'peculiar combination of law and politics, precisely in their special efficiency, lies a misspecification of human development ... which, for the time being at least, cannot be transferred to the system of world society': Luhmann, *Die Weltgesellschaft* (fn. 18), p. 71.
[20] Niklas Luhmann, *Rechtssoziologie*, 3rd ed.

110 Notes

[21] 'World society is constituted in primarily cognitive expectational settings. In speculative exaggeration of what is already visible at present, one could speak of a shift in evolutionary primacy from normative to cognitive mechanisms.' *Luhmann*, ibid, p. 340.

[22] In this context, Luhmann himself raises the question whether law will not develop differently: 'It should be considered, however, whether law itself does not change to the extent that world society consolidates and assigns its primacy to the cognitive style of human contact'. Luhmann, ibid, p. 340 f.

[23] For Rudolf Stichweh – especially at the point concerning world society – the thesis of cognitive primacy appears to be a false thesis, which for this reason is not repeated in other texts by Luhmann. Based on this statement, according to Stichweh, 'this text has actually remained a solitaire': cf. Rudolf Stichweh, Politik und Weltgesellschaft, in: Kai-Uwe Hellmann/Rainer Schmalz-Bruns (eds.), *Theorie der Politik. Niklas Luhmanns politische Soziologie*, Frankfurt am Main 2002, p. 287 ff. What Stichweh cannot explain, however, is the reason why the thesis of 1975 appears congruently again in the book *Recht der Gesellschaft (Law as a Social System)* from 1993 cited at the beginning of this article.

[24] This topic will be discussed in Chapter 2.

[25] Cf. Karl-Heinz Ladeur/Ino Augsberg, *Die Funktion der Menschenwürde im Verfassungsstaat*, Tübingen 2008, p. 105.

[26] Niklas Luhmann, *Grundrechte als Institution: Ein Beitrag zur politischen Soziologie*, 3rd ed., Berlin 1999, p. 51 f. This role assigned to fundamental rights as a structurer of independent spheres among themselves within the scheme of functional differentiation or as a repair store of this form of differentiation is particularly present in the further development of systems theory in the writings of Gunther Teubner.

[27] On the role of the figure of the katechon in Schmitt, see especially Günter Meuter, *Der Katechon. Zu Carl Schmitts fundamentalistischer Kritik der Zeit*, Berlin, 1994; and Alfons Motschenbacher, *Katechon oder Großinquisitor? Eine Studie zu Inhalt und Struktur der Politischen Theologie Carl Schmitts*, Marburg 2000.

[28] Niklas Luhmann, Globalization or World Society: How to Conceive of Modern Society?, *International Review of Sociology* 7/1 (1997), p. 67 ff.

[29] This kind of elaboration about world society can be found in several works by Niklas Luhmann. See, e.g., Niklas Luhmann, *Die Politik der Gesellschaft,* Frankfurt am Main 2002, p. 220: 'The fact of a worldwide communication system cannot be disputed'; Niklas Luhmann, *Die Wissenschaft der Gesellschaft*, 7th ed, Frankfurt am Main 2015, p. 716: 'Everything that happens, happens in the world'; Niklas Luhmann, *Soziale Systeme*, Frankfurt am Main 1984, p. 585: 'Society today is unambiguously world society, – unambiguously, at any rate, if one takes the concept of the social system proposed here as a basis'.

[30] Even before the popularisation of the Internet, Luhmann sensed that this would tangentially affect communication worldwide. Niklas Luhmann, *Systemtheorie der Gesellschaft*, Frankfurt am Main 2017, p. 213: 'Now that all human experience and action has become communicatively accessible to one another, there can only be a world-unifying social system'. It is interesting to note that the main transformation results from technology, i.e., the creation of a new medium. It is not for nothing that Thomas Vesting didactically refers to these media transformations as 'pre-adaptive advances'. See Thomas Vesting, *Rechtstheorie. Ein Studienbuch*, 2nd ed. Munich 2015, p. 167 f.

[31] Ulrich Beck/Edgar Grande, Beyond Methodological Nationalism. Non-European and European Variations of the Second Modernity, *Soziale Welt* 61 (2010), p. 187 ff.

[32] The German word 'Grenze' replaced the older 'Mark' in the course of early modern times. Mark was the demarcation marked by a stake separating village property, and therefore the marking of the national border. Cf. art. 'Mark', in: Jacob and Wilhelm Grimm (eds.), *Deutsches Wörterbuch*, vol. 12, Quellenverzeichnis Leipzig 1971, pp. 1628–1636, here p. 1633 ff.

[33] Luhmann, *Soziale Systeme* (fn. 29), p. 266: 'And incidentally, territoriality, today at any rate, is a boundary principle quite atypical for social systems, rather exotic, rather disrupting normal social mobility'.

[34] Luhmann, *Die Politik der Gesellschaft* (fn. 29), p. 220: 'The place where one is located loses its role as a condition of the possibility of seeing and hearing. It is thus trivialised in terms of information technology. Thus all space-related centralisms become transcendable – which does not exclude that thereupon an opposing regional consciousness consolidates itself.'

[35] Rudolf Stichweh, Kontrolle und Organisation des Raumes durch die Funktionssysteme der Weltgesell-schaft, in: Jörg Döring/Tristan Thielmann (Eds.), *Spatial Turn. Das Raumparadigma in den Kultur- und Sozialwissenschaften*, Bielefeld 2008, pp. 149 ff, 157.

[36] Niklas Luhmann, *Die Gesellschaft der Gesellschaft*, Frankfurt am Main 1997, p. 76.

[37] However, it is not correct to assume that systems theory ignores the concept of space. On the contrary: it is just not seen as a starting point. Marc Redepenning and Jan Lorenz Wilhelm have put the relationship between space and systems theory in a nutshell: 'spaces are therefore never significant in systems theory by themselves; rather, their significance and social relevance only arise from the specific inherent logics of the systems involved'. For example, in the economic system, investments of a company use spatial observation schemes. See Marc Redepenning/Jan Lorenz Wilhelm, Raumforschung mit luhmannscher Systemtheorie, in: Jürgen Oßenbrügge/Anne Vogelpohl (Eds.), *Theorien in der Raum- und Stadtforschung*, Münster 2014, p. 310.

[38] Luhmann, *Soziale Systeme* (fn. 29), p. 53. On the metaphor of the limit in Luhmann's work, see Albrecht Koschorke, Die Grenzen des Systems und die Rhetorik der Systemtheorie, in: Albrecht Koschorke /Cornelia Vismann (Eds.), *Widerstände der Systemtheorie. Kulturtheoretische Analysen zum Werk von Niklas Luhmann*, Berlin 1999, p. 49 ff.

[39] This 'politics of exclusion' is not only constitutive for systems theory. Kant, for example, also understands border and bordering as one of the starting points of philosophy, almost as its epistemological precondition. 'Philosophy', Kant says, consists in 'knowing its limits'. Immanuel Kant, *Werke in zwölf Bänden*, vol. 4, Frankfurt am Main 1977, p. 755. See also the role of boundaries in the accuracy of conceptualisation: 'Defining, as the expression itself gives it, should really mean only so much as originally representing the detailed concept of a thing within its boundaries'. Kant, ibid, p. 755.

[40] Rudolf Stichweh, *Die Weltgesellschaft*, Frankfurt am Main 2000, p. 27. The world society affects national law by its 'dynamism ... setting occasions for learning' or even 'exerting learning pressure' and thus limiting the arbitrariness of problem solutions. Instead of 'fidelity to norms', capacities for 'analysis and decisions' could then be built into the legal system ... as 'learning restructuring and adaptation of programs': Luhmann, *Rechtssoziologie* (fn. 20), p. 341.

[41] Luhmann, *Die Gesellschaft der Gesellschaft* (fn. 36), p. 166. 'An Argentinean may marry an Abyssinian if he loves her; a New Zealander may take out a loan in New Zealand if this is economically rational, a Berliner may tan in the Bahamas if this gives him a sense of recreation.' Luhmann, *Die Weltgesellschaft* (fn. 18), p. 66.

[42] On the distinction between success media and dissemination media, see Luhmann, *Die Gesellschaft der Gesellschaft* (fn. 36), p. 202 ff.

[43] Luhmann, *Systemtheorie der Gesellschaft* (fn. 30), p. 866.

[44] Luhmann, ibid., p. 867: 'make some subsystems grow more than others'.

[45] Luhmann, ibid, p. 868.

[46] 'Our thesis that the conditions of the performance of symbolically generalised communication media and the system formations tailored to them impose barriers to the growth of sise ...' Luhmann tests his thesis on various media such as power, truth, love and money, Luhmann, ibid, p. 867.

[47] Luhmann, *Die Gesellschaft der Gesellschaft* (fn. 36), p. 757: 'how much inward expansion society thus generates, how much monetarization, juridification, scientification, politicization it can generate and cope with, and how much of it at the same time (instead of, e.g., only monetarization)'; otherwise Teubner, *Verfassungsfragmente* (fn. 6), p. 132.

[48] Law and politics still remain regionally differentiated in the form of states. They continue to operate, if not dependent on spatial boundaries, at least dependent on institutional conditions, whose constitutionalisation processes are usually only carried out within territorial spatial boundaries. 'World society is becoming more and more a unified system – and at the same time a system that generates and has to endure immense discrepancies. This precludes political unification *without offering an alternative, a functional equivalent, for it.*' Niklas Luhmann, Die Wirtschaft der Gesellschaft, Frankfurt am Main 1994, p. 170 [emphasis added]. 'Regionally differentiable in the form of states is only the political system and with it the legal system of modern society': Luhmann, *Die Gesellschaft der Gesellschaft* (fn. 36), p. 166.

[49] Cf. Georg Schwarzenberger, *Power Politics. A Study of International Society*, 2nd ed., London 1951, p. 251: 'Modern international society is a reality for the reason that in it groups co-exist which are both interdependent and independent of each other ... The bond that holds world society together is not any vague community of spiritual interests. It is power.'

[50] Philip C. Jessup, *Transnational Law*, New Haven 1959, p. 108: 'We are here dealing of course only with transnational situations. Much existing law has developed or has been enacted with an eye merely to the local or internal problem. Modern communications and contracts have made the

transnational situations much more frequent and familiar; and actually a great deal of law has been created with a specific purpose of regulating such situations ...'.

[51] Morton Kaplan, *System and Process in International Politics*, New York 1957, p. 12.

[52] Talcott Parsons, *Order and Community in the International Social System*, in: Talcott Parsons, *Politics and Social Structure*, New York 1969, pp. 292 ff, 305 ff. Parsons, however, reserves the term society for the national state. This is related to his concept of society, which goes back to Aristotelian collective formation. For a society to qualify as a society, effective forms of enforcing normative structures, such as a central power within a territory, must exist for that society. 'Private' transnational law, UN law, and international law do not exhibit these characteristics. See Talcott Parsons, *Societies. Evolutionary and Comparative Perspectives*, Prentice-Hall 1966. p. 9; Talcott Parsons, *The Systems of Modern Societies*, Prentice Hall 1971, p. 8 ff; Talcott Parsons, Polarization of the World and International Order, in: Talcott Parsons, *Sociological Theory and Modern Society*, New York 1967, p. 478 ff.

[53] Based on a thesis by Karl Marx about capitalist development and a probable dynamic that reproduces itself beyond the borders of European nation-states, Immanuel Wallerstein developed a comprehensive theory of world society. 'It was thus the world system and not the individual "societies" that "developed". That is, once it had come into being, the capitalist world economy was first consolidated, and then gradually the influence of its basic structures on the social processes within its borders deepened and broadened. The whole notions of the process of growth from acorn to oak, from germ to its unfolding, gives meaning, if at all, only when applied to the unique capitalist world economy as a historical system.' Immanuel Wallerstein, Social Development or Development of the World System?, in Burkart Lutz (Ed.), *Sociology and Social Development*, Frankfurt am Main/ New York 1985, pp. 76 ff, 85. On the initial thesis, see Karl Marx, *Grundrisse der Kritik der politischen Ökonomie* (1857–1858), Berlin 1953, p. 175.

[54] What is decisive for his concept of world society is that it is 'depoliticised', 'just as it is, after all, also de-economised, de-sacralised, de-juridified and de-identified' – André Kieserling, Makropolitik, Mikropolitik. Politik der Protestbewegungen, in: Armin Nassehi/Markus Schroer (Eds.), *Der Begriff des Politischen*, Baden-Baden 2003, p. 419 ff.

[55] Luhmann, *Die Weltgesellschaft* (fn. 18), pp. 78–79.

[56] Luhmann, ibid, p. 79.

[57] Luhmann, *Die Gesellschaft der Gesellschaft* (fn. 36), p. 150.

[58] Luhmann, ibid. Here he distances himself from the concept of integration he applied in the 1971 essay.

[59] Luhmann, ibid, p. 80; Stichweh, *Die Weltgesellschaft* (fn. 40), p. 249: 'World society is in fact the only society that still exists on earth'.

[60] Luhmann, *Die Gesellschaft der Gesellschaft* (fn. 36), p. 145 ff.; Stichweh, *Die Weltgesellschaft* (fn. 40).

[61] Luhmann, *Die Gesellschaft der Gesellschaft* (fn. 36), p. 171; Luhmann, *Die Weltgesellschaft* (fn. 18), p. 11.

[62] Luhmann, *Die Gesellschaft der Gesellschaft* (fn. 36), p. 24 ff. See also Jens Greve/Bettina Heintz, Die 'Entdeckung' der Weltgesellschaft. Entstehung und Grenzen der Weltgesellschaftstheorie, Zeitschrift für Soziologie, special issue 'Weltgesellschaft' 2005, p. 89 ff. (89).

[63] Beck/Grande, *Jenseits des methodologischen Nationalismus* (fn. 31), p. 187 ff.

[64] The functional systems are designed for a universalism whose expansive tendency, its momentum and its own logic do not stop at national borders: Luhmann, *Die Weltgesellschaft* (fn. 18), p. 63; Luhmann, *Die Gesellschaft der Gesellschaft* (fn. 36), pp. 149, 809.

[65] Stichweh, *Die Weltgesellschaft* (fn. 40), p. 13: 'Luhmann has insisted that the performance of the theory of world society will have to be proven precisely by its success in proving differences in the system of world society to be internal differentiations of this system'.

[66] Niklas Luhmann, Moderne Systemtheorien als Form gesamtgesellschaftlicher Analyse, in: Jürgen Habermas/Niklas Luhmann (Eds.), *Theorie der Gesellschaft oder Sozialtechnologie: Was leistet die Sys-temforschung*. Frankfurt am Main 1971, p. 7 ff, 15: 'Society is that level of system formation from which there is functional differentiation'.

[67] However, the position of the regions or the different stages of development of the globe is not faded out by the worldwide functional differentiation. On the contrary: the given differences are then measured or, depending on the region, strengthened or weakened and linked with the world-societal specifications. Participation in world-societal processes, however, is established on the conceptual level of world-societal functional differentiation through the operation mode of communication and

not through the specificity of a regional concept of society. It is rather a methodological decision to start from the world society concept. Luhmann, *Die Gesellschaft der Gesellschaft* (fn. 36), p. 161 ff. Specifically on the relationship between regional and world functional differentiation, see Luhmann, ibid, p. 166: 'A primarily regional differentiation would contradict the modern primacy of functional differentiation'.

[68] Luhmann, ibid, p. 145 ff. and p. 609 ff. More generally, however, Luhmann, World Society as a Social System, in: Felix R. Geyer (Ed.), *Dependence and Inequality. A Systems Approach to the Problems of Mexico and Other Developing Countries*, Oxford 1982, pp. 295 ff, 298: 'The inclusion of all communicative behavior into one societal system is the unavoidable *consequence of functional differentiation*' [emphasis added]; with the same conclusion Rudolf Stichweh, Kulturelle Produktion in der Weltgesellschaft, in: Krassimira Kruškova/Nele Lipp (Eds.), *Tanz anderswo: intra- und unterkulturell, Jahrbuch Tanzforschung*, vol. 14, Münster 2004, pp. 189 et seq, 190 Rudolf Stichweh has put this development in a nutshell elsewhere: 'World society is based on the fact that the social world is dissected several times by the respective autonomous perspectives of the individual functional systems and that each of these functional perspectives today spans a worldwide communication context in its own way': Rudolf Stichweh, Der Zusammenhalt der Weltgesellschaft. Non-Normative Theories of Integration in Sociology, working paper, Lucerne 2004, p. 6.

[69] 'If society is nothing other than the comprehensive system of all connectable communication, then changes in the means of communication can be expected to strike and transform society like a blow': Luhmann, *Die Wissenschaft der Gesellschaft* (fn. 29), p. 597. On the communication revolution brought about by telegraphy: 'at the same time, telegraphy proved to be of great importance for the establishment of global functional systems, since spatial boundaries thus became increasingly irrelevant to communication, which was largely freed from its physical substrate'. Urs Stäheli, Der Takt der Börse. Inklusionseffekte von Verbreitungsmedien am Beispiel des Börsen-Tickers, *Zeitschrift für Soziologie* 33/3 (June 2004), pp. 245 ff, 248 ff; in this context also Teubner, *Verfassungsfragmente* (fn. 6), p. 73: 'as is well known, globalization means above all that the dynamics of functional differentiation, which was historically first realised in the nation-states of Europe and North America, is now taking hold of the entire globe'.

[70] Luhmann, *Die Politik der Gesellschaft* (fn. 29), p. 220.

[71] Luhmann, ibid.

[72] Luhmann, ibid, p. 221. 'Neither in the form of "domination" nor in the form of "culture" or "values" does the concept of world society presuppose centralization. Rather, what is typical is a heterarchical, connectionist, network-like linking of communications at the level of organization and profession – a type that will be reinforced in the future by the use of computers.'

[73] Luhmann, *Die Gesellschaft der Gesellschaft* (fn. 36), p. 145 ff: 'With this conceptual disposition there can be only one society, the world society'.

[74] Thomas Schwinn, *Weltgesellschaft, multiple Moderne und die Herausforderungen für die soziologische Theorie*, Zeitschrift für Soziologie, Sonderheft Weltgesellschaft 2005, pp. 205 ff, 210.

[75] Luhmann, *Das Recht der Gesellschaft* (fn. 10), p. 571. Law can only differentiate itself in the Luhmannian sense under institutional conditions – including state legislation, state jurisdiction and institutional politics – which is why law and politics remain regionally differentiated in the form of states. 'World society is becoming more and more a unified system – and at the same time a system that generates and has to endure immense discrepancies. This precludes political unification *without offering an alternative, a functional equivalent, for it*.' Luhmann, *Die Wirtschaft der Gesellschaft* (fn. 48), p. 170 [emphasis added]. 'Regionally differentiable in the form of states is only the political system and with it the legal system of modern society': *Luhmann, Die Wirtschaft der Gesellschaft* (fn. 36), p. 166.

[76] Luhmann, *The Law of Society* (footnote 10), p. 574.

[77] Andreas Fischer-Lescano, *Global Constitution. Die Geltungsbegründung der Menschenrechte*, Weilerswist 2005. Fischer-Lescano shows how scandals have become valid law through the incorporation of national and international legal proceedings, a law that ultimately goes beyond the immunity provisions by which perpetrators could protect themselves from prosecution. See also Gunther Teubner, Dreiers Luhmann, in Robert Alexy (Ed.), *Integratives Verstehen: Zur Rechtsphilosophie Ralf Dreiers*, Tübingen 2005, p. 199 ff: 'Positivity of human rights was plausible in the problem pressure of nation-state endangerments and in the consistency with firmly institutionalised legislation and state guaranteed jurisdiction. Scandalization becomes plausible in the problem pressure of international endangerments and a globally institutionalised media and protest culture.'

[78] Ladeur and Viellechner draw attention to the fact that although the scandal and the *colère public* in a certain sense denote a normative expectation from a societal point of view, without institutional anchoring from a legal point of view in the form of an 'expectation-securing institutionalization', they would not develop any legal effectiveness. See Karl-Heinz Ladeur/Lars Viellechner, *Die transnationale Expansion staatlicher Grundrechte. Zur Konstitutionalisierung globaler Privatrechtsregimes*, Archiv des Völkerrechts 46 (2008), pp. 42 ff, 52.

[79] This is not to draw the conclusion that transnational law emerges from international private law, human rights and scandals. Transnational law is a form of reflection precisely on certain structural developments and the formation of normative orders beyond the nation-state and international law. What is called into question here is the almost romantic positioning of scandals as a new form of law-making or positivity of law in global society. On transnational law, see Gralf-Peter Callies, Peer Zumbansen, *Rough Consensus and Running Code. A Theory of Transnational Private Law*, Oxford 2010, p. 27 ff.

[80] Although in later studies Luhmann pointed to secondary forms of structure formation in world society, such as regional differentiation and inclusion/exclusion, functional differentiation remains as the primary feature of the concept of world society. On inclusion/exclusion, however, see Boris Holzer, *Wie 'modern' ist die Weltgesellschaft? Funktionale Differenzierung und ihre Alternativen*, Soziale Systeme 13 (2007), p. 357 ff; Niklas Luhmann, Inklusion und Exklusion, in: Helmut Berding (Ed.), *Nationales Bewusstsein und kollektive Identität*, Frankfurt am Main 1994, pp. 15 ff, 41.

[81] Luhmann, *Die Gesellschaft der Gesellschaft* (fn. 36), p. 148 ff; Stichweh, *Die Weltgesellschaft* (fn. 40), p. 252 ff.

[82] This topic will be discussed in Chapter 2.

[83] For the domestic role of fundamental rights as an organiser of social differentiation, see Teubner, *Verfassungsfragmente* (fn. 6), p. 47: 'In the Basic Law there are at least elements – especially in the fundamental rights section and in the regulation of legislative competences – of an economic constitution, a cultural constitution, a media constitution, a military constitution, an environmental constitution, which standardised the given basic structures of these social subsectors in state terms. As objective legal principles, *fundamental rights "organised" functional subsystems* [emphasis added]'.

[84] Gunther Teubner, Die zwei Gesichter des Janus. Rechtspluralismus in der Spätmoderne, in: Eicke Schmidt (Ed.), *Liber Amicorum Josef Esser*, Heidelberg 1995, pp. 91 ff, 208. In later publications, the tones shift towards a constitutionalisation of the systems of meaning, so that the formula '*ubi societas, ibi ius*' is transformed into '*ubi societas, ibi constitutio*'. Teubner, *Verfassungsfragmente* (fn. 6), p. 63; the same, Transnational Constitutional Pluralism. Nine Variations on a Theme by David Sciulli, ZaöRV 76 (2016), p. 661 ff. For Latin explanations of the contexts of origin, see Detlef Liebs, *Lateinische Rechtsregeln und Rechtssprichwörter*, 7th ed., Munich 2007, p. 237.

[85] Gunther Teubner, Global Bukovina. Zur Emergenz eines transnationalen Rechtspluralismus, *Rechtshistorisches Journal* 15 (1996), pp. 255 ff, 260: 'For today's global society, Eugen Ehrlich's view seems confirmed that a centrally generated political law is quite marginal in contrast to "jurist law," the practical decision of legal conflicts, and especially in contrast to the "living law" of Bukovina.' On Eugen Ehrlich's Bukovina, see Manfred Rehbinder, *Die Begründung der Rechtssoziologie durch Eugen Ehrlich*, 2nd ed., Berlin 1986, p. 64 ff; Klaus F. Röhl/Stefan Machura, *100 Jahre Rechtssoziologie: Eugen Ehrlichs Rechtspluralismus heute*, JZ 23 (2013), p. 1117 ff.

[86] 'In modern societies, however, this is understood as the emergence of legal phenomena in the context of highly specialised discourses, which are the new sources of social self-reproduction, but are misunderstood by law as sources of norm production. This process changes the character of legal pluralism in its content and dynamics.' Teubner, *Die zwei Gesichter des Janus* (fn. 84), p. 209.

[87] Gerhard Hafner, Risks Ensuing from Fragmentation of International Law, *Int'l Law Comm'n* 143 (2000), Official Records of the General Assembly, Fifty-fifth Session, Supplement No. 10 (A/55/10), pp. 726 et seq.; the same author, Pros and Cons Ensuing from Fragmentation of International Law, *Mich. J. Int'l Law* 25 (2004), pp. 849 ff, 860 ff. Anne Peters points to arguments against the inherent 'managerialism' of the fragmentation of international law while arguing for a greater politicization of international law, on which see Anne Peters, *The Refinement of International Law: From Fragmentation to Regime Interaction and Politicization*, I-CON 15/3 (2017), pp. 671 ff, 700 ff.

[88] Study Group of the Int'l Law Comm'n, Rep. on the Fragmentation of International Law: Difficulties Arising from the Diversification and Expansion of International Law, finalised by Martti Koskenniemi, U.N. Doc. A/CN.4/L.682 (Apr. 13, 2006) – zitiert: Koskenniemi, UN-Report.

[89] 'The fragmentation of the international social world has attained legal significance especially as it has been accompanied by the emergence of specialised and (relatively) autonomous rules or rulecomplexes, legal institutions and spheres of legal practices. What once appeared to be governed by "general international law" has become the field of operation for such specialist systems as "trade law", "human rights law", "environmental law", "law of the sea", "European law" and even such exotic and highly specialised knowledge as "investment law" or "international refugee law" etc. – each possessing their own principles and institutions': Koskenniemi, UN Report, p. 11; Koskenniemi, Global Legal Pluralism: Multiple Regimes and Multiple Modes of Thought. Keynote Speech, delivered at Harvard University 5 March 2005, p. 15, abrufbar unter https://sta.rl.talis.com/items/C6EC2B43-58EA-15A1-A842-0E12FEBA8612.html.

[90] Jeffrey L. Dunoff/Joel P. Trachtman, A Functional Approach to International Constitutionalization, in: Jeffrey L. Dunoff/Joel P. Trachtman (Eds.), *Ruling the World?*, Cambridge (N.Y.) 2009, pp. 3, 9; Hafner, Pros and Cons Ensuing from Fragmentation of International Law (fn. 87), pp. 849, 849 ff.; Anne-Charlotte Martineau, The Rhetoric of Fragmentation: Fear and Faith in International Law, LJL 22 (2009), p. 1 ff.

[91] There is a latent atmosphere in the discipline of international law in which the well-meaning internationalist looks for ways to constitutionalise international law, which in one way or another ends up with the UN as the centralising institution for law reproduction (a clear allusion to the centralist model developed within the institutional experience of the nation-state). Anything conceived outside of this framework is viewed with suspicion, to say the least, within the discipline itself. A similar movement can be seen in European law, migration law, etc, when criticisms of participants in the discourse are taken as an opportunity to be moralised to their detriment. Gradually, this form of discourse becomes identitarian discourse at the expense of scientific analysis. The idea of a unity of international law in the sense of Alfred Verdross (Alfred Verdross, *Die Einheit des rechtlichen Weltbildes auf Grundlage der Völkerrechtsverfassung*, Tübingen 1923) is nevertheless increasingly seen as unrealistic. See Andreas Paulus, Fragmentierung und Segmentierung der internationalen Ordnung als Herausforderung prozeduraler Gemeinwohlorientierung, in: Hans M. Heinig/Jörg P. Terhechte (Eds.), *Postnationale Demokratie, Postdemokratie, Neoetatismus. Wandel klassischer Demokratievorstellungen in der Rechtswissenschaft*, Tübingen 2013, pp. 139 ff, 141; Anne Peters, Rechtsordnung und Konstitutionalisierung: Zur Neubestimmung der Verhältnisse, ZöR 65 (2010), pp. 3 ff, 27, on the impossibility of currently thinking about international law from a unified perspective, ibid, p. 28.

[92] Koskenniemi, UN-Report (fn. 88), p. 71 Fn. 168; Koskenniemi/Päivi Leino, Fragmentation of International Law. Postmodern Anxieties?, *Leiden Journal of International Law* 15 (2002), p. 553 ff.: 'One of the features of late international modernity has been what sociologists have called "functional differentiation", the increasing specialization of parts of society and the related autonomization of those parts'; Koskenniemi, UN-Report (fn. 88), p. 11; Koskenniemi, *The Politics of International Law*, Oxford 2011, p. 349; Pemmaraju P. Rao, Multiple International Judicial Forums: A Reflection of the Growing Strength of International Law or its Fragmentation?, Mich J Int'l L 25 (2004), pp. 929, 930 ff.; Hafner, Pros and Cons Ensuing from Fragmentation of International Law (fn. 87), p. 854; Markus Böckenförde, Zwischen Sein und Wollen – Über den Einfluss umweltvölkerrechtlicher Verträge im Rahmen eines WTO-Streitbeilegungsverfahrens, ZaöRV 63 (2003), p. 971 ff.

[93] Here is one of the central points of the analysis on the emergence of global law. It no longer takes place in the traditional centre of law production, the parliament, but on the periphery of law, that is, at the borders with other sectors of global society. 'The focus of law formation is shifting to private regimes, to contracts between *global players*, private market regulation by multinational corporations, internal rule-making in international organizations, interorganizational negotiation systems, global standardization processes.' Gunther Teubner, Privatregimes. Neo-Spontanes Recht und duale Sozialverfassungen in der Weltgesell-schaft?, in: Dieter Simon/Manfred Weiss (Eds.), *Zur Autonomie des Individuums*, Baden-Baden 2000, pp. 437 ff, 440.

[94] Dieter Grimm, *The Future of the Constitution II. Auswirkungen von Europäisierung und Globalisierung*, Frankfurt am Main 2012, p. 303.

[95] The description of the new institutional constellation as a regime first appeared in political science and only then migrated into law. Cf. Robert O. Keohane, *After Hegemony. Cooperation and Discord in the World Political Economy*, Princeton 1984; Michael Zürn, *Gerechte Internationale Regime: Bedingungen und Restriktionen der Entstehung nicht-hegemonialer internationaler Regime, untersucht am Beispiel der Weltkommunikationsordnung*, Frankfurt am Main 1987.

[96] Among others William L. Twining, *General Jurisprudence. Understanding Law from a Global Perspective*, Cambridge 2009; Nico Krisch, *Beyond Constitutionalism: The Pluralist Structure of Postnational Law*, Oxford 2010; Callies/Zumbansen, *Rough Consensus and Running Code* (fn. 79).

[97] Karl Larenz, *Das Problem der Rechtsgeltung*, Berlin 1929, p. 5; Stephan Meyer, *Juristische Geltung als Verbindlichkeit*, Tübingen 2011, p. 1; and more recently Andreas Engelmann, *Rechtsgeltung als institutionelles Projekt. Zur kulturellen Verortung eines rechtswissenschaftlichen Begriffs*, Weilerswist 2020.

[98] For Savigny, sources of law are considered to be the origins of the applicable law without a direct connection to the state. See Friedrich Carl V. Savigny, *System des heutigen Römischen Rechts*, vol. 1, Berlin 1840, p. 11. Alf Ross, much later, but still following the tradition of the theory of legal sources, no longer designates the source of law as a ground of origin but as a 'ground of cognition'. See Alf Ross, *Theorie der Rechtsquellen. Ein Beitrag zur Theorie des positiven Rechts auf Grundlage dogmenhistorischer Untersuchungen*, Leipzig/Wien 1929, p. 291 ff. The transition from a conceptualisation of the source of law from a ground of origin to a ground of knowledge points to a new legal tradition characterised by a stronger identification between law and state. However, this identification weakens over time as society becomes more complex.

[99] Bernd Rüthers, *Rechtstheorie*, Munich 2005, para. 223 ff; Klaus Röhl, *Allgemeine Rechtslehre*, Munich/Cologne 1995, p. 537 ff.

[100] Ernst-Wolfgang Böckenförde, *Demokratie als Verfassungsprinzip* (§ 24), in: Josef Isensee/Paul Kirchhof (Eds.), *Handbuch des Staatsrechts der Bundesrepublik Deutschland*, Bd. II, 3rd ed.

[101] Hart partly shifts the problem to the routine of law and therefore conceives of legal validity sometimes as a 'mysterious property', sometimes as a 'prediction of future behaviour'. 'The rule of recognition exists only as a complex, but normally concordant, practice of the courts, officials, and private persons in identifying the law by reference to certain criteria. Its existence is a matter of fact': Hart, *The Concept of Law* (fn. 8), pp. 104 and 110; Aleksander Peczenik, *The Concept 'Valid Law'*, Stockholm 1972, p. 222.

[102] Jürgen Habermas, On the Internal Relationship between the Rule of Law and Democracy, in: Jürgen Habermas, *Philosophische Texte*, vol. 4: Politische Theorie, Frankfurt am Main 2009, p. 140 ff; Jürgen Habermas, *Der demokratische Rechtsstaat – eine paradoxe Verbindung widersprüchlicher Prinzipien?*, ibid, p. 154 ff.

[103] H. Kelsen, *Reine Rechtslehre. Das Problem der Gerechtigkeit* (1934), Vienna 1960, pp. 65, 196 ff; Johannes Meiners, *Rechtsnormen und Rationalität. Zum Problem der Rechtsgeltung bei Hans Kelsen, Jürgen Habermas und Niklas Luhmann*, Berlin 2015.

[104] In the Western tradition, foundation and validity are interrelated concepts. Statutory law is valid when it is founded on an authority that creates a unity of positing and presupposition. Foundation gives law a kind of original positing or beginning that creates an overarching legitimacy. The positing of the beginning first creates the normativity of further normality. For a separation of foundation and validity, see Karl-Heinz Ladeur, *Der Anfang des westlichen Rechts. The Christianization of Roman Legal Culture and the Emergence of Universal Law*, Tübingen 2018.

[105] Rainer Forst, *Normativität und Macht. Zur Analyse sozialer Rechtfertigungsordnungen*, Berlin 2015, pp. 121–127.

[106] Marie Theres Fögen, *Das Lied vom Gesetz*, Munich 2007, p. 84 f. Niklas Luhmann does not need substitutes for his theory, only camels. For this discussion, see Niklas Luhmann, The Return of the Twelfth Camel. On the Sense of a Sociological Analysis of Law, *Journal for the Sociology of Law* 21/1 (2000), p. 3 ff. Thomas Vesting, on the other hand, needs neither camels nor substitutes nor initial violence. For him, culture becomes the constant companion of law, cf. Thomas Vesting, Die innere Seite des Gesetzes. Symbolische Ordnung, Rechtssubjektivität und Umgang mit Ungewissheit, in: Ino Augsberg (Ed.), *Ungewissheit als Chance*, Tübingen 2009, p. 50 ff.

[107] Michael Stolleis, Die Legitimation von Recht und Gesetz durch Gott, Tradition, Wille, Natur, Vernunft und Verfassung, in: Martin Avenarius et al. (Eds.), *Ars Iuris. Festschrift für Okko Behrends zum 70. Geburtstag*, Göttingen 2009, p. 533 ff.

[108] Luhmann, Das Recht der Gesellschaft (fn. 10), p. 98.

[109] On the temporalisation of norm validity, see Luhmann, ibid, p. 557 ff.

[110] Vesting, Rechtstheorie (fn. 30), p. 110.

[111] Luhmann, *Das Recht der Gesellschaft* (fn. 10), p. 353 f. As Martin Shapiro notes, redundancy is the '*invisible hand*' of the legal system. Cf. Martin Shapiro, Towards a Theory of 'Stare Decisis', *Journal of Legal Studies* 1 (1972), pp. 125 ff, 131.

[112] For a discussion on the role of the camel in the closure of justice, see Gunther Teubner (Ed.), *Die Rückgabe des zwölften Kamels. Niklas Luhmann in der Diskussion über Gerechtigkeit*, Stuttgart 2000.

[113] On the topic of the necessary externalisation of (founding) paradoxes, see most recently Gunther Teubner, *Exogene Selbstbindung: Wie gesellschaftliche Teilsysteme ihre Gründungsparadoxien externalisieren, Zeitschrift für Rechtssoziologie* 35 (2015), p. 69 ff.

[114] 'A political constitution, which has emerged in the history of nation-states as a coupling of politics/law and at the same time claimed to normalise the relations of law to other subsystems, fails at the global level.' Teubner, *Privatregimes* (fn. 93), p. 440. 'The consequence is that the structural coupling of the political system and the legal system via constitutions has no equivalent at the level of global society.' Luhmann, *Das Recht der Gesellschaft* (fn. 10), p. 582.

[115] Private regimes of normative regulation are clearly outside the hierarchy of norms of law and are therefore without doubt – Savigny, *System des heutigen Römischen Rechts* (fn. 98), p. 12, has already taught it – non-law. 'These phenomena may be all sorts of things, professional norms, general terms and conditions, social rules, contractual agreements, mores, customs, intra- or interorganizational regimes, but not legal norms.' Gunther Teubner, The King's Many Bodies. The Self-Deconstruction of the Hierarchy of Law, *Social Systems* 2 (1996), pp. 229 ff, 233.

[116] 'The Great Deconstructor (of the hierarchy of rights) is not called "Jacques Derrida" or "Niklas Luhmann", it is called "globalization"': Teubner, ibid, p. 235.

[117] 'In the global private regimes, an effective self-deconstruction of law takes place that simply invalidates essential basic principles of nation-state law: the derivation of validity of legal norms in a hierarchy of legal sources, the legitimation of law by a politically set constitution, the setting of law by parliamentary bodies, the safeguarding by institutions, procedures, and principles of the rule of law, and the guarantee of individual freedoms by politically fought-for basic rights.' Teubner, *Privatregimes* (fn. 93), p. 441. Luhmann, *Globalization or World Society?* (fn. 28), p. 76: 'In our context, where we have to decide between assuming a global system of regional societies or a world society, we now have clear and theoretically consistent arguments for a single world society. The autopoietic system of this society can be described without any reference to regional particularities.'

[118] 'Contrary to what the current debate presupposes, therefore, it is *not at all the case that* the emergence of the world society gives rise to a completely new constitutional problem.' Teubner, *Verfassungsfragmente* (fn. 6), p. 20 [emphasis added]. Qualitatively, this means that the same fundamental and human rights that make up the tradition of national state and constitutional law must be generalised and respecified for the law of global society. The essential difference of Teubner's constitutional concept from Luhmann's thus lies precisely in the fact that it is not ontologised in terms of its state reference.

[119] At this point, in the transition from the national to the global, Luhmann repeatedly questions the function of law as a counterfactual stabiliser of normative expectations in global society. In this context, he speaks clearly of a 'change of leadership' in which law would be transformed from its traditional form, related to the conventional normative type of expectation, to a technology- and economy-like type of expectation, so that its form would approach greater malleability and adaptability in the face of the increase in the cognitive dimension of society, to the detriment of the normative. Luhmann, *Die Weltgesellschaft* (fn. 18), p. 1 ff. This view is presumably also followed by Gunther Teubner and Andreas Fischer-Lescano. Cf. Andreas Fischer-Lescano/Gunther Teubner, *Regime-Kollisionen. Zur Fragmentierung des globalen Rechts*, Frankfurt am Main 2006, p. 7 ff.

[120] Teubner, *Transnational Constitutional Pluralism* (fn. 84), p. 686: 'The constitutive and the limitative services of constitutions are not primarily provided by legal norms, but by the reflexivity of social communication media. Here, law becomes effective only in a subsidiary way by supporting this reflexivity and, in the best case, enforcing it. Its contribution is to institutionalise what is actually crucial media reflexivity within different social spheres by prescribing procedures of self-limitation and reconstructing social norms as legal constitutional norms.'

[121] Luhmann, *Das Recht der Gesellschaft* (footnote 10), p. 586.

[122] With medial reflexivity or double reflexivity, an inner politicisation of the self-dynamics of the subsystems is intended, which particularly amounts to limiting the systems' horizons of action through the role of law. The attribution of this function to the law of world society goes beyond the limits imposed on law by systems theory as given by Niklas Luhmann. See only Teubner, *Transnational Constitutional Pluralism* (fn. 84), p. 686: 'On the way to a world society, law – as Luhmann *clairvoyantly* formulated – assumes the constitutional function of supporting the medial reflexivity of

social systems ...' [emphasis added]. On the double reflexivity, see Teubner, Codes of Conduct multinationaler Unternehmen: Unternehmensverfassung jenseits von Corporate Governance und gesetzlicher Mitbestimmung, in Armin Höland et al. (Eds.), *Arbeitnehmermitwirkung in einer sich globalisierenden Arbeitswelt: liber amicorum* Manfred Weiss Berlin 2005, pp. 109 ff, here p. 112; and Teubner, *Verfassungsfragmente* (fn. 6), p. 158 ff.

[123] Luhmann, *Die Weltgesellschaft* (fn. 18), p. 63.

[124] Teubner, *Verfassungsfragmente* (fn. 6), p. 256 'If it is true that political and social partial constitutions establish double reflexivity, i.e. the medial reflexivity of the respective social sphere and that of law, then it becomes the genuine task of their constitutions to create the normative preconditions for their inner politicization. And inner politicization means arguing and deciding both about the role of the social sphere in society as a whole and about its possible dangers vis-à-vis the natural, social, and human environments and about its positive contributions to these environments.'

[125] According to Luhmann, approaching a cognitive law focused on procedural methods, especially within the nation-state, would mean the abolition of the operational closure and autonomy of the legal system. At this point, the limitations of the law of the nation-state vis-à-vis the conditions of global society become particularly clear, and are well expressed in the anomaly thesis. See Luhmann, *Das Recht der Gesellschaft* (fn. 10), pp. 88 ff. and 345.

[126] The connection between the organisational form and legal normativity for the production of action parameters in hybrid social practices is the topic of Chapter 5 below. On proceduralisation as a form of knowledge generation, see Ricardo Campos, Prozeduralisierung als Wissens-Fertigung im Recht, in: Dan Wielsch (Ed.) *Breaches of Law. Spiegelungen der Rechtskritik Rudolf Wiethölters*, Baden-Baden 2019, p. 400 ff.

[127] In this respect, also the diagnosis of Grimm, *Die Zukunft der Verfassung II* (fn. 94), p. 308: 'His concept of constitution is therefore not the diluted one of supranational constitutionalism, but a thoroughly ambitious one, which is expressly based on the achievement of the state constitution. Civil constitutions are supposed to accomplish vis-à-vis globally exercised private power what the state constitution accomplished vis-à-vis territorially bound political power.'

[128] This is precisely the point of criticism of the 'social constitutionalism' of most teachers of constitutional law. In this respect, it is also incomprehensible why the traditional teachers of constitutional law criticised Gunther Teubner's constitutional model so harshly, because Teubner could be understood as a 'messenger', 'mediator', or even 'catechist' who wants to save the tradition of the rule of law, the tradition of traditional constitutionalism that has made a career in the nation-state, for the development of the law of world society.

[129] 'What is called for, as already stated, is to generalise the concept of the constitutional subject, which is tailored to the nation-state, and to respecify it, on the one hand, to transnational equivalents and, on the other, to civil society equivalents.' Teubner, *Verfassungsfragmente* (fn. 6), p. 99.

[130] Rainer Wahl, Verfassungsdenken jenseits des Staates, in: Ivo Appel/Georg Hermes (Eds.), Mensch – Staat – Umwelt, Berlin 2008, p. 135 ff.

[131] Gunther Teubner, Globale Zivilverfassungen. Alternativen zur staatszentrierten Verfassungstheorie, ZaöRV 63 (2003), p. 1 ff, 6: 'The thesis is called: emergence of a multiplicity of civil constitutions. The constitution of world society does not realise itself exclusively in the proxy institutions of international politics, but neither can it take place in a global constitution spanning all social spheres, *but it emerges incrementally in the constitutionalization of a multiplicity of autonomous world-societal subsystems* [emphasis added].'

[132] Gunther Teubner, Das Projekt der Verfassungssoziologie. Irritationen des nationalstaatlichen Konstitutionalismus, *Zeitschrift für Rechtssoziologie* 32 (2011), p. 189.

[133] For a multilevel cosmopolitan-global political system, see Jürgen Habermas, The Constitutionalization of International Law and the Legitimation Problems of a Constitution of the World Society, *Constellations* 14/4 (2008), p. 444 ff. For a later, more liberal reading of a world constitution, see Jürgen Habermas, *Der gespaltene Westen. Kleine politische Schriften X*, 2004, p. 137. On a possible complementarity between the universality of the legality code in the context of the fragmentation of world law, see Klaus Günther, Legal Pluralism or Uniform Concept of Law? Globalization as a Problem of Legal Theory, *No Foundations – Journal of Extreme Legal Positivism*, No. 5, April 2008, p. 5 ff, 15 ff.

[134] Inspired by Talcott Parsons, the method of generalisation and respecification differs from simple analogy and has become the most important methodological bridge in the transition from elements of the tradition of state constitutionalism to a constitutionalism focused on the specifics of global society. See Talcott Parsons/Charles Ackerman, *The Concept of 'Social System' as a Theoretical*

Device, in Gordon J. DiRenzo (Ed.), *Concepts, Theory and Explanation in the Behavioral Sciences*, New York 1966, p. 24 ff.

[135] Teubner, *Verfassungsfragmente* (fn. 6), p. 120 ff.

[136] Teubner, ibid, p. 161 ff: 'Constitutions emerge only when phenomena of double reflexivity emerge – reflexivity of the self-constituting social system and reflexivity of the law supporting the self-constitution.'

[137] Niklas Luhmann, Verfassung als evolutionäre Errungenschaft, *Rechtshistorisches Journal* 9 (1990), p. 176 ff; Niklas Luhmann, Political Constitutions in the Context of the Social System, *Der Staat* 1973, p. 1 ff. See also Chris Thornhill, State Building, Constitutional Rights and Social Construction of Norms. Outline for a Sociology of Constitutions, in Mikael R. Madsen/Gert Verschraegen (Eds.), *Making Human Rights Intelligible. Towards a Sociology of Human Rights*, Oxford/Portland 2013, p. 25 ff.

[138] 'Not only politics, but also other social systems found themselves through self-referential processes in which they constitute their autonomy in a paradoxical way. The specific method of constitutionalism to deal practically with the self-referential paradoxes arising here is to externalise them to the environment. Autonomy of social systems is never pure; it always contains a moment of heteronomy.' Teubner, *Verfassungsfragmente* (fn. 6), p. 108.

[139] 'Under this condition, which with reference to the social system is to be understood as functional differentiation, the systems dissolve the circular structure of their self-reference by externalization.' Luhmann, *Das Recht der Gesellschaft* (fn. 10), p. 480.

[140] Luhmann, ibid., p. 468 ff.

[141] 'Similarly, the legal system is exposed to political initiatives, which it must continually work through in procedures of legislation, administrative regulation, and adjudication (including the jurisprudence of constitutional courts).' Luhmann, ibid, p. 479.

[142] 'The world-societal constitutionalism that exists today thus aims at two things: to break the tight structural couplings of functional systems to nation-state politics and law, and to build constitutional structures insofar as it is necessary for a worldwide networking of function-specific communications.' Teubner, *Verfassungsfragmente* (fn. 6), p. 122.

[143] Teubner, ibid., p. 139 ff.

[144] Gunther Teubner/Andreas Fischer-Lescano, Fragmentierung des Weltrechts: Vernetzung globaler Regimes statt statischer Rechtseinheit, in: Mathias Albert/Rudolf Stichweh (Eds.), *Weltstaat und Weltstaatlichkeit: Beobachtungen globaler politischer Strukturbildung*, Wiesbaden 2007, p. 37 ff., 50.

[145] Teubner, *Verfassungsfragmente* (fn. 6), p. 225 ff; Christian Joerges, A New Type of Conflict of Laws as the Legal Paradigm of the Postnational Constellations, in: Christian Joerges/Josef Falke (Eds.), *Karl Polanyi. Globalization and the Potential of Law in Transnational Markets*, Oxford/Portland 2011, p. 465 ff; Paul S. Berman, Conflict of Laws, Globalization, and Cosmopolitan Pluralism, *Wayne Law Review* 51 (2005), p. 1105 ff. Early on Rudolf Wiethölter, Begriffs- oder Interessenjurisprudenz – falsche Fronten im IPR und Wirtschaftsverfassungsrecht, in: Peer Zumbansen/Marc Amstutz (Eds.), *Recht in Recht-Fertigungen. Ausgewählte Schriften von Rudolf Wiethölter*, Berlin 2014, p. 373 ff.

[146] Gunther Teubner, Fragmented Foundations, in: Petra Dobner/Martin Loughlin (Eds.), *The Twilight of Constitutionalism?*, Oxford 2010, p. 327 ff., 330: 'The primary driver of this development is the functional differentiation of society. Each of several autonomous functional subsystems of society escapes its territorial confines and constitutes itself globally. This process is not confined to economic markets alone; it also encompasses science, culture, technology, health, the military, transport, and sport, as well as, albeit in a somewhat retarded manner, politics, law and welfare. Today, each of these systems operates autonomously at the global level.' See also Teubner, *Verfassungsfragmente* (fn. 6), p. 73 'As is well known, globalization means, above all, that the dynamics of functional differentiation, historically first realised in the nation-states of Europe and North America, are now taking hold of the entire globe' ('*Bekanntlich bedeutet Globalisierung vor allem, dass die Dynamik der funktionalen Differenzierung, die historisch zuerst in den Nationalstaaten Europas und Nordamerikas realisiert wurde, nun den gesamten Erdball ergreift*').

[147] Thomas Schwinn's view of Luhmann's 'world society' adresses an important point. In Luhmann's view, the existence of world society is indeed always defined in terms of worldwide 'communicative accessibility'. 'Communication and order ... are not on the same level. To subsume the different qualities of the social all under the concept of society is not very helpful and goes along with a loss of analytical precision': Schwinn, *Weltgesellschaft, multiple Moderne und die Herausforderungen für die soziologische Theorie* (fn. 74), p. 210.

[148] Georg Wilhelm F. Hegel, *Phänomenologie des Geistes, Theorie-Werkausgabe*, vol. 3, Frankfurt am Main 1970, p. 78.
[149] Quentin Meillassoux, *After Finitude. An Essay on the Necessity of Contingency*, London 2008, p. 34; Levi R. Bryant, Art. 'Correlationism', in: Paul Ennis/Peter Gratton (Eds.), *The Meillassoux Dictionary*, Edinburgh 2015, p. 46 ff.
[150] Meillassoux, *After Finitude* (fn. 149), p. 5.
[151] Armen Avanessian (Ed.), Realismus Jetzt, Berlin 2013, p. 28.
[152] Jürgen Habermas proposes extending the limited concept of linguistic competence in terms of action theory and thus tries to show that the correct understanding of linguistic competence contributes decisively to overcoming the problem of justifying norms. Cf. Jürgen Habermas, Was heißt Universalpragmatik, in: Jürgen Habermas, *Vorstudien und Ergänzungen zur Theorie des kommunikativen Handelns*, Frankfurt am Main 1995, pp. 353 ff, 387; Jürgen Habermas, *Theorie des kommunikativen Handelns*, vol. 2, Frankfurt am Main 1988, p. 182; Hans J. Schneider, Gibt es eine 'Transzendental'- bzw. 'Universalpragmatik'?, *Zeitschrift für philosophische Forschung* 36/2 (1982), p. 208 ff.
[153] Luhmann, Soziale Systeme (fn. 29), p. 13; Dirk Baecker, Es gibt keine sozialen Systeme. 8 Thesen, in: Dirk Baecker, *Wozu Theorie?, Aufsätze*, Berlin 2016, p. 194 ff.
[154] World society, 'as far as system differentiation is concerned, is characterised by a primacy of functional differentiation': Luhmann, *Das Recht der Gesellschaft* (fn. 10), p. 572.
[155] Teubner, *Verfassungsfragmente* (fn. 6), p. 20: 'Rather, the social constitutionalism that has long existed in reality in the nation-states is today faced with the question of whether and how it must transform itself under conditions of globality. The continuity of the problem is related to the functional differentiation of society, which has been extended to the whole world in transnationalization.'
[156] Armen Avanessian/Suhail Malik (Eds.), *Genealogies of Speculation. Materialism and Subjectivity since Structuralism*, London/New York 2016; Martin Küpper, Quentin Meillassoux's Denklandschaft des spekulativen Materialismus, *Vorschein* 34 (2017), p. 205 ff.
[157] There is also a form of ambivalence inherent in this approach, according to which modern law emerged as a response to the transformation of the time regime and, at the same time, the emergence of a global society with the demise of the form of modern law was due to the transformation of the time regime. In other words, on the one hand, Niklas Luhmann presents law as a form of time-binding that appears as a response to the orientation of social action after the transformation of the time regime of modernity. On the other hand, this transformation is also seen as a fundamental factor in the emergence of world society and, in this context, is even considered the 'unbeatable evidence of world society.' See Luhmann, *Die Gesellschaft der Gesellschaft* (fn. 36), p. 149.

CHAPTER 2
LAW AS A FORM OF TIME BINDING

[158] Niklas Luhmann, *Soziologie des Risikos*, Berlin 2003, p. 41: 'Ideas about time have no observation-independent object. As observations and descriptions of temporal relations, they are temporal observations and descriptions.'
[159] Jan Assmann, 'Zeit', in: Karlfried Gründer/Joachim Ritter (Eds.), *Historisches Wörterbuch der Philosophie*, Basel 2004, p. 1186.
[160] Aleida Assmann, *Ist die Zeit aus den Fugen? Aufstieg und Fall des Zeitregimes der Moderne*, Munich 2013, p. 21.
[161] Bruno Latour, *Wir sind nie modern gewesen. Versuch einer symmetrischen Anthropologie*, Frankfurt am Main 2008, p. 18. Latour points out that the adjective 'modern' is primarily meant to indicate a rupture and the emergence of a new time regime of modernity.
[162] Although it always goes back to Koselleck, today there is a kind of inflation of the concept of acceleration that accentuates precisely this temporal dimension of society. David Harvey, *The Condition of Postmodernity. An Enquiry into the Origins of Cultural Change*, Malden (Mass.) 2004; Hartmut Rosa, *Acceleration. Die Veränderung der Zeitstruktur der Moderne*, Frankfurt am Main 2005, p. 49 f., summarises the position affirming: 'that the social acceleration constitutively inherent in modernity exceeds a critical point in "late modernity," beyond which the claim to social synchronization and social integration can no longer be sustained'; Thomas Hylland Eriksen, *Tyranny of the Moment. Fast and Slow. Time in the Information Age*, London 2001; Peter

Borscheid, *The Speed Virus. A Cultural History of Acceleration*, Frankfurt am Main 2004; Oliver D. Bidlo, *Rastlose Zeiten. Die Beschleunigung des Alltags*, Essen 2009.

[163] 'Since the second half of the 18th century, one can imagine that semantic traditions, and be they of the most sacred kind, vary with social development.' Niklas Luhmann, *Gesellschaftliche Struktur und semantische Tradition*, in: Niklas Luhmann, *Social Structure and Semantics. Studien zur Wissenssoziologie der modernen Gesellschaft*, vol. 1, Frankfurt am Main 1980, p. 9 ff. (9).

[164] Luhmann, *Die Gesellschaft der Gesellschaft* (fn. 36), p. 149.

[165] Luhmann, ibid, p. 1014: 'These changes in the semantics of time will become irreversible for the foreseeable future because the mass media have taken over the description of the world and society as a functional system of their own kind.'

[166] Vanessa Ogle, *The Global Transformation of Time: 1870–1950*, Cambridge (Mass.) 2015.

[167] Wolfgang Kaschuba, *Die Überwindung der Distanz. Zeit und Raum in der europäischen Moderne*, Frankfurt am Main 2004, p. 33 ff.

[168] 'But in contrast to older Aristotelian, Stoic, and canon law conceptions of natural law as moral law or the objective law of reason, they elaborate a minimalist conception of natural law centered on sociability, self-interest, and the subjective right of self-preservation': Victoria Kahn, *Wayward Contracts. The Crisis of Political Obligation in England. 1640–1674*, Princeton 2004, p. 33.

[169] Joachim Ritter, *Hegel und die Französische Revolution*, Cologne/Opladen 1957.

[170] The point Victoria Kahn focuses on is the collapse of social trust as a result of the wars and turmoil that swept through Europe in the seventeenth century. New rhetorical figures articulated themselves in a process of discovering a new social knowledge that was largely decoupled from 'grand narratives' such as religion or tradition. What Kahn calls 'linguistic contracts' is a mixture of everyday contractual logic, the power of metaphorical language and world views transformed to enable new forms of rule-making beyond the Christian Aristotelian tradition. The mode of founding commitment shifts from a more or less stable basis of society formation to an increasingly uncertain and artificial ordering of a provisional society. See Kahn, *Wayward Contracts* (fn. 168), p. 35 ff.

[171] Horst Bredekamp, *Thomas Hobbes' visuelle Strategien. Der Leviathan: Urbild des modernen Staates*, Berlin 1999.

[172] Philip Manow, Die Menschwerdung des Menschen unter dem Leviathan, in: Philip Manow. *Politische Ursprungsphantasien. Der Leviathan und sein Erbe*, Konstanz 2011, p. 137 ff.

[173] Still within the framework of Hobbes scholarship, Collins and Tuck show that the aim was not to demonstrate the autonomisation of secular power in images, but rather to build a state through treaty-making in such a way that the powers of the church were placed in a heteronomous relationship with the secular spheres. In this vein, Richard Tuck, The Civil Religion of Thomas Hobbes, in Nicholas Phillipson/Quentin Spinner (Eds.), *Political Discourse in Early Modern Britain*, Cambridge 1993, p. 120 ff; Jeffrey Collins, *The Allegiance of Thomas Hobbes*, Oxford 2005.

[174] For Terry Eagleton, the discourse of aesthetics first emerged in the eighteenth century as he grappled with the tension of capturing the world of the subject's perception without compromising absolute sovereignty. This gave rise to an aesthetic subject. Victoria Kahn also shows a neglected side of contract theory by pointing out the hierarchical features of the emergence of the modern subject: 'mimesis and aesthetics – poetics and the passions – these are the neglected terms in the dry judicial discourse of the later history of liberalism': Kahn, *Wayward Contracts* (fn. 168), p. 284. For the English context, see John Brewer, *The Pleasures of the Imagination. English Culture in the Eighteenth Century*, London 2013. For the German context, Terry Eagleton, *The Ideology of the Aesthetic*, Oxford 1990, p. 19 ff.

[175] Kahn, *Wayward Contracts* (fn. 168), p. 283.

[176] James Gordley, *The Philosophical Origins of Modern Contract Doctrine*, Oxford 1991.

[177] Kahn, *Wayward Contracts* (fn. 168), p. 6.

[178] Jonathan Sheehan/Dror Wahrman, *Invisible Hands. Self-Organization and the Eighteenth Century*, Chicago 2015, p. xvii.

[179] Reinhart Koselleck, Vergangene Zukunft. Zur Semantik geschichtlicher Zeiten, Frankfurt am Main 1989, p. 359 ff. As early as 1965 Joachim Ritter touched on the problem with the formula 'divisiveness of origin and future'. According to Ritter, the cause of the divisiveness, following Hegel, is the newness that modern bourgeois society brings into history and puts into the world. Here the concept of legitimacy is gradually replaced or recast by the concept of novelty. However, there would only be a 'divisiveness of origin and future' when society designs itself with a view to a future and thus there is a break with previous history 'in the setting of orders which, according to their principle, without presuppositions, like a radical new beginning, which is to be preceded by nothing,

exclude from themselves everything that is given, historical and handed down'. Ritter, *Hegel und die Französische Revolution* (fn. 169), p. 45 ff. (90).

[180] Arno Seifert, 'Verzeitlichung'. Zur Kritik einer neueren Frühneuzeitkategorie, *Zeitschrift für historische Forschung* 10 (1983), p. 447 f.; Theo Jung, Das Neue der Neuzeit ist ihre Zeit. Reinhart Koselleck's Theory of Verzeitlichung and its Critics, Moderne. *Kulturwissenschaftliches Jahrbuch* 6 (2010/2011), p. 172 ff.

[181] Reinhart Koselleck, Wie neu ist die Neuzeit?, in: Reinhart Koselleck, *Zeitgeschichten. Studien zur Historik*, Frankfurt am Main 2000, p. 225 ff.

[182] John G. A. Pocock, *The Machiavellian Moment. Florentine Political Thought and the Atlantic Republican Tradition* Princeton 1975, p. 423 ff.

[183] 'A profound historicity penetrates into the heart of things, isolates them and defines them in their own coherence, imposes on them forms of order implied by the continuity of time.' Michel Foucault, *Ordnung der Dinge. Eine Archäologie der Humanwissenschaften*, Frankfurt am Main 1974, p. 26. For the German-speaking world Wolf Lepenies, *Das Ende der Naturgeschichte. Wandel kultureller Selbstverständlichkeiten in den Wissenschaften des 18. und 19. Jahrhunderts*, Munich 1976, p. 18.

[184] Foucault, *Ordnung der Dinge* (fn. 183), p. 81.

[185] Hans-Ulrich Gumbrecht, Modern, Modernität, Moderne, in: Reinhart Koselleck/Werner Conze/Otto Brunner (Eds.), *Geschichtliche Grundbegriffe. Historisches Wörterbuch zur politisch-sozialen Sprache*, vol. 4, Stuttgart 1978, p. 93 ff.

[186] Cf. Luhmann's reproach to Habermas: '… that Habermas concentrates at this point on the social dimension *and immobilises time*.' [Author's emphasis] in Niklas Luhmann, 'Quod omnes tangit …' Notes on Jürgen Habermas's Theory of Law, *Rechtshistorisches Journal* 12 (1993), p. 36 ff, 42.

[187] Koselleck, *Wie neu ist die Neuzeit* (fn. 181), p. 10.

[188] Martin Sabrow, *Die Zeit der Zeitgeschichte*, Göttingen 2012, p. 15 ff.

[189] Cf. Jan Assmann, Zeit und Geschichte in frühen Kulturen, in: Friedrich Stadler/Michael Stöltzner (Eds.), *Time and History. Proceedings of the 28th International Ludwig Wittgenstein Symposium Kirchberg am Wechsel, Austria* 2005, p. 489 ff.

[190] What Latour meant by 'modern' is precisely this break in the time dimension, see Latour, *Wir sind nie modern gewesen* (fn. 161), p. 18. On this also Luhmann, Weltzeit und Systemgeschichte, in: Luhmann, *Soziologische Aufklärung* 2 (fn. 18), p. 128 ff, 134 ff.

[191] A. Assmann, *Ist die Zeit aus den Fugen?* (fn. 160), p. 25.

[192] Luhmann, *Die Gesellschaft der Gesellschaft* (fn. 36), p. 997 ff.

[193] Gerhart Husserl, *Recht und Zeit*, Frankfurt am Main 1955.

[194] In sociology, it is not uncommon to find authors devoted to the constellation of time and its form of influence in modern society, as is the case with Hartmut Rosa and Armin Nassehi. In jurisprudence, however, this is rather rare. Even Luhmann, at the beginning of his career, saw the primacy of economics as the rationale for the shift to future orientation and did not equate it with functional differentiation as such. 'Economy [is] more dependent on an articulable future as a result of its need for calculation.' Niklas Luhmann, *Selbst-Thematisierungen des Gesellschaftssystems. Über die Kategorie der Reflexion aus Sicht der Systemtheorie*, Zeitschrift für Soziologie 2/1 (1973), p. 21 ff, 37.

[195] Luhmann, *Gesellschaftliche Struktur und semantische Tradition* (fn. 163), p. 17 ff.

[196] Peter Fuchs, Die Unbeeindruckbarkeit der Gesellschaft – Ein Essay zur Kritikabilität sozialer Systeme, in: Andreas Fischer-Lescano/Marc Amstutz (Eds.), *Critical Systems Theory: On the Evolution of a Normative Theory*, Bielefeld 2013, p. 100 ff.

[197] Luhmann, *Die Gesellschaft der Gesellschaft* (fn. 36), p. 116 ff.; Luhmann, *Das Recht der Gesellschaft* (fn. 10), pp. 49, 58 and 107.

[198] Luhmann, ibid, p. 110.

[199] Monetisation is the second-coding of having/not having that puts the institution of property into liquid form, see Luhmann, *Soziologie des Risikos* (fn. 158), p. 73.

[200] Luhmann, *Die Wirtschaft der Gesellschaft* (fn. 48), p. 22 '… all these systems therefore develop ways of observing themselves in time horizons, that is, of distinguishing their current world-contemporaneous operation as "present" from past and future'. There is also the role of trust as a reference point for the normative support of behavioural expectations. The point is not to focus on trust in modern societies as a personal trust between individuals, but rather that a new dimension of trust emerges through the conduct of exchange relations using the medium of money, thus focusing on trust in the functioning of the use of money as a system. See Niklas Luhmann, *Trust. Ein Mechanismus der Reduktion sozialer Komplexität*, Stuttgart 1968, p. 64.

[201] Cf. Luhmann, 'Quod omnes tangit ...' (fn. 186), p. 42.

[202] Ronald Dworkin, *Freedom's Law: The Moral Reading of the American Constitution*, Cambridge 1997; see *Law's Empire* (fn. 14), pp. 256 and 279. For Niklas Luhmann's criticism of the attempt to address modern problems through the medium of morality, see Luhmann, *Die Gesellschaft der Gesellschaft* (fn. 36), p. 359: 'There is no super-medium ... for modern society. But the attempt to cure all moral weaknesses of society with ethics (i.e., with a reflection on morality) borders on the ridiculous.'

[203] In the first edition of 'Reine Rechtslehre', Hans Kelsen vividly shows how tracing norms back to norms becomes his central concept for explaining legal normality. The imprisonment of a person goes back to a judgment ('an individual norm'), the judgment to the penal code, this in turn to a 'state constitution', etc, see Kelsen, *Reine Rechtslehre* (fn. 103), p. 65.

[204] For a reading in which subjective rights play an important and central role in the production of social capital, see Ladeur, *Negative Freiheitsrechte und gesellschaftliche Selbstorganisation* (fn. 3).

[205] For example, in the Anglo-American debate of legal theory, the temporal structure of modern society is obscured by some distinctions. One of these is the distinction between 'internal point of view' and 'external point of view' that characterises the debate on Anglo-American legal theory. Cf. Scott J. Shapiro, What Is the Internal Point of View?, 75 *Fordham Law Review* (2006). P. 1157 et seq.

[206] 'It [the time reference of law] lies in the function of norms, namely, in the fact that one tries to adjust oneself, at least on the level of expectation, to a still unknown, genuine future. Therefore, along with norms, the extent to which society itself generates an uncertain future is also lost.' Luhmann, *Das Recht der Gesellschaft* (fn. 10), p. 130.

[207] The concept of time binding does not intend to neglect the social dimension. On the contrary, forms of time commitment take factual and social meaning and influence social distribution and changing forms. Every time binding has social costs. Even the basis of law's validity is intimately bound up with time. 'The only indispensable basis of validity therefore lies in *time*': Luhmann, ibid, p. 110.

[208] Luhmann, ibid, p. 39.

[209] Niklas Luhmann, *Positivität des Rechts als Voraussetzung einer modernen Gesellschaft*, in: Niklas Luhmann, *Ausdifferenzierung des Rechts*, Frankfurt am Main 1999, pp. 113 ff., 129 ff.: 'The regulative access of law is now no longer bound to the proof that it has always been this way, and thus many new behaviors or even new aspects of old behaviors become ripe for law: drunk driving or premium for destroying apples, extension of compulsory education or establishment of staff councils in the public service.'

[210] Gunther Teubner, *Der Wahnsinn der Rechtsenzyklopädien*, ARSP 91 (2005), pp. 587 et seq. (592).

[211] Luhmann, *Rechtssoziologie* (fn. 20), p. 217 ff.

[212] Luhmann, *Das Recht der Gesellschaft* (fn. 10), pp. 71 ff. and 163 ff. 'Only the two achievements, function and coding taken together, have the effect that the operations specific to law can be clearly distinguished from other communications and thus, with only marginal marginal blurring, reproduce themselves out of themselves.' Luhmann, ibid, p. 40 f.

[213] This, however, in contrast to risk: 'Risk cannot be contravened'. Luhmann, ibid, p. 67. Luhmann distinguishes between three different forms of disposition of the future: legal norms (law), appropriation of scarce goods (economy), and risk (not assigned to any system). Time commitment in the form of risk is the most difficult structural form of coordination to find when dealing with the disposition of the future. Luhmann, *Soziologie des Risikos* (fn. 158), p. 80: 'The fixation of legal norms or the appropriation of scarce goods ensures something certain for the future and exposes itself to dangers at best with their realizations. With the form of risk, on the other hand, one exploits precisely the indeterminacy of the future, indeed one's own ignorance, as it were, in order to bring the present to forms that can be confirmed or also refuted by future presences.'

[214] Luhmann, *Das Recht der Gesellschaft* (fn. 10), p. 129.

[215] Klaus Günther, Vom Zeitkern des Rechts, *Rechtshistorisches Journal* 14 (1995), p. 13 ff, 23.

[216] Luhmann, *Rechtssoziologie* (fn. 20), p. 343.

[217] Luhmann, *Das Recht der Gesellschaft* (fn. 10), p. 199: 'The commitment to the form of the conditional program is related to the function of law, that is, to the stabilization of counterfactual expectations.'

[218] Luhmann, ibid, p. 191: 'The risk of the law/unlaw coding is accepted, but the level of programming is used to reintegrate law into society. The level of programming then acts as a level of compensation for any discrepancies between law and society.'

[219] Luhmann, ibid, p. 197: 'In this respect, the legal system always operates as an afterthought, as a downstream system'.
[220] Luhmann, ibid, p. 283: 'Only mediated by the legislator does the protectability of legal goods enter the law'.
[221] Victoria Kahn, *The Future of Illusion. Political Theology and Early Modern Texts*. Chicago 2014, p. 3 ff. From a cultural studies perspective, Koschorke et al. point out that 'fact and fiction in the space of the political can hardly be divorced in the usual way'. Albrecht Koschorke et al., *The Fictive State. Konstruktionen des politischen Körpers in der Geschichte Europas*, Frankfurt am Main 2007, p. 56.

CHAPTER 3
THE DISINTEGRATION OF THE OLD ORDER

[222] Luhmann, *Das Recht der Gesellschaft* (fn. 10), p. 586.
[223] Luhmann, *Die Weltgesellschaft* (fn. 18); see, *World Society as a Social System* (fn. 68). For a discussion of legal theory, see Teubner/Fischer-Lescano, *Fragmentation of World Law* (fn. 144).
[224] For Spaemann, Hegel appears in Luhmann's theory not only as a historical object, but 'as a competitor against whose performance it is measured'. See Robert Spaemann, *Niklas Luhmann als Herausforderung der Philosophie*, in Niklas Luhmann, *Paradigm lost. Über die ethische Reflexion der Moral – Rede anlässlich der Ver-leihung des Hegel-Preises*, Frankfurt 1990, pp. 51 ff, 62.
[225] Koschorke, *Die Grenzen des Systems und die Rhetorik der Systemtheorie* (fn. 38), p. 49 ff.
[226] Jessup, *Transnational Law* (fn. 50).
[227] Jessup, ibid, p. 1.
[228] See Pieter H. F. Bekker/Rudolf Dolzer/Michael Waibel (Eds.), *Making Transnational Law Work in the Global Economy. Essays in Honor of Detlev Vagts*, Cambridge 2010; Detlef von Daniels, *The Concept of Law from a Transnational Perspective*, Ashgate 2010; Callies/Zumbansen, *Rough Consensus and Running Code* (fn. 79).
[229] Callies/Zumbansen, ibid, p. 2.
[230] Jessup's essay on transnational law has made a career. Later authors refer to Jessup, but make some minor variations. For example, Slaughter: 'Transnational Law has many definitions. I mean to include here simply national law that is designed to reach actors beyond national borders: the assertion of extraterritorial jurisdiction. Extraterritorial jurisdiction provisions are often the first effort a national government is inclined to make to regulate activity outside its borders with substantial effects within its borders': Anne-Marie Slaughter, *A Liberal Theory of International Law*, in: American Society of International Law (Ed.), Proceedings of the Annual Meeting 94 (2000), p. 240 ff., 245. Hathaway accentuates another aspect: 'transnational law includes all law that cross-border effect, whereas international law refers only to treaties or other law that governs interactions between states': Oona A. Hathaway, Between Power and Principle. An Integrated Theory of International Law, *University Chicago Law Review* 72 (2005), p. 469 ff., 473. Harold Koh fokussiert auf die grenzüberschreitenden Effekte des Transnationalen, see Harold Hongju Koh, International Law as Part of Our Law, *American Journal of International Law* 98 (2004) p. 43 ff., 53. Anne-Marie Slaughter also makes direct reference to Jessup's concept of the transnational. 'I define transnational law to include all municipal law and a subset of intergovernmental agreements that directly regulate transnational activity between individuals and between individuals and state governments': Anne-Marie Slaughter (Burley), International Law and International Relations Theory. A Dual Agenda, *American Journal of International Law* 87 (1993), p. 205 ff.
[231] Pierrick Le Goff, Global Law: A Legal Phenomenon Emerging from the Process of Globalization, *Indiana Journal of Global Legal Studies* 14 (January 2007), p. 119 ff.
[232] Teubner, *Globale Bukowina* (fn. 85); Clive Schmitthoff, International Business Law. A New Law Merchant, *Current Law and Social Problems* 2 (1961), p. 129 ff.
[233] Gralf-Peter Calliess, *Grenzüberschreitende Verbraucherverträge. Rechtssicherheit und Gerechtigkeit auf dem elektronischen Weltmarktplatz*, Tübingen 2006, p. 182 et seq.
[234] Klaus J. Hopt/Gunther Teubner (Eds.), Corporate Governance and Director's Liabilities. *Legal, Economic and Sociological Analyses on Corporate Social Responsibility*, Berlin 1985.
[235] Anna Beckers, *Enforcing Corporate Social Responsibility Codes. On Global Self-Regulation and National Private Law*, London 2015.

[236] Hanna L. Buxbaum, *Transnational Regulatory Litigation*, Virginia Journal of International Law 46 (2006), p. 251 ff.

[237] For Seinecke, legal pluralism was something inherent in law before the emergence of the modern state. For a long time, the concept was avoided by the necessity of legal unity. Now, the concept of pluralism is returning primarily due to the increase in the normative intensity of the transnational level. Seinecke writes, 'Law has always been plural in its constitution'. It is just that the legal world did not need the word legal pluralism earlier 'for its self-description'. For, '... before modernity, legal pluralism was all too self-evident'. See Ralf Seinecke, Das Recht des Rechtspluralismus, Tübingen 2015, pp. 1, 54, 70 ff. See also, from the perspective of legal history, Michael Stolleis, *Vormodernes und postmodernes Recht*, Merkur 5 (2008), p. 425 ff.

[238] Keebet von Benda-Beckmann/Bertram Turner, Legal Pluralism, Social Theory, and the State, *The Journal of Legal Pluralism and Unofficial Law* 50/3 (2018), p. 255 ff.; Paul S. Berman, A Pluralist Approach to International Law, Yale J. Int'l L. 32 (2007); Teubner, Verfassungsfragmente (fn. 6); Seinecke, *Das Recht des Rechtspluralismus* (fn. 237), p. 296 ff.

[239] Stephan Leibfried/Michael Zürn (Eds.), *Transformation of the State?*, Cambridge 2005; see also Renate Mayntz, Die Handlungsfähigkeit des Nationalstaats in Zeiten der Globalisierung, in: Ludger Heidbrink/Alfred Hirsch (Eds.), *Staat ohne Verantwortung? Zum Wandel der Aufgaben von Staat und Politik*, Frankfurt/M. 2007, and Philipp Genschel/Bernhard Zangl, Die Zerfaserung von Staatlichkeit und die Zentralität des Staates, TranState Working Papers No. 62, Bremen 2007.

[240] Anonymus (C. Schmitt), Völkerrecht, Nr. 3, in: Heinrich Freymark (Ed.), *Das juristische Repetitorium. Öffentliches Recht*, Serie B, Nr. 17, Salzgitter 1949, p. 49 f.

[241] Carl Schmitt describes the process of the emergence of the modern state as an inner ambivalent moment of renouncing features of sovereignty. This emerges from the central thesis of his book on the separation of the inner (private) and outer (public) worlds in Hobbes' *Leviathan* (1938), which discusses the question of whether the state should punish wonder and miracle. At this point, Schmitt sees Hobbes making the fundamental distinction between inner belief and outer confession, where he holds that 'the absolute state can demand anything, but only outwardly'. Carl Schmitt, *Der Leviathan in der Staatslehre des Thomas Hobbes. Sinn und Fehlschlag eines politischen Symbols*, Stuttgart 1982, p. 92. This is also the central difference between Schmitt and the 'transformation of the state' approach. Whereas for Schmitt the formation of the modern state involves a constitutive moment of abstention from sovereignty, which offers a first constitutive moment of openness to the private, in the 'Transformation of the State' approach there is an idealised form of absolute sovereignty, which may never have existed in this way and which is also deconstructed by the discovery of the transnational since the 1970s of the last century.

[242] 'The former has as its content the objective, historical ... the natural being of the state, the latter, on the other hand, the legal norms that are to be expressed in that real being.' Georg Jellinek, Allgemeine Staatslehre, Berlin 1914, p. 20.

[243] Hans Kelsen, *Das Problem der Souveränität und die Theorie des Völkerrechts. Beitrag zu einer Reinen Rechtslehre* (2nd ed. 1928), Aalen 1960, p. 105, see also p. 288. 'Sovereignty is a property of law *because it is a* property of the state': ibid, p. 102 ff.

[244] Hermann Heller, Die Krise der Staatslehre (1926), in: Hermann Heller, *Gesammelte Schriften* 2, Tübingen 1971, p. 3 ff. (18).

[245] In Kelsen's case, this is reflected in several building blocks or pillars of his theory, including above all the central dualism of ought and being. The incommunicability between the two levels, i.e., a normative level of the legal order and a cognitive level of the social order that ensures the functioning of the theory, is simply assigned as something given in people's consciousness. The arbitrariness of this separation – including its justification – clearly shows the attitude of indifference of a part of modern legal reflection to the implicit presuppositions of modern law itself, which come to light even more vehemently with the development of today's digital society. Kelsen, *Reine Rechtslehre* (fn. 103), p. 5: 'The difference between being and ought cannot be further explained. It is immediately given to our consciousness.'

[246] Stephan Leibfried/Michael Zürn, Reconfiguring the National Constellation, in: Stephan Leibfried/Michael Zürn (Eds.), *Transformation of the State* (fn. 239), pp. 1 ff., 17.

[247] Raphael Gross, *Carl Schmitt und die Juden: Eine deutsche Rechtslehre*, Frankfurt am Main 2005, p. 7.

[248] Hannah Arendt, *Elemente und Ursprünge totaler Herrschaft*, Berlin 1986, p. 544.

[249] Jan-Werner Müller, *A Dangerous Mind: Carl Schmitt in Post-war European Thought*, New Haven/London 2003, p. 221 ff.

[250] Fredric Jameson, Notes on the Nomos, *South Atlantic Quarterly* 2/104 (Spring 2005), p. 199; Anthony Carty, Carl Schmitt's Critic of Liberal International Order between 1933 and 1945, *Leiden Journal of International Law* 14 (2001), p. 24.

[251] Jameson, Notes on the Nomos (fn. 250); Ino Augsberg, *Schmitt-Lektüren: Vier Versuche über Carl Schmitt*, Berlin 2020, p. 7.

[252] Carl Schmitt, *Völkerrechtliche Großraumordnung: mit Interventionsverbot für raumfremde Mächte. Ein Beitrag zum Reichsbegriff im Völkerrecht* (1941), Berlin 1991, p. 41.

[253] A prominent author who updates Carl Schmitt's thinking for the sake of radical democracy is Chantal Mouffe. See Chantal Mouffe, *The Democratic Paradox*, London/New York 2000, p. 90 ff; also Chantal Mouffe, Deliberative Democracy or Agonistic Pluralism?, *Social Research* 66/3 (1999), pp. 745 ff, 752 ff; Mouffe, On the Political. Wider die kosmopolitische Illusion, Frankfurt am Main 2007, pp. 11 and 22; Chantal Mouffe, Carl Schmitt and the Paradox of Liberal Democracy, in: Chantal Mouffe (Ed.), *The Challenge of Carl Schmitt*, London/New York 1999, pp. 38 ff., 39.

[254] Martti Koskenniemi, *From Apology to Utopia. The Structure of International Legal Argument*, Cambridge 2006, p. 226 ff.; Martti Koskenniemi., International Law as Political Theology: How to Read *Nomos der Erde*?, *Constellations* 11/4 (2006), p. 492 ff.; Martti Koskenniemi, Carl Schmitt and International Law, in: Jens Meierhenrich/Oliver Simons (Eds.), *The Oxford Handbook of Carl Schmitt*, Oxford Handbooks Online, April 2015, pp. 4 and 12–15.

[255] Antony Anghie, Identifying Regions in the History of International Law, in: Bardo Fassbender/Anne Peters (Eds.), *The Oxford Handbook of the History of International Law*, Oxford 2012, p. 1058 ff., 1074; John de Blanco/Ivonne del Valle, Reorienting Schmitt's Nomos. Political Theology and Colonial (and Other) Exceptions in the Creation of Modern and Global Worlds, *Politica Común* 5 (2014), pp. 1 ff., 4; Achille Mbembe, Critique de la raison nègre, Paris 2013, p. 87; Walter D. Mignolo, *The Darker Side of Western Modernity. Global Futures, Decolonial Options*, Durham/London 2011, p. 28; Antony Anghie, The Evolution of International Law: Colonial and Postcolonial Realities, *Third World Quarterly* 27/5 (2006), pp. 739 ff., 742 ff.

[256] Martti Koskenniemi, *From Apology to Utopia* (fn. 254), p. 89 and fn. 66.

[257] Schmitt distinguishes between effective occupation and the legal title of *occupatio*. In this sense, he connects the occupation and *dominium of* the overseas soil with a network of a few European countries, out of which a concrete order of the Volksgemeinschaft is formed. In this way, he succeeds in distinguishing the occupation by brute force from the seizure of possession with legal legitimacy. Only in this concrete sense can it be said that the entire spatial structure of the earth in European international law was based on the special territorial status of the colonial overseas countries. Carl Schmitt, *Der Nomos der Erde im Völkerrecht des Jus Publicum Europaeum*, Berlin 1997, p. 100 ff. 'The distinction between the civilised and uncivilised was to be made, then, not in the realm of sovereignty, but of society.' Antony Anghie, *Imperialism, Sovereignty and the Making of International Law*, Cambridge 2004, p. 59.

[258] Dean M. Mitchell, A Political Mythology of World Order. Carl Schmitt's Nomos, *Theory, Culture & Society* 23 (2006), p. 1 ff.

[259] 'Yet the Peace of Westphalia in its entirety contains a body of regulations that could serve as a model for later generations and which, in practice, with its pacification of the confessionally divided center of Europe, became in fact one of the fundamental laws not only of the Holy Roman Empire but also of the "Droit public de l'Europe" (Ius publicum Europaeum), as the international law unifying the Christian community of states was also fondly called in the 18th century.' Karl-Heinz Ziegler, The Significance of the Peace of Westphalia of 1648 for European International Law, *International Law Archive* 37 (1999), p. 129 ff. (150); Martti Koskenniemi/Anne Orford, 'We do not need to always look to Westphalia …': A Conversation with Martti Koskenniemi and Anne Orford, *Journal of the History of International Law* 7 (2015), p. 1 ff.

[260] 'The spatial order has essentially emerged not from internal European land acquisitions and from territorial changes, but from the European land acquisition of a non-European New World …': Schmitt, *Der Nomos der Erde* (fn. 257), p. 155.

[261] 'Both parts recognise each other as states. This makes it possible to distinguish the enemy from the criminal. The concept of the enemy becomes capable of legal formation. The enemy ceases to be something "that must be destroyed". Aliud est hostis, aliud rebellis. This also makes a peace treaty with the defeated possible. Thus, European international law has succeeded in elevating war by means of the concept of the state.' Schmitt, ibid, p. 114.

[262] Giorgio Agamben, *Homo Sacer: Sovereign Power and Bare Life*, Stanford (Cal.) 1998, p. 36; William Rasch, Human Rights as Geopolitics: Carl Schmitt and the Legal Form of American

Supremacy, *Cultural Critique* 54 (2003), pp. 120 ff, 124 ff; Carl Schmitt, *Raum und Großraum im Völkerrecht*, in: *Carl Schmitt, Staat, Großraum, Nomos. Arbeiten aus den Jahren 1916–1969*, Berlin 1995, pp. 234 ff., 241–242; Carl Schmitt, *Der Nomos der Erde* (fn. 257), p. 171 ff. See also Carl Schmitt, Cambio de estructura del derecho internacional, *Revista de Estudios Politicos* 5 (1943), pp. 3 ff, 7. 'In several respects, the shielding of Europe from a conflict-ridden periphery decided upon at the Congress of Vienna was an ingenious peacemaking idea.' Jürgen Osterhammel, *Die Verwandlung der Welt. Eine Geschichte des 19. Jahrhunderts*, Munich 2009, p. 679.

[263] Carl Schmitt, Nomos Nahme Name, in: Carl Schmitt, *Staat, Großraum, Nomos* (fn. 262), p. 584.

[264] Niklas Luhmann has described an ecology of paradoxical externalisation for such constellations leading to a final question of validity, which is played out in every system due to internal necessities. For the question of externalisation of reasons of validity of law beyond the state, see Teubner, *Exogene Selbstbindung* (fn. 113).

[265] Thomas Schestag, Namen nehmen. Zur Theorie des Namens bei Carl Schmitt, MLN 122/3 (April 2007), pp. 544 et seq., 561 et seq.

[266] Annelise Riles, Aspiration and Control: International Legal Rhetoric and the Essentialization of Culture, *Harvard Law Review* 106 (1993), p. 723 ff.

[267] Thomas J. Lawrence, *Principles of International Law*, Boston 1900, § 1, p. 1. It is clear from the enumeration of sources of international law in his book that even the most elementary principles of international law are rather indeterminate and uncertain, and that their enforcement must depend on the voluntary compliance of the 'civilised' nations of the world.

[268] 'Thus the European system of states, as a spatial order of territorially delimited power formations of the European soil, had found its firm structure. Not the precarious ties of the "self-binding" sovereign wills, but the affiliation to a spatial equilibrium system perceived as common and the hedging of the European war thereby made possible, constituted the actual hold of this international legal order. The basis was the self-contained area with specific state order.' Schmitt, *Der Nomos der Erde* (fn. 257), p. 137.

[269] '... for European international law the difference of colonial and overseas land status was self-evident and the whole spatial structure of the earth was based on this distinction': Schmitt, ibid, p. 195.

[270] 'Intellectual superiority was entirely on the European side, and so strong that the New World could simply be "taken," while in the non-Christian old world of Asia and Islamic Africa only the regime of capitulations and extraterritoriality of the Europeans developed.' Schmitt, ibid, p. 103.

[271] Riles, *Aspiration and Control* (fn. 266), p. 736.

[272] Riles, ibid, p. 723.

[273] Anghie, *Imperialism, Sovereignty and the Making of International Law* (fn. 257), p. 56 ff.

[274] Gradually, the obviousness of a single centre of power in Europe around the *ius publicum europaeum* lost credibility. A new tension, described by Osterhammel, gained ground. 'In the later 19th century, opposing tendencies confronted each other: on the one hand, a growing certainty that all international relations had to be seen as elements of a single global system; on the other, a persisting conceptual separation of the "periphery" from the sphere of "actual," inner-European politics.' Osterhammel, *Die Verwandlung der Welt* (fn. 262), p. 680.

[275] 'The use of international law to further imperial policies is, I have argued, a persistent feature of the discipline. The civilizing mission, the dynamic of difference, continues now in this globalised, terror-ridden world, as international law seeks to transform the internal characteristics of societies, a task which is endless, for each act of bridging generates resistances, reveals further differences that must in turn be addressed by new doctrines and institutions': Anghie, *The Evolution of International Law* (fn. 255), p. 751.

[276] Peter Gratton, *The State of Sovereignty. Lessons from the Political Fictions of Modernity*, Albany (NY) 2012, p. 162 ff. (162); Giorgio Agamben, *Die Macht des Denkens*, Frankfurt am Main 2013, p. 9 ff. For a critique of Agamben see Michèle Lowrie, Sovereignty before the Law: Agamben and the Roman Republic, *Law and Humanities* 1 (2007), p. 40 ff.

[277] The role of law as an orchestrator of social spheres of freedom in global society becomes clear from the thesis that the media – money, power, technology, etc – are not only institutionalised – functionally – in global society, but inevitably carry within them a destructive, expansive tendency. The role of a more social constitutionalism would exist precisely through the functioning of the legal code in limiting these expansions or expansion, which would orchestrate and guarantee the zones and spheres of freedom in global society. On this point, see Teubner, *Verfassungsfragmente* (fn. 6),

p. 15: 'Does a social constitutionalism have the potential, beyond limiting the expansion tendencies of the political system, to contain the expansion tendencies of numerous social subsystems, which are no less problematic today and which endanger individual and institutional integrity? Can constitutions effectively combat centrifugal dynamics of subsystems in global society and thereby contribute to societal integration – quite different from the classical understanding of integration through constitution?' The role of law as a conductor against the undesirable advance of expansive tones of one social logic over another is carried out in particular through the central role of fundamental rights. See Teubner, ibid, p. 215: 'Fundamental rights, unlike general subjective rights, define themselves neither from the fundamentality of the legal good concerned nor from their privileging in constitutional texts, but as social and legal counter-institutions to expansionist tendencies of social systems'.

[278] This is one of the central issues addressed in Chapter 1 above.

[279] Luhmann, *Das Recht der Gesellschaft* (fn. 10), p. 584.

[280] 'This fixation on humans as independent subjects is, we are told, the source of our own current mess': Frank Trentmann, *The Empire of Things. How We Became a World of Consumers, from the Fifteenth Century to the Twenty-first*, London 2016, p. 95 ff.; see also Bruno Latour, 'From Realpolitik to Dingpolitik' or How to Make Things Public, in: Bruno Latour/Peter Weibel (Eds.), *Making Things Public: Atmospheres of Democracy*, Cambridge/Karlsruhe 2005, p. 14 ff., und Frank Trentmann, Materiality in the Future of History: Things, Practices, and Politics, *Journal of British Studies* 48/2 (2009), p. 283 ff. This is also a blind spot of the Frankfurter critical tradition: it does not seem to contain any theoretical observation potential beyond the distinction between instrumental and communicative reason.

[281] Christopher A. Bayly, *The Birth of the Modern World, 1780–1914. Global Connections and Comparisons*, Oxford 2004.

[282] Koskenniemi/Orford, 'We do not need to always look to Westphalia …' (fn. 259), p. 15.

[283] One could also assume in this context that the 'thinking in networks' promoted by computer technology has given important impulses to the science of history, which led here to the foundation of the approach of global history. On this, see John R. McNeill/William H. McNeill, *The Human Web. A Birds-Eye View of World History*, New York 2003. On global history, see also Thomas Duve, *Von der Europäischen Rechtsgeschichte zu einer Rechtsgeschichte Europas in globalhistorischer Perspektive, Rechtsgeschichte – Legal History* (Rg) 20 (2012), p. 18 ff. Jürgen Osterhammel, Higher Madness. Universalhistorische Denkstile im 20. Jahrhundert, in: Jürgen Osterhammel, *Geschichtswissenschaft jenseits des Nationalstaats. Studien zu Beziehungsgeschichte und Zivilisationsvergleich*, Göttingen 2001, p. 170 ff; Roxann Prazniak, Is World History Possible? An Inquiry, in: Vinay Bahl et al. (Eds.), *History After the Three Worlds. Post-Eurocentric historiographies*, Boulder 2000, p. 221 ff.

[284] Heinz Duchhardt, *Westphalian System. Zur Problematik einer Denkfigur, Historische Zeitschrift* 269 (1999), p. 305 ff.

[285] 'With these treaty-like arrangements made in Paris and Aachen, the legal basis was laid for the decision-making authority in the major "European" questions subsequently claimed by the "European Concert," albeit under partly altered composition, and exercised at congresses and conferences, under the direct direction of the sovereign rulers of the participating states, through their ministers or even only at the ambassadorial level, until the outbreak of the First World War in 1914.' Christian Hillgruber, *Die Aufnahme neuer Staaten in die Völkerrechtsgemeinschaft. Das völkerrechtliche Institut der Anerkennung von Neustaaten in der Praxis des 19. und 20. Jahrhunderts*, Frankfurt am Main 1998, p. 17.

[286] Carl Schmitt, Staatliche Souveränität und freies Meer. Über den Gegensatz von Land und See im Völkerrecht der Neuzeit, in: Carl Schmitt, *Staat, Großraum, Nomos* (fn. 262), p. 401 ff; Schmitt, *Der Nomos der Erde* (fn. 257), p. 96 ff.

[287] 'My broad argument is that colonialism was central to the constitution of international law …': Anghie, *Sovereignty and the Making of International Law* (fn. 257), pp. 3, 34; Brett Levinson, The Coming Nomos; or, the Decline of Other Orders in Schmitt, *The South Atlantic Quarterly* 104/2 (2005), p. 205 ff.; Srinivas Aravamudan, Carl Schmitt's The Nomos of the Earth: Four Corollaries, *The South Atlantic Quarterly* 104/2 (2005), p. 231 f.; Mitchell, *A Political Mythology of World Order* (fn. 258), p. 8; Stephen Legg, *Interwar Spatial Chaos? Imperialism, Internationalism and the League of Nations*, in: Stephen Legg (Ed.), *Spatiality, Sovereignty, and Carl Schmitt. Geographies of the Nomos*, London/New York 2011, p. 106 ff., 109.

[288] Jörg Fisch, *Die europäische Expansion und das Völkerrecht. Die Auseinandersetzungen um den Status der überseeischen Gebiete vom 15. Jahrhundert bis zur Gegenwart*, Wiesbaden/Stuttgart 1984.

[289] Roberto Ago, on the other hand, argues for the parallel existence of three distinct, separate, international communities: the Western Catholic, the Byzantine Orthodox, and the Arab-Islamic. See Roberto Ago, The Pluralistic Beginnings of the International Community, in: P. Fischer/ H. F. Köck et al. (Eds.), *International Law and Philosophy of Law. Internationale Festschrift für Stephan Verosta zum 70. Geburtstag*, Berlin 1980, p. 54 ff.

[290] 'Not the precarious ties of the "self-binding" sovereign wills, but the affiliation to a spatial equilibrium system perceived as common and the hedging of the European war made possible by it, constituted the actual hold of this international legal order … It is an essential part of the spatial basis of the hedging of the war that the war remains within the framework of the European ground order and its system of equilibrium.' Schmitt, *Der Nomos der Erde* (fn. 257), pp. 137 and 139.

[291] Schmitt, ibid, pp. 112 ff, 155.

[292] For the historical side, see Albert F. Berner, Art. 'Völkerrecht', in Johann C. Bluntschli/Carl L. Brater (Eds.), *Deutsches Staats-Wörterbuch*, vol. 11, Stuttgart and Leipzig 1870, p. 76 ff. (79): 'For some time now, the five great powers have in fact formed a kind of tribunal of nations and supervise the observation of the great treaties of states and the customs of international law'. See also Miloš Vec, Legalization of International Dispute Settlement in the 19th and 20th Centuries? Observations and Questions on the Structures of International Law Conflict Resolution, in Serge Dauchy/Miloš Vec (Eds.), *Les conflits entre peuples. De la résolution libre à la résolution imposée*, Baden-Baden 2011, p. 3 ff.

[293] The controversy over methods during the Weimar period had a profound impact on constitutional doctrine in the postwar period. Gerhard Anschütz and Richard Thoma, who advocated constitutional positivism, were Schmitt's antipodes, as was Rudolf Smend, who for his part, however, rejected the prevailing formalist positivism. Concrete order thinking was Schmitt's conceptual position in the discussion. Michael Stolleis, *Geschichte des Öffentlichen Rechts in Deutschland*, vol. 3, Munich 1999, p. 153 ff; Manfred Friedrich, Der Methoden- und Richtungsstreit. Zur Grundlagendiskussion der Weimarer Staatsrechtslehre, AöR 102 (1977), p. 161 ff; Christoph Möllers, Der Methodenstreit als politischer Generationenkonflikt: Ein Angebot zur Deutung der Weimarer Staatsrechtslehre, *Der Staat* 43 (2004), p. 399 ff; Rudolf Smend, Die Vereinigung der Staatsrechtslehrer und der Richtungsstreit, in: Horst Ehmke et al. (Eds.), *Festschrift für U. Scheuner*, Berlin 1973, p. 575 ff.

[294] Ernst-Wolfgang Böckenförde, Art. 'Ordnungsdenken, konkretes', in: *Historisches Wörterbuch der Philosophie*, Ed. by Joachim Ritter and Karlfried Gründer, vol. 6, Basel/Stuttgart 1984, pp. 1312–1315; Joseph H. Kaiser, Konkretes Ordnungsdenken, in: Helmut Quaritsch (Ed.), *Complexio Oppositorum. Über Carl Schmitt*, Berlin 1988, p. 319 ff.

[295] 'The norm or rule does not create the order; rather, it has only on the ground and within the framework of a given order a certain regulating function with a relatively small measure in itself of independent validity, independent of the situation of the matter.' Carl Schmitt, *On the Three Kinds of Jurisprudential Thought*, Berlin 2006, p. 13. 'The worst cross of its vocabulary, however, is the word *law*': Schmitt, *Der Nomos der Erde* (fn. 257), p. 41.

[296] Schmitt, *Nomos Nahame Name* (footnote 263), p. 578 ff. He refers here to a statement by Alvaro d'Or. 'But "nomos," like "law," does not mean law, rule, or norm, but law, which is norm, as well as decision, as above all order; and terms like king, ruler, overseer, or governor, as well as judge and court, immediately transport us to concrete institutional orders that are no longer mere rules.' Schmitt, *Über die drei Arten des rechtswissenschaftlichen Denkens* (fn. 295), p. 13.

[297] Nomos can be interpreted as a sharpening of the distinction between constitutional law and constitution already made by Carl Schmitt in his Verfassungslehre (1928), in which an instance preceding the law is determinative for the practical legal forms. On this, see Carl Schmitt, *Verfassungslehre*, Berlin 1983, p. 21 ff.

[298] 'The nomos in the original sense, however, is precisely the full immediacy of a legal force not mediated by laws; it is a constituting historical event, an act of *legitimacy that* makes the legality of mere law meaningful in the first place.' Schmitt, *Der Nomos der Erde* (fn. 257), p. 42.

[299] Homogeneity also plays a central role in Carl Schmitt's construction of the concept of democracy along the lines of the construction of international law by the concept of nomos. On this, see Carl Schmitt, *Die geistesgeschichtliche Lage des heutigen Parlamentarismus*, Berlin 1926, p. 13 ff. 'Every real democracy is based on the fact that not only what is equal is treated equally, but, with

inevitable consequence, what is not equal is not treated equally. Democracy therefore necessarily involves, first, homogeneity, and secondly – if necessary – the elimination or annihilation of the heterogeneous.'

[300] 'The inter-state order has not reached this degree of organization even in the longest European peace, while the earth-encompassing inter-state international law has never been even close to a concrete order at all.' Carl Schmitt, Die Auflösung der europäischen Ordnung im 'International Law', in: Carl Schmitt. *Staat, Großraum, Nomos* (fn. 262), pp. 372 ff, 382.

[301] Bernd Rüthers, *Carl Schmitt im Dritten Reich. Wissenschaft als Zeitgeist-Verstärkung?*, Munich 1989; Gross, *Carl Schmitt und die Juden* (fn. 247).

[302] Matthias Schmoeckel, *Die Großraumtheorie: ein Beitrag zur Geschichte der Völkerrechtswissenschaft im Dritten Reich, insbesondere der Kriegszeit*, Berlin 1994.

[303] Koskenniemi, *Carl Schmitt and International Law* (fn. 254), p. 3 f.

[304] Carl Schmitt, Der Völkerbund und Europa, in: Carl Schmitt, *Positionen und Begriffe. Im Kampf mit Weimar – Genf – Versailles 1923–1939*, Berlin 1988, p. 88 ff.

[305] Abnormality because the Rhineland and regulated demilitarisation were not to be normalised by the subjection of a large part of German territory to a special international regulation or special organisation (League of Nations). The 'intervention treaties' of the League of Nations no longer use the old semantics of territorial annexation, but that of intervention. Thus Schmitt: 'The intervening state then decides on the essential existing questions of the "controlling" state, in particular on the concrete determination of what "public order and security" means.' Carl Schmitt, Völkerrechtliche Probleme im Rheingebiet, in: Carl Schmitt, *Positionen und Begriffe im Kampf mit Weimar – Genf – Versailles 1923–1939* (fn. 304), pp. 111 ff, 120.

[306] 'The United States is not present at Geneva; but where the Monroe Doctrine is recognised and other American states are present, they cannot in fact be absent either.' Schmitt, *Der Völkerbund und Europa* (fn. 304), p. 104.

[307] Carl Bilfinger, *Das wahre Gesicht des Kellogg-Paktes. Angelsächsischer Imperialismus im Gewande des Rechts*, Berlin 1942, p. 62 ff.; Carl Schmitt, *Das politische Problem der Friedenssicherung*, Vienna 1993, p. 43 ff.

[308] M. Schulz speaks in this context of 'cultural practices of peace management'. See Matthias Schulz, *Normen und Praxis: Das Europäische Konzert der Großmächte als Sicherheitsrat 1815–1860*, Munich 2009, p. 2; Paul W. Schroeder, *The Transformation of European Politics, 1763–1848*, Oxford 1994; Winfried Baumgart, *Europäisches Konzert und nationale Bewegung: Internationale Beziehungen 1830–1878*, Paderborn 1999.

[309] 'The prohibition of future European colonization in America postulated by the United States practically decided the fate of the former Spanish colonies in Central and South America, which they themselves had already recognised as independent, by leaving the European powers no choice but to recognise the new status quo under international law sooner or later as well.' Hillgruber, *Die Aufnahme neuer Staaten in die Völkerrechtsgemeinschaft* (fn. 285), p. 406 f.

[310] 'Ethiopia and Liberia were according to the positivist doctrine civilised States which belonged to the Family of Nations since the second half of the 19th century': Charles H. Alexandrowicz, *The European-African Confrontation*, Leiden 1973, p. 71; see also James Crawford, *The Creation of States in International Law*, Oxford 1979, p. 5 ff. On the increasingly central role of the United Nations in the postwar period in the recognition of states within the international community, see John Dugard, *Recognition and the United Nations*, Cambridge 1987.

[311] Schmitt, *Der Nomos der Erde* (fn. 257), p. 172: 'To the extent, however, that overseas colonial soil was indiscriminately equated with state territory in the sense of European soil, the structure of international law also changed and the previous, specifically European international law came to an end.'

[312] Schmitt, *Die Auflösung der europäischen Ordnung* (fn. 300), p. 377: 'What took its place was not a "system" of states, but a systemless juxtaposition of norms; moreover, a disorderly, spatially and ethnically incoherent juxtaposition of 50 heterogeneous, but supposedly equally entitled sovereign states, for which, in the end, not even the concept of "civilization" could be regarded as the substance of a certain homogeneity. The previous distinction of civilised, semi-civilised (barbarian) and savage peoples (sauvages), fundamental to colonial European international law, became as "legally irrelevant" as the fact of spatial continental interrelations.'

[313] Schmitt, ibid, p. 373.

[314] Schestag, *Namen nehmen* (fn. 265).

[315] 'Cities are nodes of relationships and interconnections. They organize their surrounding regions – whether through the market, a superior state apparatus, or through diplomatic hierarchies and submissive associations among multiple cities. No city is an island. Influences enter societies from the outside through cities; they are "gateways to the world".' Osterhammel, *Die Verwandlung der Welt* (fn. 262), p. 357.

[316] Karl Löwith, *Der okkasionelle Dezisionismus von C. Schmitt* (1935), in: Karl Löwith, *Sämtliche Schriften*, vol. 8: *Heidegger – Denker in dürftiger Zeit*, Stuttgart 1984, p. 60 ff. Karl Löwith has held his own in the secondary literature on Occasionalism. His long and profound remarks on Gogarten, Heidegger and Kierkegaard and their connection to the concept of the political are instructive. But his initial thesis – namely, that Schmitt's political romanticism is not least self-explanatory because his own decisionism is an occasional one – misses Schmitt's theory. This book attempts to distance itself both from readings that primarily seek to expose Schmitt's connection to National Socialism and from the traditional reading that reduces Carl Schmitt's writings to pure decisionism. Rather, by moving away from these two lines, an attempt is made to reconstruct the dimension of cultural theory in Carl Schmitt.

[317] Ino Augsberg, Carl Schmitt's Fear: Nomos – Norm – Network, *Leiden Journal of International Law* 23 (2010), p. 741 ff.

[318] For a historical account of the shielding of legal legitimacy, see Stolleis, *Die Legitimation von Recht und Gesetz* (fn. 107).

[319] The thinking and feeling of the Romantics differed from the convictions of Enlightenment rationalism. For them, the creator was at the centre of aesthetic and social activity. They shared not a particular style but a worldview – to remain true to oneself – and therefore did not align themselves with a fixed representative instance of the social, rather they were more concerned with an experimental openness. See Tim Blanning, *The Romantic Revolution*, Oxford 2011.

[320] Tim Blanning, *The Culture of Power and the Power of Culture. Old Regime Europe 1660–1789*, Oxford 2002, p. 123 f.; Brewer, *The Pleasures of the Imagination* (fn. 174), p. 2 ff.

[321] The emergence of an impersonal network of subjects that do not come from a centre themselves, and challenge traditional social (subject) boundaries presupposes the growth of literacy. On the rise of literacy, see Keith Thomas, The Meaning of Literacy in Early Modern England, in: Gerd Baumann (Ed.), *The Written Word: Literacy in Transition*, Oxford 1986, p. 102. For figures, see Blanning, *The Culture of Power and the Power of Culture* (fn. 320), p. 112 ff.

[322] 'But their chief attraction was that they became centers of conversation and "intelligence", commercial premises and places of private exchange where deals were cut and money, goods and information traded. As the number of coffee houses grew, they became more specialised': Brewer, *The Pleasures of the Imagination* (fn. 174), p. 49 ff.

[323] The highest expression of this re-presented centralised culture is Versailles. Blanning calls the form 'representational culture', in which the production of the new within the arts, whether in music or theatre, served the court and the king's centralised form of self-representation. 'The rest of Europe succumbed too, with varying degrees of enthusiasm. The sophistication, self-confidence, and sheer quality of Louis XIV's achievement made most foreign cultures come to seem old-fashioned, dull and – fatal stigma – provincial. Those who could not travel to Versailles to experience its wonders at first hand could make their acquaintance through the numerous descriptions and illustrations which were published': Blanning, *The Culture of Power and the Power of Culture* (fn. 320), p. 49.

[324] In his lectures on aesthetics, Hegel divides the epochal forms of art into symbolic art, classical art and romantic art. According to Hegel, romantic art is a pejorative form of art, since the dominance of inwardness leads to subjective distortions that appear 'grimacing'. Only in Greek-ancient art is the function of art, as a conception of the absolute instead of free subjectivity, fulfilled. 'The true content of the romantic is absolute inwardness, the corresponding form spiritual subjectivity, as grasping its independence and freedom.' Georg W. F. Hegel, *Vorlesungen über die Aesthetik*, vol. II, Berlin 1843, pp. 122 ff, 129.

[325] This position could also be occupied by other supreme authorities, such as the state, the people, by the proletariat in Marxism, or historically such as in the French Revolution by the nation.

[326] Carl Schmitt, *Politische Romantik*, Berlin 1991, p. 16 f.

[327] In the Roman Catholic Church, according to Schmitt, *ratio* and *repraesentatio*, form and idea, correspond optimally. Therefore, he uses the concept of *complexio oppositorum* to distinguish two dimensions of the political power of Roman Catholicism: the theological and the dogmatic. 'In the fact that it has the capacity for juridical form lies one of its sociological secrets. But it has the power

of this, as of any form, only because it has the power of representation. It represents the *civitas humana*, it represents at every moment the historical connection with the historical moment of Christ's Incarnation and sacrifice on the Cross, it represents Christ himself, personally, God made man in historical reality. In the representative lies its superiority over an age of economic thought': Carl Schmitt, Römischer Katholizismus und politische Form, Stuttgart 2008, p. 39 f.

[328] Schmitt links the modern economic sphere with Protestantism by following Max Weber's argument that 'inner-worldly' asceticism basically paves the way for impersonal economic rationalism. In doing so, he attempts to counter the political potential of the Catholic Church for this development. Carl Schmitt, Das Zeitalter der Neutralisierungen und Entpolitisierungen, 1929, in: Carl Schmitt, Der Begriff des Politischen, Munich/Leipzig 1932, p. 66 ff; Reinhard Mehring, Politische Ethik in Max Weber's 'Politik als Beruf' und Carl Schmitt's 'Der Begriff des Politischen', *Politische Vierteljahresschrift*, 31 (1990), p. 608 ff.

[329] In this aspect there is a point of contact of different dimensions of the debate of modernity. First, there is the question of the release of subjective energies (see Max Weber's argument about the inner-worldly question and romantic productivity). There is also the growth dimension of the impersonal institutions of modern liberalism in the Weimar Republic. Finally, there is the question of the role of the state in this scenario. The Catholic Church as *complexio oppositorium* is a political response on these three fronts: the subjective (individual), the objective (economy) and the institutional (state).

[330] There is a certain connection between the subjective and objective fronts, which arises especially from the theological discussion around Rudolph Sohm and his influence on Max Weber and Carl Schmitt. See fn. 107.

[331] Schmitt, Römischer Katholizismus und politische Form (fn. 327), p. 32. Here lies an important difference between Kantorowicz and Schmitt concerning the concept of the mystical. For Ernst Kantorowicz, Thomas Aquinas' *'corpum mysticum'* or *'persona mystica'* is close to the *'persona ficta'* of the jurists. In other words, 'mystical' for Kantorowicz is almost synonymous with 'fictive', while for Schmitt the mystical inevitably embodies a moment of personification.

[332] Schmitt, Politische Romantik (fn. 326), p. 15.

[333] Schmitt, ibid., p. 14.

[334] Schmitt, ibid., p. 18 f.

[335] Many museums were founded in the nineteenth century and contribute to the autonomy of art, such as the Alte Pinakothek in Munich (1824–1836), the Prado in Madrid (1819), the Altes Museum in Berlin (1823–1830), the Fitzwilliam Museum in Cambridge (1837–1847), the Historical Museum in Moscow (1874–1883), and the Rijksmuseum in Amsterdam (founded c. 1800, first exhibition 1877–1885); see Tim Blanning, The Commercialization and Sacralization of European Culture in the Nineteenth Century, in: Tim Blanning (ed.), *The Oxford History of Modern Europe*, Oxford 2000, p. 126 ff.

[336] Schmitt, Römischer Katholizismus und politische Form (fn. 327), p. 16.

[337] J. B. Schneewind describes the emergence of the autonomous subject and the invention of autonomy on a level of the history of ideas, which he traces back to Kant. Dror Wahrman, on the other hand, argues for embedding the explanation of the emergence of modern subjectivity in social contexts. As an example, he connects the explanation of the demise of an *'ancien régime* of identity' that relied on collective representations and the emergence of a new regime of (personal) identity with the Romantic movement. 'After all, many of the developments routinely associated with literary Romanticism are precisely those I have identified for the new regime of identity: the characterization of self in terms of psychological depth; the emphasis on human difference and individuality; the rekindled interest in innate, intuitive, and instinctive traits or behaviors; the developmental perspective on human growth.' Dror Wahrman, *The Making of the Modern Self. Identity and Culture in Eighteenth-Century England*, New Haven (Conn.) 2006, p. 290. Jerome B. Schneewind, *The Invention of Autonomy. A History of Modern Moral Philosophy*, Cambridge 1998.

[338] Osterhammel, Die Verwandlung der Welt (fn. 262).

[339] On the history of department stores, see Uwe Spiekermann, *Warenhaussteuer in Deutschland, Mittelstandbewegung, Kapitalismus und Rechtsstaat im späten Kaiserreich*, Frankfurt am Main 1994, p. 29 ff; and Walter Benjamin, *Passagen, Kristalle: Die Axt der Vernunft und des Satans liebster Trick*, Hamburg 2011.

[340] Norman J. G. Pounds, *Hearth & Home. A History of Material Culture*, Bloomington 1989, p. 394 ff; Uwe Spiekermann, *Basis der Konsumgesellschaft. Entstehung und Entwicklung des modernen Kleinhandels in Deutschland 1850 bis 1914*, Munich 1999, p. 199; Osterhammel, *Die Verwandlung der Welt* (fn. 262).

[341] Franco Moretti, *The Bourgeois. Between History and Literature*, London/New York 2014, p. 94 ff. For a consistent reading on legal theory, see Thomas Vesting, Eine Versetzung des Objektiven in die Subjektivität. Ein Beitrag zu Recht und Literatur, in Inka Mülder-Bach/Jens Kersten (Eds.), *Prosa schreiben. Literatur – Geschichte – Recht*, Paderborn 2019, p. 75 ff.

[342] In an earlier book, Franco Moretti expresses the effect that the city brings to literature, namely: 'But the underlying rule of the big laissez-faire city has the peculiarity of furthering *an incessant shift in classification*: specially in that tumultuous development of heterogeneous forms of power – financial, political, and cultural: each in turn divided between conflicting groups – which characterised Paris in the mid nineteenth century. A constantly shifting classification implies at least two consequences. First of all, it becomes almost impossible to define the monstrous ... But the second, and much more far-reaching consequence is that what engages the reader is no longer the "state of exception" of a symbolic system (the monster indicates a taxonomy that is no longer obeyed: the falling apart of all symbolic "laws") and, thereby, of represented life – but the unpredictability harboured *in ordinary administration and "everyday life"*': Franco Moretti, Balzac's Novels and Urban Personality, in: Franco Moretti, *Signs Taken for Wonders. On the Sociology of Literary Forms*, London/New York 1983, p. 115.

[343] Moretti, ibid., p. 116 f.

[344] Schmitt, *Politische Romantik* (fn. 326), p. 111.

[345] Schmitt, ibid., p. 18.

[346] Koskenniemi, *International Law as Political Theology* (fn. 254).

[347] Schmitt, *Politische Romantik* (fn. 326), p. 122.

[348] Friedrich Balke, *Der Staat nach seinem Ende. Die Versuchung Carls Schmitts*, Munich 1996, p. 131.

[349] Schmitt, *Die Auflösung der europäischen Ordnung* (fn. 300), p. 373.

CHAPTER 4
THE BIRTH OF THE NEW WORLD FROM THE CULTURE OF DISPERSION

[350] Benedict Anderson, *Imagined Communities. Reflections on the Origin and Spread of Nationalism*, London 1992.

[351] Imagining, however, is not arbitrary. It presupposes pre-existing experiences and limits. For a recent reading of the role of imagination for modern democracy, see Yaron Ezrahi, *Imagined Democracies. Necessary Political Fictions*, Cambridge 2012, p. 7: 'The imagination does not, of course, create our worlds *ex nihilo*. Its creativity lies not merely in inventing, but also in reconfiguring and restructuring the fabrics of our experience and thought, and in its capacity to modify earlier modes of imagining'.

[352] Bayly, *The Birth of the Modern World* (fn. 281).

[353] 'Large numbers of professional bodies of specialists had emerged. These were common across the globe, but the picture in itself was more varied. In China, the descendants of the old mandarin class were now lawyers, accountants, newspaper editors, surgeons, pharmacists, and university lectures': Bayly, ibid., p. 483.

[354] Sheehan/Wahrman, *Invisible Hands* (fn. 178), p. xv.

[355] International Law Commission, 'Fragmentation of International Law: Difficulties arising from the Diversification and Expansion of International Law' (fn. 88). For the current debate, also see Anne Peters, Fragmentation and Constitutionalization, in: *The Oxford Handbook of the Theory of International Law*, Oxford/New York 2016, p. 1011 ff.

[356] The fragmentation and constitutionalisation debates are only two sides of the same coin. Both narratives counterfactually assume the spectre of a discourse of unity: fragmentation as a consequence of broken unity and constitutionalisation as a desired unity. This latent semantics of unity affects the self-description of a phenomenon that can no longer be described as unitary. On this, see Anne Peters, Compensatory Constitutionalism. The Function and Potential of Fundamental International Norms and Structures, LJIL 19 (2006), p. 579 ff, 610 (602 f.).

[357] Cf. Fabian Steinhauer, *Medienverfassung. Untersuchung zur Verfassungswissenschaft nach 1990, Habilitationsmanuskript*, Frankfurt am Main 2015, p. 132 ff. Fabian Steinhauer uses the concept of dispersion to address the debate about the concept of constitution in particular.

[358] Karl-Heinz Ladeur, Soziale Epistemologie der Demokratie. Theoretische Überlegungen zur Bindung von Unbestimmtheit durch Institutionen in der postmodernen Gesellschaft, in: Ino Augsberg (Ed.), *Ungewissheit als Chance*, Tübingen 2009, pp. 135 ff., 141.

[359] Siegfried Kracauer, Kult der Zerstreuung, in: Siegfried Kracauer, *Das Ornament der Masse*, Frankfurt am Main 1977, p. 311 ff. Here Kracauer engages in an analysis of mass culture, where dispersion not only describes the viewer, but also concerns the dispersed structure of the medium. For Benjamin, dispersion is also not primarily a deficiency, but a property of art or works of art that is conditioned by the masses; the collective of art is also only made possible by dispersion. Walter Benjamin, Das Kunstwerk im Zeitalter seiner technischen Reproduzierbarkeit, in: Walter Benjamin, *Gesammelte Schriften*, vol. I/2, Frankfurt am Main 1980, pp. 502–504.

[360] While the semantics of the fragment still represents a part of the whole, just as a shard is a part of the original glass, the notion of dispersion seeks to observe the effects of fragility itself. The point is not that the *ius publicum europaeum* is dismantled or divided into small parts, but that through the medium of sovereignty and through a technique of subjectivation, emerge new ambivalences and possibilities for imagining, as well as new possibilities for action (*Handlungsmöglichkeiten*) of a society, that are situated beyond the centralised concrete order of the *ius publicum europaeum* and its fragmentation.

[361] Here also lies the added value of a cultural-theoretical approach within legal theory. The foundation of the relationship between individuals and society is interpreted in terms of a constructive and performative function of legal concepts and institutions. However, law's participation in this construction is not purposeful, but only prepares the ground for new variations and interpretations of the real. Lawrence Rosen, *Law as Culture. An Invitation*, Princeton 2006, p. 92 ff; Clifford Geertz, *Local Knowledge: Further Essays in Interpretative Anthropology*, New York 1982, pp. 184 and 232.

[362] David Armitage, Globalizing Jeremy Bentham, *History of Political Thought* 32 (2011), p. 63. The South American Andrés Bello, who came in contact with Jeremy Bentham during Bello's stay in London (1810–1829), was also one of the first to introduce this semantic change into the law of global society. He first published his book on international law as 'Derecho de Jentes' in Santiago de Chile in 1832, but by 1844 he had already published the second edition under the title 'Derecho international' (Andrés Bello, *Principios del Derecho Internacional*, Lima 1844).

[363] Ingo Hueck, The Disciple of the History of International Law. New Trends and Methods on the History of International Law, *Journal of History of International Law* 3 (2001), p. 194 ff., 200 ff.; Koskenniemi, *From Apology to Utopia* (fn. 254), p. 122.

[364] 'A modernization of the science of international law took place and the new technique focused primarily on historical sources, treaties, and customs, instead of the eternity of natural law': Miloš Vec, Sources in the 19th Century European Tradition: The Myth of Positivism, in: Samantha Besson/Jean d'Aspremont (Eds.), *The Sources of International Law*, Oxford 2017, p. 121 ff., 129. See also Luigi Nuzzo/Miloš Vec (Eds.), *Constructing International Law – The Birth of a Discipline*, Frankfurt am Main 2012.

[365] However, it cannot be denied that international law did not emerge until the nineteenth century. The preliminary achievements of the second scholasticism, Grotius' and Vattel's, were of course decisive. However, its establishment at the university level as a separate discipline was only possible because of certain social developments. With increasing social complexity due to the emergence of new technologies, intensification of trade, and mass immigration, international law could no longer treat its object as a general part of philosophy (natural law – Grotius) or as a commentary on diplomatic practices (Vattel). Not even the semantic distinction between the civilised world and the uncivilised world could guide the discussions on international law during the dispersion of sovereignty around the globe after the disintegration of the *ius publicum europaeum*, although this distinction had until then structured the system of rights in world society. See *Luigi Nuzzo*, Un modo senza nemici: La costruzione del diritto internazionale e la negazione delle differenze, Quaderni Fiorentini 39 (2009), pp. 1311 ff.

[366] Koskenniemi, *From Apology to Utopia* (fn. 254), p. 98 ff. On the 'case' of natural law as a source of the new international law, see Mónica García-Salmones Rovira, *The Project of Positivism in International Law. The History and Theory of International Law*, Oxford 2013, pp. 30–35.

[367] The ambivalent role of the nationality principle with regard to the emergence and resolution of conflicts in nineteenth-century international law scholarship is discussed by Luigi Nuzzo. See Luigi Nuzzo, The Principle of Nationality: The Italian Way to International Law, in Serge Dauchy/Miloš Vec (Eds.), *Les conflits entre peuples* (fn. 292), p. 93 ff. Michael Stolleis, *Nationalität und Internationalität: Rechtsvergleichung im öffentlichen Recht des 19. Jahrhunderts*, Stuttgart 1998.

[368] Peter Macalister-Smith/Joachim Schwietzke, Bibliography of the Textbooks and Comprehensive Treatises on Positive International Law of the 19th Century, *Journal of History of International Law* 3 (2001), p. 75 ff.

[369] Ingo Hueck, Die Gründung völkerrechtlicher Zeitschriften in Deutschland im internationalen Vergleich, in: Michael Stolleis (Ed.), *Juristische Zeitschriften. Die neuen Medien des 18.-20. Jahrhunderts*, Frankfurt am Main 1999, pp. 379 ff, 388 ff.

[370] The international law of treaties also contributed to the transformation or even the emergence of modern subjectivity. As F. Trentmann accentuates, in the nineteenth-century free trade agreements put the consumer on the political map. 'The new civic persona of the consumer was crucial for completing the synergy between freedom of trade and civil society': Frank Trentmann, *Free Trade Nation. Commerce, Consumption and Civil Society in Modern Britain*, Oxford 2008, p. 16.

[371] 'It was also the tendency to multilateralism, the conclusion of law-making treaties, the allotment of new fields of international cooperation, the institutionalizations, particularly within the flourishing nineteenth-century sciences, in economy and technology': Edward Keene, The Treaty-making Revolution of the Nineteenth Century, *The International History Review* 34 (2012), p. 475 ff.

[372] Keene, ibid.

[373] 'The jurists believed to experience a reception of the non-Europeans, which was very flattering for Europe, and did not even notice that they dissolved all bases of a reception, because the previous, good or bad, but at least as a certain concrete order, i.e. above all as a spatial order, a really existing housing cooperative (*Hausgenossenschaft*) of European principalities, states and nations disappeared, and disappeared without replacement. What took its place was not a "system" of states – but a spatially and systemless interweaving and juxtaposition of factual relations, a disorderly, spatially and spiritually incoherent interweaving and juxtaposition of more than fifty heterogeneous, supposedly equally entitled, equally sovereign states and their scattered possessions, a structureless chaos that was no longer capable of any common management of war and for which, finally, not even the term "civilization" could be regarded as the substance of a certain homogeneity.' Schmitt, *Der Nomos der Erde* (fn. 257), p. 206 f.

[374] Crawford, *The Creation of States in International Law* (fn. 310), p. 14 ff.

[375] On the problem of the organism metaphor in the nineteenth century debate on constitutional law, see Koschorke et. al. *Der fiktive Staat* (fn. 221); Hubert Rottleuthner, Biological Metaphors in Legal Thought, in: Gunther Teubner (Ed.), *Autopoietic Law*, Berlin 1987, p. 97 ff.

[376] Gunther Teubner, in clear distinction to Max Weber and Talcott Parsons, points to the dynamic social reality of the social substrate of the legal person. Translated into the language of systems theory: the essence of the legal person lies precisely in the fact that it is a 'pulsating sequence of meaningfully interrelated communicative events that constantly reproduce themselves': Gunther Teubner, Unternehmenskorporatismus. New Industrial Policy and the 'Essence' of the Legal Person, KritV 3 (1987), p. 67 ff. For an extension of the debate to algorithms, see Gunther Teubner, Digitale Rechtssubjekte? Zum privatrechtlichen Status autonomer Softwareagenten. *Ar-chiv für Civilistische Praxis*, AcP 2018, p. 155 ff.

[377] Janne E. Nijman, *The Concept of International Legal Personality. An Inquiry into the History and Theory of International Law*, Den Haag 2004, p. 31 ff.

[378] Jan H. W. Verzijl, International Persons, in Jan H. W. Verzijl, *International Law in Historical Perspective*, Vol. II, Leiden 1969, p. 2 ff. See also Patrick Riley, *Leibniz' Universal Jurisprudence. Justice as the Charity of the Wise*, Cambridge (Mass.) 1996.

[379] The *res publica christiana* – if one applies the method of periodisation – was under pressure due to the fact that the supremacy of the pope and the emperor was challenged by the inclusion of new actors involved in power. The order that emerged from this limited expansion was presented above as *ius publicum europaeum*. Legal personality, in this sense, is a legal form of access to global society, both for the constitution and, in decay, for the *ius publicum europaeum*. Wilhelm Grewe, *Epochen der Völkerrechtsgeschichte*, Baden-Baden 1984, p. 91 ff; Randall Lesaffer, The Grotian Tradition Revisited. Change and Continuity in the History of International Law, BYIL 73 (2002), pp. 103 ff, 112.

[380] This led to a thematisation of the current state and was called 'state theory' from the nineteenth century onwards, see *Riley*, Introduction, in: Riley, *Leibniz's Political Writings*, 2nd ed, Cambridge 1988, p. 12 ff.

[381] David Kennedy, International Law and the Nineteenth Century. History of an Illusion, *Nordic Journal of International Law* 65 (1996), p. 385 ff.

[382] Kennedy, ibid.

[383] Schmitt, *Römischer Katholizismus und politische Form* (fn. 327), p. 31 f.: 'The church, too, is a "legal person," but different from a corporation. The latter, the typical product of the age of production, is a mode of calculation, but the church is a concrete, personal representation of concrete personality ... In the representative lies its superiority over an age of economic thought.'

[384] Schmitt, Der Nomos der Erde (fn. 257), p. 116.

[385] Niklas Luhmann, Staat und Staatsräson im Übergang von traditioneller Herrschaft zu moderner Politik, in: Niklas Luhmann, Gesellschaftsstruktur und Semantik, Frankfurt am Main 1993, pp. 65 ff, 127 f.: 'The theory of the state is gradually changed from virtus to ius and finally becomes the theory of that legal person which determines that legal persons exist and what they can do with legal effect.'

[386] The concept of culture is not understood here in the sense of postcolonial international lawyers, for whom the old distinction between civilised and uncivilised peoples, anchored in the *ius publicum europaeum*, still lives on latently in world law. Instead, 'culture' here is meant to refer to the constitutive and acentric relationship between individuals and society in the production of the social.

[387] Rosen, *Law as Culture* (fn. 361), p. 93.

[388] Yan Thomas, Les opérations du Droit, Paris 2011. According to Yan Thomas, legal operations and legal techniques were invented to 'artificially' connect people and things, thereby reshaping the architecture of the social world in new and open ways. For the application of this interpretation of law claimed here, this amounts to the proliferation of the sovereign fictitious legal entities that endowed new relations beyond the *ius publicum europaeum*.

[389] Aldo Schiavone, *Ius. L'invenzione del diritto in Occidente*, Turin 2005.

[390] The fiction of the personalisation of the state also has a tradition in state theory, and behind it lies an important evolutionary achievement. Kantorowicz's study, 'The Two Bodies of the King', focuses on how the distinction between crown and body became the distinction between person and office. The Fiction of the Crown shows how medieval glossators used the Roman legal tradition to guarantee the continuity of the replacement of the predecessor by the successor. The continuity or finality of temporal authority was not confused with the continuity of the crown itself. Thus, in particular, the concepts of Roman law and legal fictions used in fiscal matters began to acquire a constitutional significance that had not been given to them before. The figure of legal fictional crowns is not simply an analogy to the idea of personification of the state in the nineteenth century, but rather presents itself as a semantic advance. Personification suggests a rupture between symbolic power and real (actual) power, in which new abstract, semantic artifacts replace or supplement 'real' units of attribution. Ernst H. Kantorowicz, *The King's Two Bodies. A Study in Mediaeval Political Theory*, Princeton (N.J.) 1957, p. 319.

[391] 'Overall, it is clear that extra-European treaty-making accounts for a substantial part of the total level of treaty-making, and that any explanation for the treaty-making revolution that does not account for the significance of extra-European treaty-partners will be too narrow.' See Keene, *The Treaty-making Revolution of the Nineteenth Century* (fn. 371), p. 491.

[392] Trust is at the centre of even the contract theories. The state arises from the sources of mistrust or because of the negative side of trust. Without trust, no (social) contract comes into being. In Hobbes, the security problem becomes the trust problem through the establishment of a central rule to eliminate generalised trustlessness (the state of nature). In other contract theories, trust is also the centre of theorising.

[393] '... *ius gentium* delimits political power within the sphere of territorial sovereignty and liberates private *dominium* to express itself as ownership so as to contribute to the creation of a world-wide capitalist economy': Martti Koskenniemi, Ius Gentium and the Birth of Modernity, in: Nuzzo/Vec (Eds.), *Constructing International Law* (fn. 364), p. 22.

[394] *Koskenniemi*, ibid, p. 23.

[395] Gradually, also due to the increasing complexity of decentralised relations, another relational form of superiority is emerging instead of that of states. Organizations assume a central role in the production of sectoral social knowledge in society on a constant basis. This will be the topic of the next chapter.

[396] Bayly, *The Birth of the Modern World* (fn. 281), p. 238; also see Carlos Petit, *Historia del Derecho Mercantil*, Madrid 2016, p. 354 ff.

[397] Trentmann, *Free Trade Nation* (fn. 370), p. 16.

[398] István Hont, *Jealousy of Trade. International Competition and the Nation-State in Historical Perspective*, Cambridge (Mass.) 2010.

[399] Hont, ibid., p. 5 ff.

[400] '... in all times, kings, and persons of sovereign authority, because of their independency, are in continual jealousies, and in the state and posture of gladiators; having their weapons pointing, and their eyes fixed on one another.' Thomas Hobbes, *Leviathan*, Kap. XIV, p. 89.

[401] See James E. King, The Origin of the Term 'political economy', *Journal of Modern History* 20 (1948), p. 230 f.; Henry C. Clark, Commerce, the Virtues, and the Public Sphere in Early-Seventeenth-Century France, *French Historical Studies* 21 (1998), p. 415 ff.

[402] Richard Tuck, *The Rights of War and Peace. Political Thought and the International Order from Grotius to Kant*, Oxford, 1999, pp. 1–15.

[403] It is astonishing that in Machiavelli there is not a word on 'trade' or 'commerce,' especially since Florence was a commercial city, see Hont, *Jealousy of Trade* (fn. 398), p. 9 ff. On the one hand, constitutive spheres of sovereignty imply deprivation of sovereignty in those spheres that actually possessed sovereignty; on the other hand, paradoxically, they become incessantly political or state affairs. Economics – and especially the emergence of a global market – is a good example of this constitutive paradoxical process of constitution of statehood through withdrawal of statehood. On the constitutive relationship between public knowledge and private interest in the agency of the state, see John Brewer, *The Sinews of Power. War, Money and the English State 1688–1783*, Cambridge 1990, p. 221 ff.

[404] Ritter, *Hegel und die Französische Revolution* (fn. 169).

[405] Joseph Vogl also draws on traditional theories of sovereignty, but in his most recent book he focuses on a qualitative shift in the constitutive split of modern sovereignty. This qualitative shift, in which, according to Vogl, sovereignty is gradually juxtaposed with a new form of (economic) governance, is first found in the invention of government finance through a cycle of borrowing and debt service by credit. Vogl even locates the birth of the modern state in the spirit of public credit, which was first created by state debt or, better, self-debt. To put it more pointedly, one could say with Vogl that such forms of state financing – state debt and public credit – gave rise to the complex modern financial economy, but also to the state itself. Joseph Vogl, *Der Souveränitätseffekt*, Zurich 2015.

[406] In Kantorowicz's study of the double body of law, the split or divorce between crown and body is the centre in which the fiction of the crown by the medieval glossators, with reference to Roman law, guaranteed the continuation of secular rule to the heir. In Bodin, the recognition of certain property rights was the basis of the coming rule. In Hobbes, the split took place in the distinction between internal faith and external confession. *Cuius regio, eius religio*, but above all one sees the division in the formula: no obedience without protection. The division of sovereignty is more constitutive than the conventionally asserted absolute rule of a sovereign. On the cultural technique of divorce, see Fabian Steinhauer, *Vom Scheiden. Geschichte und Theorie einer juristischen Kulturtechnik*, Berlin 2015.

[407] German modernity is characterised by a path of anchoring culture as the cultivation of the individual and thereby, above all, by the figure of the educated citizen. However, this did not take place without preconditions. The Bildungsbürgertum first consisted of the petty bourgeoisie, which represented an intermediate level between the industrialists and the proletariat. As Friedrich Engels correctly observed, it was only with the expansion of the Zollverein, internal competition and external rapprochement with various states that the commercial class of the petty bourgeoisie emerged. At the same time, the extension and consolidation of the Zollverein, the general introduction of steam power into traffic, and the growing competition in the internal market led to the mutual rapprochement of the commercial classes of the various states and provinces, the equalisation of their interests, and the centralisation of their power. Friedrich Engels in Karl Marx/Friedrich Engels Gesamtausgabe (MEGA), Berlin 2009, vol. 8, p. 9.

[408] 'But as long as the struggle had to be waged against such ridiculously antiquated remnants of the Middle Ages, as they fettered the material bourgeois development of Germany until 1830, no German political economy was possible. Only with the establishment of the Zollverein did the Germans come into a position in which they could only understand political economy at all.' Karl Marx / Friedrich Engels – *Werke*, Vol. 13, 7th ed., Berlin 1971, pp. 460–477, here pp. 465–466.

[409] Thomas Duve, '... how there is still room for a happy existence for millions of people ...' Der Freundschafts-, Handels- und Schiffahrtsvertrag zwischen Preußen und den übrigen Staaten des Zollvereins und der Argentinischen Konföderation von 1858, in: Hans-Georg Hermann/Thomas Gutmann et al. (Eds.), *Von den Leges Barbarorum bis zum ius barbarum des Nationalsozialismus*, Vienna 2008, p. 269 ff; Hans-Otto Kleinmann, Der atlantische Raum als Problem des europäischen Staatensystems, *Jahrbuch für Geschichte Lateinamerikas* 38 (2001), p. 7 ff.

[410] Marcel Gauchet, De l'avènement de l'individu à la découverte de la société, Annales E. p. C. 3/1979, p. 461 ff.

138 Notes

[411] This opening for the new is presented by F. Trentmann in the context of a 'culture of improvement' of behaviour. 'The culture of politeness gave consumption an additional lift. Coffee houses and the taste for exotic beverages were just one part of an expanding universe of social spaces – from clubs and restaurants to promenades and pleasures gardens – that were simultaneously dedicated to leisurely entertainment and genteel self-fashioning ... Politeness put the enlightenment ideals of sympathy and sensibility into material practice': Trentmann, *The Empire of Things* (fn. 280), p. 107.

[412] Even with Hegel, the juxtaposition was intended to open up to world society. See G. W. F. Hegel, *Grundlinien der Philosophie des Rechts* (1821), *Werkausgabe* vol. 7, Frankfurt am Main 1970, p. 360 (§ 280). See also Walter Pauly, Hegel und die Frage nach dem Staat, *Der Staat* 39 (2000), pp. 381 ff, here p. 393: 'Since, according to Hegel, bourgeois society also tends toward expansion and colonization, the concept of world society is by no means far removed from his approach'; and, not least, Ritter, *Hegel und die Französische Revolution* (fn. 169), 1965, p. 62 ff.

[413] Argentine Confederation (1856); Uruguay (1856); Paraguay (1860); 1827 with Brazil (Prussia); Mexico (1855); Netherlands (1839); Britain (1841); Belgium (1844); Chile (1862).

[414] There was a legal controversy, since the Zollverein did not have its own legal personality. Nevertheless, on the German side, all members of the German Customs Association were contracting parties. The Zollverein was thus seen as the embodiment of the German Confederation. It was not until 1867 and 1871 that the North German Confederation and the German Empire, respectively, absorbed the powers of the individual states. See Duve, '... as there is still room there ...' (fn. 409), p. 279 ff.

[415] There was one or more functions of these mutual treaties under international law that went beyond economic intercourse. On the one hand, one wanted to secure the unsettled constitutional situation and the often precarious international recognition of these states and nations, and on the other hand, one wanted to eliminate certain internal power constellations through centered monopolies of force by means of international recognition.

[416] See Hans-Joachim König, Free Trade in Exchange for Political Recognition? The Special Case of the Negotiations between Greater Columbia and the Hanseatic Cities, in: Renate Piper/Peer Schmidt (Eds.), *Latin America and the Atlantic World. The Atlantic World and Latin America (1500–1850)*, Köln 2005, p. 403 ff.; Felix Becker, Treaties of Friendship, Commerce and Navigation and the Integration of the American Independent States into the International System, in: Inge Buisson/Gunther Kahle/Hans König/Horst Pietschmann (Eds.), *The Formation of the State and the Nation in Latin America*, Köln-Wien 1984, p. 247 ff.

[417] 'Nevertheless, the similarity in the overall pattern suggests that, insofar as we are initially concerned with a general increase in the incidence of treaty-making during the nineteenth century, we cannot treat it as an exclusively European or Euro-American phenomenon. The treaty-making revolution was a global one, even if there were significant regional variations.': Keene, *The Treaty-making Revolution of the Nineteenth Century* (fn. 371), p. 493.

[418] Schmitt, Die Auflösung der europäischen Ordnung im 'International Law' (fn. 300).

[419] The generation of a new kind of trust was not only linked to economic conditions, such as foreign trade, economic growth, revenue from taxes, customs, and duties (although these were an important part of it), but also formed the basis of trust for mass long-distance migration from Europe in the nineteenth century. Without a conversion of the basis of trust, which consisted of unstable and insecure networks of families, small dynasties, and local rulers, to one based on minimal protection of personal property, freedom of belief, and freedom of settlement, which depended on a more or less state and bureaucratic structure, large-scale German and European immigration would have been little more than an adventure. See Osterhammel, *Die Verwandlung der Welt* (fn. 262), pp. 235 ff. and p. 1010 ff.; Duve, '... as there is still room there ...' (fn. 409).

[420] Bayly, *The Birth of the Modern World* (fn. 281), p. 194: 'During the course of the nineteenth century, however, global urban culture emerged as a more uniform and distinct pattern of living ... In addition to the profusion of urban societies, clubs, meeting halls, and community associations, the café provided a potent symbol for the urban public space, both as a meeting point for men and women and as a scene of political and philosophical discussion.'

[421] Bayly, ibid., p. 197: 'The tension between old royal and religious centers, and the need for the state to proclaim its modernity in the great arena of the city, was particularly sharp in the non-European world. The khedives of Egypt and the post-Tanzimat rulers of the Ottoman Empire made a special project of establishing boulevards, opera houses, public squares adorned with statuary, and flower gardens adjoining the new railways stations in their cities.'

[422] Osterhammel, *Die Verwandlung der Welt* (fn. 262).

CHAPTER 5
THE LAW OF ORGANISATIONS

[423] This was the subject of Chapter 1.
[424] That was the subject of Chapter 2.
[425] The increase in juridification in the national and transnational framework was a correlate of the mechanisation of living conditions. An interesting example of the handling of law and technology is the steam boiler legislation in the nineteenth century. On this, see Ina vom Feld, *Kontrollierte Staatsentlastung im Technikrecht. Dampfkesselgesetzgebung und Dampfkesselüberwachung in Preußen 1831–1914*, Frankfurt am Main 2007, p. 36 ff. For a general discussion of the topic, see Miloš Vec, Kurze Geschichte des Technikrechts, in: Martin Schulte/Rainer Schröder (Eds.), *Handbuch des Technikrechts. Allgemeine Grundlagen Umweltrecht – Gentechnikrecht – Energierecht – Telekommunikations- und Medienrecht Patentrecht – Computerrecht*, 2nd ed.
[426] The emergence of new normative orders in a globalised arena, driven by new norm producers, transnational regulatory networks, and decision makers was not an invention of the late 1980s and early 1990s. As early as the nineteenth century, development was crucial to the emergence of a global dynamic society. For the legal context, see Teubner, Global Bukovina (fn. 85). For the historical context, see Osterhammel, *Die Verwandlung der Welt* (fn. 262), esp. pp. 437–440.
[427] Thomas Duve, What is 'Multinormativity'? Introductory Remarks, Rechtsgeschichte – *Legal History* Rg 25 (2017), p. 88 ff. Legal pluralism as an approach offers propositions for an alternative self-description of law. On this as a concept of reflection, see Seinecke, *Das Recht des Rechtspluralismus* (fn. 237).
[428] Karl Marx/Friedrich Engels: *Gesamtausgabe, Dritte Abteilung, Briefwechsel*, vol. 10: September 1859 to May 1860, Berlin 2000.
[429] Johann Wolfgang von Goethe, *Goethes sämtliche Werke*, vol. 39, Stuttgart/Tübingen 1854, p. 377.
[430] Hans Barion et al. (Eds.), *Epirrhosis. Festgabe für Carl Schmitt*, Berlin 1968.
[431] See the correspondence between Ernst Forsthoff and Carl Schmitt in: Dorothee Mußgnug/Reinhard Mußgnug/Angela Reinstahl (Eds.), *Briefwechsel Ernst Forsthoff Carl Schmitt (1926–1974)*, Berlin 2007.
[432] Carl Schmitt, *Theorie des Partisanen. Zwischenbemerkungen zum Begriff des Politischen*, 7th ed.
[433] Briefwechsel Ernst Forsthoff/Carl Schmitt (fn. 431), p. 303 f.
[434] Hasso Hofmann, Feindschaft – Grundbegriff des Politischen, Zeitschrift für Politik 12 (1965), pp. 17 ff, 23 ff, 35 ff. See also Schmitt, *Der Begriff des Politischen* (fn. 328), Preface, p. 18. Helmut Ridder speaks at this point of a necessary fantasy in the Schmitt interpretation. For this, see Helmut Ridder, Schmittiana (II), *Neue Politische Literatur* 12 (1967), pp. 137 ff, 144.
[435] Carl Schmitt, Die letzte globale Linie, in: Egmont Zechlin (Ed.), *Völker und Meere*, Leipzig 1944, p. 342 ff, here p. 348: 'Against the claims of a universal, planetary world control and world domination defends itself another nomos of the earth, the basic idea of which is the division of the earth into several large areas filled by their historical, economic and cultural substance.'
[436] Mathias Schmoeckel, Carl Schmitt's Concept of Partisan (31 March 2006), forum historiae iuris, https://forhistiur.de/2006-03-schmoeckel/.
[437] Hasso Hofmann, *Legitimacy versus Legality. Der Weg der politischen Philosophie Carl Schmitts*, 2nd edition, Berlin 1992, p. 163 ff.
[438] Schmoeckel, *Carl Schmitt's Concept of the Partisan* (fn. 436); Schmitt, *Theorie des Partisanen* (fn. 432), p. 89.
[439] Chapter 2 discussed at length Carl Schmitt's equation of German liberalism with political romanticism from a cultural-theoretical perspective. For a discussion of Schmitt's critique of liberalism, see Klaus Hansen/Klaus Lietzmann (Eds.), *Carl Schmitt und die Liberalismuskritik*, Opladen 1988.
[440] The interpretation that the modern weak state would not rule but only administer was widespread in the Schmittian circle. On this, see Felix Grossheutschi, *Carl Schmitt und die Lehre vom Katechon*, Berlin 1996, p. 108.
[441] The topic of technological development was discussed again and again. The central issue was whether the political-constitutional decision-making systems of parliamentary democracy would adequately deal with technical development. Fritz Ossenbühl, Die Not des Gesetzgebers im naturwissenschaftlich-technischen Zeitalter, Wiesbaden 2000, p. 30.

442 From the point of view of state organisations, the trend toward the expansion of administrative law from the nineteenth century onward is striking and has progressed continuously to the present. Cf. Franz Wieacker, Privatrechtsgeschichte der Neuzeit, 2nd ed., Göttingen 1967/1996, p. 543 ff; summarising Rainer Schröder, *Rechtsgeschichte*, 5th ed., Münster 2000, p. 156 f.

443 Forsthoff always emphasises a dualistic legal and constitutional structure, according to which the constitutional state and the social state exist simultaneously. Ernst Forsthoff, Begriff und Wesen des sozialen Rechtsstaates, in: Ernst Forsthoff, *Rechtsstaat im Wandel*. *Verfassungsrechtliche Abhandlungen 1950–1964*, Stuttgart 1964, 27 ff, 50 ff, 53 ff; Ernst Forsthoff, Von der sozialen zur technischen Realisation, *Der Staat* 9 (1970), pp. 145 ff., 149 and 160.

444 'The independence of the institutions of the rule of law vis-à-vis the change of ambience was achievable only through the mechanization of these institutions. In modern mass democracy, whose thinking in terms of equality opposes the recognition of independent political forces, the structures of the constitutional state under the rule of law necessarily assume a technical character. The mechanization can be demonstrated in all institutions of the constitutional state ... A constitutional system which has become technical in the sense indicated ... lays claim ... to being taken particularly strictly in its institutions. In isolation from the change of ambience, the elements of the constitutional state under the rule of law become an intrinsic value.' Forsthoff, *Begriff und Wesen des sozialen Rechtsstaates* (fn. 443), p. 50 ff.

445 Even the Weimar discussion on legality and legitimacy has become obsolete for Forsthoff due to the technical conditionality of the new society: '... the constitutional policy designated by the relationship between legality and legitimacy is obsolete at present': Ernst Forsthoff, Der introvertierte Staat, in: Ernst Forsthoff, *Rechtsstaat im Wandel* (fn. 443), pp. 213 ff, 114; 'Under the circumstances of 1961, to continue to spin the humanistic thread of about 1930 is an anachronism, the reality of which the constitutional jurist is least permitted to miss': Ernst Forsthoff, *Zur Problematik der Verfassungsauslegung*, Stuttgart 1961.

446 Ernst Forsthoff, *Der Staat der Industriegesellschaft. Dargestellt am Beispiel der Bundesrepublik Deutschland*, Munich 1971, p. 19.

447 At this point, Ernst Forsthoff and Niklas Luhmann seem to share the same view, with Luhmann making it particularly clear that a new problematic would arise from the non-juridifiability of these new problems stemming from the (technical) 'age of realization' Cf. Niklas Luhmann, *Rechtssoziologie*, vol. 2, Reinbek bei Hamburg 1972, p. 338; Forsthoff, *Zur Problematik der Verfassungsauslegung* (fn. 445).

448 Ernst Forsthoff, *Die Verwaltung als Leistungsträger*, Stuttgart/Berlin 1938, pp. 9, 13 ff. On the transformation and trajectory of the concept of Daseinsvorsorge in Forsthoff's work, see Jens Kersten, Die Entwicklung des Konzepts der Daseinsvorsorge im Werk von Ernst Forsthoff, *Der Staat* 44 (2005), p. 543 ff.

449 Ernst Forsthoff, Von der Aufgabe der Verwaltungsrechtswissenschaft, *Deutsches Recht* 5 (1935), p. 398. On the subject of the transition from a public law based on intervention to an administrative law based on provision for the public good, see also Stolleis, *Geschichte des öffentlichen Rechts in Deutschland*, vol. 3 (fn. 293), p. 367 f.

450 'This people is not only a peasant people, but also and essentially a people of the radio, of sports, of the weekend, of settlements, of machine shops, of highways, and as such bound to special forms and needs of life essentially determined by technology and machine. A real people's order must do justice to this extraordinary diversity.' Cf. Ernst Forsthoff, *Der totale Staat*, 2nd edition, Hamburg 1934, p. 47.

451 Peter Häberle rightly points out that Forsthoff's concept of the constitution and the rule of law is contradictory to his theory of administration. Peter Häberle, *Zum Staatsdenken Ernst Forsthoffs*, ZSR 95 I (1976), p. 477 ff.

452 Forsthoff, *Die Verwaltung als Leistungsträger* (fn. 448), p. 9.

453 A first glance reveals a framework of influence from three different authors: Hegel, Schmitt, and Weber. In Hegel's case, it is about the concept of precaution from § 188 of Hegel's 'Basic Lines of the Philosophy of Law', in Weber's case, it is about the analysis of bureaucracy and law, and *last but not least*, in Schmitt's case, it is about his change from decision-making to concrete order thinking.

454 See the difference between 'effective' and 'dominated' space: Forsthoff, *Die Verwaltung als Leistungsträger* (fn. 448), p. 5. As a result of industrial-technical development at the turn of the twentieth century, modern transportation increased the effective living space and decreased the dominated living space in Forsthoffian categories. The latter had been the space where the subject himself had power of disposal over spaces and things, such as the farm, the field or in their house.

The transition from the court to the city, mentioned here several times, is alluded to by Forsthoff in terms of a necessary adaptation of administrative law to the new reality of large cities.

[455] *Daseinsvorsorge* presents itself as a structural change experienced by municipalities in the industrial revolution, especially through urbanisation, or, as Forsthoff puts it, 'great transformation of Dasein through technology and the big city': Ernst Forsthoff, *Führung und Bürokratie*, Dt. Adelsblatt 1935, p. 1339; see also Ernst Forsthoff, *Die Krise der Gemeindeverwaltung im heutigen Staat*, Berlin 1932, p. 53 ff.

[456] Forsthoff, *Von der Aufgabe der Verwaltungswissenschaft* (fn. 449), p. 399.

[457] 'There is no authority of accountants, millers, locksmiths, chauffeurs, meat inspectors, since these are partial functions in which the wholeness of man does not appear. Therefore, to the extent that the world becomes divided into parts of labour, a dwindling of authority occurs.' Ernst Forsthoff, The Political Problem of Authority, in: Ernst Forsthoff, *Rechtsstaat im Wandel* (fn. 443), p. 100 ff.

[458] In the lecture series 'Genealogy of the Modern State', Foucault is less concerned with a historical reconstruction of the emergence and transformation of political structures. Rather, he is concerned with the institutionalisation of state and legal forms and their formative role in processes of subjectivation – in short, with the connection between the history of the state and its relationship to the history of the subject. Michel Foucault, *Geschichte der Gouvernementalität*, vol. I: *Sicherheit, Territorium, Bevölkerung*, Frankfurt am Main 2004, p. 508. See also Michel Foucault, *Dits et Ecrits. Schriften*, vol. 4, Frankfurt am Main 2005, p. 900; Thomas Lemke, *Gouvernementalität und Biopolitik*, Wiesbaden 2006.

[459] Foucault does not conceive of the modern state as a centralised structure. Instead, he understands it as a 'complex connection between the technique of individualization and totalizing procedures'. Foucault, *Dits et Ecrits* (fn. 458), p. 277.

[460] Forsthoff, ibid., pp. 34 and 41.

[461] Forsthoff, *Der Staat der Industriegesellschaft* (fn. 446), p. 36.

[462] For the case of associations, see Forsthoff, ibid, p. 19.

[463] Michel Foucault, *Ästhetik der Existenz. Schriften zur Lebenskunst*. Frankfurt am Main 2007, p. 26.

[464] 'The normal establishes itself as a coercive principle in teaching along with the introduction of standardised education and the establishment of normal schools; it establishes itself in the effort to create a uniform corpus of medicine and universal hospital care for the nation, thereby enforcing general health standards; it establishes itself in the regulation and regimentation of industrial processes and products.' Michel Foucault, *Überwachen und Strafen. Die Geburt des Gefängnisses*, Frankfurt am Main 1976, p. 237.

[465] Friedrich Balke, Disziplinartechnologien, Normalität, Normalisierung, in: Clemens Kammler/Rolf Parr/Ulrich Johannes Schneider (Eds.), *Foucault Handbuch. Leben, Werk, Wirkung*, Stuttgart 2014, p. 243.

[466] 'The definition of the relationship between body and machine in the factories under the auspices of economy, rationalization and surveillance forms a problem that runs through the 19th and 20th centuries', Werner Sohn, Bio-Macht und Normalisierungsgesellschaft. Versuch einer Annäherung, in: Werner Sohn/Herbert Mehrtens (Eds.), *Normalität und Abweichung: Studien zur Theorie und Geschichte der Normalisierungsgesellschaft*, Opladen/Wiesbaden 1999, pp. 9 ff, 19.

[467] Foucault, *Überwachen und Strafen* (fn. 464), p. 362.

[468] Foucault, ibid.

[469] Markus Krajewski, *ZettelWirtschaft. Die Geburt der Kartei aus dem Geiste der Bibliothek*, Berlin 2002, p. 14.

[470] Foucault, *Überwachen und Strafen* (fn. 464), p. 363 fn. 49.

[471] For a detailed definition of a dispositif, see the conversation with Jacques-Alain Miler. See Foucault, *Dits et Ecrits*, vol. 3, 2003, p. 392 ff. For the case of the panopticon as a form of power without a centre and personalised command (genuine *dispositif*), see Matteo Pasquinelli, Was ein Dispositiv nicht ist: Archäologie der Norm bei Foucault, Canguilhem und Goldstein, in Lorenz Aggermann/Georg Döcker/Gerald Siegmund (Eds.) *Theater als Dispositiv*, Frankfurt am Main 2017, p. 123 ff.

[472] Gilles Deleuze, Postscriptum zur Kontrollgesellschaft, in: Gilles Deleuze, *Unterhandlungen. 1972–1999*, Frankfurt am Main 1993, p. 240.

[473] Sohn, *Bio-Macht und Normalisierungsgesellschaft* (fn. 466), p. 9 ff.

[474] Michel Foucault, *Sexualität und Wahrheit. Der Wille zum Wissen*, vol. I, Frankfurt am Main 1987, p. 171 f.

[475] Sebastian Conrad/Jürgen Osterhammel, Einleitung, in: Sebastian Conrad/Jürgen Osterhammel (Eds.) *Das Kaiserreich transnational. Deutschland in der Welt 1871–1914*, Göttingen 2004, p. 7 ff; Niels P. Peterson, *Das Kaiserreich in Prozessen ökonomischer Globalisierung*, ibid, p. 49 ff.

[476] Miloš Vec, *Recht und Normierung in der Industriellen Revolution. Neue Strukturen der Normsetzung in Völkerrecht, staatlicher Gesetzgebung und gesellschaftlicher Selbstnormierung*, Frankfurt am Main 2006, pp. 165–291; Jan O. Kehrberg, *Die Entwicklung des Elektrizitätsrechts in Deutschland. Der Weg zum Energiewirtschaftsgesetz von 1935*, Frankfurt am Main 1997, p. 21 ff.

[477] Lorenz Jellinghaus, *Zwischen Daseinsvorsorge und Infrastruktur. Zum Funktionswandel von Verwaltungswissenschaften und Verwaltungsrecht in der zweiten Hälfte des 19. Jahrhunderts*, Frankfurt am Main 2006, p. 13 ff.

[478] 'Thinking about the origins of international institutions seems to demand a vision of war, of peace, and of the process by which war gives way to peace ... As comprehended by the discipline, the year 1918 originates the international institution in three ways. First, it executes a break between a pre-institutional and an institutional moment': David W. Kennedy, The Move to Institutions, *Cardozo L. Rev.* 8 (1987), p. 841 ff., 845.

[479] Gerard J. Mangone, *A Short History of International Organization*, New York 1954, p. 34: 'The havoc of international war has compelled statesman to turn their attention to the positive construction of peace by international organizations'.

[480] Among others, Wilhelm G. Grewe, Peaceful Change, in: Rudolf Bernhardt (Ed.) *Max Planck Encyclopedia of Public International Law* 3, Oxford 1997, p. 971 ff; Edgar Wolfrum/Cord Arendes, *Globale Geschichte des 20. Jahrhunderts*, Stuttgart 2007, p. 64 ff; Jost Dülffer, Art. 'Völkerbund', in: Helmut Vogler (Ed.), *Lexikon der Vereinten Nationen*, Munich 2000, p. 609 ff; Winfried Baumgart, *Vom europäischen Konzert zum Völkerbund. Friedensschlüsse und Friedenssicherung von Versailles bis Wien*, Darmstadt 1987.

[481] 'War embodying disorganization, is often identified with violence and passion. Peace, the antithesis of war, is seen to embody organization': Henry Brailsford, *A League of Nations 1–2* (1917), New York 2018, p. 324.

[482] Akira Iriye, *Global Community. The Role of International Organization in the Making of the Contemporary World*, Berkeley 2004; John Boli/George M. Thomas (Eds.), *Constructing World Culture. International Nongovernmental Organizations since 1875*, Stanford (Cal.) 1999.

[483] Miloš Vec, Weltverträge für Weltliteratur. Das Geistige Eigentum im System der rechtsetzenden Konventionen des 19. Jahrhunderts, in: Louis Pahlow/Jens Eisfeld (Eds.), *Grundlagen und Grundfragen des geistigen Eigentums*, Tübingen 2008, pp. 107 ff., 127 ff.

[484] Madeleine Herren, Governmental Internationalism and the Beginning of a New World Order in the Late Nineteenth Century, in: Martin H. Geyer/Johannes Paulmann (Eds.), *The Mechanics of Internationalism. Culture, Society, and Politics from the 1840s to the First World War*, Oxford 2001, p. 121 ff.; Madeleine Herren-Oesch, *Internationale Organisationen seit 1865. Eine Globalgeschichte der internationalen Ordnung*, Darmstadt 2009.

[485] For the case of jurisprudence oriented toward sociology, see Bertram Lomfeld (Ed.), *Die Fälle der Gesellschaft. Eine neue Praxis soziologischer Jurisprudenz*, Tübingen 2017. For an approach to jurisprudence oriented toward media theory, see the four-volume work by Thomas Vesting, *Die Medien des Rechts*, Weilerswist 2011-2015; Cornelia Vismann, *Akten. Medientechnik und Recht*, Frankfurt am Main 2010; Cornelia Vismann, *Das Recht und seine Mittel. Ausgewählte Schriften*, Frankfurt am Main 2012. p. 394.

[486] See Chapter 1.

[487] See Chapter 1.

[488] Traditionally Josef Kohler, *Die Idee des geistigen Eigenthums, Archiv für die Civilistische Praxis* 82 (1894), p. 141 ff; Matthias Leistner/Gerd Hansen, Die Begründung des Urheberrechts im digitalen Zeitalter – Versuch einer Zusammenführung von individualistischen und utilitaristischen Rechtfertigungsbemühungen, Gewerblicher Rechtsschutz und Urheberrecht 2006, p. 479 ff. For a development of intellectual property beyond the exclusive right, see Karl-Heinz Ladeur/Thomas Vesting, Geistiges Eigentum im Netzwerk – Anforderungen und Entwicklungslinien, in: Martin Eifert/Wolfgang Hoffmann-Riem (Eds.), *Innovationsrecht: Geistiges Eigentum und Innovation. Innovation und Recht I*, Berlin 2008, p. 123 ff.

[489] Intellectual property (or intangible property law) is a generic term that includes copyright, patent, trademark, utility model and design law. On the relationship between reproducibility

and juridification, see Alexander Peukert, Die Herausbildung der normativen Ordnung 'geistiges Eigentum'. Diskurstheoretische und andere Erklärungsansätze, in: Rainer Forst/Klaus Günther (Eds.), *Theorien normativer Ordnungen*, Berlin: '... the emergence and worldwide expansion of intellectual property, however, it is now generally acknowledged that legal development can be seen as a repeated reaction to new reproductive technologies ...', para. 13.

[490] See Chapter 4.

[491] Ludwig Gieseke, *Vom Privileg zum Urheberrecht. Die Entwicklung des Urheberrechts in Deutschland bis 1845*, Göttingen 1995, p. 39 ff; Elmar Wadle, Der langsame Abschied vom Privileg: Das Beispiel des Urheberrechts, in: Barbara Dölemeyer/Heinz Mohnhaupt (Eds.), *Das Privileg im europäischen Vergleich*, vol. 1, Frankfurt am Main 1997, p. 377 ff.

[492] Peter Burke, *Papier und Marktgeschrei. Die Geburt der Wissensgesellschaft*, Berlin 2001, pp. 139-205. The transformation of the production system and the dissemination of cultural goods through a more open public sphere of cities are also described by Jacques Attali. For this, see Jacques Attali, *Noise. The Political Economy of Music*, Minneapolis 1985.

[493] Henrich Bosse, *Autorschaft ist Werkherrschaft. Über die Entstehung des Urheberrechts aus dem Geist der Goethezeit*, Paderborn 1981.

[494] For a description of this situation from the 1980s onward, see Teubner, Globale Bukowina (fn. 85).

[495] For a philosophical critique of the hermeneutic tradition, see Martin Gessmann, *Zur Zukunft der Hermeneutik*, Munich 2012, p. 35 ff.

[496] Hans Ulrich Gumbrecht, Rhythmus und Sinn, in: Hans Ulrich Gumbrecht/Karl Ludwig Pfeiffer (Eds.), *Materialität der Kommunikation*, Frankfurt am Main 1995, p. 714 ff.

[497] Monika Dommann, *Authors and Apparatuses. Die Geschichte des Copyrights im Medienwandel*, Frankfurt am Main 2014, pp. 45–46.

[498] Attali, Noise (fn. 491), p. 87.

[499] D. L. LeMahieu writes that the sound recording is one of 'a score of new technologies thrust upon a population increasingly accustomed to mechanical miracles. In a decade when men learned to fly, the clock-sprung motor of a portable gramophone or the extended playing time of a double-sided disk hardly provoked astonishment. Indeed, what may be most remarkable was the rapidity with which technological innovations became absorbed into everyday, commonplace experience': Daniel L. LeMahieu, *A Culture for Democracy: Mass Communication and the Cultivated Mind in Britain between the Wars*, Oxford 1988, p. 81; see also Donald M. Lowe, *History of Bourgeois Perception*, University of Chicago Press, Chicago 1982, pp. 111–117; Roland Gelatt, *The Fabulous Phonograph*, 1877–1977, New York 1977, p. 68 ff.

[500] Gelatt, ibid., p. 58 ff.

[501] Timothy Day, *A Century of Recorded Music. Listening to Musical History*, New Haven/London 2000.

[502] Jonathan Sterne, *The Audible Past. Cultural Origins of Sound Reproduction*, Durham/London 2003, p. 195 ff. The thesis of the book is that modern ways of hearing prefigure modern ways of seeing. Taking seriously the role of sound and hearing in modern life, we argue, means challenging the visualist definition of modernity. For the history of the phonogram, see p. 195 ff.

[503] William H. Kenney, *Recorded Music in American Life. The Phonograph and Popular Memory*, 1890–1945, New York 1999.

[504] Friedrich A. Kittler, *Aufschreibsysteme. 1800–1900*, Munich 2003, p. 314.

[505] Bernhard Siegert, Kulturtechnik, in: Harun Maye/Leander Scholz (Eds.), *Einführung in die Kulturwissenschaft*, Munich 2011, pp. 95 ff., 98: 'Media become describable as a cultural technique when the chains of action, in which they are integrated, which they configure, or which they constitutively produce, are reconstructed'. Although there is a clear difference between script, writing and reading, media become a cultural technique when they become the enabling condition of writing, reading and communicating.

[506] The characterisation of postindustrial society is always conceptualised in counterpoint to the industrial society that preceded it. In postindustrial society, labour and capital resources are replaced by knowledge and information as the main sources of economic value creation. See Alain Touraine, *Die postindustrielle Gesellschaft*, Frankfurt am Main 1972, p. 7; Daniel Bell, *Die nachindustrielle Gesellschaft*, Frankfurt am Main 1975, p. 112: 'The concept of "postindustrial society" emphasises the centrality of theoretical knowledge as the axis around which new technologies, economic growth, and the stratification of society are organised.'

[507] On the tension between nationalism and internationalism from the perspective of legal history, see Michael Stolleis, *Der lange Abschied vom 19. Jahrhundert. Die Zäsur von 1914 aus rechtshistorischer Perspektive*, Berlin 1997, p. 10 ff; Michael Stolleis, *Nationalität und Internationalität* (fn. 367), p. 23 ff; Michael Stolleis, *Geschichte des öffentlichen Rechts in Deutschland*, vol. 3 (fn. 293), p. 41 f.

[508] Michael Zürn, Global Governance, in: Gunnar Schuppert (Ed.) *Governance-Forschung. Vergewisserung über den Stand und Entwicklungslinien*, Baden-Baden 2006, p. 121 ff; Maria Behrens/ Alexander Reichwein, Global Governance, in: Arthur Benz et al. (Eds.), *Handbuch Governance. Theoretische Grundlagen und empirische Anwendungsfehler*, Wiesbaden 2007, p. 311 ff. On the knowledge dimension of global governance, see Helmut Willke, *Global Governance*, Bielefeld 2006, p. 74 ff.

[509] Leibfried/Zürn, *Reconfiguring the National Constellation* (fn. 246), p. 17: 'Our working hypotheses assume, firstly, that *important* shifts are taking place in the different dimensions of the modern state, i.e. we are in an age of transformation that began in the 1970.' 'International institutions are the primary response to the denationalization of the problematic situation. Never before has the number of international institutions been as large as it is today, and never before have international institutions intervened so deeply in social transaction as they do today.' Michael Zürn, On the Characteristics of Postnational Politics, in Markus Jachtenfuchs/Michèle Knodt (Eds.) *Governing in International Institutions*, Opladen 2002, p. 230.

[510] Arthur Nussbaum, *Geschichte des Völkerrechts*, Munich 1960, p. 224: 'The emergence of multilateral, law-setting, open-ended treaties serving organizational goals as well as the new type of international "conferences" were characteristic symptoms of a deep structural change in international law'; Vec, *Recht und Normierung in der industriellen Revolution* (fn. 476), p. 107: 'The real increase and functional change of international law treaties in the course of the nineteenth century have so far only been explored in rudimentary form by modern international law history'.

[511] Bardo Fassbender, Heinrich Triepel und die Anfänge der dualistischen Sicht von 'Völkerrecht und Landesrecht' im späten 19, in: Lukas Gschwend et al. (Eds.), *Recht im digitalen Zeitalter. Festgabe Schweiserischer Juristentag 2015*, pp. 463–464. 'With trade treaties, treaties on shipping and railroads, postal and telegraph services, mutual legal assistance and extradition, freedom of movement and settlement, new matters were made the subject of international law regulation. Particularly fundamental agreements were identified as "law-making treaties" that fulfilled a "legislative" function at the international level. In the late nineteenth century, standardisation intensified in a first wave of what we now call globalisation. Enabled and driven by new technology, international communication, migration, and international trade multiplied and accelerated. This gave rise to a need for regulation that was satisfied by intensified international lawmaking.' Klaus Dicke, *International Law Policy and International Lawmaking. Grundlagen – Verfahren – Entwicklungstendenzen*, ZG 3 (1988), p. 193 ff.

[512] '[The administrative agreement] is one of the specific means by which industrial-bureaucratic society has for more than 150 years created for itself, across national borders, the law assigned to it, what Lorenz von Stein called international administrative law.' Hartwig Bülck, Internationale Verwaltungsgemeinschaften, in: Karl Strupp/Hans-Jürgen Schlochauer (Eds.), *Wörterbuch des Völkerrechts*, vol. 3, 2nd ed., Berlin 1962, p. 560 ff, here p. 562.

[513] For the significance of this form of treaty for the present, see Georg Dahm/Jost Delbrück/Rüdiger Wolfrum, *Völkerrecht, Vol. I: Die Grundlagen; Die Völkerrechtssubjekte*, 2nd edition, Berlin 1989, p. 50 ff.

[514] Vec, *Recht und Normierung in der Industriellen Revolution* (fn. 476), p. 134.

[515] John Dugard, Diplomatic Protection, in: J. Crawford/A. Pellet/S. Olleson (Eds.), *The Law of International Responsibility*, Oxford 2010, p. 1051 ff.

[516] Sebastian Kneisel, *Schiedsgerichtsbarkeit in Internationalen Verwaltungsunionen (1874–1914)*, Baden-Baden 2009, p. 67 ff.

[517] Koselleck does not find any evidence that alliances of a technical and economic nature existed before 1800. Reinhart Koselleck, Art. 'Bund, Bündnisse, Föderalismus, Bundesstaat', in: Otto Brunner/Werner Conze/Reinhart Koselleck (Eds.) *Geschichtliche Grundbegriffe. Historisches Wörterbuch zur politisch-sozialen Sprache*, vol. I, Stuttgart 1972, p. 582 ff.

[518] Jürgen Osterhammel/Niels P. Peterson, *Geschichte der Globalisierung. Dimensionen, Prozesse, Epochen*, Munich 2003, p. 74.

[519] Martti Koskenniemi, *The Gentle Civiliser of Nations. The Rise and Fall of International Law 1870–1960*, Cambridge 2001, p. 4.

[520] Bodo Richter, *Völkerrecht, Außenpolitik und internationale Verwaltung bei Stein*, Hamburg 1973, p. 224 ff; Arthur Nussbaum, Lorenz von Stein on International Law and International Administration, in: Max Gerwig/August Simonius (Eds.), Festschrift für Hans Lewald, Basel 1953, pp. 555 ff, 559; Klaus Vogel, Der räumliche Anwendungsbereich der *Verwaltungsrechtsnorm. Eine Untersuchung über die Grundfragen des sog. Internationalen Verwaltungs- und Steuerrechts*, Frankfurt am Main 1965, p. 156 ff.

[521] Claus Dieter Classen, Die Entwicklung eines Internationalen Verwaltungsrechts als Aufgabe der Rechtswissenschaft, VVDStRL, 2008, p. 365 ff; Klaus Vogel, Art. 'Administrative Law, International Aspects', in: Rudolf Bernhardt. (Ed.), *Encyclopedia of Public International Law*, vol. 9, Amsterdam 1992, pp. 22 ff. On the variant meaning of the term, see Heinhard Steiger, Art. 'Völkerrecht', in: Joachim Ritter/Karlfried Gründer et al. (Eds.) *Historisches Wörterbuch der Philosophie*, vol. 11, Basel 2003, pp. 1096–1100.

[522] Fassbender, *Heinrich Triepel und die Anfänge der dualistischen Sicht von 'Völkerrecht und Landesrecht' im späten 19. Jahrhundert* (fn. 510), pp. 464 ff.

[523] Cf. Alfred Verdross/Bruno Simma, *Universelles Völkerrecht. Theorie und Praxis*, Berlin 1984, p. 915.

[524] Carl Schmitt, Abwandlung eines schlimmem Wortes von Proudhon, Staatsethik und pluralistischer Staat, 1930, in: Carl Schmitt, *Positionen und Begriffe im Kampf mit Weimar – Genf – Versailles 1923–1939* (fn. 304), pp. 133 ff, here p. 143.

[525] Vec, *Kurze Geschichte des Technikrechts* (fn. 425), p. 47.

[526] Isabella Löhr, *Die Globalisierung geistiger Eigentumsrechte. Neue Strukturen internationaler Zusammenarbeit 1886–1952*, Göttingen 2010, p. 67 f.

[527] Dommann, *Autoren und Apparate* (fn. 496), p. 299.

[528] Dommann, ibid, p. 301 f. The account of the interaction between hardware and container providers in the formative stages of the European and American music industries, and their mobilisation of particular industrial and trade interests of the actors involved in the process of international lawmaking demonstrates the strength of Dommann's book.

[529] 'In the most important areas of social activity with a cross-border character, administrative unions were established to harmonise or recognise nation-state regulations. The organizational structure of the unions, which became more and more solidified over time, was largely homogeneous: the Conference of States acted as the main body, responsible for fundamental political decisions, and was supported in the technical field by conferences of delegates with more closely spaced meetings. Furthermore, there were international offices (secretariats) to handle the day-to-day administrative work, whose independence was partly ensured by their localization in neutral states (Switzerland, Belgium).' Christian Tietje, *Internationalisiertes Verwaltungshandeln*, Berlin 2001, p. 129.

[530] Vec, *Recht und Normierung in der industriellen Revolution* (fn. 476), p. 107 ff.

[531] Roland Wenzlhuemer, The History of Standardization in Europe. Europäische Geschichte Online, 03.12.2010, p. 5: 'Therefore, Scientists were among the chief lobbyists for standardization in the late eighteenth and the nineteenth century.'

[532] Miloš Vec, *Weltverträge für Weltliteratur* (fn. 483), p. 109: 'For this area of protection, the problems in the transnational handling of printed matter were the forerunner, which in turn became internationalised in their dissemination, so that one could formulate with some brevity that world treaties for world literature were concluded here.'

[533] In the general international literature of the time, no special attention was paid to these unions in most cases. One of the few authors who drew attention to this development at that time was Georg Jellinek. He made it clear that without this form of organisation, the growing interaction between different sectors of global society would have been unthinkable. See Anne Peters/Simone Peter, International Organizations: Between Technocracy and Democracy, in: B. Fassbender/A. Peters (Eds.), *The Oxford Handbook of the History of International Law*, Oxford 2012, pp. 170 ff, 175: 'In any case, we are at the beginning of an epoch of international administrative alliances which will put a new stamp on the intercourse of the civilised world'; Georg Jellinek, *Die Lehre von den Staatenverbindungen* (1882), Aalen 1969, p. 111.

[534] Löhr, *Die Globalisierung geistiger Eigentumsrechte* (fn. 525), p. 266.

[535] Ogle, *The Global Transformation of Time* (fn. 166), p. 177 f. Classic contribution in this regard, Edward P. Thompson, Time, Work-Discipline, and Industrial Capitalism, *Past & Present* 38 (1967), p. 56 ff.

[536] Ian R. Bartky, The Adoption of Standard Time, *Technology and Culture* Vol. 30/1 (Jan. 1989), pp. 25–56 ff.; Wenzlhuemer, *The History of Standardization in Europe* (fn. 530), p. 18: 'As trains of

different companies had to be coordinated and timetables had to be harmonised whenever possible, other railway companies followed suit. Due to the rising importance of railway transport and travel, many towns in the railway network adjusted their local time to "railway time" – and, thereby, to GMT – and by 1855, 98% of all public clocks in Britain were already set to GMT. The successful laying of the transatlantic telegraph cable in 1866 brought the United States of America and Europe into almost immediate contact (and, for instance, intimately linked the stock exchanges in New York and London), thus necessitating the synchronization of time at both ends of the wire.'

[537] Albrecht Weber, *Geschichte der internationalen Wirtschaftsorganisationen*, Wiesbaden 1983, p. 39.

[538] Petra Buck-Heeb, *Geistiges Eigentum und Völkerrecht – Contributions of International Law to the Further Development of the Protection of Intellectual Property*, Berlin 1994, p. 108 ff.

[539] Löhr, *Die Globalisierung geistiger Eigentumsrechte* (fn. 525), p. 63 ff.; James Foreman-Peck, The Emergence and Growth of International Organizations, in: Richard H. Tilly/Paul J. J. Welfens (Eds.), *Economic Globalization, International Organizations and Crisis Management. Contemporary and Historical Perspectives on Growth, Impact and Evolution of Major Organizations in an Interdependent World*, Berlin et al. 2000, p. 73 ff.

[540] Buck-Heeb, *Geistiges Eigentum und Völkerrecht* (fn. 537), p. 73 ff.

[541] Buck-Heeb, ibid., p. 53 ff.

[542] Ernst Brem, Das Verhältnis der Berner Übereinkunft zu anderen völkerrechtlichen Verträgen, in: Schweiserische Vereinigung für Urheberrecht (ed.), *Die Berner Übereinkunft und die Schweiz. Schweiserische Festschrift zum einhundertjährigen Bestehen der Berner Übereinkunft zum Schutze von Werken der Literatur und Kunst*, Bern 1986, p. 99 ff.

[543] Madeleine Herren-Oesch, *Hintertüren zur Macht. Internationalisierung und modernisierungsorientierte Außenpolitik in Belgien, der Schweiz und den USA 1865-1914*, Munich 2000, p. 11 ff.

[544] 'The aim of this International Administrative Union was thus not the unification of legislation, but rather the approximation of standards for the protection of intellectual property, which could also be regulated by administrative regulations.' Kneisel, *Arbitration in International Administrative Unions* (fn. 515), p. 56.

[545] Craig N. Murphy, *International Organization and Industrial Change. Global Governance since 1850*, Cambridge 1994.

[546] Armin von Bogdandy/Ingo Venzke, *In wessen Namen?: Internationale Gerichte in Zeiten globalen Regierens*, Berlin 2014, p. 107.

[547] von Bogdandy/Venzke, ibid., p. 108.

CHAPTER 6

THE LAW OF PLATFORMS

[548] Luhmann, *Die Gesellschaft der Gesellschaft* (fn. 36), p. 826. Elena Esposito, *Social Forgetting. Forms and Media of the Memory of Society*. Frankfurt am Main 2002, p. 364: 'And when machines are used as communication media, a network of virtually simultaneous operations and events emerges that are mutually interdependent because they are simultaneous but cannot be causally controlled'.

[549] That was the subject of Chapter 1.

[550] That was the subject of Chapter 3.

[551] Thomas Vesting, *Die Medien des Rechts, Vol. 4: Computernetzwerke*, Weilerswist 2015, p. 12 ff.

[552] Oliver Stengel/Alexander van Looy/Stephan Wallaschkowski (Eds.), Digitalzeitalter – Digitalgesellschaft. Das Ende des Industriezeitalters und der Beginn einer neuen Epoche, Wiesbaden 2017.

[553] Aleida Assmann, *Einführung in die Kulturwissenschaft. Grundbegriffe, Themen, Fragestellungen*. 4th ed., Cologne 2011, p. 59; Vesting, *Die Medien des Rechts*, vol. 4 (fn. 550), p. 50.

[554] It is not just the respective sensations of privacy, politics, friendship, etc that change through the new transparency and contact possibilities provided by the Internet. Even the physical body as corporeality experiences a change of meaning through virtual reality, which becomes a reality of life. See Christiane Funken, Der Körper im Internet, in: Markus Schroer (Ed.), *Sociology of the Body*, Frankfurt am Main 2005, p. 215 ff.

[555] Michael Mahoney, The Histories of Computing(s), *Interdisciplinary Science Reviews* 30 (2005), p. 119 ff.; Michael Mahoney, *The Histories of Computing*, Cambridge 2011. David Gugerli varies Mahoney and says that what happened is a real move of the world into its digital reality. See David Gugerli, *How the World Came into the Computer. Zur Entstehung digitaler Wirklichkeit*, Frankfurt am Main 2018, p. 16.

[556] Koselleck, Vergangene Zukunft (fn. 179), p. 359. As early as 1965, Joachim Ritter used the formula 'Divorcing origin and future', see Ritter, *Hegel und die Französische Revolution* (fn. 169), p. 45.

[557] It is not a historical caesura consisting of various visible incisions or distinctive points within a historical continuum, i.e. historical events, such as the October Revolution in 1917 or the end of World War I in 1918, the turnaround in the GDR in 1989, the end of World War II in 1945, the French Revolution (1789–1799), and so on. The epochal caesura concept mentioned here aims, on the one hand, to avoid the periodisation problem and, on the other hand, to refer to the medial injection of more social complexity and relations, which at first seems counterintuitive in the transition of organisations and their inherent technologies to the digital. Frank Bösch, Upheavals into the Present. Global Events and Crisis Responses around 1979, *Zeithistorische Forschungen/Studies in Contemporary History* 9 (2012), no. 1, p. 8 ff. On the change in the understanding of time in modern times, see Rüdiger Graf, Zeit und Zeitkonzeptionen in der Zeitgeschichte, version 2.0, in Docupedia Zeitgeschichte, online at http://docupedia.de/zg/Zeit_und_Zeitkonzeptionen_Version_2.0_R. C3.BCdiger_Graf?oldid=84945.

[558] Thomas Vesting, *Die Medien des Rechts*, vol. 3: Buchdruck, Weilerswist 2012, p. 167. It is 'precisely the recognition of the impersonal and objective as a precondition of the form of subjectivity that is at stake in the culture of printing'. At this point, the culture of printing differs from the culture of the digital. It is not a matter of consolidating the impersonal and objective, which thoroughly connected with a kind of advance performance of the organizations. Instead, in the culture of the digital, the personal and the subjective are added back to the social. This change is reflected in the form of public representation by the current crisis of political parties (organizations) and also, for example, by the emergence of a flat-earth movement as a new form of deobjectification (and detachment from science) caused by the disposability of a new medium, the digital, which offers the possibility of making social knowledge (or social ignorance) to be disseminated at high speed, almost indefinitely, and at low cost, leading to a massive decentralization of knowledge production, which until then had been essentially the preserve of organizations (universities, research centers, journal publications, and large media organizations). With the increase in communication possibilities between lay people via online platforms, there is now also the possibility of producing knowledge that is decoupled from the scientific base, with serious social implications. The generation of artificial "opinion waves" via bots is also emerging in the new digital context. On this, see Alexander Roßnagel/Lena Isabell Löber, Kennzeichnung von Social Bots – Transparenzpflichten zum Schutz integrer Kommunikation, MMR 21/8 (2019), p. 493 et seq.

[559] On economics and consumer law, see Ariel Ezrachi/Maurice E. Stucke, *Virtual Competition. The Promise and Perils of the Algorithm-Driven Economy*, Cambridge (Mass.) 2016.

[560] Felix Stalder, *Kultur der Digitalität*, Berlin 2016.

[561] Jacques Le Goff, Zeit der Kirche und Zeit des Händlers im Mittelalter, in: Claudia Honegger et al. (Eds.), *Scripture and the Matter of History. Proposals for the Systematic Appropriation of Historical Processes*, Frankfurt am Main 1977, p. 393 ff; Lucian Hölscher, *The Discovery of the Future*, Frankfurt am Main 1999; Zachary Schiffmann, *The Birth of the Past*, Baltimore 2011, Achim Landwehr, *Geburt der Gegenwart. Eine Geschichte der Zeit im 17*, Frankfurt am Main 2014.

[562] 'Accordingly, personal memory, including artificially trained memory, loses its position at the bottleneck of the transmission of culture, and mnemosyne is deleted from the genealogy of the muses.' Luhmann, *Die Wissenschaft der Gesellschaft* (fn. 29), p. 605 f.

[563] Niklas Luhmann, *Gesellschaftliche Struktur und semantische Tradition* (fn. 163), p. 49: 'The transitional period is certainly very long. It begins, for instance, in the operation of law or in monasteries, long before the modern era begins, and here it produces functionally specific terminologies which, as a kind of intellectual preparation, as "preadaptive advances," facilitate later generalizations and reformulations.'

[564] The problem of systems theory in dealing with knowledge lies in how to assign knowledge within the theory's construction. Knowledge is described as the 'overall result of structural couplings of the social system', i.e., it lies within the 'feature of social autopoiesis' as something that emerges from the 'resonance to structural coupling of the social system'. See Luhmann, *Die Wissenschaft der*

Gesellschaft (fn. 29), p. 122 ff. Everything that does not fit into the theory plan cannot be observed by the theory.

[565] Luhmann, *Soziologie des Risikos* (fn. 158), p. 78 ff.

[566] Luhmann, ibid, p. 57.

[567] This era of the digital has various facets. The most important, which is clearly expressed in the everyday world, is called the 'sharing economy', 'platform revolution', 'gig economy', and 'disruptive innovation', among others. This concrete increase in platform-centred technology has transformed people's lives and institutions in the most mundane form of their experiences. To cite just a few examples: as patients, people increasingly avoid looking at books or waiting for a consultation to learn about their conditions. Experiences are shared on the PatientsLikeMe platform. To have personal intimate relationships, people no longer meet randomly in nightclubs, but first on Tinder. The old public, which was tied to newspapers and television (large organisations), is migrating to Twitter, Facebook and WhatsApp groups.

[568] For the positive impact of platforms on society, cf. Geoffrey Parker/Marshall W. Van Alstyne/Sangeet P. Choudary, *Platform Revolution: How Networked Markets are Transforming the Economy – and How to Make them Work for You*, New York 2016; Arun Sundararajan, *The Sharing Economy: The End of Employment and the Rise of Crowd-Based Capitalism*, Cambridge 2016. Enthusiastic expressions are also made about the impacts of new technologies on democratic participation in Daniele Archibugi/Andrea Filippetti/Marion Frenz, The Impact of the Economic Crises on Innovation. Evidence from Europe, *Technological Forecasting and Social Change* 80/7 (2013), p. 1673 ff.; Philippe Aigrain, *Sharing: Culture and the Economy in the Internet Age*, Amsterdam 2012.

[569] Hans Blumenberg, *Die Legitimität der Neuzeit*, Frankfurt am Main 1988, p. 545: '[t]he epochal turn ... an imperceptible time, not evidently bound to any concise date or event. But in a differential consideration a threshold marks itself, which can be determined as either not yet reached or already crossed'.

[570] Elizabeth Brient, Epochenschwelle, in: Daniel Weidner/Robert Buch (Eds.), *Blumenberg lesen. Ein Glossar*, Berlin 2014, p. 72 ff.

[571] Blumenberg, *Die Legitimität der Neuzeit* (fn. 568), p. 545.

[572] For his epochal threshold studies, Hans Blumenberg has sought out two witnesses who are linked by both continuity and difference: Nicholas of Cues (1401–1464) and Giordano Bruno (1548-1600). The two thinkers transferred the traditionally theological attribute of God's infinity to the universe. Blumenberg, ibid., p. 555 ff.

[573] In order to examine the thresholds located in the indifference zone of organisations and platform societies, it is necessary to trace the change in the social basis of experience. There are several perspectives to draw on at this point that represent the indeterminacy of the transitions addressed here: for example, those of economists Fritz Machlup (1940–1983) and Edward Bernay (1891–1995). These are two scholars who reflect on this threshold between organisation and platform economy in terms of the information, knowledge, or network society. Fritz Machlup, in the context of his research on the patent system, notes that a new kind of economy has emerged with the growth of government agencies, development institutions, corporate laboratories, universities, and media sectors since Roosevelt's New Deal. Reflecting on the emergence of a (new) economy based predominantly on the generation, exchange and application of abstract and codified knowledge, he coined the term 'knowledge economy'. At the same time, Edward Bernay, Sigmund Freud's nephew, 'discovered' the concept of market research that resulted from merging ideas about unconscious drives with sociological methods of opinion polling. In this context, communication, which used to be used purely to convey information, became a strategic field in which politics and economics also had to adapt to the new logic. This contributed to the emergence of a new media industry, based on the (analogue) collection of data and targeted (analogue) applications. For an empirical and detailed study of economic change in the 1960s in the U.S., see Fritz Machlup, *The Production and Distribution of Knowledge in the United States*, Princeton 1962; Fritz Machlup, *The Political Economy of Monopoly. Business, Labor and Government Policies*, Baltimore 1952; James Beniger, *The Control Revolution: Technological and Economic Origins of the Information Society*, Cambridge (Mass.) 1986, p. 350.

[574] Yochai Benkler, *The Wealth of Networks. How Social Production Transforms Markets and Freedom*, New Haven/London 2006, p. 3 ff.

[575] Manuel Castells, *The Rise of the Network Society*, 2nd ed., Oxford 2010. For jurisprudence, see Karl-Heinz Ladeur, *Der Staat der 'Gesellschaft der Netzwerke'*. On the further development of the paradigm of the 'guarantee state', in Thomas Vesting/Ino Augsberg (Eds.), *Ladeur. Das*

Recht der Netzwerkgesellschaft, Tübingen 2013, p. 353 ff; Vesting, *Die Medien des Rechts*, vol. 4 (fn. 550). For private law, see Gunther Teubner, *Netzwerk als Vertragsverbund: Virtuelle Unternehmen, Franchising, Just-in-time in sozialwissenschaftlicher und juristischer Sicht*, Baden-Baden 2004.

[576] The most commonly cited anti-network theory comes from Richard Buxbaum: 'network is not a legal concept'. Indeed, 'network' is not a legal concept. But that says nothing about its theoretical or dogmatic processing. On the contrary, all legal concepts are concepts of other provenance – be it from medicine, like 'constitution', be it from biology, like 'organism' in the nineteenth-century discussion of constitutional law, or concepts from theology, as Carl Schmitt has repeatedly emphasised – as a *terminus technicus*, 'network' is like all other legal concepts: in the end, it is not the law itself that decides, but a complex social translation process that is actually decentralised. See Richard Buxbaum, Is Network a Legal Concept?, JITE 149/4 (1993), p. 698 ff.

[577] Cf. Sebastian Gießmann, *Die Verbundenheit der Dinge. Eine Kulturgeschichte der Netze und Netzwerke*, Berlin 2014; Bernhard Siegert, *Passage des Digitalen. Zeichenpraktiken der neuzeitlichen Wissenschaften 1500-1900*, Berlin 2003; Joseph Vogl (Ed.), *Poetologien des Wissens um 1800*, Munich 1999.

[578] See Albert-László Barabási, *Linked: How Everything Is Connected to Everything Else and What It Means for Business, Science, and Everyday Life*, New York 2014. Barabási points out that the nodes and nodal points of networks are the greatest strength and also greatest weakness of the network. Because of the diverse and decentralised nature of a network, it can easily respond to changes in its environment. Networks have a high tolerance for change and internal errors.

[579] Andreas Wald/Dorothea Jansen, Netzwerke, in: Arthur Benz et al. (Eds.), *Handbuch Governance* (fn. 507), p. 93 ff.

[580] Koschorke, *Die Grenzen des Systems und die Rhetorik der Systemtheorie* (fn. 38), p. 50.

[581] For media law, see Karl-Heinz Ladeur/Tobias Gostomzyk, *Das Medienrecht und die Herausforderung der technologischen Hybridisierung, Kommunikation und Recht* 2018, p. 686 ff; see also Möllers, *Die Möglichkeit der Normen* (fn. 5), p. 440 ff.

[582] In Ladeur's work, this is primarily addressed through the explanation of a veiling between the normative and the cognitive. Cf. Karl-Heinz Ladeur, The Postmodern Condition of Law and Societal 'Management of Rules'. Facts and Norms Revised, *Zeitschrift für Rechtssoziologie* 27 (2006), p. 87 ff: 'The intrinsic complexity of the "semantic artifacts" with which the system carries out its descriptions of itself and others, as well as interpretation, necessarily contains far more complex entanglements than the term "second-order observation/description" is identified with'; *id.*, *Postmodern Legal Theory. Selbstreferenz – Selbstorganisation – Prozeduralisierung*, Berlin 1995, p. 162. In this respect also Thomas Vesting, *Die Medien des Rechts*, vol. 1: Sprache, Weilerswist 2011, p. 67 ff. For a critique of functional differentiation and the normative phenomena therein in the field of economics, see Jens Beckert, Die sittliche Einbettung der Wirtschaft. From Efficiency and Differentiation Theory to a Theory of Economic Fields, *Berliner Journal für Soziologie* 22 (2012), p. 247 ff.

[583] Ladeur, *Negative Freiheitsrechte und gesellschaftliche Selbstorganisation* (fn. 3), p. 275 et seq.; *Der Staat gegen die Gesellschaft. Zur Verteidigung der Rationalität der 'Privatrechtsgesellschaft'*, Tübingen 2006, p. 296 ff.

[584] The classic distinction that the network concept seeks to break with is the distinction between organisation and market. The dissolution of this distinction occurs through the practice of relational contracts. Cf. Walter Powell, Neither Market Nor Hierarchy, *Research in Organizational Behavior* 12 (1990), p. 295 ff. On the garage logic of Internet law, see Karl-Heinz Ladeur, 'Rechte gegen Rechte' – Kann diese Konfrontation dem Prozessieren des Rechts gerecht werden?, in: Ino Augsberg/Steffen Augsberg/Ludger Heidbrink (Eds.), *Recht auf Nicht-Recht. Rechtliche Reaktionen auf die Juridifizierung der Gesellschaft*, Weilerswist 2020, p. 211 ff. 'Much today is simply "done" ("l'âge du faire"), and only ex post, with the help of lawyers, is a legal construction of the process asked for': ibid, p. 232. On relational contracts, see Thomas Vesting, Einbau von Zeit. Rechtsnormativität im relationalen Vertrag, KJ 52 (2019), p. 626 ff. 'In the new contract models of the high-tech industry, unwritten informal mechanisms play an important role in the interaction between the parties (in contrast to the formal and judicially enforceable contract). These contracts are often referred to as "relational contracts," but the terminology is not uniform': ibid, p. 632.

[585] Cf. Thomas Vesting, Die Staatsrechtslehre und die Veränderung ihres Gegenstandes: Consequences of Europeanization and Internationalization, VVDStRL 63 (2004), p. 41 ff; Karl-Heinz Ladeur, A Law of Networks for the World Society or Constitutionalization of the Community of Nations?, *International Law Archive*, 49/3 (September 2011), p. 246 ff; Udo Di Fabio, *Das Recht*

offener Staaten, Tübingen 1998; *id. Der Verfassungsstaat in der Weltgesellschaft*, Tübingen 2001. 'The name of the great paradoxifier is neither "Jacques Derrida" nor "Niklas Luhmann". Its name is "globalization". The recurrent doubts about law's hierarchy so easily silenced in the nation-states' past can be silenced no more. They explode in the face of the "statelessness" of *lex mercatoria* and other practices that produce global laws without the state. It is globalization of law that is killing the sovereign-father and making the legal paradox visible': Gunther Teubner, The King's Many Bodies: The Self-Deconstruction of Law's Hierarchy, *Law & Society Review* 31/4 (1997), pp. 763 ff, here p. 769.

[586] On territoriality Saskia Sassen, *Territory, Authority, Rights. From Medieval to Global Assemblages*, Princeton 2008.

[587] On the overreaching of state regulators with respect to private emergent regimes, see Calliess/Zumbansen, *Rough Consensus and Running Code* (fn. 79), esp. p. 109.

[588] Ino Augsberg, *Das Gespinst des Rechts*, Rechtstheorie 38 (2007), p. 479 ff, (480); Jean N. Druey, Das Recht als Netz für Netzwerke. A road sketch, KritV 89 (2006), p. 163 ff. Ino Augsberg argues for a shift in the meaning of the concept of network to a non-hierarchical concept based on the metaphor of the rhizome. On this, see Augsberg, *Schmitt-Lektüren* (fn. 251), p. 37 ff.

[589] Alexandra Kemmerer, Der normative Knoten. Über Recht und Politik im Netz der Netzwerke, in: Sigrid Boysen et al. (Eds.), *Netzwerke*, Baden-Baden 2007, p. 195 ff, here p. 221: 'At nodes, approaches to action and questions of responsibility and attribution of legal design are open. This is where a "normative recalibration" of the network can start, which does justice to the "stubbornness" of law."' On nodes as basic elements of the network from a cultural theory perspective, see Hartmut Böhme, Introduction: Networks. On the Theory and History of a Construction, in: Jürgen Barkhoff/Hartmut Böhme/Jeanne Riou (Eds.), *Netzwerke. Eine Kulturtechnik der Moderne*, Cologne 2004, p. 17 ff.

[590] Christoph Möllers, Netzwerk als Kategorie des Organisationsrechts. Zur juristischen Beschreibung dezentraler Steuerung, in: Janbernd Oebbecke (Ed.), *Nicht-Normative Steuerung in dezentralen Systemen*, Berlin 2005, p. 285 ff. Already early Karl-Heinz Ladeur, Von der Verwaltungshierarchie zum administrativen Netzwerk?, *Die Verwaltung* 26 (1993), p. 137 ff.

[591] Teubner, *Netzwerk als Vertragsverbund* (fn. 574), p. 204 ff.

[592] Lars Viellechner, *Transnationalisierung des Rechts*, Weilerswist 2013.

[593] On a supposed tendential metamorphosis of constitutional law teachers into 'cosmopolitan network experts', see Josef Isensee, *Diskussionsbeitrag*, VVDStRL 63 (2004), p. 91 ff; Matthias Ruffert, *Diskussionsbeitrag*, VVDStRL vol. 63 (2004), p. 90.

[594] Janet Abbate, *Inventing the Internet*, Cambridge 1999; Michael Friedewald, Vom Experimentierfeld zum Massenmedium: Gestaltende Kräfte in der Entwicklung des Internets, *Technikgeschichte* 67/4 (2000), p. 331 ff. The technical infrastructure of the Internet is the main pillar of its functionality, and the protocols are its operating system. Some of the major protocols that support the Internet are Internet Protocol (IP), Transmission Control Protocol (TCP), User Datagram Protocol (UDP), Hypertext Transfer Protocol (HTTP), Simple Mail Transfer Protocol (SMTP), File Transfer Protocol (FTP), and Domain Name System (DNS). David Yates, *Turing's Legacy: A History of Computing at the National Physical Laboratory 1945–1995*, London 1997, pp. 126–146.

[595] Martin Campbell-Kelly, Data Communications at the National Physical Laboratory (1965–1975), IEEE Annals of the History of Computing, 9/3–4 (July-Sept 1987), p. 221 ff.

[596] Tim Berners-Lee, Long Live the Web, in: Tilman Baumgärtel (Ed.), *Texte zur Theorie des Internets*, Stuttgart 2020, p. 74 ff, 83 'Manufacturers can improve refrigerators and printers without changing the way electricity works, and utilities can improve the power grid without changing the way appliances work. The two levels of technology work together but can evolve independently. The same is true for the Web and the Internet. Separating the layers is critical to innovation'.

[597] José van Dijck, *The Culture of Connectivity. A Critical History of Social Media*. Oxford 2013, p. 5 'Until the turn of the millennium, networked media were mostly generic services that you could join or actively utilise to build groups, but the service itself would not automatically connect you to others. With the advent of Web 2.0, shortly after the turn of the millennium, online services shifted from offering channels for networked communication to becoming interactive, two-way vehicles of networked sociality.'

[598] David S. Evans/Andrei Hagiu/Richard Schmalensee, *Invisible Engines: How Software Platforms Drive Innovation and Transform Industries*, Cambridge 2006; Parker/Van Alstyne//Choudary, *Platform Revolution* (fn. 567); Mark de Reuver/Carsten Sørensen/Rahul C. Basole, The Digital Platform: A Research Agenda, *Journal of Information Technology* 33/2 (2018), p. 124 ff.

[599] Julie E. Cohen, *Law for the Platform Economy*, U.C. Davis L. Rev. 15 (2017), pp. 133, 143: '... platforms are not the same as networks, nor are they simply infrastructures ... For most practical purposes, however, the "network of networks" is becoming a network of platforms; Internet access and use are intermediated from beginning to end'.

[600] Nick Couldry/Andreas Hepp, *The Mediated Construction of Reality*, Cambridge 2017, p. 139.

[601] Couldry/Hepp, ibid.

[602] Sebastian Gießmann, *Netze und Netzwerke. Archäologie einer Kulturtechnik, 1740–1840*, Bielefeld 2006, p. 14.

[603] Tarleton Gillespie, The Politics of 'Platforms', *New Media & Society* 12/3 (2010), p. 347 ff.

[604] Dal Yong Jin, The Construction of Platform Imperialism in the Globalization, *Journal for a Global Sustainable Information Society* 11/1 (2013), p. 145 ff.; Christian Fuchs, New Imperialism: Information and Media Imperialism, *Global Media and Communication* 6/1 (2010), p. 33 ff.

[605] Jean Rochet and Jean Tirole, for example, emphasise the creative side of digital platforms. For them, platforms are surfaces for technical innovation on which new players can develop additional services or products; in many ways, they are utilities that generate new social functions and business opportunities; and in economic terms, they are so-called '*multisided markets*'. Jean C. Rochet/Jean Tirole, Platform Competition in Two-Sided Markets, *Journal of the European Economic Association* 1/4 (2003), p. 990 ff; Jean C. Rochet, Two-Sided Markets: A Progress Report, *RAND Journal of Economics* 35 (2006), p. 645 ff.

[606] Cf. Gugerli, *Wie die Welt in den Computer kam* (fn. 554).

[607] Maria Eriksson et al. also argue in this sense for the duality and ambivalence of digital platforms: 'platform affordances simultaneously allow and constrain expressions'. See Maria Eriksson/Rasmus Fleischer/Anna Johansson/Pelle Snickars/Patrick Vonderau, *Spotify Teardown: Inside the Black Box of Streaming Music*, Cambridge (Mass.) 2019.

[608] Anne Holmond, The Platformization of the Web: Making Web Data Platform Ready, *Social Media + Society* July-December 2015, p. 1 ff.

[609] Even recent authors confirm the view that the technological and transnational conditions of the new business model of digital platforms present themselves as a barrier to the semantics of traditional law. Gillespie, *The Politics of 'Platforms'* (fn. 602), p. 358 f.; see also Jonas A. Schwarz, Platform Logic: An Interdisciplinary Approach to the Platform-Based Economy, Pol'y & Int. Aug. 3 (2017), p. 4 ff; Cohen, *Law for the Platform Economy* (fn. 598), p. 144 f.

[610] Holmond, *The Platformization of the Web* (fn. 607).

[611] Alessandro Roncaglia, *Petty: The Origins of Political Economy*, New York 1985, p. 118. On the concept of the ancient European economy of the whole house as a landed aristocratic society or large peasant farm in contrast to the modern urban economic order, see Otto Brunner, *Land und Herrschaft. Grundfragen der territorialen Verfassungsgeschichte Südostdeutschlands im Mittelalter*, Darmstadt 1990.

[612] Jean-Jacques Rousseau, *Politische Ökonomie*, Frankfurt am Main 1977.

[613] Joseph A. Schumpeter/Elizabeth B. Schumpeter (Eds.), *Geschichte der ökonomischen Analyse*. First Partial Volume. Göttingen 1965, p. 73.

[614] For Max Weber, see Wolfgang Schluchter, *Die Entstehung des modernen Rationalismus. Eine Analyse von Max Weber's Entwicklungsgeschichte des Occzidents*, Frankfurt am Main 1998, p. 13.

[615] Karl Marx, *Zur Kritik der politischen Ökonomie*, in: Karl Marx/Friedrich Engels (fn. 401).

[616] Hont, *Jealousy of Trade* (fn 398), p. 9.

[617] Cary Nederman/Guillaume Bogiaris, Niccolò Machiavelli, in: Daniel M. Robinson/Chad Meister/Charles Taliaferro (Eds.), *The History of Evil in the Early Modern Age: 1450–1700 CE*, London 2018, p. 53 ff.; Peter Schröder, *Niccolò Machiavelli*, Frankfurt 2004, p. 44.

[618] Hont, *Jealousy of Trade* (fn. 398), p. 8 ff. David Hume noted in his notebook, visibly surprised, that although his city of Florence was created and kept alive by trade, the word 'trade' does not even appear in his writings. See Ernest C. Mossner, Hume's Early Memoranda, 1729–1740: The Complete Text, *Journal of the History of Ideas* 9/4 (1948), p. 508: 'There is not a Word of Trade in all Machiavel, which is strange considering that Florence rose only by Trade'.

[619] This is the subject of Chapter 2.

[620] Osterhammel, *Die Verwandlung der Welt* (fn. 262), p. 235. 'No other epoch in history has been an age of mass long-distance migration to the same extent as the 19th century. Between 1815 and 1914, at least 82 million people *voluntarily* traveled across borders.'

[621] Trentmann, *The Empire of Things* (fn. 280), p. 165. On the circulation of ideas see Bayly, *The Birth of the Modern World* (fn. 281).

[622] Istvan Hont, *Politics in Commercial Society*. Jean-Jacques Rousseau and Adam Smith, Cambridge 2015.
[623] Trentmann, *The Empire of Things* (fn. 280), p. 107: 'The culture of politeness gave consumption an additional lift. Coffee houses and the taste of exotic beverages were just one part of an expanding universe of social spaces – from clubs and restaurants to promenades and pleasures gardens – that were simultaneously dedicated to leisurely entertainment and genteel self-fashioning. Fashionable clothes, tea sets, the latest novel and appropriate wallpaper and furnishings were vital to the polite lifestyle through which the expanding middling sort defined itself and asserted its place in a fluid, post-aristocratic society.'
[624] Trentmann, ibid., p. 101: 'Hume's project was nothing less than "a science of man," and his positive view of luxury was part of a larger appreciation of the role of objects in the making of self and civil society ... By nourishing commerce and industry, it brought them together in clubs, conversation and entertainment, all of which made them "feel an increase of humanity." "Thus," Hume concluded, "industry, knowledge, and humanity, are linked together by an indissoluble chain, and are found, from experience as well as reason, to be peculiar to the more polished, and ... more luxurious ages."'.
[625] This point is addressed in Chapter 3 using the example of intellectual property and its form of production and reproduction in relation to the knowledge generated in organisations with an impact on the adaptation of global and national law.
[626] Charles Perrow, A Society of Organizations, in Max Haller/Hans-Jürgen Hoffmann-Nowotny/Wolfgang Zapf (Eds.), *Kultur und Gesellschaft: Verhandlungen des 24. Deutschen Soziologentags, des 11. Österreichischen Soziologentags und des 8. Kongresses der Schweizerischen Gesellschaft für Soziologie in Zürich 1988*, Frankfurt am Main 1989, p. 265 ff., 269: 'These elements, which constitute the definition of the modern form of bureaucracy – centralization, hierarchy, formalization, standardization and specialization – were only gradually introduced.'
[627] 'With the upgrading of products and services to knowledge-based, professional goods, the conventional factors of production (land, chapter, labor) dramatically lose their importance vis-à-vis implicit or built-in expertise, and thus the modern capitalist economy gradually mutates into a post-capitalist, knowledge-based form of production.' Helmut Willke, *Studies in Utopian Society*, Frankfurt am Main 2001, p. 129.
[628] Viktor Mayer-Schönberger, *Big Data: A Revolution that Will Transform How We Live, Work and Think*, Boston 2013.
[629] Cohen, *Law for the Platform Economy* (fn. 598), p. 157; Danah Boyd/Kate Crawford, *Critical Questions for Big Data: Provocations for a Cultural, Technological, and Scholarly Phenomenon, Information, Communication & Society* (2012), p. 662 ff., here p. 665; Lisa Gitelman (Ed.), *'Raw Data' is an Oxymoron*, Cambridge (Mass.) 2013.
[630] Julie E. Cohen, *Between Truth and Power. The Legal Constructions of Informational Capitalism*, New York 2019, p. 37.
[631] Aleida Assmann, *Einführung in die Kulturwissenschaft. Grundbegriffe, Themen, Fragestellungen*. 4th ed., Cologne 2011.
[632] Mireille Hildebrandt, *Smart Technologies and the End(s) of Law. Novel Enlargements of Law and Technology*, Cheltenham 2015, pp. 67–61; Ian Kerr/Jessica Earle, *Prediction, Preemption, Presumption: How Big Data Threatens Big Picture Privacy*, 66 Stan. L. Rev 2013, online, pp. 65 ff., 68–71.
[633] Cohen, *Between Truth and Power* (fn. 629), p. 41 '... the "network of networks" is becoming a network of platforms; for most users, Internet access and use are intermediated from beginning to end'.
[634] Cohen, ibid., p. 40: 'Platforms represent infrastructure-based strategies for introducing frictions into networks. Those strategies both rely on and reinforce the centrality of a particular way of (re)configuring networked digital communications infrastructures for data-based surplus extraction.'
[635] Lina Khan, Amazon's Antitrust Paradox, *Yale Law Journal*, 126 (2017), p. 710 ff. David Evans/Richard Schmalensee, The Antitrust Analysis of Multi-Sided Platform Businesses, in: Roger Blair/Daniel Sokol (Eds.) *Oxford Handbook on International Antitrust Economics*, Oxford 2013.
[636] Niklas Luhmann, *Die Realität der Massenmedien*, Wiesbaden 1996, p. 9.
[637] Brewer, *The Pleasures of the Imagination* (fn. 174), p. 15 ff. 'The coffee house was the precursor of the modern office, but once you were there you were as likely to talk about matters of general interest – the latest play, sexual scandal or political quarrel – as carry on business': ibid., pp. 38–39.

[638] This is the subject of Chapter 2. On cities as 'gateways to the world', see Osterhammel, Die Verwandlung der Welt (fn. 262), p. 357.

[639] Brewer, *The Pleasures of the Imagination* (fn. 174), p. 7: 'As many foreign commentators and visitors to England recognised, the rise of the arts in England was the triumph of a commercial and urban society, not the achievement of a royal court. It was the political as well an economic condition of England – its weak monarchy, free constitution and rule of law – which helped to create literature and performing arts that aimed for a public and were organised commercially rather than being confined to a few.'

[640] On the centrality of the court, see 'Der Hof als Gesellschaftsmodell' in: Steffen Martus, *Aufklärung. The German 18th Century. Ein Epochenbild*, Berlin 2015, p. 71: 'According to the idea, the prince stood in the center on a lonely post above all others; he was surrounded by circles and fields of power that competed and coalesced with each other'.

[641] 'The increased emphasis on the right of individual subjects was a natural concomitant of the legislature's claim to absolute authority. As the legislature came to look more and more a part of the state apparatus and less and less like the representative of the people (a function it nevertheless succeeded in retaining), so political debate expanded into the public sphere. This trend, always encouraged by some members of the legislature and made possible by a national infrastructure of print, was exploited by those interest groups the state itself had largely brought into being': Brewer, *The Sinews of Power* (fn. 403), p. 247. See also on the rise of the mass press Martin Kohlrausch, Medienskandale und Monarchie. The Development of the Mass Press and 'Big Politics' in the Empire, in Jörg Requate (Ed.) *Das 19. Jahrhundert als Mediengesellschaft*, Munich 2009, p. 116 ff; the *same author*, *Der Monarch im Skandal. Die Logik der Massenmedien und die Transformation der wilhelminischen Monarchie*, Berlin 2005, p. 66: 'The monarch, court and government could not possibly ignore this development. Parallel to the media revolution described above, therefore, a profound change in the relationship of state institutions to the public took place at the turn of the 19th and 20th centuries. Although there was a long tradition of state influence on the media, government action only now had to be publicly legitimised in order to make it feasible at all in many cases.'

[642] Osterhammel, *Die Verwandlung der Welt* (fn. 262), p. 357: 'The city is of mouldering origin and at the same time the birthplace of modernity'.

[643] Jürgen Habermas, *Strukturwandel der Öffentlichkeit. Untersuchung zu einer Kategorie der bürgerlichen Gesellschaft*, Frankfurt am Main 1990, p. 69 ff.

[644] The Enlightenment societies served as media of early bourgeois culture, see Richard van Dülmen, *Die Gesellschaft der Aufklärer*, Frankfurt am Main 1986, p. 120 ff.

[645] 'Finally, society and the state became increasingly intertwined with the rise of "welfare state mass democracy" in the 20th century. The public sphere, in the sense of a critical view of the state, was displaced by *public relations*, by mass media-orchestrated pronouncements, and by the industrialised "production" and manipulation of public opinion. In the early 1960s, Habermas concluded from this that the public sphere had been "refeudalised".' Nancy Fraser, Theory of the Public Sphere. Strukturwandel der Öffentlichkeit (1961), in: Hauke Brunkhorst/Regina Kreide/Cristina Lafont (Eds.), *Habermas Handbuch*, Stuttgart 2009, p. 149.

[646] 'Certainly, this problem does not arise today primarily as a technical one. The loss of publicity within the large organizations, both state and social, and even more so the flight of publicity in their intercourse, results from the unresolved pluralism of competing interests, which in any case makes it doubtful whether a general interest can ever emerge from it in such a way that a public opinion would find its yardstick in it.' Habermas, *Strukturwandel der Öffentlichkeit* (fn. 642), p. 340. Again, it would probably be appropriate to establish better criteria for comparing the public sphere of coffee houses with the public sphere of large organisations. Intuitively, it seems that the internal dynamics and competition between organisations and technologies exhibited a greater plurality than the few spaces in salons and coffee houses that were frequented by 'mannered men'. In other words, both in the field of participation and in the field of democratisation of information, the idealisation of the bourgeois public sphere before the public sphere of organisations lacks at least greater elements of comparison for a sweeping assertion of its decay. Habermas's reading of it as decadence can only be read in the context of the Frankfurt School's critique of mass culture. Martin Jay, *The Dialectical Imagination. A History of the Frankfurt School and The Institute of Social Research. 1923–1950*, London 1996, p. 173 ff.

[647] Vesting, *Die Medien des Rechts*, vol. 4 (fn. 550), p. 13: 'Since the late 19th century, mass culture has integrated letterpress culture into a new kind of media constellation, into diverse and tense

forms of interweaving different media, to which telegraphy, photography, radio, film, and television are now newly added, before the rise of the computer confronts mass culture in its turn with a new kind of network culture'.

[648] Georg Christoph Tholen, *Die Zäsur der Medien. Kulturphilosophische Konturen*, Frankfurt am Main 2002, p. 7 ff.

[649] The current difficulty of public broadcasting in Germany in maintaining a public integration broadcasting structure stems from the inherent tensions arising from the confusing teleological direction of meaning resulting from the emergence of new media. The new ecosystem of communication is far removed from the usual connection between media (radio, television, and others) and the organisational form as collective actor and knowledge generator. On this, see Thomas Vesting, *Die Rundfunkfreiheit und die neue Logik der 'Content-Curation' in elektronischen Netzwerken*, JZ 2020, p. 975 ff.

[650] In Germany, there has been a strong influence of a special version of a culture state on the modelling of the regulatory communication framework since 1871. This version of a culture state, which guarantees cultural homogeneity to the population, differs from the non-state-centric American model. Even in the American system, however, there is a clear administrative regulatory framework, centred on the one hand on licences issued by government agencies and on the other hand on the Federal Communications Commission (FCC), the federal agency that regulates broadcasting. Regulatory systems similar to the US one can be found in several countries, such as Brazil. On the cultural state, see Dieter Grimm/Udo Steiner, *Kulturauftrag im staatlichen Gemeinwesen. Die Steuerung des Verwaltungshandelns durch Haushaltsrecht und Haushaltskontrolle*, Berlin/New York 1984, p. 110 ff. On the American context, see Lili Levi, The Four Eras of FCC Public Interest Regulation, Admin. L. Rev. 60 (2008), p. 813 et seq.

[651] This was the topic of Chapter 1 above. On this topic see also Vaios Karavas, *The Force of Code: Law's Transformation under Information-Technological Conditions*, 2009, pp. 478–479: 'This new media-dependency of law paves the way for the emergence of what I would like to call "techno-digital normativity", i.e., the amalgamation of normative and digital expectations inside the digital medium, resulting out of what we have described above as calculability of normativity. This means, however, that this techno-digital normativity cannot be assessed anymore according to Luhmann's distinction between cognitive openness and normative closure of the legal system, as it neglects the fact that inside the digital medium a strict distinction between digital and normative expectations is not possible.'

[652] Cf. Lawrence Lessig, *Code and Other Laws of Cyberspace*, New York 1999, pp. 89–91; Lawrence Lessig, Code: Version 2.0, New York 2006, p. 125.

[653] Shoshana Zuboff, *The Age of Surveillance Capitalism*, London 2019, pp. 103–104: 'A key element of Google's freedom strategy was its ability to discern, construct, and stake its claim to unprecedented social territories that were not yet subject to law ... [L]awlessness has been a critical success factor in the short history of surveillance capitalism.' Her book focuses in particular on the development of the Google company with its new behavioural advertising system. Julie Cohen also criticises this vision of a legal vacuum. See Julie E. Cohen, *Surveillance Capitalism as Legal Entrepreneurship*, Surveillance & Society 17 (2019), p. 240.

[654] Luhmann, *Gesellschaftliche Struktur und semantische Tradition* (fn. 163). See also Cohen, *Between Truth and Power* (fn. 629), p. 1: '... as our political economy transforms, our legal institutions too are undergoing transformation, and the two sets of processes are inextricably related'.

[655] On access rights, see Dan Wielsch, *Access Rules. Die Rechtsverfassung der Wissensteilung*, Tübingen 2008.

[656] Clayton M. Christensen/Michael E. Raynor/Rory McDonald, What Is Disruptive Innovation?, *Harvard Business Review* December 2015, https://hbr.org/2015/12/what-is-disruptive-innovation.

[657] Data capitalism aims to describe the consequences of the shift from an e-commerce model based on the online sale of goods to a different advertising model based on the 'sale of audiences' – or, more precisely, on the sale of individual behavioural profiles tied to user data. See Sarah Myers West, Data Capitalism: Redefining the Logics of Surveillance and Privacy, *Business & Society* 58/1 (2019), pp. 20 ff, 23.

[658] Section 230 of the Communications Decency Act (CDA) of 1996 is a common name for Title V of the Telecommunications Act of 1996 in the United States. On the history of Section 230 of the CDA, see Danielle Keats Citron, Cyber Civil Rights, *Boston University Law Review* 89 (2009), p. 61 ff, and Robert Cannon, The Legislative History of Senator Exon's Communications Decency Act: Regulating Barbarians on the Information Superhighway, *Fed. Comm. Law Journal* 49 (1996), pp. 52 f.

[659] In the US context, as presidents, both Joe Biden and Donald Trump, have shown an interest in repealing Section 230 of the CDA. There are also currently several proposals to amend immunity liability based on Section 230 of the CDA in the US Congress.

[660] Jeff Kosseff, *The Twenty-Six Words That Created the Internet*, London 2019.

[661] This remains the central problem of the limits of the protection of freedom of expression in the digital world. See Karl-Heinz Ladeur's critique of the recent development of the case law of the Federal Constitutional Courts on this issue: Karl-Heinz Ladeur, Die Kollision von Meinungsfreiheit und Ehrenschutz in der interpersonalen Kommunikation – Was stellt die 'Klarstellung' der Zweiten Kammer des BVerfG vom 19.6.2020 klar?, JZ 2020, p. 943 ff.

[662] 'The First Amendment first came to life in the early twentieth century, when the main threat to the nation's political speech environment was state suppression of dissidents. The jurisprudence of the First Amendment was shaped by that era. It presupposes an information-poor world, and it focuses exclusively on the protection of speakers from government, as if they were rare and delicate butterflies threatened by one terrible monster'... 'The safeguarding of political speech is widely understood to be the core function of the First Amendment': Tim Wu, Is the First Amendment Obsolete?, *Michigan Law Review* 117 (2018), p. 547 ff.

[663] To justify this delineation of large organisations, Jack M. Balkin explicitly points to the crucial role of *New York Times Co. v. Sullivan* and *New York Times Co. v. United States* (Pentagon Papers) as foundational to the regulatory contours of First Amendment jurisprudence over the course of the twentieth century. Jack M. Balkin, Old-School/New-School Speech Regulation, Yale Law School, Public Law Research Paper No.491, ssrn.com. See also *Cantrell v. Forest City Publ'g Co.*, 419 U.S. 245, 253–54 (1974), which permitted the imposition of vicarious liability on a publisher for the knowing falsehoods of its staff writer. On publisher liability, see the classic case of *Blumenthal v. Drudge*, 992 F. Supp. 44, 49 (D.D.C. 1998).

[664] For the location of the protection of freedom of expression in the political dimension, cf. Owen Fiss, Free Speech and Social Structure, *Iowa Law Review* 71/5 (1986) p. 1405 ff., 1409 f.: 'The purpose of free speech is not individual self-actualisation, but rather the preservation of democracy, and the right of a people, as a people, to decide what kind of life it wishes to live.' Owen Fiss also emphasises that the concern of the First Amendment about autonomy is primarily instrumental: 'Autonomy may be protected, but only when it enriches public debate' (Owen Fiss, Why the State?, 100 *Harvard Law Review* (1987), p. 781 ff., 786.).

[665] Balkin points out that the jurisprudential construction of the First Amendment in the second half of the twentieth century was centred on a communication infrastructure, that is, on a collective dimension of communication centred on journalistic organisations. The scenario of the contemporary collective dimension of communication, he argues, denotes a different 'social epistemology'. See Balkin, Old-School/New-School Speech Regulation (fn. 662), p. 2296: 'Half a century later, the impact of these two decisions has been weakened by significant changes in the practices and technologies of free expression, changes that concern a revolution in the infrastructure of free expression. That infrastructure, largely held in private hands, is the central battleground over free speech in the digital era.'

[666] This is a central problem of First Amendment jurisprudence, which focuses on a 'state action' theory in which the application of the right to free speech is conditioned by a state element in its relationship to the individual. Since Marsh, however, First Amendment jurisprudence has moved closer to a functionalist reading of free speech, treating private entities – such as shopping malls – as if they were public entities. See Developments in the Law: State Action and the Public/Private Distinction, *Harvard Law Review* 123/5 (2010), pp. 1248–1314, here pp. 1303 et seq. In Germany, too, there is a trend toward a functional reading of the right to freedom of expression that extends its application to private spaces that do not focus solely on the relationship between the state and the individual.

[667] These are bookstores, newsstands, libraries, and other intermediaries. The most important case that guided the jurisprudential construction of the First Postwar Amendment was *Smith v. California*, 361 U.S. 147 (1959), which was not about the right of the speaker or author, but about the right of the intermediary as a bookseller. The First Amendment granted limited protection to the intermediary in the distribution of books, videos, or other content to the extent that the companies did not know that the content distributed was illegal.

[668] In the first case, *Cubby, Inc. v. CompuServe, Inc*, the court held that CompuServe could not be held liable for the defamatory content in part because the intermediary had not reviewed or moderated any of the content posted to the forum. In the second case discussed, *Stratton Oakmont, Inc. v. Prodigy Services Co*, the court held that Prodigy was liable as a publisher for all posts on its website

because it had actively moderated some forum posts. On this point, see David S. Ardia, Free Speech Savior or Shield for Scoundrels: An Empirical Study of Intermediary Immunity Under Section 230 of the Communications Decency Act, *Loyola of Los Angeles Law Review* 43/2 (2010), p. 406 et seq.

[669] 'Relying on a tangled web of First Amendment decisions dating to the 1950s, the judge ruled that because Prodigy moderated some content and established online community policies, and it failed to delete posts that allegedly defamed the plaintiff, Prodigy could be sued for those posts regardless of whether it knew of them': Kosseff, *The Twenty-Six Words That Created the Internet* (fn. 659), p. 2.

[670] 'Though distributor-publisher distinctions were an established analogy in tort liability, the difficulty of using this model for online intermediaries quickly became apparent': Kate Klonick, The New Governors: The People, Rules, and Processes Governing. Online Speech, *Harvard Law Review* 131/6 (2018), p. 1599 ff., here p. 1605.

[671] 'Accordingly, the cases created a strong disincentive for online intermediaries to expand business or moderate offensive content and threatened the developing landscape of the internet': Klonick, ibid. 'If a company like Prodigy or CompuServe even had a policy of deleting posts that accused others of serious crimes such as murder, the company could risk losing its status as "distributor" and be held liable for every hateful utterance of millions of customers': Kosseff, *The Twenty-Six Words that Created the Internet* (fn. 659), p. 56.

[672] Eric Goldman, Why Section 230 Is Better than the First Amendment, 95 *Notre Dame L. Rev. Reflection* 33 (2019), pp. 36 et seq, noting that the substantive and procedural protections of Section 230 CDA far exceed those of the First Amendment. Kosseff, in turn, makes clear the practical importance of Section 230 of the CDA as a framework for opening up new discovery methods for the new economy: 'Section 230 acted as an incubator, allowing them to develop business models based on user content without the fear of lawsuits and regulation.' Kosseff, *The Twenty-Six Words that Created the Internet* (fn. 659), p. 147.

[673] Ardia, *Free Speech Savior or Shield for Scoundrels* (fn. 667), p. 452.

[674] Kosseff, *The Twenty-Six Words that Created the Internet* (fn. 659), p. 9: 'Section 230 has rightly earned a reputation as a kind of super-First Amendment ... But the paradox of Section 230 is that it also encourages online services to moderate user content as they see fit. Chris Cox and Ron Wyden made it clear in the brief text of Section 230'; and ibid., p. 239: 'Congress passed Section 230 because the First Amendment did not adequately protect large online platforms that process vast amounts of third-party content'.

[675] Cf. *Batzel v. Smith*, 333 F.3d 1018, 1026 (9th Cir. 2003): 'Congress decided not to treat providers of interactive computer services like other information providers such as newspapers, magazines or television and radio stations, all of which may be held liable for publishing or distributing obscene or defamatory material written or prepared by others.'

[676] Kosseff, *The Twenty-Six Words That Created the Internet* (fn. 659), p. 248: 'Section 230 reflects an implicit contract between Congress and the technology community: if online platforms develop responsible and reasonable moderation procedures, Congress will grant them extraordinary legal immunity'. This was also the original intention of Senators Chris Cox and Ron Wyden, who drafted Section 230 CDA: 'We want to encourage people like Prodigy, CompuServe, like America Online, like the new Microsoft network, to do everything possible for us, the customer, to help us control, at the portals of our computer, at the front door of our house, what comes in and what our children see'. Also Kosseff, ibid., p. 250.

[677] David Post, A bit of Internet history, or how two members of Congress helped create a trillion or so dollars of value, 27 August 2015, https://www.washingtonpost.com/news/volokhconspiracy/wp/2015/08/27/a-bit-of-internet-history-or-how-two-members-of-congresshelped-create-a-trillion-or-so-dollars-of-value/. Also in this sense see Balkin, Old-School/New-School (fn. 662), p. 2313. 'An early version of Google or Facebook might not have survived a series of defamation lawsuits if either had been treated as the publisher of the countless links, blogs, posts, comments, and updates that appear on their facilities.'

[678] This is a development that begins with the 1998 American Statute and continues to this day with Directive 2019/790 on Copyright in the Digital Single Market. See Peukert, *The Formation of the Normative Order 'Intellectual Property'* (fn. 488), para. 16: 'Namely, while in the early days of the Internet a heterarchical access culture was favored that corresponded to the technology and shielded commercially acting intermediaries such as access and host providers from liability risks, it has now been replaced by an exclusivity culture that transforms neutral intermediaries into perpetually

liable platforms and aims to ensure that every perception of protected content, even if only fleetingly via stream, must be individually licensed and remunerated'; *id.*, 'Intellectual Property Law and Development', in Philipp Dann/Stefan Kadelbach/Markus Kaltenborn (Eds.), *Development and Law. Eine systematische Einführung*, Baden-Baden 2014, p. 189 et seq.

[679] 'The ability of private platforms to moderate content comes from § 230 of the Communications Decency Act (CDA), which gives online intermediaries broad immunity from liability for user-generated content posted on their sites': Klonick, *The New Governors* (fn. 669), p. 1602.

[680] Herbert Kopp-Oberstebrink, *Umbesetzung, in: Daniel Weidner/Robert Buch* (fn. 569), pp. 350 ff.

[681] Tarleton Gillespie, *Custodians of the Internet. Platforms, Content Moderation and the Hidden Decisions that Shape Social Media*, New Haven/London 2018, p. 211: 'Given the immense amount of data they collect, platforms could use that data to make more visible the lines of contestation in public discourse and offer spaces in which they can be debated, informed by the everyday traces of billions of users and the value systems they imply.'

[682] Gillespie, ibid, p. 213.

[683] The concept of 'translation' is increasingly conceived as an alternative to the transitional concepts of transfer and reception. Translation is not the circulation of something (theory, normativity) that does not change, it is not a copy/model relationship, it is not a relationship of influence, but a kind of relationship in which system A creates something of its own out of system B. Translation is emphasised as the production of what was previously perceived as passive, as reception. On this, see Duve, Von der europäischen Rechtsgeschichte zu einer Rechtsgeschichte Europas in globalhistorischer Perspektive (fn. 283), p. 56 f.: 'Here the potential of a heuristic of translational processes reflected in cultural studies could also be realised for the synthesis of a frame of reference. One might then in turn call the totality or an excerpt of the conditions under which a process of translation takes place "legal culture"'; Duve, *Wie schreibt man eine Geschichte der Globalisierung von Recht?* JZ 15/16 (2020), p. 757 ff.

[684] Martin Eifert, Das Netzwerkdurchsetzungsgesetz und Plattformregulierung, in: Martin Eifert/Tobias Gostomzyk (Eds.), *Netzwerkrecht. Die Zukunft des NetzDG und seine Folgen für die Netzwerkkommunikation*, Baden-Baden 2018, p. 11. Gerald Spindler, Rechtliche Verantwortlichkeit nach Maßgabe technischer Kontrollmöglichkeiten? The Example of the Responsibility of Internet Providers, in: Martin Eifert/Wolfgang Hoffmann-Riem (Eds.), *Innovation, Recht und öffentliche Kommunikation*, Baden-Baden 2011, p. 79 et seq. On the liability privilege of Section 10 TMG, see Gerald Spindler, in: Schmitz (Ed.), *Telemediengesetz*, 2nd ed., Munich 2018, Section 10 paras. 1-118. See also Jaani Riordan, *The Liability of Internet Intermediaries*, Oxford 2016, p. 37.

[685] Aleksandra Kuczerawy, *Intermediary Liability and Freedom of Expression in the EU: From Concepts to Safeguards*, Cambridge 2018, p. 73. 'The Directive builds upon the German Multimedia Act of 1997 but it is strongly influenced by the US instrument.'

[686] Vesting, *Die Rundfunkfreiheit und die neue Logik der 'Content-Curation'* (fn. 648(; on Konrad Hesse, see also Andreas Voßkuhle/Jakob Schemmel, *Der Staatsrechtslehrer Konrad Hesse als Richter des Bundesverfassungsgerichts*, AöR 144/3 (2019), p. 425 ff.

[687] Konrad Hesse, *Grundzüge des Verfassungsrechts der Bundesrepublik Deutschland (1966)*, Munich 1999, para. 150. On the difference between the subjective aspects of freedom of expression and freedom of broadcasting, see para. 388.

[688] The intransparency of the way content is sorted presents itself as a glaring difference in the way intermediaries within the society of organisations produce their content – at least in the German model of broadcasting. Tarleton Gillespie, Governance of and by Platforms, in: Jean Burgess/Thomas Poell/Alice Marwick Sage (Eds.), *SAGE Handbook of Social Media*, London 2017, p. 57: '… they organise information through algorithmic sorting, privileging some content over others, in opaque ways. And it includes what is not permitted, and how and why they police objectionable content and behavior.' See also James Grimmelmann, The Virtues of Moderation, *Yale Journal of Law and Technology* 17 (2015), p. 42 ff.

[689] Ladeur, *Die Kollision von Meinungsfreiheit und Ehrenschutz in der interpersonalen Kommunikation* (fn. 660).

[690] 'But it is genuinely new, simply because it has so many more voices, so much more information, and such broad participation, with overlapping and unpredictable networks, leading to cascade effects, and suddenly visible bits of information whose popularity no one could have foreseen': Cass Sunstein, *#Republic. Divided Democracy in the Age of Social Media*, Oxford 2018, p. 154; Jill Lepore, 'We have got the Internet … We have got talk radio. We have got social media. We've got the ability to go directly around, and directly to the people', *The New Yorker*, February 2016.

[691] On this role within the German public law model, see BVerfG, Urteil des Ersten Senats v. 25. 3. 2014–1 BvF 1/11 = BVerfGE 136, 9, 33 Rn. 38 ff. = JZ 2014, p. 560, 562 f. (on this, Christian Starck, Das ZDF-Gremien-Urteil des Bundesverfassungsgerichts und seine gesetzliche und staatsvertragliche Umsetzung, JZ 2014, p. 552 ff.

[692] On media as 'pre-adaptive advances', see Vesting, *Rechtstheorie* (fn. 30), p. 144 ff.

[693] Terry Flew, The Platformised Internet: Issues for Internet Law and Policy, *Journal of Internet Law* 22/11 (2019), p. 3 ff.

[694] Dan Wielsch, Responsibility of Digital Intermediaries for Third-Party Infringements, *Journal of Intellectual Property* 10 (2018), p. 1 ff, here p. 32.

[695] Yochai Benkler, Communications infrastructure regulation and the distribution of control over content, *Telecommunications Policy* 22/3 (1998), p. 183 ff.; Robert B. Horwitz, The First Amendment meets some new technologies, *Theory and Society* 20/1 (1991), p. 21ff.

[696] Edward Castronova/Travis L. Ross/Isaac Knowles, Policy Questions Raised by Virtual Economies, *Telecommunications Policy* 39 (2015), p. 787 ff.; Sandra Braman, Where has Media Policy Gone? Defining the field in the twenty-first century, *Communication Law and Policy* 9/2 (2004), p. 153 ff.; R. MacKinnon/E. Hickok//A. Bar/H. Lim, Fostering Freedom Online: The Roles, Challenges and Obstacles of Internet Intermediaries, United Nations Educational 2014.

[697] This development can be seen in various decisions of nation states and supranational courts. These are decisions that involve intermediaries in their various functions. See BGH, judgment of 14.05.2013, VI ZR 268/12 – Autocomplete (NJW 2013, p. 2348). On the BGH's new liability model, Vera von Pentz, Ausgewählte Fragen des Medien- und Persönlichkeitsrechts im Lichte der aktuellen Rechtsprechung des VI. Zivilsenats, AfP 2014, p. 8 et seq. At the European level, cf. ECJ, Case C-131/12, para. 80 'Google Spain'.

[698] Rebecca Tushnet, Power without Responsibility: Intermediaries and the First Amendment, *George Washington Law Review* 76 (2008), p. 1001 ff., 1009: 'The flip side of this legislative grace is that the corporation's powers and freedoms stem from laws designed to give it special advantages, but those need not include the ability to claim both speaker status as against the government and also immunity from treatment as a speaker as against private claimants'.

[699] Karl-Heinz Ladeur, *Helmut Ridders Konzeption der Meinungsfreiheit als Prozessgrundrecht*, KJ 53/2 (2020), p. 178; Gunther Teubner, Zum transsubjektiven Potential subjektiver Rechte. Gegenrechte in ihrer kommunikativen, kollektiven und institutionellen Dimension, in: Hanna Franzki/Johann Horst/Andreas Fischer-Lescano (Eds.), *Gegenrechte: Recht jenseits des Subjekts*, Tübingen 2018, p. 357 ff.

[700] Horst Bredekamp, *Political Time. The Two Bodies of Thomas Hobbes's Leviathan*, in: Wolfgang Ernst/Cornelia Vismann (Eds.), *Geschichtskörper. Zur Aktualität von Ernst H. Kantorowicz*, Wilhelm Fink Verlag, 1998, p. 105 ff. On this also Wolfgang Ernst/Cornelia Vismann, On the Prehistory of the Modern State, in: Hans-Jörg Rheinberger et al. (Eds.), *Räume des Wissens. Repräsentation, Codierung, Spur*, Berlin 1997, p. 22 ff.

[701] Kahn, *The Future of Illusion* (fn. 221), p. 63.

[702] This is the subject of Chapter 1.

[703] Luhmann, *Das Recht der Gesellschaft* (fn. 10), p. 191: 'The risk of law/unlaw coding is accepted, but the level of programming is used to reintegrate law into society. The level of programming then acts as a level of compensation for any discrepancies between law and society.'

[704] Luhmann, ibid., p. 196: 'The form of the conditional program is one of the great evolutionary achievements of social development ... In a rapidly expanding world, they offer the possibility of imagining orders in the form of fixed couplings, and this equally in areas where (in contemporary terms) knowledge or normative regulations matter.'

[705] Vilém Flusser, *Medienkultur*, 5th ed., Frankfurt am Main 2008. p. 202 ff.

[706] Flusser, ibid, p. 206.

[707] '... data-driven, algorithmic processes multiply both obstacles to accountability and opportunities for cooptation of accountability structures. Smart digital technologies produce decisions that are ad hoc, personalised, and pattern-based rather than principled and generalizable.' Julie E. Cohen, Internet Utopianism and the Practical Inevitability of Law, *Duke Law & Technology Review* (2019), pp. 85 ff, here p. 95; Wolfgang Hoffmann-Riem, Digital Disruption and Transformation. Herausforderung für das Recht und Rechtswissenschaft, in: Martin Eifert (Ed.) *Digitale Disruption und Recht. Workshop in Honor of the 80th Birthday of Wolfgang Hoffmann-Riem*, Baden-Baden 2020, p. 189. 'Thus, they [algorithms] lack the ability to use the tacit knowledge that is important for human action. Deficient is the ability to develop creativity, emotions, and the use

of intuition, or, importantly for lawyers, justice. In the argumentatively guided interpretation of meaning, which is important for the interpretation of norms, algorithms encounter limitations (at least so far).'

[708] Thomas Vesting emphasises a dimension of dispersion and enabling of new social experiences through the written constitution as an effect of printing beyond the generation of social bonds through the 'if-then' form of conditional programmes. This is particularly evident, not least, in the open semantics of fundamental rights. Vesting, *Die Medien des Rechts*, vol. 3 (fn. 557), p. 136 ff: 'Thus the authority of constitutional law inevitably opens itself to the dispersed experiences of the "bearers of fundamental rights" and the generation of bonds in the practical fields of everyday civic life, to bonds that – like the speaking of a natural language – become completely naturalised in social relations as a totality of actions and ideas and (must) create a kind of second nature.'

[709] Luhmann, *Das Recht der Gesellschaft* (fn. 10), p. 199: 'The commitment to the form of the conditional program is related to the function of law, that is, to the stabilization of counterfactual expectations'.

[710] Luhmann, *Das Recht der Gesellschaft* (footnote 10), p. 197.

[711] Rosa, *Beschleunigung* (fn. 162), p. 365: '*Verzeitlichung der Zeit* means that the duration, sequence, rhythm, and tempo of actions, events, and bonds are decided only in the process, that is, *in time itself*; they no longer follow a predefined schedule'.

[712] Ino Augsberg, *Die Normalität der Normativität*, manuscript p. 11.

[713] Luca Belli/Cristiana Sappa, *The Intermediary Conundrum: Cyber-Regulators, Cyber-Police or Both?*, 8 (2017), p. 183 (185).

[714] Dan Wielsch, Die Ordnung der Netzwerke. AGB – Code – Community Standards, in: Eifert/Gostomzyk (fn. 683), pp. 67–68. Dan Wielsch argues that the new network technology brings about an indifference between 'dissemination medium' and 'success medium' in the Luhmannian sense. However, the article does not elaborate on this idea. This could be a form description of the current movement of platformisation of the Internet in the sense of the present work – albeit starting from the conceptual arsenal of systems theory.

[715] For the context of regulation as an interconnection of different levels, see Rebecca Schmidt, *Regulatory Integration Across Borders: Public-Private Cooperation in Transnational Regulation*, Cambridge 2018, p. 205: 'Building on the work of organisational theorists, as well as private law literature, the book pointed to the inherent dichotomy of networks to combine the imperatives of both co-operation and competition. Thus, networks transform external contradictions into a tense, but sustainable, "double orientation" within the operational system, which acknowledges both the market (competition) as well as the corporate aspects of interactions.'

[716] On a productive relationship between conflict resolution on the platform itself and the traditional legal way of resolving conflicts, see Karl-Heinz Ladeur, Netzwerkrecht als neues Ordnungsmodell des Rechts, in: Eifert/Gostomzyk (fn. 683), p. 172 ff.

OUTLOOK

[717] Steinhauer, *Vom Scheiden* (fn. 406), pp. 163–164: 'No law without writing, no law without graphological process. All this, then, belongs to the external things of law, which are indeed the most external things, but only because there are none more external. Even their superlative stems from a deficiency.'

[718] Thomas, *Les opérations du droit* (fn. 388). Thomas noted that 'the present development of our history has not given law a place to ask in principle the questions that arise from the normative function through its fictional aspects', Thomas, 'Droit', in André Burguière (Ed.), *Dictionnaire des sciences historiques*, Paris 1986, pp. 205 ff, here p. 211.

[719] Kantorowicz, *The King's Two Bodies* (fn. 390), p. 336 ff.

[720] Kahn, *The Future of Illusion* (fn. 221), p. 81: 'Whereas racism and religious fundamentalism attempt to give society a body, the usefulness of the category of fiction is that it complicates any attempt to locate power in one particular body or one particular place'.

[721] A network of institutional conditions supported by legal fictions helped limit the extent of the damage done by the Nazi regime, as Timothy Snyder indicated. 'Thus citizenship, bureaucracy, and foreign policy hindered the Nazi drive to have all European Jews murdered.' Timothy Snyder, *Black Earth. The Holocaust as History and Warning*, New York 2015, p. 225.

[722] Cohen, *Between Truth and Power* (fn. 629), p. 144: 'The gradual but accelerating movement to informational capitalism has confronted the judicial system with two large and interrelated problems: a proliferation of asserted harms that are intangible, collective, and highly informationalized; and an unmanageably large and ever-increasing number of claimants and interests'.

[723] This is the subject of Chapter 1 above.

[724] Marie Theres Fögen, *Die Enteignung der Wahrsager. Studien zum kaiserlichen Wissensmonopol in der Spätantike*, Frankfurt am Main 1997, p. 315 ff.

[725] Jill Lepore, *If Then? How the Simulmatics Corporation Invented the Future*. New York 2020, p. 323. 'By the early twenty-first century, the mission of Simulmactis had become the mission of many corporations, from manufactures to banks to predictive policing consultants. Collect data. Write code. Detect patterns. Target ads. Predict behavior. Direct action. Encourage consumption. Influence elections. It became impossible to read a newspaper or open a refrigerator or buy shampoo or cast a vote or sign a petition or go to the dentist without having had one's probable human behavior estimated by the use of computer technology.'

Bibliography

Abbate, Janet. *Inventing the Internet*. Cambridge (MA): MIT Press, 1999.

Agamben, Giorgio. *Homo Sacer: Sovereign Power and Bare Life* – transl. by Daniel Heller-Roazen. Stanford (Cal.): Stanford University Press, 1998.

Agamben, Giorgio. *Die Macht des Denkens*. Frankfurt am Main: Fischer, 2013.

Ago, Roberto. 'Die pluralistischen Anfänge der internationalen Gemeinschaft'. In: P. Fischer/ H. F. Köck et al. (Coord.). *Völkerrecht und Rechtsphilosophie. Internationale Festschrift für Stephan Verosta*. Berlin: Duncker & Humblot, 1980.

Aigrain, Philippe. *Sharing: Culture and the Economy in the Internet Age*. Amsterdam: Amsterdam Univ. Press, 2012.

Alexandrowicz, Charles H. *The European-African Confrontation. A Study in Treaty Making*. Leiden: Sijthoff, 1973.

Alexiadis, P.; De Streel, A. Designing an EU intervention standard for digital platforms. EUI Working Papers RSCAS 2020/14, vol. 1, n° 1, 2020.

Anderson, Benedict. *Imagined Communities. Reflections on the Origin and Spread of Nationalism*. London: Verso, 1992.

Anghie, Antony. *Imperialism, Sovereignty and the Making of International Law*. Cambridge: Cambridge University Press, 2004.

Anghie, Antony. 'The Evolution of International Law: Colonial and Postcolonial Realities.' *Third World Quarterly*, Vol. 27, No. 5, 2006, 739–753. JSTOR, http://www.jstor.org/stable/4017775. Accessed 2 Apr. 2025.

Anghie, Antony. 'Identifying Regions in the History of International Law'. In: B. Fassbender/A. Peters (Coord.). *The Oxford Handbook of the History of International Law*. Oxford: Oxford University Press, 2012.

Anonymus (C. Schmitt). Völkerrecht, Nr. 3. In: Heinrich Freymark (Coord.). *Das juristische Repetitorium. Öffentliches Recht*, Serie B, Nr. 17, Salzgitter 1949.

Aravamudan, Srinivas. 'Carl Schmitt's The Nomos of the Earth: Four Corollaries'. In: *South Atlantic Quarterly* 104/2, 2005.

Archibugi, Daniele; Filippetti, Andrea; Frenz, Marion. 'The Impact of the Economic Crises on Innovation'. Evidence from Europe. In: *Technological Forecasting and Social Change* 80/7, 2013.

Ardia, David S. 'Free Speech Savior or Shield for Scoundrels: An Empirical Study of Intermediary Immunity under Section 230 of the Communications Decency Act'. In: *Loyola of Los Angeles Law Review* 43/2, 2010.

Arendt, Hannah. *Elemente und Ursprünge totaler Herrschaft*. Frankfurt am Main: Europ. Verlagsanstalt, 1955.

Armitage, David. 'Globalizing Jeremy Bentham'. In: *History of Political Thought* 32, 2011.

Assmann, Aleida. *Einführung in die Kulturwissenschaft. Grundbegriffe, Themen, Fragestellungen*. Berlin: Erich Schmitt Verlag, 2011.

Assmann, Aleida. *Ist die Zeit aus den Fugen? Aufstieg und Fall des Zeitregimes der Moderne*, München: Hanser, 2013.

Assmann, Jan. 'Zeit und Geschichte in frühen Kulturen'. In: F. Stadler/M. Stöltzner (Coord.). *Time and History. Proceedings of the 28. International Ludwig Wittgenstein Symposium Kirchberg am Wechsel*. Austria: Österr. Ludwig-Wittgenstein-Gesellschaft, 2005.

Assmann, Jan. 'Art. Zeit'. In: J. Ritter/K. Gründer (Coord.). *Historisches Wörterbuch der Philosophie Bd. 12*. Basel: Schwabe AG, 2004.

162   Bibliography

AttalI, Jacques, *Noise. The Political Economy of Music*. Minneapolis: University of Minnesota, 1985.
Augsberg, Ino. 'Das Gespinst des Rechts'. In: *Rechtstheorie* 38, 2007.
Augsberg, Ino. 'Carl Schmitt's Fear: Nomos – Norm – Network'. In: *Leiden Journal of International Law* 23/04, 2010.
Augsberg, Ino. Schmitt-Lektüren: Vier Versuche über Carl Schmitt. *Wissenschaftliche Abhandlungen und Reden zur Philosophie, Politik und Geistes-geschichte*, vol. 99. Berlin: Duncker & Humblot, 2020.
Augsberg, Ino. *Die Normalität der Normativität*, Manuskript, 2020. Avanessian, Armen. *Realismus Jetzt*. Berlin: Merve, 2013.
Avanessian, Armen; Malik, Suhail. *Genealogies of Speculation. Materialism and Subjectivity since Structuralism*. London: Bloomsbury, 2016.
Baecker, Dirk. 'Es gibt keine sozialen Systeme'. 8 Thesen. In: Baecker, Dirk. (Coord.). *Wozu Theorie? Aufsätze*. Berlin: Suhrkamp, 2016.
Balke, Friedrich. *Der Staat nach seinem Ende. Die Versuchung Carl Schmitts*. München: Fink, 1996.
Balke, Friedrich. 'Disziplinartechnologien, Normalität, Normalisierung'. In: C. Kammler et al. (Coord.). *Foucault Handbuch. Leben, Werk, Wirkung*. Stuttgart: Metzler, 2014.
Balkin, Jack M. Old-School/New-School Speech Regulation. In: Yale Law School, Public Law Research Paper N. 491.
Barabási, Albert-László. *Linked: How Everything is Connected to Everything Else and What It Means for Business, Science, and Everyday Life*. New York: Basic Books, 2014.
Barion, Hans; Böckenförde, Ernst-Wolfgang; Forsthoff, Ernst; Weber, Werner (Coord.). *Epirrhosis. Festgabe für Carl Schmitt*. Berlin: Duncker & Humblot, 1968.
Bartky, Ian R. 'The Adoption of Standard Time'. In: *Technology and Culture*. vol. 30/1, 1989.
Baumgart, Winfried. *Vom europäischen Konzert zum Völkerbund. Friedensschlüsse u. Friedenssicherung von Versailles bis Wien*. Darmstadt: Wiss. Buchges, 1987.
Baumgart, Winfried. *Europäisches Konzert und nationale Bewegung. Internationale Beziehungen 1830–1878*. Paderborn: Schöningh, 1999.
Bayly, Christopher A. *The Birth of the Modern World 1780–1914. Global Connections and Comparisons*. Malden (MA)/Oxford (UK): Blackwell Publishing, 2004.
Beck, Ulrich; Grande, Edgar. Jenseits des methodologischen Nationalismus. Aussereuropäische und europäische Variationen der Zweiten Moderne. In: *Soziale Welt* 61, 2010.
Becker, Felix. 'Los tratados de amistad, comercio y navegación y la integración de los estados independientes americanos en el sistema internacional'. In: I. Buisson; G.Kahle; H. König; H. Pietschmann (Coord.). *La formación del Estado y la nación en América Latina*. Köln/Wien: Bohlau, 1984.
Beckers, Anna. *Enforcing Corporate Social Responsibility Codes. On Global Self-Regulation and National Private Law*. London: Hart Publishing, 2015.
Beckert, Jens. 'Die sittliche Einbettung der Wirtschaft. Von der Effi-zienz- und Differenzierungstheorie zu einer Theorie wirtschaftlicher Felder'. In: *Berliner Journal für Soziologie* 22, 2012.
Bekker, Pieter H. F.; Dolzer, Rudolf; Wailbel, Michael. *Making Transnational Law Work in the Global Economy. Essays in Honor of Detlev Vagts*. Cambridge: Cambridge University Press, 2010.
Bell, Daniel. *Die nachindustrielle Gesellschaft*. Frankfurt am Main: Campus, 1975.
Belli, Luca; SAPPA, Cristiana. 'The Intermediary Conundrum: Cyber-Regulators, Cyber-Police or both?' In: *Journal of Intellectual Property, Information Technology and Electronic Commerce Law* 8, 2017.
Bello, Andrés. *Principios del Derecho Internacional*. Lima: Librería de Moreno, 1844.
Benda-Beckmann, Keebet von; Turner, Bertram. 'Legal Pluralism, Social Theory, and the State'. In: *The Journal of Legal Pluralism and Unofficial Law* 50/3, 2018.
Behrens, Maria; Reichwein, Alexander. 'Global Governance'. In: A. Benz; S. Lütz; U. Schimank; G. Simonis (Coord.). *Handbuch Governance. Theoretische Grundlagen und empirische Anwendungsfelder*. Wiesbaden: VS Verlag f. Sozialwiss, 2007.

Beniger, James. *The Control Revolution: Technological and Economic Origins of the Information Society*. Cambridge (Mass.): Harvard University Press, 1986.
Benjamin, Walter. 'Das Kunstwerk im Zeitalter seiner technischen Reproduzierbarkeit'. In: Benjamin, Walter. Gesammelte Schriften, Bd. I/2. Frankfurt am Main: Suhrkamp, 1980.
Benjamin, Walter. *Passagen, Kristalle: Die Axt der Vernunft und des Satans liebster Trick*. Edited by J. Otte. Hamburg: Corso, 2011.
Benkler, Yochai. Communications Infrastructure Regulation and the Distribution of Control over Content. *Telecommunications Policy*, 22/3, 1998.
Benkler, Yochai. *The Wealth of Networks. How Social Production Transforms Markets and Freedom*. New Haven/London: Yale University Press, 2006.
Berman, Paul S. 'Conflict of Laws, Globalization, and Cosmopolitan Pluralism'. In: *Wayne Law Review* 51, 2005.
Berman, Paul S. 'A Pluralist Approach to International Law'. In: *Yale J. Int'l L*. 32, 2007.
Berner, Albert. 'Art: Völkerrecht'. In: J. C. Bluntschli; Brater, Carl L. T. (Coord.). *Deutsches Staats-Wörterbuch*, Bd. 11. Stuttgart/Leipzig: Expedition des Staats-Wörterbuch, 1870.
Berners-Lee, Tim. 'Lang lebe das Web'. In: Tilman Baumgärtel (Coord.). *Texte zur Theorie des Internets*. Stuttgart: Reclam, 2020.
Bidlo, Oliver D. *Rastlose Zeiten. Die Beschleunigung des Alltags*. Essen: Oldib-Verlag, 2009.
Bilfinger, Carl. *Das wahre Gesicht des Kellogg-Paktes. Angelsächsischer Imperialismus im Gewande des Rechts*. Berlin: Haka-Dr., 1942.
Blanco, John D.; Del Valle, Ivonne. 'Reorienting Schmitt's Nomos. Political Theology and Colonial (and Other) Exceptions in the Creation of Modern and Global Worlds'. In: *Política Común* 5, 2014.
Blanning, Tim C. 'The Commercialization and Sacralization of European Culture in the Nineteenth Century'. In: Blanning, Tim C. *The Oxford History of Modern Europe*. Oxford: Oxford University Press, 2000.
Blanning, Tim C. *The Culture of Power and the Power of Culture. Old Regime Europe, 1660–1789*. Oxford: Oxford University Press, 2002.
Blanning, Tim C. *The Romantic Revolution*. Oxford/London: Phoenix, 2011. Blumenberg, Hans. Die Legitimität der Neuzeit. 2nd Ed. Frankfurt am Main: Suhrkamp, 1988.
Böckenförde, Ernst-Wolfgang. 'Art. Ordnungsdenken, konkretes'. In: J. Ritter; K. Gründer (Coord.). *Historisches Wörterbuch der Philosophie*, Bd. 6. Basel/Stuttgart: Schwabe, 1984.
Böckenförde, Ernst-Wolfgang. 'Demokratie als Verfassungsprinzip'. In: J. Isensee/P. Kirchhof (Coord.). *Handbuch des Staatsrechts der Bundesrepublik Deutschland*, Bd. 2. Heidelberg: Müller, 3rd Ed, 2004.
Böckenförde, Markus. 'Zwischen Sein und Wollen: über den Einfluss umweltvölkerrechtlicher Verträge im Rahmen eines WTO-Streitbeilegungsverfahrens'. In: *ZaöRV* 63, 2003.
Böhme, Hartmut. 'Einführung: Netzwerke. Zur Theorie und Geschichte einer Konstruktion'. In: J. Barkhoff/ Böhme, Hartmut/Jeanne Riou (Coord.). *Netzwerke. Eine Kulturtechnik der Moderne*. Köln: Böhlau, 2004.
Boli, John; Thomas, George M. *Constructing World Culture. International Nongovernmental Organizations Since 1875*. Stanford (Cal.): Stanford University Press, 1999.
Borscheid, Peter. *Das Tempo-Virus. Eine Kulturgeschichte der Beschleunigung*. Frankfurt am Main: Campus-Verlag, 2004.
Bösch, Frank. 'Umbrüche in die Gegenwart. Globale Ereignisse und Krisenreaktionen um 1979'. In: *Zeithistorische Forschungen/Studies in Contemporary History* 9. N. 1, 2012.
Bosse, Henrich. *Autorschaft ist Werkherrschaft. Über die Entstehung des Urheberrechts aus dem Geist der Goethezeit*. Paderborn: Schöningh, 1981.
Boyd, Danah; Crawford, Kate. 'Critical Questions for Big Data: Provocations for a Cultural, Technological, and Scholarly Phenomenon'. In: *Info. Comm. Society* 15/5, 2012.
Brailsford, Henry. *A League of Nations 1–2* (1917). New York: Forgotten Books, 2018.
Braman, Sandra. 'Where has Media Policy Gone? Defining the Field in the Twenty-first century'. In: *Communication Law and Policy*, 9/2, 2004.

Bredekamp, Horst. 'Zur Vorgeschichte des modernen Staates'. In: Hans-Jörg Rheinberger et al. (Coord.). *Räume des Wissens. Repräsentation, Codierung, Spur.* Berlin: Akademie-Verlag, 1997.
Bredekamp, Horst. Politische Zeit. 'Die zwei Körper von Thomas Hobbes's Leviathan'. In: Wolfgang Ernst; Cornelia Vismann (Coord.). *Geschichtskörper. Zur Aktualität von Ernst H. Kantorowicz.* München: Wilhelm Fink Verlag, 1998.
Bredekamp, Horst. *Thomas Hobbes' visuelle Strategien. Der Leviathan: Urbild des modernen Staates. Werkillustrationen und Portraits.* Berlin: Akademie-Verlag, 1999.
Brem, Ernst. 'Das Verhältnis der Berner Übereinkunft zu anderen völkerrechtlichen Verträgen'. In: *Schweizerische Vereinigung für Urheberrecht (Coord.). Die Berner Übereinkunft und die Schweiz. Schweizerische Festschrift zum einhundertjährigen Bestehen der Berner Übereinkunft zum Schutze von Werken der Literatur und Kunst.* Bern, 1986. (reprinted in: Buck-Heeb, Petra (Coord.). *Geistiges Eigentum und Völkerrecht,* Berlin: Duncker & Humblot, 1994).
Brewer, John. *The Sinews of Power. War, Money and the English State 1688–1783.* Cambridge: Harvard University Press, 1988.
Brewer, John. *The Pleasures of the Imagination. English Culture in the Eighteenth Century.* London: Routledge, 2013.
Brient, Elizabeth. 'Epochenschwelle'. In: D. Weidner; R. Buch (Coord.). *Blumenberg lesen. Ein Glossar.* Berlin: Suhrkamp 2014.
Brunner, Otto. *Land und Herrschaft. Grundfragen der territorialen Verfassungsgeschichte Südostdeutschlands im Mittelalter.* Darmstadt: Wissenschaftliche Buchgesellschaft, 1990.
Bryant, Levi R. Art. 'Correlationism'. In: P. Ennis/P. Gratton (Coord.). *The Meillassoux Dictionary.* Edinburgh: Edinburgh University Press, 2015.
Buck-Heeb, Petra. *Geistiges Eigentum und Völkerrecht – Beiträge des Völkerrechts zur Fortentwicklung des Schutzes von geistigem Eigentum.* Berlin: Duncker & Humblot, 1994.
Bülck, Hartwig. 'Internationale Verwaltungsgemeinschaften'. In: K. Strupp; H.-J. Schlochauer (Coord.). *Wörterbuch des Völkerrechts,* Bd. 3. 2nd Ed. Berlin: de Gruyter, 1962.
Burke, Peter. *Papier und Marktgeschrei. Die Geburt der Wissensgesellschaft.* Berlin: Wagenbach, 2001.
Buxbaum, Hannah L. 'Transnational Regulatory Litigation'. In: *Virginia Journal of International Law* 46, 2006.
Buxbaum, Richard. 'Is Network a Legal Concept?' In: *Journal of Institutional and Theoretical Economics (JITE).* vol. 149/4, 1993.
Calliess, Gralf-Peter. *Grenzüberschreitende Verbraucherverträge. Rechtssicherheit und Gerechtigkeit auf dem elektronischen Weltmarktplatz.* Tübingen: Mohr Siebeck, 2006.
Calliess, Gralf-Peter; Zumbansen, Peer. *Rough Consensus and Running Code. A Theory of Transnational Private Law.* Oxford: Hart Publishing, 2010.
Campbell-Kelly, Martin. Data Communications at the National Physical Laboratory (1965–1975), *IEEE Annals of the History of Computing.* vol. 9/Issue 3–4, July–Sept,1987.
Campos, Ricardo. 'Prozeduralisierung als Wissens-Fertigung im Recht'. In: D. Wielsch (Coord.). *Rechtsbrüche. Spiegelungen der Rechtskritik Rudolf Wiethölters.* Baden-Baden: Nomos, 2019.
Cannon, Robert. 'The Legislative History of Senator Exon's Communications Decency Act: Regulating Barbarians on the Information Superhighway'. In: 49 Fed. Comm. L. J., 1996.
Carty, Anthony. 'Carl Schmitt's Critic of Liberal International Order between 1933 and 1945'. In: *Leiden Journal of International Law* 14, 2001.
Castells, Manuel. *The Rise of the Network Society.* 2nd Ed. Oxford: Wiley Blackwell, 2010.
Castronova, Edward; Knowles, Isaac; ROSS, Travis L. 'Policy Questions Raised by Virtual Economies'. In: *Telecommunications Policy* 39/9, 2015.
Clark, Henry C. 'Commerce, the Virtues, and the Public Sphere in Early-Seventeenth-Century France'. In: *French Historical Studies* 21, 1998.
Classen, Claus D. 'Die Entwicklung eines Internationalen Verwaltungsrechts als Aufgabe der Rechtswissenschaft'. In: VVDStRL, 2008.

Cohen, Julie E. *Law for the Platform Economy*. 51 U.C. Davis L. Rev. 15, 2017.
Cohen, Julie E. 'Surveillance Capitalism as Legal Entrepreneurship'. In: *SurVeillance & Soc'y* 17, 2019.
Cohen, Julie E. *Between Truth and Power. The Legal Constructions of Informational Capitalism*. New York: 2019.
Cohen, Julie E. 'Internet Utopianism and the Practical Inevitability of Law'. In: *Duke Law & Technology Review*, 2019.
Collins, Jeffrey. *The Allegiance of Thomas Hobbes*. Oxford: Oxford University Press, 2005.
Conrad, Sebastian; Osterhammel, Jürgen. 'Einleitung'. In: *Conrad, Sebastian. (Coord.). Das Kaiserreich transnational. Deutschland in der Welt 1871–1914*. Göttingen: Vandenhoeck und Ruprecht, 2004.
Couldry, Nick/Hepp, Andreas, *The Mediated Construction of Reality*, Cambridge: Polity Press, 2017.
Crawford, James. *The Creation of States in International Law*. Oxford: Clarendon Press, 1979.
Dahm, Georg; Delbrück, Jost; Wolfrum, Rüdiger. Völkerrecht, Bd. 1: *Die Grundlagen; Die Völkerrechtssubjekte*. 2nd Ed. Berlin: de Gruyter, 1989.
Daniels, Detlef von. *The Concept of Law from a Transnational Perspective*. Ashgate: Burlington, 2010.
Danto, Arthur C. 'Wiedersehen mit der Kunstwelt: Komödien der Ähnlichkeit'. In: Danto, Arthur C. *Kunst nach dem Ende der Kunst*. München: Fink, 1996.
Danto, Arthur C. *What Art Is*. New Haven (Conn.): Yale University Press, 2013.
Day, Timothy. *A Century of Recorded Music. Listening to Musical History*. New Haven/London: Yale University Press, 2000.
Deleuze, Gilles. 'Postscriptum zur Kontrollgesellschaft'. In: Deleuze, Gilles. Unterhandlungen 1972–1999. Frankfurt am Main: Suhrkamp, 1993.
Descombes, Vincent. *Die Rätsel der Identität*. Berlin: Suhrkamp, 2013.
Di Fabio, Udo. *Das Recht offener Staaten*. Tübingen: Mohr Siebeck, 1998.
Di Fabio, Udo. *Der Verfassungsstaat in der Weltgesellschaft*. Tübingen: Mohr Siebeck, 2001.
Dicke, Klaus. Völkerrechtspolitik und internationale Rechtsetzung. Grundlagen – Verfahren – Entwicklungstendenzen. ZG 3, 1988.
Dickie, George. *Introduction to Aesthetics. An Analytic Approach*. New York: Oxford University Press, 1997.
Dickie, George. *Art and Value*. Malden (Mass.): Blackwell, 2001.
Dommann, Monika. *Autoren und Apparate. Die Geschichte des Copyrights im Medienwandel*. Frankfurt am Main: Fischer, 2014.
Druey, Jean N. 'Das Recht als Netz für Netzwerke. Eine Wegskizze'. In: KritV, vol. 89, 2006.
Duchhardt, Heinz. 'Westphalian System. Zur Problematik einer Denkfigur'. In: *Historische Zeitschrift* 269, 1999.
Dugard, John. *Recognition and the United Nations*. Cambridge: Grotius Publications, 1987.
Dugard, John. 'Diplomatic Protection'. In: J. Crawford/A. Pellet/S. Olleson (Coord.). *The Law of International Responsibility*. Oxford: Oxford University Press, 2010.
Dülffer, Jost. 'Art. Völkerbund'. In: H. Vogler (Coord.). *Lexikon der Vereinten Nationen*. München: Oldenbourg, 2000.
Dunoff, Jeffrey L.; Trachtman, Joel P. 'A Functional Approach to International Constitutionalization'. In: Dunoff, Jeffrey L. (Coord.). *Ruling the World. Constitutionalism, International Law, and Global Governance*. Cambridge: Cambridge University Press, 2009.
Duve, Thomas '… wie dort noch Raum ist zu glücklichem Dasein für Millionen von Menschen … Der Freundschafts-, Handels – und Schiffahrtsvertrag zwischen Preußen und den übrigen Staaten des Zollvereins und der Argentinischen Konföderation von 1858'. In: H.-G. Hermann; T. Gutmann (Coord.). *Von den Leges Barbarorum bis zum ius barbarum des Nationalsozialismus. Festschrift für Hermann Nehlsen zum 70. Geburtstag*. Vienna: Böhlau, 2008.

Duve, Thomas. 'Von der Europäischen Rechtsgeschichte zu einer Rechtsgeschichte Europas in globalhistorischer Perspektive'. In: Rechtsgeschichte (Rg) 20, 2012.
Duve, Thomas. 'Was ist "Multinormativität"? Einführende Bemerkungen'. In: Rechtsgeschichte – Legal History Rg 25, 2017.
Duve, Thomas. 'Wie schreibt man eine Geschichte der Globalisierung von Recht?' In: Juristenzeitung 15/16, 2020.
Dworkin, Ronald. *Law's Empire*. Cambridge (Mass.)/London: Harvard University Press, 1986.
Dworkin, Ronald. *Freedom's Law. The Moral Reading of the American Constitution*, Oxford: Oxford University Press, 1999.
Eagleton, Terry. *The Ideology of the Aesthetic*. Oxford: Blackwell, 1990.
Ehrlich, Eugen. *Grundlegung der Soziologie des Rechts* (Nachdruck 1967). 4th Ed. Berlin: Duncker & Humblot, 1989.
Eifert, Martin. 'Das Netzwerkdurchsetzungsgesetz und Plattformregulierung'. In: Eifert, Martin. Tobias Gostomzyk (Coord.). *Netzwerkrecht. Die Zukunft des NetzDG und seine Folgen für die Netzwerkkommunikation*. Baden-Baden: Nomos, 2018.
Engelmann, Andreas. *Rechtsgeltung als institutionelles Projekt*. Weilerswist: Velbrück, 2020.
Engels, Friedrich. In: *Karl Marx/Friedrich Engels Gesamtausgabe* (MEGA). Berlin: Akademie-Verlag, 2009.
Eriksen, Thomas H. *Tyranny of the Moment. Fast and Slow. Time in the Information Age*. London: Pluto Press, 2001.
Eriksson, Maria; Fleischer, Rasmus; Johansson, Anna; Snickars, Pelle; Vonderau, Patrick. Spotify Teardown: Inside the Black Box of Streaming Music. Cambridge (Mass.): MIT Press, 2019.
Esposito, Elena. *Soziales Vergessen. Formen und Medien des Gedächtnisses der Gesellschaft*. Frankfurt am Main: Suhrkamp, 2002.
Evans, David S.; Hagiu, Andrei; Schmalensee, Richard. *Invisible Engines: How Software Platforms Drive Innovation and Transform Industries*. Cambridge (Mass.): MIT, 2006.
Evans, David; Schmalensee, Richard. 'The Antitrust Analysis of Multi-Sided Platform Businesses'. In: R. Blair; D. Sokol (Coord.). *Oxford Handbook on International Antitrust Economics*. Oxford: Oxford University Press, 2013.
Ezrachi, Ariel; Stucke, Maurice E. *Virtual Competition. The Promise and Perils of the Algorithm-Driven Economy*. Cambridge (Mass.): Harvard University Press, 2016.
Ezrachi, Yaron. *Imagined Democracies. Necessary Political Fictions*. Cambridge: Cambridge University Press, 2012.
Fassbender, Bardo. 'Heinrich Triepel und die Anfänge der dualistischen Sicht von "Völkerrecht und Landesrecht" im späten 19. Jahrhundert'. In: Lukas Gschwend et al. (Coord.). *Recht im digitalen Zeitalter. Festgabe Schweizerischer Juristentag*. St. Gallen: Universität St. Gallen, 2015.
Fisch, Jörg. *Die europäische Expansion und das Völkerrecht. Die Auseinandersetzungen um den Status der überseeischen Gebiete vom 15. Jahrhundert bis zur Gegenwart*. Wiesbaden/Stuttgart: Steiner, 1984.
Fischer-Lescano, Andreas. Globalverfassung. Die Geltungsbegründung der Menschenrechte. Weilerswist: Velbrück Wissenschaft, 2005.
Fischer-Lescano, Andreas; Teubner, Gunther. *Regime-Kollisionen. Zur Fragmentierung des globalen Rechts*. Frankfurt am Main: Suhrkamp, 2006.
Fiss, Owen. 'Free Speech and Social Structure'. In: 71 *Iowa Law Review*, 1986.
Fiss, Owen. 'Why the State?' In: 100 *Harvard Law Review*, 1987.
Flew, Terry. 'The Platformized Internet: Issues for Internet Law and Policy'. In: *Journal of Internet Law* 22/11, 2019.
Flusser, Vilém. *Medienkultur*. 5th Ed. Frankfurt am Main: Fischer, 2008.
Fögen, Marie Theres. *Die Enteignung der Wahrsager. Studien zum kaiserlichen Wissensmonopol in der Spätantike*. Frankfurt am Main: Verlag, 1997.
Fögen, Marie Theres. *Das Lied vom Gesetz*. München: Carl-Friedrich-von-Siemens-Stiftung, 2007.

Foreman-Peck, James. 'The Emergence and Growth of International Organizations'. In: R. Tilly; P. J. Welfens (Coord.). *Economic Globalization, International Organizations and Crisis Management: Contemporary and Historical Perspectives on Growth, Impact and Evolution of Major Organizations in an Interdependent World*. Berlin: Springer, 2000.

Forst, Rainer. *Normativität und Macht. Zur Analyse sozialer Rechtfer-tigungsordnungen*. Berlin: Suhrkamp, 2015.

Forsthoff, Ernst. *Die Krise der Gemeindeverwaltung im heutigen Staat*. Berlin: Junker u. Dünnhaupt, 1932.

Forsthoff, Ernst. *Der totale Staat*. 2nd Ed. Hamburg: Hanseat. Verl.-Anstalt, 1934.

Forsthoff, Ernst. 'Von der Aufgabe der Verwaltungsrechtswissenschaft'. In: *Deutches Recht* 5, 1935.

Forsthoff, Ernst. 'Führung und Bürokratie'. In: Dt. Adelsblatt, 1935.

Forsthoff, Ernst. *Die Verwaltung als Leistungsträger*. Stuttgart/Berlin: Kohlhammer, 1938.

Forsthoff, Ernst. *Zur Problematik der Verfassungsauslegung*. Stuttgart: Kohlhammer, 1961.

Forsthoff, Ernst. 'Der introvertierte Staat'. In: Forsthoff, Ernst. *Rechtsstaat im Wandel*. Stuttgart: Kohlhammer, 1963.

Forsthoff, Ernst. 'Begriff und Wesen des sozialen Rechtsstaates'. In: Forsthoff, Ernst. *Rechtsstaat im Wandel. Verfassungsrechtliche Abhandlungen 1950–1964*. Stuttgart: Kohlhammer, 1964.

Forsthoff, Ernst. 'Das politische Problem der Autorität'. In: Forsthoff, Ernst. *Rechtsstaat im Wandel. Verfassungsrechtliche Abhandlungen 1950–1964*. Stuttgart: Kohlhammer, 1964.

Forsthoff, Ernst. 'Von der sozialen zur technischen Realisation'. In: *Der Staat* 9, 1970.

Forsthoff, Ernst. *Der Staat der Industriegesellschaft. Dargestellt am Beispiel der Bundesrepublik Deutschland*. München: Beck, 1971.

Foucault, Michel. *Ordnung der Dinge. Eine Archäologie der Human-wissenschaften*. Frankfurt am Main: Suhrkamp, 1974.

Foucault, Michel. *Überwachen und Strafen. Die Geburt des Gefängnisses*. Frankfurt am Main: Suhrkamp, 1976.

Foucault, Michel. *Sexualität und Wahrheit. Der Wille zum Wissen I*. Frankfurt am Main: Suhrkamp, 1987.

Foucault, Michel. *Geschichte der Gouvernementalität, Bd. I: Sicherheit, Territorium, Bevölkerung*. Frankfurt am Main: Suhrkamp, 2004.

Foucault, Michel. *Dits et Ecrits. Schriften Bd. 3, 1976–1979*. Frankfurt am Main: Suhrkamp, 2003.

Foucault, Michel. *Dits et Ecrits. Schriften Bd. 4, 1980–1988*. Frankfurt am Main: Suhrkamp, 2005.

Foucault, Michel. *Ästhetik der Existenz. Schriften zur Lebenskunst*. Frankfurt am Main: Suhrkamp, 2007.

Franck, J.-U.; Peitz, M. *Market Definition and Market Power in the Platform Economy*. CERRE Report, 2019.

Fraser, Nancy. 'Theorie der Öffentlichkeit. Strukturwandel der Öffentlichkeit (1961)'. In: H. Brunkhorst; R. Kreide; C. Lafont (Coord.). *Habermas Handbuch*, Stuttgart, 2009.

Friedewald, Michael. 'Vom Experimentierfeld zum Massenmedium: Gestalende Kräfte in der Ent-wicklung des Internets'. In: *Technikgeschichte* 67, 2000.

Friedrich, Manfred. 'Der Methoden- und Richtungsstreit. Zur Grundlagendiskussion der Weimarer Staatsrechtslehre'. In: AöR 102, 1977.

Fuchs, Christian. 'New Imperialism: Information and Media Imperialism'. In: *Global Media and Communication* 6/1, 2010.

Fuchs, Peter. 'Die Unbeeindruckbarkeit der Gesellschaft – Ein Essay zur Kritikabilität sozialer Systeme'. In: A. Fischer-Lescano; M. Amstutz (Coord.). *Kritische Systemtheorie: Zur Evolution einer normativen Theorie*. Bielefeld: transcript, 2013.

Funken, Christiane. 'Der Körper im Internet'. In: M. Schroer (Coord.). *Soziologie des Körpers*. Frankfurt am Main: Suhrkamp, 2005.

García-Salmones, Rovira, Mónica. *The Project of Positivism in International Law. The History and Theory of International Law*. Oxford: Oxford University Press, 2013.

Gauchet, Marcel. 'De l'avènement de l'individu à la découverte de la société'. In: *Annales*, E. pp. C. 3, 1979.
Geertz, Clifford. *Local Knowledge. Further Essays in Interpretive Anthropology*. New York: Basic Books, 1983.
Genschel, Philipp; Zangl, Bernhard. *Die Zerfaserung von Staatlichkeit und die Zentralität des Staates*. TranState Working Papers N. 62, Bremen, 2007.
Gelatt, Roland. *The Fabulous Phonograph, 1877–1977*. New York: MacMillan, 1977.
Gerald Spindler, 'Rechtliche Verantwortlichkeit nach Maßgabe technischer Kontrollmöglichkeiten? Das Beispiel der Verantwortlichkeit von Internet-Providern'. In: M. Eifert; W. Hoffmann-Riem (Coord.). *Innovation, Recht und öffentliche Kommunikation*. Baden-Baden, 2011.
Gessmann, Martin. *Zur Zukunft der Hermeneutik*. München: Wilhelm Fink, 2012.
Gieseke, Ludwig. *Vom Privileg zum Urheberrecht. Die Entwicklung des Urheberrechts in Deutschland bis 1845*. Göttingen: Schwartz, 1995.
Giebmann, Sebastian. *Netze und Netzwerke. Archäologie einer Kulturtechnik, 1740–1840*. Bielefeld: Transcript, 2006.
Giebmann, Sebastian. *Die Verbundenheit der Dinge. Eine Kulturgeschichte der Netze und Netzwerke*. Berlin: Kulturverlag Kadmos, 2014.
Gillespie, Tarleton. 'The Politics of Platforms'. In: *New Media & Society* 12/3, 2010.
Gillespie, Tarleton. 'Governance of and by Platforms'. In: SAGE *Handbook of Social Media*, (Coord.). Jean Burgess, Thomas Poell, and Alice Marwick Sage, 2017.
Gillespie, Tarleton. *Custodians of the Internet. Platforms, Content Moderation and the Hidden Decisions that Shape Social Media*. New Haven/London: Yale University Press, 2018.
Gitelman, Lisa (Coord.). *Raw Data is an Oxymoron*. Cambridge (Mass.): MIT, 2013.
Goethe, Johann Wolfgang von. *Goethes sämtliche Werke*, Bd. 39. Stuttgart und Tübingen: Cotta'scher Verlag, 1854.
Goldman, Eric. 'Why Section 230 Is Better than the First Amendment'. In: 95 *Notre Dame L. Rev. Reflection 33*, 2019.
Gordley, James. *The Philosophical Origins of Modern Contract Doctrine*. Oxford: Clarendon Press, 1991.
Gratton, Peter. *The State of Sovereignty. Lessons from the Political Fictions of Modernity*. Albany: State University of New York Press, 2012.
Greve, Jens; Heintz, Bettina. 'Die Entdeckung der Weltgesellschaft. Entstehung und Grenzen der Weltgesellschaftstheorie'. In: *Zeitschrift für Soziologie, Sonderheft 'Weltgesellschaft'*, 2005.
Grewe, Wilhelm G. *Epochen der Völkerrechtsgeschichte*. Baden-Baden: Nomos, 1984.
Grewe, Wilhelm G. 'Peaceful Change'. In: R. Bernhardt (Coord.). *Max Planck Encyclopedia of Public International Law 3*. Oxford: Elsevier, 1997.
Grimm, Dieter. *Die Zukunft der Verfassung II. Auswirkungen von Europäisierung und Globalisierung*. Frankfurt am Main/Berlin: Suhrkamp, 2012.
Grimm, Dieter; Steiner, Udo. *Kulturauftrag im staatlichen Gemeinwesen. Die Steuerung des Verwaltungshandelns durch Haushaltsrecht und Haushaltskontrolle – Coord. von der Vereinigung der Dt. Staatsrechtslehrer*. Berlin/New York: De Gruyter, 1984.
Grimm, Jacob; Grimm, Wilhelm (Hrsg). *Deutsches Wörterbuch*. Leipzig 1854–1961. Quellenverzeichnis Leipzig 1971. Online-Version vom 05.10.2020.
Grimmelmann, James. 'The Virtues of Moderation'. In: *Yale Journal of Law and Technology* 17, 2015.
Gross, Raphael. *Carl Schmitt und die Juden. Eine deutsche Rechtslehre*. Frankfurt am Main: Suhrkamp, 2005.
Grossheutschi, Felix. *Carl Schmitt und die Lehre vom Katechon*. Berlin: Duncker & Humblot, 1996.
Gugerli, David. *Wie die Welt in den Computerkam. Zur Entstehung digitaler Wirklichkeit*. Frankfurt am Main: Fischer, 2018.
Gumbrecht, Hans-Ulrich. 'Modern, Modernität, Moderne'. In: R. Koselleck; W. Conze; O. Brunner. *Geschichtliche Grundbegriffe. Historisches Wörterbuch zur politisch-sozialen Sprache*, Bd. 4. Stuttgart: Klett Cotta, 1978.

Gumbrecht, Hans-Ulrich. 'Rhythmus und Sinn'. In: Gumbrecht, Hans-Ulrich; K. L. Pfeiffer (Coord.). *Materialität der Kommunikation*. Frankfurt am Main: Suhrkamp, 1995.
Günther, Klaus. '*Vom Zeitkern des Rechts*'. In: *Rechtshistorisches Journal* 14, 1995.
Günther, Klaus. 'Legal Pluralism or Uniform Concept of Law? Globalisation as a Problem of Legal Theory'. In: *NoFo – Journal of Extreme Legal Positivism*, N. 5, April 2008.
Häberle, Peter. *Zum Staatsdenken Ernst Forsthoffs*. In: ZSR 95/I, 1976. Habermas, Jürgen. Theorie des kommunikativen Handelns, Bd. 2. Frankfurt am Main: Suhrkamp, 1988.
Häberle, Peter. *Strukturwandel der Öffentlichkeit. Untersuchung zu einer Kategorie der bürgerlichen Gesellschaft*. Frankfurt am Main: Verlag, 1990.
Häberle, Peter. 'Was heißt Universalpragmatik'. In: Häberle, Peter. *Vorstudien und Ergänzungen zur Theorie des kommunikativen Handelns*. Frankfurt am Main: Suhrkamp, 1995.
Häberle, Peter. Der gespaltene Westen. *Kleine politische Schriften X*. Frankfurt am Main: Suhrkamp, 2004.
Häberle, Peter. 'The Constitutionalization of International Law and the Legitimation Problems of a Constitution of the World Society'. In: *Constellations* 14/4, 2008.
Häberle, Peter. 'Der demokratische Rechtsstaat – eine paradoxe Verbindung widersprüchlicher Prinzipien?' In: Häberle, Peter. Philosophische Texte, Studienausgabe in 5 Bänden, Bd. 4: *Politische Theorie*. Frankfurt am Main: Suhrkamp, 2009.
Häberle, Peter. 'Über den internen Zusammenhang von Rechtsstaat und Demokratie'. In: Häberle, Peter. Philosophische Texte. Studienausgabe in 5 Bänden, Bd. 4: *Politische Theorie*. Frankfurt am Main: Suhrkamp, 2009.
Hafner, Gerhard. Risks Ensuing from Fragmentation of International Law. In: Int'l L. Comm'n 143 (2000). Fifty-fifth Session, Supplement N. 10 (A/55/10). Official Records of the General Assembly.
Hafner, Gerhard. 'Pros and Cons Ensuing from Fragmentation of International Law'. In: *Mich J Int'l L* 25, 2003.
Hansen, Klaus; Lietzmann, Klaus (Coord.). *Carl Schmitt und die Liberalismuskritik*. Opladen: Leske + Budrich, 1988.
Hart, Herbert L. A. *The Concept of Law*. Oxford/New York: Clarendon Press, 1997.
Harvey, David. *The Condition of Postmodernity. An Enquiry into the Origins of Cultural Change*. Malden (Mass.): 2004.
Hathaway, Oona A. 'Between Power and Principle: An Integrated Theory of International Law'. In: *University Chicago Law Review* 72, 2005.
Hegel, Georg W. F. *Vorlesungen über die Aesthetik*, Bd. II. Berlin: Duncker & Humblot, 1843.
Hegel, Georg W. F. Vorlesung über die Ästhetik I. in: Werke 13. Frankfurt am Main: Suhrkamp, 1986.
Hegel, Georg W. F. *Grundlinien der Philosophie des Rechts* (1821), Werkausgabe Bd. 7. Frankfurt am Main, 1970.
Hegel, Georg W. F. *Phänomenologie des Geistes* (1807). Theorie-Werkausgabe (Coord. von Eva Moldenhauer und Karl Markus Michel) Bd. 3. Frankfurt am Main: Suhrkamp, 1970.
Heller, Hermann. 'Die Krise der Staatslehre (1926)'. In: Heller, Hermann. *Gesammelte Schriften 2: Recht, Staat, Macht – Coord. von Christoph Müller*. Tübingen: Mohr, 1971.
Herren, Madeleine. 'Governmental Internationalism and the Beginning of a New World Order in the Late Nineteenth Century'. In: M. H. Geyer; J. Paulmann (Coord.). *The Mechanics of Internationalism. Culture, Society, and Politics from the 1840s to the First World War*. Oxford: de Gruyter, 2001.
Herren-Oesch, Madeleine. *Hintertüren zur Macht. Internationalismus und modernisierungsorientierte Außenpolitik in Belgien, der Schweiz und den USA 1865–1914*. München: Oldenbourg, 2000.
Herren-Oesch, Madeleine. *Internationale Organisationen seit 1865. Eine Globalgeschichte der internationalen Ordnung*. Darmstadt: Wiss. Buchgesellschaft 2009.
Hesse, Konrad. Grundzüge des Verfassungsrechts der Bundesrepublik Deutschland (1966). *Neudruck* 20, 1999.
Hildebrandt, Mireille. *Smart Technologies and the End(s) of Law. Novel Enlargements of Law and Technology*. Cheltenham: Edgar Elgar Publishing, 2015.

Hillgruber, Christian. *Die Aufnahme neuer Staaten in die Völkerrechtsgemeinschaft. Das völkerrechtliche Institut der Anerkennung von Neustaaten in der Praxis des 19. und 20. Jahrhunderts*. Frankfurt am Main: Lang, 1998.
Hobbes, Thomas. *Leviathan*. Oxford University Press, New York, 1996.
Hoffmann-Riem, Wolfgang. 'Digitale Disruption und Transformation. Herausforderung für das Recht und Rechtswissenschaft'. In: Martin Eifert (Coord.). *Digitale Disruption und Recht. Workshop zu Ehren des 80. Geburtstags von Wolfgang Hoffmann-Riem*. Baden-Baden: Nomos, 2020.
Hofmann, Hasso. 'Feindschaft – Grundbegriff des Politischen'. In: *Zeitschrift für Politik* 12, 1965.
Hofmann, Hasso. *Legitimität gegen Legalität. Der Weg der politischen Philosophie Carl Schmitts*. Berlin 2. Ed. 1992.
Holmond, Anne. 'The Platformization of the Web: Making Web Data Platform Ready'. In: *Social Media + Society* July–December 2015.
Hölscher, Lucian. *Die Entdeckung der Zukunft*. Frankfurt am Main: Fischer, 1999.
Holzer, Boris. 'Wie "modern" ist die Weltgesellschaft? Funktionale Differenzierung und ihre Alternativen'. In: *Soziale Systeme* 13, 2007.
Hont, Istvan. *Jealousy of Trade. International Competition and the Nation-State in Historical Perspective*. Cambridge (Mass.): Harvard University Press, 2010.
Hont, Istvan. *Politics in Commercial Society. Jean-Jacques Rousseau and Adam Smith*. Cambridge: Harvard University Press, 2015.
Hopt, Klaus J.; Teubner, Gunther (Coord.). *Corporate Governance and Director's Liabilities. Legal, Economic and Sociological Analyses on Corporate Social Responsibility*. Berlin: De Gruyter, 1985.
Horwitz, 'Robert B. The First Amendment Meets Some New Technologies'. In: *Theory and Society* 20/1, 1991.
Hueck, Ingo. 'Die Gründung völkerrechtlicher Zeitschriften in Deutschland im internationalen Vergleich'. In: M. Stolleis (Coord.). *Juristische Zeitschriften. Die neuen Medien des 18.–20. Jahrhunderts*. Frankfurt am Main: Klostermann, 1999.
Hueck, Ingo. 'The Disciple of the History of International Law. New Trends and Methods on the History of International Law'. In: *Journal of History of International Law* 3, 2001.
Husserl, Gerhart. *Recht und Zeit*. Frankfurt am Main: Klostermann, 1955.
Iriye, Akira. *Global Community. The Role of International Organization in the Making of the Contemporary World*. Berkeley: University of California Press, 2004.
Isensee, Josef. 'Diskussionsbeitrag'. In: VVDStRL 63, 2004.
Jameson, Frederic. 'Notes on the Nomos'. In: *South Atlantic Quarterly*, vol. 104/2, 2005.
Jay, Martin. *The Dialectical Imagination. A History of the Frankfurt School and The Institut of Social Research*. 1923–1950. London: 1996.
Jellinek, Georg. *Allgemeine Staatslehre*. Berlin: Häring, 1914.
Jellinek, Georg. *Die Lehre von den Staatenverbindungen* (1882). Aalen: Scientia, 1969.
Jellinghaus, Lorenz. *Zwischen Daseinsvorsorge und Infrastruktur. Zum Funktionswandel von Verwaltungswissenschaften und Verwaltungsrecht in der zweiten Hälfte des 19. Jahrhunderts* (*Studien zur europäischen Rechtsgeschichte* 202; *Recht in der Industriellen Revolution* 3). Frankfurt am Main: Klostermann, 2006.
Jessup, Philip C. *Transnational Law*. New Haven: Yale University Press, 1959.
Jin, Dal Yong. 'The Construction of Platform Imperialism in the Globalization'. In: *Journal for a Global Sustainable Information Society* 11/1, 2013.
Joerges, Christian. 'A New Type of Conflict of Laws as the Legal Paradigm of Postnational Constellations'. In: Joerges, Christian; J. Falke (Coord.). *Karl Polanyi. Globalization and the Potential of Law in Transnational Markets*. Oxford/Portland: Hart Publishing, 2011.
Jung, Theo. 'Das Neue der Neuzeit ist ihre Zeit. Reinhart Kosellecks Theorie der Verzeitlichung und ihre Kritiker'. In: *Moderne. Kulturwis-senschaftliches Jahrbuch* 6, 2010–2011.
Kahn, Victoria A. *Wayward Contracts. The Crisis of Political Obligation in England, 1640–1674*. Princeton: Princeton University Press, 2004.

Kahn, Victoria A. *The Future of Illusion. Political Theology and Early Modern Texts.* Chicago: Chicago University Press, 2014.
Kaiser, Josef H. 'Konkretes Ordnungsdenken'. In: H. Quaritsch (Coord.). *Complexio Oppositorum. Über, Carl Schmitt. Vorträge u. Diskussionsbeitrag d. 28. Sonderseminars 1986 d. Hochschule für Verwaltungswissenschaften Speyer.* Berlin: Duncker & Humblot, 1988.
Kant, Immanuel. *Werke in zwölf Bänden.* Frankfurt am Main: Suhrkamp, 1977.
Kantorowicz, Ernst H. 'The King's Two Bodies'. Kantorowicz, Ernst H. *A Study in Mediaeval Political Theory.* Princeton: Princeton University Press, 1957.
Kaplan, Morton. *System and Process in International Politics.* New York: Wiley, 1957.
Kaschuba, Wolfgang. *Die Überwindung der Distanz. Zeit und Raum in der europäischen Moderne.* Frankfurt am Main: Fischer, 2004.
Karavas, Vaios. The Force of Code: Law's Transformation under Information-Technological Conditions, 2009.
Keats Citron, Danielle. 'Cyber Civil Rights'. In: *Boston University Law Review* 89, 2009.
Keene, Edward. 'The Treaty-making Revolution of the Nineteenth Cen-tury'. In: *The International History Review* 34, 2012.
Kehrberg, Jan. O. *Die Entwicklung des Elektrizitätsrechts in Deutschland. Der Weg zum Energiewirtschaftsgesetz von 1935 – Rechtshistorische Reihe 157.* Frankfurt am Main: Lang, 1997.
Kelsen, Hans. *Reine Rechtslehre.* Berlin/Vienna: Deuticke, 1934. 2nd, completely revised and expanded edition. Vienna: Deuticke, 1960.
Kelsen, Hans. Das Problem der Souveränität und die Theorie des Völkerrechts. Beitrag zu einer Reinen Rechtslehre. *Aalen: Scientia*, 2. Ed. 1928, Neudruck 1960.
Kemmerer, Alexandra. 'Der normative Knoten. Über Recht und Politik im Netz der Netzwerke'. In: *Sigrid Boysen*, et al. (Coord.). Netzwerke. 47. *Assistententagung Öffentliches Recht.* Baden-Baden: Nomos.
Kennedy, David W. 'International Law and the Nineteenth Century. History of an Illusion'. In: *Nordic Journal of International Law* 65, 1996.
Kennedy, David W. 'The Move to Institutions'. In: *Cardozo Law Rev.* 8, 1987.
Kenney, William Howland. *Recorded Music in American Life. The Phonograph and Popular Memory, 1890–1945.* New York: Oxford University Press, 1999.
Keohane, Robert O. *After Hegemony. Cooperation and Discord in the World Political Economy.* Princeton: Princeton University Press, 1984.
Kersten, Jens. 'Die Entwicklung des Konzepts der Daseinsvorsorge im Werk von Ernst Forsthoff'. In: *Der Staat* 44, 2005.
Kerr, Ian; Earle, Jessica. 'Prediction, Preemption, Presumption: How Big Data Threatens Big Picture Privacy', 66 Stan. L. Rev. Online 65, 2013.
Khan, Lina. 'Amazon's Antitrust Paradox'. In: *Yale Law Journal*, 126, 2017.
Kieserling, André. 'Makropolitik, Mikropolitik. Politik der Protestbewegungen'. In: A. Nassehi; M. Schroer (Coord.). *Der Begriff des Politischen* (Soziale Welt, Sonderband 14). Baden-Baden: Nomos, 2003.
King, James E. 'The Origin of the Term Political Economy'. In: *Journal of Modern History 20*, 1948.
Kittler, Friedrich A. *Aufschreibsysteme. 1800–1900.* München: Fink, 2003.
Kleimann, Hans-Otto. 'Der atlantische Raum als Problem des europäischen Staatensystems'. In: *Jahrbuch für Geschichte Lateinamerikas* 38, 2001.
Klonick, Kate. The New Governors: The People, Rules, and Processes Governing. Online Speech. In: *Harvard Law Review* 131/6, 2018.
Kneisel, Sebastian. Schiedsgerichtsbarkeit in *Internationalen Verwaltungsunionen (1874–1914).* Baden-Baden: Nomos, 2009.
Koh, Harold Hongju. International Law as Part of Our Law. In: *American Journal of International Law* 98, 2004.
Kohler, Josef. 'Die Idee des geistigen Eigenthums'. In: Ar*chiv für die Civilistische Praxis* 82, 1894.

Kohlrausch, Martin. *Der Monarch im Skandal. Die Logik der Massenmedien und die Transformation der wilhelminischen Monarchie*. Berlin: Akad.-Verl, 2005.

Kohlrausch, Martin. *Medienskandale und Monarchie. Die Entwicklung der Massenpresse und die 'große Politik' im Kaiserreich*. In: Jörg Requate (Coord.). *Das 19. Jahrhundert als Mediengesellschaft*, München: 2009.

König, Hans-Joachim. '¿Comercio Libre a cambio de Reconocimiento político? El caso especial de las negociaciones entre la Gran Colombia y las Ciudades Hanseática'. In: R. Piper/P. Schmidt (Coord.). *Latin America and the Atlantic Word. El mundo atlantico y America latina (1500–1850). Essays in Honor of Horst Pietschmann*. Köln: Böhlau, 2005.

Kopp-Oberstebrink, Herbert. 'Umbesetzung'. In: Weidner, Daniel/Buch, Robert (Coord.). *Blumenberg lesen. Ein Glossar*. Berlin: Suhrkamp, 2014.

Koschorke, Albrecht. 'Die Grenzen des Systems und die Rhetorik der Systemtheorie'. In: Koschorke, Albrecht; C. Vismann (Coord.). *Widerstände der Systemtheorie. Kulturtheoretische Analysen zum Werk von Niklas Luhmann*. Berlin: Akademie-Verlag, 1999.

Koschorke, Albrecht; Lüdemann, Susanne; Thomas, Frank; Matala De Mazza, Ethel. *Der fiktive Staat. Konstruktionen des politischen Körpers in der Geschichte Europas*. Frankfurt am Main: Fischer, 2007.

Koselleck, Reinhart. 'Art. Bund, Bündnisse, Föderalismus, Bundesstaat'. In: *Koselleck, Reinhart; W. Conze; O. Brunner. Geschichtliche Grundbegriffe. Historisches Wörterbuch zur politischsozialen Sprache*, Bd. I. Stuttgart: Klett-Cotta, 1972.

Koselleck, Reinhart. Vergangene Zukunft. Zur Semantik geschichtlicher Zeiten. Frank-furt am Main: Suhrkamp, 1989.

Koselleck, Reinhart. 'Wie neu ist die Neuzeit?'. In: Koselleck, *Reinhart. Zeitgeschichten. Studien zur Historik*. Frankfurt am Main: Suhrkamp, 2000.

Koskenniemi, Martti. *The Gentle Civilizer of Nations. The Rise and Fall of International Law 1870–1960*. Cambridge: Cambridge University Press, 2001.

Koskenniemi, Martti. *From Apology to Utopia. The Structure of International Legal Argument*. Cambridge: Cambridge University Press, 2006.

Koskenniemi, Martti. International Law as Political Theology. How to Read Nomos der Erde?. In: *Constellations* 11/4, 2006.

Koskenniemi, Martti. *The Politics of International Law*. Oxford: Hart Publishing, 2011.

Koskenniemi, Martti. 'Ius Gentium and the Birth of Modernity'. In: L. Nuzzo; M. Vec (Coord.). *Constructing International Law. The Birth of a Discipline*. Frankfurt am Main: Klostermann, 2012.

Koskenniemi, Martti. 'Carl Schmitt and International Law'. In: J. Meierhenrich/O. Simons (Coord.). *The Oxford Handbook of Carl Schmitt*. Oxford Handbooks Online (April 2015).

Koskenniemi, Martti; Leino, Päivi. 'Fragmentation of International Law'. Postmodern Anxieties?. In: *Leiden Journal of International Law* 15, 2002.

Koskenniemi, Martti; Orford, Anne. '"We do not Need to Always Look to Westphalia ..." A Conversation with Martti Koskenniemi and Anne Orford'. In: *Journal of the History of International Law* 7, 2015.

Kosseff, Jeff. *The Twenty-Six Words That Created the Internet*. London: Cornell University Press, 2019.

Krajewski, Markus. *ZettelWirtschaft. Die Geburt der Kartei aus dem Geiste der Bibliothek*. Berlin: Kulturverlag Kadmos, 2002.

Kracauer, Siegfried. 'Kult der Zerstreuung'. In: Kracauer, Siegfried. *Das Ornament der Masse*. Frankfurt am Main: Suhrkamp, 1977.

Krich, Nico. *Beyond Constitutionalism: The Pluralist Structure of Post-national Law*. Oxford: Oxford University Press, 2010.

Küpper, Martin. 'Quentin Meillassoux: Denklandschaft des spekulativen Materialismus'. In: *Vorschein* (Jahrbuch der Ernst-Bloch-Assoziation – Coord. von Doris Zeilinger), 34, 2017.

Kuczerawy, Aleksandra. *Intermediary Liability and Freedom of Expression in the EU: From Concepts to Safeguards*. Cambridge: Intersentia, 2018.
Ladeur, Karl-Heinz. 'Von der Verwaltungshierarchie zum administrativen Netzwerk?' In: *Die Verwaltung* 26, 1993.
Ladeur, Karl-Heinz. *Postmoderne Rechtstheorie. Selbstreferenz – Selbstorganisation – Proceduralisierung*. Berlin: Duncker & Humblot, 1995.
Ladeur, Karl-Heinz. *Negative Freiheitsrechte und gesellschaftliche Selbstorganisation. Die Erzeugung von Sozialkapital durch Institutionen*. Tübingen: Mohr Siebeck, 2000.
Ladeur, Karl-Heinz. 'The Postmodern Condition of Law and Societal Management of Rules'. *Facts and Norms Revised*. In: Zeitschrift für Rechtssoziologie 27, 2006.
Ladeur, Karl-Heinz. *Der Staat gegen die Gesellschaft. Zur Verteidigung der Rationalität der Privatrechtsgesellschaft*. Tübingen: Mohr Siebeck, 2006.
Ladeur, Karl-Heinz. 'Soziale Epistemologie der Demokratie. Theoretische Überle-gungen zur Bindung von Unbestimmtheit durch Institutionen in der postmodernen Gesellschaft'. In: I. Augsberg (Coord.). *Ungewissheit als Chance*. Tübingen: Mohr Siebeck, 2009.
Ladeur, Karl-Heinz. Ein Recht der Netzwerke für die Weltgesellschaft oder Konstitutionalisierung der Völkergemeinschaft?. In: *Archiv des Völkerrechts* 49/3, September 2011.
Ladeur, Karl-Heinz. 'Der Staat der Gesellschaft der Netzwerke. Zur Fortentwicklung des Paradigmas des Gewährleistungsstaat'. In: T. Vesting/I. Augsberg (Coord.). *Ladeur. Das Recht der Netzwerkgesellschaft*. Tübingen: Verlag, 2013.
Ladeur, Karl-Heinz. *Der Anfang des westlichen Rechts. Die Christianisierung der römischen Rechtskultur und die Entstehung des universalen Rechts*. Tübingen: Mohr Siebeck, 2018.
Ladeur, Karl-Heinz. 'Netzwerkrecht als neues Ordnungsmodell des Rechts'. In: M. Eifert; T. Gostomzyk, Gostomzyk (Coord.). *Netzwerkrecht. Die Zukunft des NetzDG und seine Folgen für die Netzwerkkommunikation*. Baden-Baden: Nomos, 2018.
Ladeur, Karl-Heinz. 'Rechte gegen Rechte' – Kann diese Konfrontation dem Prozessieren des Rechts gerecht werden? In: I. Augsberg/S. Augsberg/L. Heidbrink (Coord.). Recht auf Nicht Recht. Rechtliche Reaktionen auf die Juridifizierung der Gesellschaft. Weilerswist: Velbrück, 2020.
Ladeur, Karl-Heinz. 'Helmut Ridders Konzeption der Meinungsfreiheit als Prozessgrundrecht'. In: KJ 53 (2020) Heft 2.
Ladeur, Karl-Heinz. Die Kollision von Meinungsfreiheit und Ehrenschutz in der interpersonalen Kommunikation – Was stellt die Klarstellung der Zweiten Kammer des BVerfG vom 19.6.2020 klar?. JZ, 2020.
Ladeur, Karl-Heinz; Augsberg, Ino. *Die Funktion der Menschenwürde im Verfassungsstaat. Humangenetik, Neurowissenschaft, Medien*. Tübingen: Mohr Siebeck, 2008.
Ladeur, Karl-Heinz; Gostomzyk, Tobias. 'Das Medienrecht und die Herausforderung der technologischen Hybridisierung'. In: *Kommunikation und Recht*, 2018.
Ladeur, Karl-Heinz; Vesting, Thomas. 'Geistiges Eigentum im Netzwerk – Anforderungen und Entwicklungslinien'. In: M. Eifert/W. Hoffmann-Riem (Coord.). *Geistiges Eigentum und Innovation. Innovation und Recht I*. Berlin: Duncker & Humblot, 2018.
Ladeur, Karl-Heinz; Viellechner, Lars. Die transnationale Expansion staatlicher Grundrechte. Zur Konstitutionalisierung globaler Privatrechtsregimes, *Archiv des Völkerrechts* 46, 2008.
Landwehr, Achim. *Geburt der Gegenwart. Eine Geschichte der Zeit im 17. Jahrhundert*. Frankfurt am Main: Fischer, 2014.
Larenz, Karl. *Das Problem der Rechtsgeltung*. Berlin: Junker & Dünnhaupt, 1929.
Latour, Bruno. 'From Realpolitik to Dingpolitik or How to Make Things Public'. In: Latour, Bruno; P. Weibel (Coord.). *Making Things Public. Atmospheres of Democracy*. Karlsruhe: Zentrum für Kunst und Medientechnologie, 2005.
Latour, Bruno. *Wir sind nie modern gewesen. Versuch einer symmetrischen Anthropologie*. Frankfurt am Main: Suhrkamp, 2008.
Lawrence, Thomas J. *Principles of International Law*. Boston: D.C. Heath, 1900.

174 Bibliography

Legg, Stephen. 'Interwar Spatial Chaos? Imperialism, Internationalism and the League of Nations'. In: Legg, Stephen. (Coord.). *Spatiality, Sovereignty, and Carl Schmitt. Geographies of the Nomos.* London/New York: Routledge, 2011.

Le Goff, Jacques. 'Zeit der Kirche und Zeit des Händlers im Mittelalter'. In: C. Honegger; M. Bloch; F. Braudel; L. Febvre et al. (Coord.). *Schrift und Materie der Geschichte. Vorschläge zur systematischen Aneignung historischer Prozesse.* Frankfurt am Main: Suhrkamp, 1977.

Le Goff, Pierrick. 'Global Law: A Legal Phenomenon Emerging from the Process of Globalization'. In: *Indiana Journal of Global Legal Studies* 14, 200.

Leibfried, Stephan; Zürn, Michael. 'Reconfiguring the National Constellation'. In: Leibfried, Stephan. (Coord.). *Transformation of the State?* Cambridge: Cambridge University Press, 2005.

Leistner, Matthias; Hansen, Gerd. 'Die Begründung des Urheberrechts im digitalen Zeitalter – Versuch einer Zusammenführung von individualistischen und utilitaristischen Rechtfertigungsbemühungen'. In: *Gewerblicher Rechtsschutz und Urheberrecht*, 2006.

Lemahieu, Daniel L. *A Culture for Democracy: Mass Communication and the Cultivated Mind in Britain between the Wars.* Oxford: Clarendon Press, 1988.

Lemke, Thomas. *Gouvernementalität und Biopolitik.* Wiesbaden: Verl. für Sozialwiss, 2006.

Lepenies, Wolf. *Das Ende der Naturgeschichte. Wandel kultureller Selbstverständlichkeiten in den Wissenschaften des 18. und 19. Jahrhunderts.* München: Hanser, 1976.

Lepore, Jill. 'We have got the Internet ... We have got talk radio. We have got social media. We've got the ability to go directly around, and directly to the people'. In: *The New Yorker*, 22. February, 2016.

Lepore, Jill. *If Then? How the Simulmatics Corporation Invented the Future.* New York: Norton & Company, 2020.

Lesaffer, Randall. 'The Grotian Tradition Revisited: Change and Continuity in the History of International Law'. In: BYIL 73, 2002.

Lawrence, Lessig. *Code and Other Laws of Cyberspace.* New York; Basic Books, 1999.

Lawrence, *Lessig. Code: Version 2.0.* New York: Basic Books, 2006.

Levi, Lili. 'The Four Eras of FCC Public Interest Regulation', *Admin. L. Rev.* 60, 2008.

Levinson, Brett. 'The Coming Nomos; or, the Decline of Other Orders in Schmitt'. In: *The South Atlantic Quarterly* 104/2, 2005.

Liebs, Detlef. *Lateinische Rechtsregeln und Rechtssprichwörter.* 7a Ed. München: Beck, 2007.

Löhr, Isabella. *Die Globalisierung geistiger Eigentumsrechte. Neue Strukturen internationaler Zusammenarbeit 1886–1952 – Kritische Studien zur Geschichtswissenschaft* 195. Göttingen: Vandenhoeck & Ruprecht, 2010.

Lomfeld, Bertram (Coord.). *Die Fälle der Gesellschaft: eine neue Praxis soziologischer Jurisprudenz.* Tübingen: Mohr Siebeck, 2017.

Lowe, Donald M. *History of Bourgeois Perception.* Chicago: University of Chicago Press, 1982.

Löwith, Karl. 'Der okkasionelle Dezisionismus von C. Schmitt (1935)'. In: Löwith, Karl. *Sämtliche Schriften, Bd. 8: Heidegger – Denker in dürftiger Zeit. Zur Stellung der Philosophie im 20. Jahrhundert.* Stuttgart: J.B. Metzler, 1984.

Lowrie, Michèle. Sovereignty before the Law. Agamben and the Roman Republic. In: *Law and Humanities* 1, 2017.

Luhmann, Niklas. *Vertrauen. Ein Mechanismus der Reduktion sozialer Komplexität.* Stuttgart: Enke, 1968.

Luhmann, Niklas. 'Moderne Systemtheorien als Form gesamtgesellschaftlicher Analyse'. In: J. Habermas; Luhmann, Niklas. (Coord.). *Theorie der Gesellschaft oder Sozialtechnologie: Was leistet die Systemforschung.* Frankfurt am Main: Suhrkamp, 1971.

Luhmann, Niklas. *Rechtssoziologie*, Bd. 2. Reinbek bei Hamburg: Rowohlt, 1972.

Luhmann, Niklas. Politische Verfassungen im Kontext des Gesellschaftssystems. Teil 1. In: *Der Staat* 1 (1973); Teil 2. In: *Der Staat* 2 (1973).

Luhmann, Niklas. Selbst-Thematisierungen des Gesellschaftssystems. Über die Kategorie der Reflexion aus Sicht der Systemtheorie. In: *Zeitschrift für Soziologie* 2/1, 1973.

Luhmann, Niklas. 'Gesellschaftliche Struktur und semantische Tradition'. In: Luhmann, Niklas. *Gesellschaftsstruktur und Semantik. Studien zur Wissenssoziologie der modernen Gesellschaft*, Band 1. Frankfurt am Main: Suhrkamp, 1980.
Luhmann, Niklas. World Society as a Social System. In: F. R. Geyer/J. v. d. Zouwen (Coord.). *Dependence and Inequality. A Systems Approach to the Problems of Mexico and Other Developing Countries*. Oxford: Pergamon Press, 1982.
Luhmann, Niklas. *Soziale Systeme*. Frankfurt am Main: Suhrkamp, 1984.
Luhmann, Niklas. *Rechtssoziologie*. 3rd Ed. Opladen: Westdeutscher Verlag, 1987.
Luhmann, Niklas. Verfassung als evolutionäre Errungenschaft. In: *Rechtshistorisches Journal 9*, 1990.
Luhmann, Niklas. *Paradigm lost. Über die ethische Reflexion der Moral – Rede anlässlich der Verleihung des Hegel-Preises 1989*. Frankfurt am Main: Suhrkamp, 1990.
Luhmann, Niklas. *Das Recht der Gesellschaft*. Frankfurt am Main: Suhrkamp, 1993.
Luhmann, Niklas. 'Quod omnes tangit ... 'Anmerkungen zur Rechtstheorie von Jürgen Habermas. In: *Rechtshistorisches Journal* 12, 1993.
Luhmann, Niklas. Staat und Staatsräson im Übergang von traditioneller Herrschaft zu moderner Politik. In: Luhmann, Niklas.*Gesellschaftsstruktur und Semantik*. Frankfurt am Main: Suhrkamp, 1993.
Luhmann, Niklas. *Die Wirtschaft der Gesellschaft*. Frankfurt am Main: Suhrkamp, 1994.
Luhmann, Niklas. Inklusion und Exklusion. In: H. Berding (Coord.). *Nationales Be-wusstsein und kollektive Identität. Studien zur Entwicklung des kollektiven Bewußtseins in der Neuzeit 2*. Frankfurt am Main: Suhrkamp, 1994.
Luhmann, Niklas. *Die Realität der Massenmedien*. Wiesbaden: VS Verlag für Sozialwissenschaften, 1996.
Luhmann, Niklas. *Die Gesellschaft der Gesellschaft*, 2 Bde. Frankfurt am Main: Suhrkamp, 1997.
Luhmann, Niklas. Globalization or World Society. How to Conceive of Modern Society?. In: *International Review of Sociology* 7/1, 1997.
Luhmann, Niklas. Positivität des Rechts als Voraussetzung einer modernen Gesellschaft. In: Luhmann, Niklas. *Ausdifferenzierung des Rechts. Beiträge zur Rechtssoziologie und Rechtstheorie*. Frankfurt am Main: Suhrkamp. 1999.
Luhmann, Niklas. *Grundrechte als Institution: Ein Beitrag zur politischen Soziologie*. Berlin: Duncker & Humblot, 3. Auf, 1999.
Luhmann, Niklas. Die Rückgabe des zwölften Kamels: Zum Sinn einer soziologischen Analyse des Rechts. In: *Zeitschrift für Rechtssoziologie 21*, 2000.
Luhmann, Niklas. Die Politik der Gesellschaft. Frankfurt am Main: Suhrkamp, 2002.
Luhmann, Niklas. *Soziologie des Risikos*. Berlin: de Gruyter, 2003.
Luhmann, Niklas. 'Die Weltgesellschaft'. In: Luhmann, Niklas. *Soziologische Aufklärung 2: Aufsätze zur Theorie der Gesellschaft*. Wiesbaden: Verlag für Sozialwissenschaften. 5th Ed, 2005.
Luhmann, Niklas. *Weltzeit und Systemgeschichte*, ebd.
Luhmann, Niklas. *Die Wissenschaft der Gesellschaft*. 7a Ed. Frankfurt am Main: Suhrkamp, 2015.
Luhmann, Niklas. *Systemtheorie der Gesellschaft*. Berlin: Suhrkamp, 2017.
Macalister-Smith, Peter; Schwietzke, Joachim. Bibliography of the Textbooks and Comprehensive Treatises on Positive International Law of the 19th Century. In: *Journal of the History of International Law* 3, 2001.
Machlup, Fritz. *The Political Economy of Monopoly. Business, Labor and Government Policies*. Baltimore: John Hopkins Press, 1952.
Machlup, Fritz. *The Production and Distribution of Knowledge in the United States*. Princeton: Princeton University Press, 1962.
Mackinnon, Rebecca; Hickok, Elonnai; BAR, Allon; LIM, Hae-in. Fostering Freedom Online: The Roles, challenges and obstacles of internet intermediaries. United Nations Educational 2014.
Mahoney, Michael. 'The Histories of Computing(s)'. In: *Interdisciplinary Science Reviews* 30, 2005.
Mahoney, Michael. *The Histories of Computing*. Cambridge: Harvard University Press, 2011.

Mangone, Gerard J. *A Short History of International Organization*. New York: McGraw-Hill, 1954.
Manow, Philip. Die Menschwerdung des Menschen unter dem Leviathan. In: Manow, Philip. *Politische Ursprungsphantasien: der Leviathan und sein Erbe*. Konstanz: Konstanz University Press, 2011.
Martineau, Anne-Charlotte. 'The Rhetoric of Fragmentation: Fear and Faith in International Law'. In: *Leiden Journal of International Law* 22, 2009.
Martus, Steffen. *Aufklärung. Das Deutsche 18. Jahrhundert. Ein Epochenbild*. Berlin: Rowohlt, 2015.
Marx, Karl. *Grundrisse der Kritik der politischen Ökonomie* (1857–58). Berlin: Dietz, 1953.
Marx, Karl; Engels, Friedrich. Gesamtausgabe (MEGA) – Coord. *von der internationalen Marx-Engels-Stiftung Amsterdam*. Berlin: Akademie Verlag, 2000.
Mayer-Schönberger, Viktor. *Big Data: A Revolution that Will Transform how we Live, Work and Think*. Boston: Houghton Mifflin Harcourt, 2013.
Mayntz, Renate. 'Die Handlungsfähigkeit des Nationalstaats in Zeiten der Globalisierung'. In: L. Heidbrink; A. Hirsch (Coord.). *Staat ohne Verantwortung? Zum Wandel der Aufgaben von Staat und Politik*. Frankfurt am Main: Campus, 2007.
Mbembe, Achille. *Critique de la raison nègre*. Paris: Édition la Découverte, 2013.
McNeill, John B.; McNeill, William H. *The Human Web. A Birds-Eye View of World History*. New York: Norton, 2003.
Mehring, Reinhard. 'Politische Ethik in Max Webers Politik als Beruf und Carl Schmitts Der Begriff des Politischen'. In: *Politische Vierteljahreszeitschrift* 31/4, 1990.
Meillassoux, Quentin. *After Finitude. An Essay on the Necessity of Contingency*. London: Continuum, 2008.
Meiners, Johannes. *Rechtsnormen und Rationalität. Zum Problem der Rechtsgeltung bei Hans Kelsen, Jürgen Habermas und Niklas Luhmann*. Berlin: Duncker & Humblot, 2015.
Meuter, Günter. *Der Katechon. Zu Carl Schmitts fundamentalistischer Kritik der Zeit*. Berlin: Duncker & Humblot, 1994.
Meyer, Stephan. *Juristische Geltung als Verbindlichkeit*. Tübingen: Mohr Siebeck, 2011.
Mignolo, Walter D. *The Darker Side of Western Modernity. Global Futures, Decolonial Options*. Durham (N.C.)/London: Duke University Press, 2001.
Mitchell, Dean M. 'A Political Mythology of World Order. Carl Schmitt's Nomos'. In: *Theory, Culture & Society* 23, 2006.
Möllers, Christoph. 'Der Methodenstreit als politischer Generationenkonflikt. Ein Angebot zur Deutung der Weimarer Staatsrechtslehre'. In: *Der STAAT* 43/3, 2004.
Möllers, Christoph. 'Netzwerk als Kategorie des Organisationsrechts. Zur juristischen Beschreibung dezentraler Steuerung'. In: Janbernd Oebbecke (Coord.). *Nicht-Normative Steuerung in dezentralen Systemen*. Stuttgart: 2005.
Möllers, Christoph. *Die Möglichkeit der Normen. Über eine Praxis jenseits von Moralität und Kausalität*. Berlin: Suhrkamp, 2015.
Moretti, Franco. 'Balzac's Novels and Urban Personality'. In: Möllers, Christoph. *Signs Taken for Won. On the Sociology of Literary Forms*. London/New York: Verso, 1983.
Moretti, Franco. *The Bourgeois. Between History and Literature*. London/New York: Verso, 2014.
Mossner, Ernest C. 'Hume's Early Memoranda, 1729–1740: The Complete Text'. In: *Journal of the History of Ideas* 9/4, 1948.
Motta, Massimo; Peitz, Martin. Intervention Triggers and Underlying Theories of Harm. In: *Market Investigations: A New Competition Tool for Europe?* Cambridge University Press, 2022.
Motschenbacher, Alfons. *Katechon oder Großinquisitor? Eine Studie zu Inhalt und Struktur der Politischen Theologie Carl Schmitts*. Marburg: Tectum-Verl., 2000.
Mouffe, Chantal. 'Carl Schmitt and the Paradox of Liberal Democracy'. In: Mouffe, Chantal. *The Challenge of Carl Schmitt*. London/New York: Verso, 1999.
Mouffe, Chantal. 'Deliberative Democracy or Agonistic Pluralism?' In: *Social Research* 66/3, 1999.
Mouffe, Chantal. *The Democratic Paradox*. London/New York: Verso, 2000.

Mouffe, Chantal. *Über das Politische. Wider die kosmopolitische Illusion*. Frankfurt am Main: Suhrkamp, 2007.
Müller, Jan-Werner. *A Dangerous Mind. Carl Schmitt in Post-war European Thought*. New Haven/London: Yale University Press, 2003.
Murphy, Craig N. *International Organization and Industrial Change. Global Governance since 1850*. Cambridge: Polity Press, 1994.
Mußgnug, Dorothee; Mußgunug, Reinhard; Reinstahl, Angela (Coord.). *Briefwechsel Ernst Forsthoff Carl Schmitt (1926–1974)*. Berlin: 2007.
Myers West, Sarah. 'Data Capitalism: Redefining the Logics of Surveillance and Privacy'. In: *Business & Society* 58/1, 2019.
Nederman, Cary; Bogiaris, Guillaume. 'Niccolò Machiavelli'. In: Daniel M. Robinson; Chad Meister; Charles Taliaferro (Coord.). *The History of Evil in the Early Modern Age: 1450–1700 CE*. London, 2018.
Nijan, Janne E. *The Concept of International Legal Personality. An Inquiry into the History and Theory of International Law*. Den Haag: Asser Press, 2004.
Nussbaum, Arthur. 'Lorenz von Stein on International Law and International Administration'. In: Gerwig, Max; Simonius, August (Coord.). *Festschrift Hans Lewald* (S. 555–560). Basel: Helbing & Lichtenhahn, 1953.
Nussbaum, Arthur. *Geschichte des Völkerrechts – in gedrängter Darstellung*. München: Beck, 1960.
Nuzzo, Luigi. 'Un modo senza nemici. La costruzione del diritto internazionale e la negazione delle differenze'. In: *Quaderni Fiorentini* 39, 2009.
Nuzzo, Luigi. 'Das Nationalitätsprinzip: der italienische Weg zum Völkerrecht'. In: Dauchy; M. Vec (Coord.). *Les conflits entre peuples. De la résolution libre à la résolution imposée*. Baden-Baden: Nomos, 2011.
Nuzzo, Luigi; VEC, Miloš (Coord.). *Constructing International Law – The Birth of a Discipline*. Frankfurt am Main: Klostermann, 2012.
Ogle, Vanessa. *The Global Transformation of Time: 1870–1950*. Cambridge (Mass.): Harvard University Press, 2015.
Ossembühl, Fritz. *Die Not des Gesetzgebers im naturwissenschaftlich – technischen Zeitalter*. Wiesbaden: Westdt. Verlag, 2000.
Osterhammel, Jürgen. *Die Verwandlung der Welt. Eine Geschichte des 19. Jahrhunderts*. München: Beck, 2009.
Osterhammel, Jürgen. 'Höherer Wahnsinn. Universalhistorische Denkstile im 20. Jahrhundert'. In: Osterhammel, Jürgen. *Geschichtswissenschaft jenseits des Nationalstaats. Studien zu Beziehungsgeschichte und Zivilisationsvergleich*. Göttingen: Vandenhoeck und Ruprecht, 2001.
Osterhammel, Jürgen; Peterson, *Niels P. Geschichte der Globalisierung. Dimensionen, Prozesse, Epochen*. München: Beck, 2003.
Parker, Geoffrey; Van Alstyne, Marshall W.; Choudary, Sangeet Paul. *Platform Revolution: How Networked Markets Are Transforming The Economy – And How To Make Them Work For You*. New York: W.W. Norton & Company, 2016.
Parsons, Talcott, *Societies. Evolutionary and Comparative Perspectives*. Englewood-Cliffs (N.J.): Prentice-Hall, 1966.
Parsons, Talcott. 'Polarization of the World and International Order'. In: Parsons, Talcott. *Sociological Theory and Modern Society*. New York: Free Press, 1967.
Parsons, Talcott. *The Systems of Modern Societies*. Englewood-Cliffs (N.J.): Prentice Hall, 1971.
Parsons, Talcott; Ackermann, Charles. 'The Concept of Social System as a Theoretical Device'. In: G. J. DiRenzo (Coord.). *Concepts, Theory and Explanation in the Behavioral Sciences*. New York: Random House, 1966.
Pasquinelli, Matteo. 'Was ein Dispositiv nicht ist: Archäologie der Norm bei Foucault, Canguilhem und Goldstein'. In: L. Aggermann; G. Döcker; G. Siegmund (Coord.). *Theater als Dispositiv. Dysfunktion, Fiktion und Wissen in der Ordnung der Aufführung*. Frankfurt am Main: Peter Lang, 2017.

Paulus, Andreas. 'Fragmentierung und Segmentierung der internationalen Ordnung als Herausforderung prozeduraler Gemeinwohlorientierung'. In: H. M. Heinig; J. P. Terhechte (Coord.). *Postnationale Demokratie, Postdemokratie, Neoetatismus. Wandel klassischer Demokratievorstellungen in der Rechtswissenschaft*. Tübingen: Mohr Siebeck, 2013.

Pauly, Walter. 'Hegel und die Frage nach dem Staat'. In: *Der Staat* 39, 2000.

Peczenik, Aleksander. *The Concept Valid Law*. Stockholm: Almquist & Wiksell, 1972.

Perrow, Charles. 'A Society of Organizations'. In: M. Haller; H. J. Hoffmann-Nowotny; W. Zapf (Coord.). *Kultur und Gesellschaft: Verhandlungen des 24. Deutschen Soziologentags, des 11. Österreichischen Soziologentags und des 8. Kongresses der Schweizerischen Gesellschaft für Soziologie in Zürich 1988*. Frankfurt am Main: Campus Verlag, 1989.

Peters, Anne. 'Compensatory Constitutionalism. The Function and Potential of Fundamental International Norms and Structures'. LJIL 19, 2006.

Peters, Anne. Rechtsordnung und Konstitutionalisierung: Zur Neubestimmung der Verhältnisse. ZöR 65, 2010.

Peters, Anne. 'Fragmentation and Constitutionalization'. In: *The Oxford Handbook of the Theory of International Law*. Oxford/New York: Oxford University Press, 2016.

Peters, Anne. *The Refinement of International Law: From Fragmentation to Regime Interaction and Politicization*. I•CON 15/3, 2017.

Peters, Anne; Peter, Simone. 'International Organizations: Between Technocracy and Democracy'. In: B. Fassbender; A. Peters (Coord.). *The Oxford Handbook of the History of International Law*. Oxford: Oxford University Press, 2012.

Peterson, Niels P. 'Das Kaiserreich in Prozessen ökonomischer Globalisierung'. In: Conrad; J. Osterhammel. *Das Kaiserreich transnational. Deutschland in der Welt 1871–1914*. Göttingen: Vandenhoeck & Ruprecht, 2004.

Petit, Carlos. *Historia del Derecho Mercantil*. Madrid: Marcial Pons, 2016.

Peukert, Alexander. 'Immaterialgüterrecht und Entwicklung'. In: Philipp Dann; Stefan Kadelbach/Markus Kaltenborn (Coord.). *Entwicklung und Recht. Eine systematische Einführung*. Baden-Baden: Nomos, 2014.

Peukert, Alexander. 'Die Herausbildung der normativen Ordnung geistiges Eigentum'. Diskurstheoretische und andere Erklärungsansätze'. In: Rainer Forst; Klaus Günther (Coord.). *Theorien normativer Ordnungen*. Berlin: Suhrkamp, i. E.

Pocock, John G. A. *The Machiavellian Moment. Florentine Political Thought and the Atlantic Republican Tradition*. Princeton: Princeton University Press, 1975.

Posner, Richard. *Economic Analysis of Law*. 8a Ed. Aspen: 2011. Pounds, Norman J. *Hearth & Home. A History of Material Culture*. Bloomington: Indiana University Press, 1989.

Powell, Walter. 'Neither Market Nor Hierarchy'. In: *Research in Organizational Behavior*. vol. 12, 1990.

Prazniak, Roxann. 'Is World History Possible? An Inquiry'. In: V. Bahl (Coord.). *History After the Three Worlds: Post-Eurocentric Historiographies*. Boulder: Rowman & Littlefield, 2000.

Rao, Pemmaraju S. 'Multiple International Judicial Forums: A Refection of the Growing Strength of International Law or its Fragmentation'. In: *Mich J Int'l L* 25, 2004.

Rasch, William. Human Rights as Geopolitics. Carl Schmitt and the Legal Form of American Supremacy. In: *Cultural Critique* 54, 2003.

Redepenning, Marc; Wilhelm, Jan L. 'Raumforschung mit luhmannscher Systemtheorie'. In: J. Oßenbrügge; A. Vogelpohl (Coord.). *Theorien in der Raumund Stadtforschung*. Münster: Westfälisches Dampfboot, 2014.

Rehbinder, Manfred. *Die Begründung der Rechtssoziologie durch Eugen Ehrlich*. 2nd Ed. Berlin: Duncker & Humblot, 1986.

Reuver, Mark de; Sørensen, Carsten; Basole, Rahul C. 'The Digital Platform: A Research Agenda'. In: *Journal of Information Technology* 33/2, 2018.

Rheinberger, Hans-Jörg. *Historische Epistemologie zur Einführung*. Hamburg: Junius, 2007.

Richter, Bodo. *Völkerrecht, Außenpolitik und internationale Verwaltung bei Lorenz von Stein*. Hamburg: Heitmann, 1973.

Ridder, Helmut. 'Schmittiana (II)'. In: *Neue Politische Literatur* 12, 1967.

Riles, Annelise. 'Aspiration and Control. International Legal Rhetoric and the Essentialization of Culture'. In: *Harvard Law Review* 106, 1993.

Rikey, Patrick. *Leibniz' Universal Jurisprudence. Justice as the Charity of the Wise*. Cambridge (Mass.): Harvard University Press, 1996.

Rikey, Patrick. Introduction. In: Rikey, Patrick. *Leibniz: Political Writings*. Cambridge: Cambridge University Press, 2. Ed. 1988.

Riordan, Jaani. *The Liability of Internet Intermediaries*. Oxford: Oxford University Press, 2016.

Ritter, Joachim. *Hegel und die Französische Revolution*. Köln/Opladen: Westdeutscher Verlag, 1957.

Rochet, Jean C.; Tirole, Jean. 'Platform Competition in Two-Sided Markets'. In: *Journal of the European Economic Association* 1/4, 2003.

Rochet, Jean C. 'Two-Sided Markets: A Progress Report'. In: *RAND Journal of Economics* 35, 2006.

Röhl, Klaus F. *Allgemeine Rechtslehre*. München/Köln: Heymann, 1995.

Röhl, Klaus F.; Machura, Stefan. '100 Jahre Rechtssoziologie: Eugen Ehrlichs Rechtspluralismus heute'. In: *JZ* 23, 2013.

Roncaglia, Alessandro. *Petty: The Origins of Political Economy*. New York: M. E. Sharpe Inc, 1985.

Rosa, Hartmut. 'Beschleunigung'. *Die Veränderung der Zeitstrukturen der Moderne*. Frankfurt am Main: Suhrkamp, 2005.

Rosen, Lawrence. *Law as Culture. An Invitation*. New York: Princeton University Press, 2006.

Ross, Alf. *Theorie der Rechtsquellen. Ein Beitrag zur Theorie des positiven Rechts auf Grundlage dogmenhistorischer Untersuchungen*. Leipzig und Vienna: F. Deuticke, 1929.

Rossnagel, Alexander; Löber, Lena Isabell. 'Kennzeichnung von Social Bots – Transparenzpflichten zum Schutz integrer Kommunikation'. In: *Multimedia und Recht* (MMR) 21/8, 2019.

Rottleuthner, Hubert. 'Biological Metaphors in Legal Thought'. In: G. Teubner (Coord.). *Autopoietic Law. A New Approach to Law and Society*. Berlin: de Gruyter, 1987.

Rousseau, Jean-Jacques. 'Vom Gesellschaftsvertrag – übersetzt von Ludwig Schmidts'. In: *Politische Schriften* Bd. 1. Paderborn: Schöningh, 1977.

Rousseau, Jean-Jacques. *Politische Ökonomie* (Text französisch – deutsch), Coord. von Hans-Peter Schneider/Brigitte Schneider-Pachaly. Frankfurt am Main: Klostermann, 1977.

Ruffert, Matthias. 'Diskussionsbeitrag'. In: VVDStRL 63, 2004. Rüthers, Bernd. *Rechtstheorie*. 2nd Ed. München: Beck, 2005.

Rüthers, Bernd. *Carl Schmitt im Dritten Reich. Wissenschaft als Zeitgeist-Verstärkung?* München: 1989.

Sabrow, Martin. *Die Zeit der Zeitgeschichte*. Göttingen: Wallstein, 2012.

Sassen, Saskia. *Territory, Authority, Rights. From Medieval to Global Assemblages*. Princeton: Princeton University Press, 2008.

Savigny, Friedrich Carl von. *System des heutigen Römischen Rechts*, Bd. 1. Berlin: Veit, 1840.

Schestag, Thomas. 'Namen nehmen. Zur Theorie des Namens bei Carl Schmitt'. In: *MLN* 122/3, 2007.

Schiavone, Aldo, Ius. *L'invenzione del diritto in Occidente*. Turin: Giuli Einaudi, 2005.

Schiffmann, Zachary. *The Birth of the Past*. Baltimore: John Hopkins University Press, 2011.

Schluchter, Wolfgang. *Die Entstehung des modernen Rationalismus. Eine Analyse von Max Webers Entwicklungsgeschichte des Okzidents*. Frankfurt am Main: Suhrkamp, 1998.

Schmidt, Rebecca. *Regulatory Integration Across Borders: Public–Private Cooperation in Transnational Regulation*. Cambridge: Cambridge University Press, 2018.

Schmitt, Carl. *Die geistesgeschichtliche Lage des heutigen Parlamentarismus*. Berlin: Duncker & Humblot, 1926.

Schmitt, Carl. 'Das Zeitalter der Neutralisierungen und Entpolitisierungen'. In: Schmitt, Carl. *Der Begriff des Politischen*. München/Leipzig: Duncker & Humblot, 1932.

Schmitt, Carl. 'Cambio de estructura del derecho internacional'. In: *Revista de Estudios Politicos* 5, 1943.
Schmitt, Carl. 'Die letzte globale Linie'. In: Egmont Zechlin (Coord.). *Völker und Meere*. Leipzig: Harrassowitz, 1944.
Schmitt, Carl. *Der Nomos der Erde im Völkerrecht des Jus Publicum Europaeum* (1950). 2nd Ed. Berlin: Duncker & Humblot, 1974.
Schmitt, Carl. *Der Leviathan in der Staatslehre des Thomas Hobbes. Sinn und Fehlschlag eines politischen Symbols*. Stuttgart: Klett-Cotta, 1982.
Schmitt, Carl. *Verfassungslehre* (1928). Berlin: 1983.
Schmitt, Carl. 'Der Völkerbund und Europa'. In: *Schmitt, Carl. Positionen und Begriffe. Im Kampf mit Weimar– Genf – Versailles 1923–1939*. Berlin: Duncker & Humblot, 1988.
Schmitt, Carl. 'Abwandlung eines schlimmen Wortes von Proudhon, Staatsethik und pluralistischer Staat'. In: *Schmitt, Carl. Positionen und Begriffe im Kampf mit Weimar, Genf, Versailles (1923–1939)*. Berlin: Duncker & Humblot, Nachdruck, 1988.
Schmitt, Carl. 'Völkerrechtliche Probleme im Rheingebiet'. In: *Schmitt, Carl. Positionen und Begriffe. Im Kampf mit Weimar – Genf – Versailles 1923–1939*. Berlin: Duncker & Humblot, 1988.
Schmitt, Carl. *Politische Romantik*. Berlin: Duncker & Humblot, 1991.
Schmitt, Carl. *Völkerrechtliche Großraumordnung: mit Interventionsverbot für raumfremde Mächte. Ein Beitrag zum Reichsbegriff im Völkerrecht* (1941). Berlin: Duncker & Humblot, 1991.
Schmitt, Carl. *Das politische Problem der Friedenssicherung*. Vienna: Karolinger, 1993.
Schmitt, Carl. 'Die Auflösung der europäischen Ordnung im International Law'. In: *Schmitt, Carl. Staat, Großraum, Nomos. Arbeiten aus den Jahren 1916–1960* – Coord. von Günther Maschke. Berlin: Duncker & Humblot, 1995.
Schmitt, Carl. 'Nomos Nahme Name'. In: *Schmitt, Carl. Staat, Großraum, Nomos. Arbeiten aus den Jahren 1916–1969* – Coord. von Günther Maschke. Berlin: Duncker & Humblot, 1995.
Schmitt, Carl. 'Raum und Großraum im Völkerrecht'. In: *Schmitt, Carl. Staat, Großraum, Nomos. Arbeiten aus den Jahren 1916–1969* – Coord. von Günther Maschke. Berlin: Duncker & Humblot, 1995.
Schmitt, Carl. 'Staatliche Souveränität und freies Meer. Über den Gegensatz von Land und See im Völkerrecht der Neuzeit'. In: *Schmitt, Carl. Staat, Großraum, Nomos. Arbeiten aus den Jahren 1916–1969* – Coord. von Günter Maschke. Berlin: Duncker & Humblot, 1995.
Schmitt, Carl. *Der Begriff des Politischen*. Berlin: Duncker & Humblot, 2002.
Schmitt, Carl. *Über die drei Arten des rechtswissenschaftlichen Denkens – 1934*. Berlin: Duncker & Humblot, 2006.
Schmitt, Carl. *Römischer Katholizismus und politische Form*. Stuttgart: Klett–Cotta, 2008.
Schmitt, Carl. *Theorie des Partisanen. Zwischenbemerkung zum Begriff des Politischen*. 7a Ed. Berlin: 2010.
Schmitthoff, Clive M. 'International Business Law: A New Law Merchant'. In: *Current Law and Social Problems* 2, 1961.
Schmoeckel, Matthias. *Die Großraumtheorie: ein Beitrag zur Geschichte der Völkerrechtswissenschaft im Dritten Reich, insbesondere der Kriegszeit*. Berlin: Duncker & Humblot, 1994.
Schneewind, Jerome B. *The Invention of Autonomy. A History of Modern Moral Philosophy*. Cambridge: Cambridge University Press, 1998.
Schneider, Hans J. 'Gibt es eine 'Transzendental' – bzw. 'Universalpragmatik'?' In: *Zeitschrift für philosophische Forschung* 36/2, 1982.
Schröder, Peter. *Niccolò Machiavelli*. Frankfurt am Main: Campus, 2004.
Schröder, Rainer. *Rechtsgeschichte*. 5th Ed. Münster: Verlag, 2000.
Schroeder, Paul W. *The Transformation of European Politics, 1763–1848*. Oxford: Clarendon Press, 1994.
Schulz, Matthias. *Normen und Praxis: Das Europäische Konzert der Großmächte als Sicherheitsrat 1815–1860. Studien zur Internationalen Geschichte* Bd. 21. München, 2009.

Schumpeter, Josef A.; Schumpeter, *Elisabeth. Geschichte der ökonomischen Analyse*, Bd. I. Göttingen: 1965.
Schwarz, Jonas A. 'Platform Logic: An Interdisciplinary Approach to the Platform-Based Economy'. In: Pol'y & Int, 2017.
Schwarzenberger, Georg. *Power Politics: A Study of International Society*. 2nd Ed. London, 1951.
Schweitzer, Heike. *The Art to Make Gatekeeper Positions Contestable and the Challenge to Know What is Fair: A Discussion of the Digital Markets Act Proposal*. Zeitschrift für Europäisches Privatrecht, vol. 3, 2021.
Schwinn, Thomas. 'Weltgesellschaft, multiple moderne und die Herausforderungen für die soziologische Theorie. Plädoyer für eine mittlere Abstraktionshöhe'. In: Zeitschrift für Soziologie, Sonderheft Weltgesellschaft, 2005.
Seel, Martin. 'Das Naturschöne und das Kunstschöne'. In: Birgit Sandkaulen (Coord.). *G. W. F. Hegel. Vorlesungen über die Ästhetik*. Berlin: De Gruyter, 2018.
Seifert, Arno. 'Verzeitlichung'. Zur Kritik einer neueren Frühneuzeitkategorie'. In: *Zeitschrift für historische Forschung* 10, 1983.
Seinecke, Ralf. *Das Recht des Rechtspluralismus*. Tübingen: Mohr Siebeck, 2015.
Shapiro, Martin. 'Towards a Theory of Stare Decisis'. In: *Journal of Legal Studies* 1, 1972.
Shapiro, Scott J. What Is the Internal Point of View?, 75 Fordham Law Review, 2006.
Sheehan, Jonathan; Wahrman, Dror. *Invisible Hands. Self-organization in the Eighteenth Century*. Chicago/London: University of Chicago Press, 2015.
Siegert, Bernhard. *Passage des Digitalen. Zeichenpraktiken der neuzeitlichen Wissenschaften 1500–1900*. Berlin: Brinkmann u. Bose, 2003.
Siegert, Bernhard. 'Kulturtechnik'. In: H. Maye; L. Scholz (Coord.). *Einführung in die Kulturwissenschaft*. München: Fink, 2011.
Slaughter Burley, Anne-Marie. 'International Law and International Relations Theory: A Dual Agenda'. In: *American Journal of International Law* 87, 1993.
Slaughter, Anne-Marie. 'A Liberal Theory of International Law'. In: American Society of International Law (Coord.). Proceedings of the Annual Meeting 94, 2000.
Smend, Rudolf. 'Die Vereinigung der Staatsrechtslehrer und der Richtungsstreit'. In: H. Ehmke et al. (Coord.). *Festschrift für Ulrich Scheuner zum. 70. Geburtstag*. Berlin: Duncker & Humblot, 1973.
Sohn, Werner. 'Bio-Macht und Normalisierungsgesellschaft. Versuch einer Annäherung'. In: Sohn, Werner.H. Mehrtens (Coord.). *Normalität und Abweichung: Studien zur Theorie und Geschichte der Normalisierungsgesellschaft*. Opladen/Wiesbaden: Westdt. Verlag, 1999.
Spaemann, Robert. 'Niklas Luhmann als Herausforderung der Philosophie – Laudatio'. In: N. Luhmann, *Paradigm lost. Über die ethische Reflexion der Moral – Rede anlässlich der Verleihung des Hegel-Preises 1989*. Frankfurt am Main: Suhrkamp, 1990.
Spiekermann, Uwe. *Warenhaussteuer in Deutschland, Mittelstandbewegung, Kapitalismus und Rechtsstaat im späten Kaiserreich*. Frankfurt am Main: Lang, 1994.
Spiekermann, Uwe. Basis der Konsumgesellschaft. *Entstehung und Entwicklung des modernen Kleinhandels in Deutschland 1850 bis 1914*. München: Beck, 1999.
Spiekermann, Uwe. Kommentierung in: Spiekermann/Schmitz et al. (Coord.). *Telemediengesetz mit Netzwerkdurchset-zungsgesetz*. 2nd Ed. München: Beck, 2018.
Stäheli, Urs. 'Der Takt der Börse. Inklusionseffekte von Verbreitungsmedien am Beispiel des Börsen-Tickers'. In: *Zeitschrift für Soziologie* 33/3, 2004.
Stalder, Felix. *Kultur der Digitalität*. Berlin: Suhrkamp, 2016.
Starck, Christian. *Das ZDF-Gremien-Urteil des Bundesverfassungsgerichts und seine gesetzliche und staatsvertragliche Umsetzung*. In: JZ, 2014.
Steiger, Heinhard. 'Art. Völkerrecht'. In: J. Ritter; K. Gründer et al. (Coord.). *Historisches Wörterbuch der Philosophie*, Bd. 11. Basel: Schwabe, 2003.
Steinhauer, Fabian. Vom Scheiden. *Geschichte und Theorie einer juristischen Kulturtechnik*. Berlin: Duncker & Humblot, 2015.

182 Bibliography

Steinhauer, Fabian. *Medienverfassung. Untersuchung zur Verfassungswissenschaft nach 1990*, Habilitationsmanuskript. Frankfurt am Main, 2015.
Snyder, Timothy. *Black Earth. The Holocaust as History and Warning*. New York: Tim Duggan Books, 2015.
Stengel, Oliver; Van Looy, Alexander; Wallaschkowki, Stephan (Coord.). *Digitalzeitalter – Digitalgesellschaft. Das Ende des Industriezeitalters und der Beginn einer neuen Epoche*. Wiesbaden: Springer VS, 2017.
Sterne, Jonathan. *The Audible Past. Cultural Origins of Sound Reproduction*. Durham/London: Duke University Press, 2003.
Stichweh, Rudolf. *Die Weltgesellschaft*. Frankfurt am Main: Suhrkamp, 2000.
Stichweh, Rudolf. 'Politik und Weltgesellschaft'. In: K.-U. Hellmann; R. Schmalz-Bruns (Coord.). *Theorie der Politik. Niklas Luhmanns politische Soziologie*. Frankfurt am Main: Suhrkamp, 2002.
Stichweh, Rudolf. *Der Zusammenhalt der Weltgesellschaft. Nicht-normative Integrationstheorien in der Soziologie*. Unveröffentl. Arbeitspapier, Luzern, 2004.
Stichweh, Rudolf. 'Kulturelle Produktion in der Weltgesellschaft'. In: K. Kruškova; N. Lipp (Coord.). *Tanz anderswo: intra- und unterkulturell, Jahrbuch Tanzforschung*, Bd. 14. Münster: LIT, 2004.
Stichweh, Rudolf. 'Kontrolle und Organisation des Raumes durch die Funktions-systeme der Weltgesellschaft'. In: J. Döring; T. Thielmann (Coord.). *Spatial Turn. Das Raumparadigma in den Kultur- und Sozialwissenschaften*. Bielefeld: transcript, 2008.
Stolleis, Michael. *Der lange Abschied vom 19. Jahrhundert. Die Zäsur von 1914 aus rechtshistorischer Perspektive; Vortrag gehalten vor der Juristischen Gesellschaft zu Berlin am 22*. Berlin/New York: De Gruyter, 1997.
Stolleis, Michael. *Nationalität und Internationalität: Rechtsvergleichung im öffentlichen Recht des 19*. Jahrhunderts. Stuttgart: Steiner, 1998.
Stolleis, Michael. *Geschichte des öffentlichen Rechts in Deutschland, Bd. 3 – Staats- und Verwaltungsrechtswissenschaft in Republik und Diktatur*. München: C.H. Beck, 1999.
Stolleis, Michael. 'Vormodernes und postmodernes Recht'. In: *Merkur* 5, 2008.
Stolleis, Michael. 'Die Legitimation von Recht und Gesetz durch Gott, Tradition, Wille, Natur, Vernunft und Verfassung'. In: M. Avenarius; R. Meyer-Pritzl; C. Möller (Coord.). *Ars Juris. Festschrift für Okko Behrends zum 70. Geburtstag*. Göttingen: Wallstein, 2009.
Study Group of The Int'l Law Comm'n f. b. (Apr. 13, 2006).
Rep. on the Fragmentation of International Law: Difficulties Arising from the Diversification and Expansion of International Law. U.N. Doc. A/CN/.4/L.682.
Sundararajan, Arun. *The Sharing Economy: The End of Employment and the Rise of Crowd-Based Capitalism*. Cambridge: MIT Press, 2016.
Sunstein, Cass R. *#Republic. Divided Democracy in the Age of Social Media*. Oxford. Princeton: Princeton University Press, 2018.
Teubner, Gunther. 'Unternehmenskorporatismus. New Industrial Policy und das "Wesen" der Juristischen Person'. In: KritV 3, 1987.
Teubner, Gunther. 'Die zwei Gesichter des Janus. Rechtspluralismus in der Spätmoderne'. In: E. Schmidt (Coord.). *Liber amicorum Josef Esser zum 85. Geburtstag*. Heidelberg: Müller, 1995.
Teubner, Gunther. 'Des Königs viele Leiber'. In: *Soziale Systeme* 2, 1996.
Teubner, Gunther. 'Globale Bukowina. Zur Emergenz eines transnationalen Rechtspluralismus'. In: *Rechtshistorisches Journal* 15, 1996.
Teubner, Gunther. 'The King's Many Bodies: The Self-Deconstruction of Law's Hierarchy'. In: *Law & Society Review*, vol. 31/4, 1997.
Teubner, Gunther. (Coord.). *Die Rückgabe des zwölften Kamels. Niklas Luhmann in der Diskussion über Gerechtigkeit*. Stuttgart: Lucius & Lucius, 2000.
Teubner, Gunther. 'Privatregimes. Neo-Spontanes Recht und duale Sozialverfassungen in der Weltgesellschaft?' In: D. Simon; M. Weiss. *Zur Autonomie des Individuums. Liber Amicorum Spiros Simitis*. Baden-Baden: Nomos, 2000.

Teubner, Gunther. 'Globale Zivilverfassungen. Alternativen zur staatszentrierten Verfassungstheorie'. In: ZaöRV 63, 2003.
Teubner, Gunther. *Netzwerk als Vertragsverbund: Virtuelle Unternehmen, Franchising, Just-in-time in sozialwissenschaftlicher und juristischer Sicht*. Baden-Baden: Nomos, 2004.
Teubner, Gunther. 'Der Wahnsinn der Rechtsenzyklopädien'. In: ARSP 91/4, 2005.
Teubner, Gunther. 'Dreiers Luhmann'. In: R. Alexy (Coord.). *Integratives Verstehen. Zur Rechtsphilosophie Ralf Dreiers*. Tübingen: Mohr Siebeck, 2005.
Teubner, Gunther. 'Codes of Conduct multinationaler Unternehmen: Unternehmensverfassung jenseits von Corporate Governance und gesetzlicher Mitbestimmung'. In: Höland, A. (Coord.). Arbeitneh*mermitwirkung in einer sich globalisierenden Arbeitswelt: Liber Amicorum Manfred Weiss*. Berlin: Berliner Wiss.-Verlag, 2005.
Teubner, Gunther. 'Fragmented Foundations'. In: P. Dobner; M. Loughlin (Coord.). The *Twilight of Constitutionalism?* Oxford: Oxford University Press, 2010.
Teubner, Gunther. 'Das Projekt der Verfassungssoziologie. Irritationen des nationalstaatlichen Konstitutionalismus'. In: *Zeitschrift für Rechtssoziologie* 32, 2011.
Teubner, Gunther. *Verfassungsfragmente. Gesellschaftlicher Konstitutionalismus in der Globalisierung*. Frankfurt am Main: Suhrkamp, 2012.
Teubner, Gunther. 'Exogene Selbstbindung: Wie gesellschaftliche Teilsysteme ihre Gründungsparadoxien externalisieren'. In: *Zeitschrift für Rechtssoziologie* 35, 2015.
Teubner, Gunther. 'Transnationaler Verfassungspluralismus. Neun Variationen über ein Thema von David Sciulli'. In: ZaöRV 76, 2016.
Teubner, Gunther. *Digitale Rechtssubjekte? Zum privatrechtlichen Status autonomer Softwareagenten*. Archiv für Civilistische Praxis – AcP 2018.
Teubner, Gunther. 'Zum transsubjektiven Potential subjektiver Rechte. Gegenrechte in ihrer kommunikativen, kollektiven und institutionellen Dimension'. In: H. Franzki; J. Horst/A. Fischer-Lescano (Coord.). *Gegenrechte: Recht jenseits des Subjekts*. Tübingen: Mohr Siebeck, 2018.
Teubner, Gunther; Fischer-Lescano, Andreas. 'Fragmentierung des Weltrechts: Vernetzung globaler Regimes statt statischer Rechtseinheit'. In: M. Albert; R. Stichweh (Coord.). *Weltstaat und Weltstaatlichkeit: Beobachtungen globaler politischer Strukturbildung*. Wiesbaden: Verlag für Sozialwissenschaft, 2007.
Tholen, Georg Christoph. *Die Zäsur der Medien. Kulturphilosophische Konturen*. Frankfurt am Main: Suhrkamp, 2002.
Thomas, Keith. 'The Meaning of Literacy in Early Modern England'. In: G. Baumann (Coord.). *The Written Word. Literacy in Transition*. Oxford: Clarendon, 1986.
Thomas, Yan. 'Droit'. In: André Burguière (Coord.). *Dictionnaire des sciences historiques*. Paris: Verlag, 1986.
Thomas, Yan. *Les opérations du Droit*. Paris: Le Seuil, 2011.
Thompson, Edward. P. Time, Work-Discipline, and Industrial Capitalism. *Past & Present* 38, 1967.
Thornhill, Chris, State Building. 'Constitutional Rights and Social Construction of Norms. Outline for a Sociology of Constitutions'. In: M. R. Madsen; G. Verschraegen (Coord.). *Making Human Rights Intelligible. Towards a Sociology of Human Rights*. Oxford/Portland Oregon: Hart Publishing, 2013.
Tietje, Christian. *Internationalisiertes Verwaltungshandeln*. Berlin: Duncker & Humblot, 2001.
Touraine, Alain. *Die postindustrielle Gesellschaft*. Frankfurt am Main: Suhrkamp, 1972.
Trentmann, Frank. *Free Trade Nation. Commerce, Consumption and Civil Society in Modern Britain*. Oxford: Oxford University Press, 2018.
Trentmann, Frank. *The Empire of Things. How We Became a World of Consumers, from the Fifteenth Century to the Twenty-First*. London: Allen Lane, 2016.
Trentmann, Frank. 'Materiality in the Future of History: Things, Practices, and Politics'. In: *Journal of British Studies* 48/2, 2009.
Tuck, Richard. 'The Civil Religion of Thomas Hobbes'. In: N. Phillipson; Q. Spinner (Coord.). *Political Discourse in Early Modern Britain*. Cambridge: Cambridge University Press, 1993.

Tuck, Richard. *The Rights of War and Peace. Political Thought and the International Order from Grotius to Kant*. Oxford: Oxford University Press, 1999.

Tushnet, Rebecca. Power without Responsibility: Intermediaries and the First Amendment. *George Washington Law Review* 76, 2008.

Twining, William L. *General Jurisprudence. Understanding Law From A Global Perspective*. Cambridge: Cambridge University Press, 2009.

Van Dijck, José. *The Culture of Connectivity. A Critical History of Social Media*. Oxford: Oxford University Press, 2013.

Vec, Miloš. 'Verrechtlichung internationaler Streitbeilegung im 19. Und 20. Jahrhundert? Beobachtungen und Fragen zu den Strukturen völkerrechtlicher Konfliktaustragung'. In: Serge Dauchy; Vec, Miloš. (Coord.). *Les conflits entre peuples. De la résolution libre à la résolution imposée*. Baden-Baden: Nomos, 2011.

Vec, Miloš. 'Kurze Geschichte des Technikrechts'. In: M. Schulte; R. Schröder (Coord.). *Handbuch des Technikrechts. Allgemeine Grundlagen Umweltrecht – Gentechnikrecht – Energierecht Telekommunikations- und Medienrecht Patentrecht – Computerrecht*. Heidelberg: Springer, 2nd Ed., 2011.

Vec, Miloš. *Recht und Normierung in der Industriellen Revolution. Neue Strukturen der Normsetzung in Völkerrecht, staatlicher Gesetzgebung und gesellschaftlicher Selbstnormierung (Studien zur europäischen Rechtsgeschichte 200; Recht in der Industriellen Revolution I*. Frankfurt am Main: Klostermann, 2006.

Vec, Miloš. 'Weltverträge für Weltliteratur. Das Geistige Eigentum im System der rechtsetzenden Konventionen des 19. Jahrhunderts'. In: L. Pahlow; J. Eisfeld (Coord.). *Grundlagen und Grundfragen des Geistigen Eigentums*. Tübingen: Mohr Siebeck, 2008.

Vec, Miloš. 'Sources in the 19th Century European Tradition: The Myth of Positivism'. In: pp. Besson/J. d'Aspremont (Coord.). *The Sources of International Law*. Oxford: Oxford University Press, 2017.

Verdross, Alfred. *Die Einheit des rechtlichen Weltbildes auf Grundlage der Völkerrechtsverfassung*. Tübingen: Mohr, 1923.

Verdross, Alfred; Simma, Bruno. *Universelles Völkerrecht. Theorie und Praxis*. Berlin: Duncker & Humblot, 1984.

Verzijl, Jan H. 'International Persons'. In: Verzijl, Jan H. *International Law in a Historical Perspective*, vol 2. Leyden: A.W. Sijthoff, 1969.

Vesting, Thomas. 'Die Staatsrechtslehre und die Veränderung ihres Gegenstandes: Konsequenzen von Europäisierung und Internationalisierung'. In: VVDStRL 63, 2004.

Vesting, Thomas. 'Die innere Seite des Gesetzes. Symbolische Ordnung, Rechtssubjektivität und Umgang mit Ungewissheit'. In: I. Augsberg (Coord.). *Ungewissheit als Chance. Perspektiven eines produktiven Umgangs mit Unsicherheit im Rechtssystem*. Tübingen: Mohr Siebeck, 2009.

Vesting, Thomas. *Die Medien des Rechts*, Bd. 1: Sprache. Weilerswist: Velbrück, 2011.

Vesting, Thomas. *Die Medien des Rechts*. Bd. 3: Buchdruck. Weilerswist: Velbrück, 2013.

Vesting, Thomas. Die Medien des Rechts. Bd. 4: *Computernetzwerke*. Weilerswist: Velbrück, 2015.

Vesting, Thomas. 'Eine Versetzung des Objektiven in die Subjektivität. Ein Beitrag zu Recht und Literatur'. In: I. Mülder-Bach; J. Kersten (Coord.). *Prosa Schreiben. Literatur – Geschichte – Recht*. Paderborn: Wilhelm Fink, 2019.

Vesting, Thomas. *Rechtstheorie. Ein Studienbuch*. 2nd Ed. München: C.H. Beck, 2015.

Vesting, Thomas. *Staatstheorie. Ein Studienbuch*. München: C.H. Beck, 2018.

Vesting, Thomas. 'Einbau von Zeit. Rechtsnormativität im relationalen Vertrag'. In: KJ Kritische Justiz 52, 2019.

Vesting, Thomas. 'Die Rundfunkfreiheit und die neue Logik der "Content-Curation" in elektronischen Netzwerken'. In: JZ, 2020.

Vesting, Thomas. *Gentleman, Manager, Homo Digitalis. Der Wandel der Rechtssubjektivität in der Moderne*. Weilerswist: Velbrück, 2021.

Vesting, T Campos, R. *Content Curation Medienregulierung für das 21. Jahrhundert.* KritV, 2022 (no prelo).
Viellechner, Lars. *Transnationalisierung des Rechts.* Weilerswist: Velbrück, 2013.
Vismann, Cornelia. *Akten: Medientechnik und Recht.* Frankfurt am Main: Fischer, 2010.
Vismann, Cornelia. *Das Recht und seine Mittel. Ausgewählte Schriften.* Frankfurt am Main: Fischer, 2012.
Vogel, Klaus. *Der räumliche Anwendungsbereich der Verwaltungsrechtsnorm. Eine Untersuchung über die Grundfragen des sog. Internationalen Verwaltungs- und Steuerrechts.* Frankfurt am Main: Metzner, 1965.
Vogel, Klaus. 'Art. Administrative Law, International Aspects'. In: R. Bernhardt (Coord.). *Encyclopedia of Public International Law*, Bd. 9. Amsterdam: North Holland, 1992.
Vogl, Joseph (Coord.). *Poetologien des Wissens um 1800.* München: Fink, 1999.
Vogl, Joseph. *Der Souveränitätseffekt.* Zürich: Diaphanes, 2015.
Voßkuhle, Andreas; Schemmel, Jacob. 'Der Staatsrechtslehrer Konrad Hesse als Richter des Bundesverfassungsgerichts'. In: *Archiv des öffentlichen Rechts* (AöR), 144/3, 2019.
Van Dülmen, Richard. *Die Gesellschaft der Aufklärer.* Frankfurt am Main: 1986.
Vom Feld, Ina. *Kontrollierte Staatsentlastung im Technikrecht. Dampfkesselgesetzgebung und Dampfkesselüberwachung in Preußen 1831–1914.* Frankfurt am Main: Klostermann, 2007.
Von Bogdandy, Armin; Venzke, Ingo. *In wessen Namen? Internationale Gerichte in Zeiten globalen Regierens.* Berlin: Suhrkamp, 2014.
Von Pentz. Vera. 'Ausgewählte Fragen des Medien- und Persönlichkeitsrechts im Lichte der aktuellen Rechtsprechung des VI. Zivilsenats'. In: AFP, 2014.
Wadle, Elmar. 'Der langsame Abschied vom Privileg: Das Beispiel des Urheberrechts'. In: B. Dölemeyer; H. Mohnhaupt (Coord.). *Das Privileg im europäischen Vergleich.* Frankfurt am Main: Klostermann, 1997.
Wahl, Rainer. 'Verfassungsdenken jenseits des Staates'. In: I. Appel/G. Hermes (Coord.). *Mensch – Staat – Umwelt.* Berlin: Duncker & Humblot, 2008.
Wahrman, Dror. *The Making of the Modern Self. Identity and Culture in Eighteenth-Century England.* New Haven (Conn.): Yale University Press, 2006.
Wald, Andreas; Dorothea, Jansen. 'Netzwerke'. In: A. Benz et al. (Coord.). *Handbuch Governance. Theoretische Grundlage und empirische Forschungsfelder.* Wiesbaden: VS Verlag f. Sozialwissenschaften, 2007.
Wallerstein, Immanuel. 'Gesellschaftliche Entwicklung oder Entwicklung des Weltsystems?' In: B. Lutz (Coord.). *Soziologie und gesellschaftliche Entwicklung. Verhandlungen des 22. Deutschen Soziologentages in Dortmund.* Frankfurt am Main/New York: Campus, 1984.
Weber, Albrecht. *Geschichte der internationalen Wirtschaftsorganisationen.* Wiesbaden: Steiner, 1983.
Weber, Max. *Wirtschaft und Gesellschaft. Grundriß der verstehenden Soziologie* (1921). 5th Ed. Tübingen: Mohr, 1972.
Weigel, Sigrid. *Walter Benjamin. Die Kreatur, das Heilige, die Bilder.* Frankfurt am Main: Fischer, 2008.
Wenzlhuemer, Roland. *The History of Standardization in Europe.* Europäische Geschichte online. Von: The History of Standardization in Europe, accessed on 12.03.2010.
Wieacker, Franz. *Privatrechtsgeschichte der Neuzeit.* 2nd Ed. Göttingen: Vandenhoeck & Ruprecht, 1996.
Wielsch, Dan. *Zugangsregeln.* Tübingen: Mohr Siebeck, 2008.
Wielsch, Dan. 'Verantwortung von digitalen Intermediären für Rechtsverletzungen Dritter'. In: *Zeitschrift für Geistiges Eigentum* 10, 2018.
Wielsch, Dan. 'Die Ordnung der Netzwerke. AGB – Code – Community Standards'. In: Martin Eifert; Tobias Gostomzyk (Coord.). *Netzwerkrecht. Die Zukunft des NetzDG und seine Folgen für die Netzwerkkommunikation.* Baden-Baden: Nomos, 2018.

Wiethölter, Rudolf. 'Begriffsoder Interessenjurisprudenz – falsche Fronten im IPR und Wirtschaftsverfassungsrecht'. In: P. Zumbansen;M. Amstutz (Coord.). *Recht in Recht-Fertigungen. Ausgewählte Schriften Rudolf Wiethölters*. Berlin: Berliner Wissenschaftsverlag, 2013.
Willke, Helmut. *Studien zur utopischen Gesellschaft*. Frankfurt am Main: Verlag, 2001.
Willke, Helmut. *Global Governance*. Bielefeld: transcript, 2006.
Wolfrum, Edgar; Arendes, Cord. *Globale Geschichte des 20. Jahrhunderts*. Stuttgart: Kohlhammer, 2007.
Wu, Tim. 'Is the First Amendment Obsolete?' In: *Michigan Law Review* 117, 2018.
Yates, David. *Turing's Legacy: A History of Computing at the National Physical Laboratory 1945–1995*. London, 1997.
Ziegler, Karl-Heinz. 'Die Bedeutung des Westfälischen Friedens von 1648 für das europäische Völkerrecht'. In: *Archiv des Völkerrechts* 37/2, 1999.
Zuboff, Shoshana. *The Age of Surveillance Capitalism*. London: Profile Books Ltd., 2019.
Zürn, Michael. *Gerechte Internationale Regime: Bedingungen und Restriktionen der Entstehung nichthegemonialer internationaler Regime, untersucht am Beispiel der Weltkommunikationsordnung*. Frankfurt am Main: Haag und Herchen, 1987.
Zürn, Michael. 'Zu den Merkmalen postnationaler Politik'. In: M. Jachtenfuchs; M. Knodt. Regieren in internationalen Institutionen. Opladen: Leske + Budrich, 2002.
Zürn, Michael. 'Global Governance'. In: Gunnar Schuppert (Coord.). *Governance-Forschung. Vergewisserung über den Stand und Entwicklungslinien*. Baden-Baden: Nomos, 2006.
Zürn, Michael; Leibfried, Stephan. 'Reconfiguring the National Constellation'. In: *European Review*, vol. 13, 2005.

Index

algorithmisation, xxiii, 82–83
allocation of social goods, 69
anomaly thesis, 8, 9–10, 13, 16, 18, 28, 29, 34, 37–38, 40, 46, 91, 103–4
   see also Luhmann, Niklas; Teubner, Gunther
Arendt, Hannah, 42
Aristotelian tradition:
   collective formation, 112n52
   natural law, 121n168
   semantics of time, 30
artificial intelligence, xxiii, 82–83, 84
   social order, impact on, 84, 93
authors' rights, 73–74
   copyright compared, 78–81
   cross-border recognition, 78–81

Bayly, Chris, xix
   birth of modernity, 43, 47, 59, 60–61, 64, 138n420–421
Bello, Andrés, 134n362
Bentham, Jeremy, 57, 134n362
big data, xxiii, 82–83
Blumenberg, Hans, 100
   epochal thresholds, 85, 89, 91, 148n572
boundaries:
   boundary hygiene, 39, 40, 86
   communication media, effect of, 15, 17–18, 25, 51
   disciplinary boundaries, 4
   dissolution of boundaries, 34
   functional boundaries, primacy of, 12–13
   ius publicum europaeum, 55–56
   network research, 86–87
   power dynamics, 45–46, 47
   social differentiations, 37–38
   spatial boundaries, 11–12
   systems theory, 11–12
      economy of the boundary, 12–13, 40
   territorial boundaries, 12, 15
   unity crisis and social fragmentation, 86–87
bourgeois society, 121n179
   emergence of, xxi, 63
   industrial development, relationship with, 66–68

   Daseinsvorsorge, 68–69
   Zollverein, 63, 137n407–408
   mass culture and crisis of bourgeois consciousness, 95–96
   political romanticism, 52, 53
   public sphere, 95

centralisation, 65
   centralisation of the concrete order, 54, 62
   legal normativity, relationship with, 87
   political romanticism, 51
cognitive dimension of society, 65–66, 84–85, 117n119
collective dimension of communication, 94, 155n665
   Communications Decency Act, 100–1
   platform society, 97, 105–6
   public sphere, 97, 98
   society of organisations, 96, 97
   transnational regulation, 101–2
collective will, 1
common law:
   English soil versus other, 44
communication and order-forming, 5–6, 15–16, 25–26
   culture of correspondence, 66–71
Communications Decency Act s.230 (USA), 98–99
   collective dimension of communication, 100–1
   prevailing legal accountability structures, 99–100
conditional programmes, 23–24, 37–38, 104, 105, 158n704, 159n708
consumer, persona of, 61, 135n370
consumer protection, 40–41
content moderation, 100
contract, 13
   global law, 115n93
   international law, 76–77
   network theory, 87–88
   non-Eurocentric contractual relations, 50
   political obligation as, 30–32, 102–3
   relational contracts, 87–88, 149n584

semantics of time, 30
social trust, collapse of, 121n170, 136n392
copyright, xxii–xxiii
  authors' rights compared, 78–81, 78–79
  state-centred to organisation-centred global society, transition from, 71–72
  technology, 72–74
    recording media, 74–75
  transnational juridification, 78–81
correlationism, xviii–xix, 26–28, 38, 56
cross-border effects of law, 3–4, 37, 71, 77, 78–81, 100, 124n230, 145n529
cultural goods:
  juridification of cultural goods, xxii, 72–74, 75, 78–79
cultural property, protection of, 78
culture of digitality:
  experience versus expectation, xi–xii
    cognitive and normative expectation, 84

Dasein concept, 34–35
  possibilities of shaping and reshaping *Dasein*, 68–69
Daseinsvorsorge concept, 68–69, 141n455
datafication, 89
  knowledge compared, 93
decentralised dynamics of contacts, xxi, 31–32
decentralised self-organisation, 31–32
decision-making systems, 4, 37, 76, 107–8, 128n285, 139n441, 140n453
decolonisation:
  ius publicum europaeum, 43–44
degradation:
  essence of law, 4–5
  spiritual, 2–3
  Teubner's systems theory, 18
determinism of law, 1–3
  dispersion of sovereignty, 62–63
  economic colonisation of law, 97
digital platforms:
  authoritarian versus libertarian regulation, 89–90
  cognitive mechanisms of rapid adaptation and learning, 84–85
  culture of digitality
    cognitive and normative expectation, 84
    experience versus expectation, 84
  knowledge-generation structures, 82–83
  law and time, relationship between, 108
  media and law, 83–84, 85
  organisation-based social order compared, 82–85

platform society, 88–89, 90–91
  law and the future, relationship between, 108
  new platform society, 91, 93–95
platformisation of the Internet, 88–89, 90, 97
political economy, 91–93
public and private interests, conflict between, 90–91
semantics, 90
structuring of transnational public sphere, 100–1
typology, 90
uninfluenceability of simultaneous events, 82, 84
disintegration of old legal order, *see* fragmentation; law and politics, relationship between
dispersion of global society, 56–57, 84
dispersion of legal normativity, 5–6
dispersion of sovereignty, xx–xxi, 54, 56–57, 58, 60–61, 62–63, 92, 134n365
division of labour, 69
dominance of the political, 6
  dominance of the relational, relationship with, xx–xxi, 50, 54, 55–56, 57, 60–61, 64
  Schmitt, 42–44
  trust, 60–61
dominance of the relational:
  dominance of the political, relationship with, xx–xxi, 50, 54, 55–56, 57, 60–61, 64
  new legal order, 50, 55–56, 57, 60–61, 64
Dworkin, Ronald, 35

epochal thresholds, 83–84, 85–89, 148n572
equal treatment, 80
Eurocentricism, 48, 54
  Eurocentric concept of culture, 44, 45, 50
  nomos, 54
  non-Eurocentric contractual relations, 50
European sovereign countries, 43–44, 50
exclusionary inclusion, 44, 114n80
experience versus expectation, 32–33
  cognitive and normative expectation, 36–37, 84
  culture of digitality, 84
  time-binding, relationship with, 35–37
  uninfluenceability of simultaneous events, 84
existential unease, xv, 2–3

Forsthoff, Ernst, 140n443, 140n445
  Dasein concept, 68–69
  Daseinsvorsorge concept, 68–69, 141n455
  'effective' and 'dominated' space, 140n454
  normalisation and standardisation, 70
  Schmitt, correspondence with, xxi, 66–67
    allocation of social goods, 69
    Daseinsvorsorge concept, 68–69
    governmentality, 69
    partisan and industrial society, relationship between, xxi–xxii, 67–68
    society of organisations, rise of, 68
    technology, 68–69
Foucault, Michel:
  governamentality, xxi, 69–70
  political-power, xxi
  possibilities of shaping and reshaping Dasein, 69–70
  society of organisations, 69–70
    generation of knowledge, 70
    normalisation and standardisation, 70–71
  space and time, 33
fragmentation of global society:
  dispersion of global society compared, 56–57
  international law, 56
  ius publicum europaeum, 47–50
  unity crisis and social fragmentation, 86–87
functional differentiation, 37–38, 39, 115n92
  Luhmann, 8–10, 12–13, 15–16, 83–84, 86–87, 110n26, 112n67–n69, 114n80, 122n194
  Teubner, xviii–xix, 17, 19, 25–26, 27, 119n146, 120n154–n55

German Zollverein, 63, 137n407–409, 138n414
Goethe, Johann Wolfgang von, 66
governmentality, xxi, 69
Großraum doctrine, 67

Habermas, Jürgen, xvi–xvii
  communicative action, 26–27, 95, 120n152
  correlations, 26–27
  functional differentiation, 15
  justification of law, 20–21, 22
  public sphere, xxiv, 95, 153n645–646
  social dimension and temporal dimension compared, 35, 122n186
  society of individuals, xxiv, 95
Hart, HLA, 2
  secondary rules, 20

Hegel, Georg Wilhelm Friedrich, 2, 26, 40
  absolute subjectivity, 51
  aesthetics and romantic art, 51, 131n324
  bourgeois society, 121n179
  nature and freedom distinguished, 30
  political economy, 62
  semantics of time, 30
Heidegger, Martin:
  temporalised normativity of law, 105
Heller, Hermann, 41–42
Hobbes, Thomas, 137n406
  sovereignty, 62, 125n241
  semantics of time, 30
  trust and social contract, 136n392
Hume, David:
  political economy, 62
Husserl, Gerhart, 34
hybrid legal concepts, xxiii, xxv, 23–24, 106
hybridisation of global society, xi, xvi, xix, 4, 38–39, 46, 87, 104

inclusion through exclusion, 44, 114n80
intellectual property rights, 72–74, 78–81, 100, 142n489
international law:
  development of, 57–58
  fragmentation of international law, 56
  juridification of international relations, 76
  legal personality of states, 58–60
  natural law, relationship with, 57
  scientification and professionalisation, 57
  treaty law, 57–58
    bilateral/multilateral agreements compared, 76–77
    interstate international law treaties compared, 76–77
interventionalism as moral war, 42
ius and virtus, relationship between, 60, 136n385
ius gentium, 61, 136n393
ius publicum europaeum, 5–6
  decolonisation, 43–44, 47–48
    reconstruction of cultural dimension of global relations, 48–49
  demise, 49–50
  disintegration, 6, 47–50
    emerging global society, 50–54
    political romanticism, relationship with, 50–54
  dispersion of sovereignty, relationship with, 60–61, 62–63, 134n360, 135n365

Eurocentrism, 44, 48, 50, 54
  Eurocentric concept of culture, 45
  Europe versus other, 44
  fragmentation, 47–50
  land-grabbing, 44–45, 54
  modern liberal rights, relationship with, 44
  nomos and concrete order, 48–49
  power and language, 45–46

Jellinek, George, xx, 41, 145n533
  statehood, 41–42
Jessup, Philip C:
  transnational law, 13, 40–41, 111n50, 124n230
juridification of international relations, 57–58, 76, 79–81
just war concept:
  "humanitarian wars" as just wars, 42

Kellogg Pact, 49
Kelsen, Hans, xvi–xvii, xx
  connectivity of norms, 35
  justification of law, 20–21
  statehood, 41–42, 125n245
knowledge-generation structures, 4–5
  culture of digitality, 84, 93
  datafication compared, 93
  digital economy, 82–83, 93
Koselleck, Reinhart:
  experience and expectation, 32–33, 108
  saddle time (*Sattelzeit*) theory, 29, 83–84
  semantics of time, 83–84, 108, 120n162
Koskenniemi, Martti, 43, 49
  fragmentation of international law, 19, 56, 77
  ius publicum europaeum, 47–50
  legal realism, 43

land-grabbing and giving names, 44–45
language of world society law, 44–47
  power and language, 45–46
law and politics, relationship between, 6, 37, 47–50
  emerging global society, 50–54
  Eurocentric concept of culture, 44, 45, 50
  ius publicum europaeum, 5–6, 42–44
  language of world society law, 44–47
    power and language, 45–46
  legal pluralism, 40–41
  linguistic dimension of the law of global society, 44–47
    power and language, 45–46

nomos and concrete order, relationship between, 48–49
  political romanticism, relationship with, 50–54
  state theory, 40–42
  statehood concept, 41–42
  transnational law concept, 40–41
law as social time binding, 34–38
law and technology, 5, 65–66, 68–69
  copyright, 72–74
    recording media, 74–75
  Daseinsvorsorge concept, 68–69
  intellectual property rights, 72–74
    existing law, challenges to, 74–75
  new technologies and cross-border effects, 3–4
  reproduction techniques, 72–73, 74–75
  semantics of law
    time from perspective of law, 105–6
  sovereignty, relationship with, 66
  technological innovations and social relations, 72
  see also digital platforms; technology
law as society, 2
law enforcement, xvii–xviii, 104
League of Nations, 49, 71, 130n305
legal normativity, 6–7
  legal fictions, xxi, 46, 59–60, 107
    Roman law, 60–61, 136n390
  legal normativity in global society, 65
  nation-state legislation, 71–72, 74–75
  organisational management of, 75
    bilateral/multilateral agreements, 76–77
    dispute resolution, 77
    governance structures, 76
    'international administrative law', 77–78
    semantics, 77–78
    standardisation procedures, instruments and institutes, 77–78
  private law, 75–78
  temporal binding, xvi–xviii, xxv, 5, 17–18, 21–22, 34–38, 123n207
    platform society, 105–6, 108
    see also semantics of time; temporal binding
  temporalised normativity of law, 35, 105
  treaty law, 57–58
    bilateral/multilateral agreements compared, 76–77
    interstate international law treaties compared, 76–77

legal personality/personhood, 58–60, 79–80, 135n379
  Zollverein, 138n414
legal pluralism, 25, 40–41, 68, 125n237, 139n427
  Teubner, xviii, 19–20, 27, 114n86
legal realism, 43, 62
legitimacy of law, xviii, 3, 21–22, 24, 140n445
  occupation and possession, 126n257
liberal individualism, xx–xxi
liberalism, 30–31, 62, 64, 91, 121n174, 132n329
linguistic dimension of the law of global society, 44–47
  power and language, 45–46
Luhmann, Niklas:
  anomaly thesis, 8, 9–10, 13, 16, 18, 28, 29, 34, 37–38, 40, 46, 91, 103–4
  evolution of law, 2–3
  law and technology, 96–97, 103–4
  law from the perspective of time, 34, 36–38
  Luhmannian unease, 3–4, 5, 46
  mass media, 94–95
  self-evidence of a world society, 10–13
  semantics of time, *see* semantics of time
  systems theory, xvi–xix
  virtus and *ius*, 60
  world society, 10–11
    growth, 12–13
    linguistic dimension, 44–47
    national systems, relationship with, 11, 12–13
    post-colonial lens, 46–47
    spatial boundaries, 11–12
    systems theory, 13–17
  see also individual entries

malaise, *see* Luhmannian unease
materiality of intelligent technology, xix
media and law, 83–84
metamorphoses/transformation of law, xix–xxv, 1–2, 3, 38–39, 70, 92, 107–8
modern law, xvi, 1–3, 9–10, 13, 16–17, 107–8, 120n157
  anomaly thesis, 18, 34
  correlationism, 27–28
  dispersion of sovereignty, 57
  legal fiction, relationship with, 107
  political temporality, 103
  semantics of modern law, 103–5
  semantics of time, 29, 35–37
Monroe Doctrine, 49–50

natural law, 36, 121n168, 134n365
  international law, relationship with, 57
network theory, 85–89
  boundary-making, 86–87
  digital as a concept, 89
  epochal thresholds, 85–86
  heterarchical and hierarchical moments, 88–89
  plasticity, 87–88
  technical protocols, 88–89
  unity and hierarchy of law, 86–87
  web versus internet, 88
new technologies and cross-border effects, 3–4
nomos:
  concept, 48–49, 129n296–299
  concrete order, relationship with, 48–49
  law formation, 50–51
  Eurocentricism, 54
  Großraum doctrine, relationship with, 67
  land-grabbing and name, relationship with, 44
normalisation and standardisation, 70–71
normativity of law, *see* legal normativity

occasionalism, 51–52, 53–54
  causation, relationship with, 54
organisational theory:
  decentralised self-organisation, 31–32
  legal normativity, 75
    bilateral/multilateral agreements, 76–77
    dispute resolution, 77
    governance structures, 76
    'international administrative law', 77–78
    semantics, 77–78
    standardisation procedures, instruments and institutes, 77–78
  organisation-based social order, xxi, 68–70, 75, 80
    digital era, 82–85, 89
    self-organisation
    society of organisations, 69–70
    emergence, 68
    generation of knowledge, 70
    normalisation and standardisation, 70–71
orientation instability, 29, 33–34, 61

partisan and industrial society, relationship between, xxi, 66, 67–68
personification:
  legal personality of states, 58–60, 136n390
platform society, 88–89, 90–91

collective dimension of communication, 97, 105–6
law and the future, relationship between, 108
legal normativity and temporal binding, 105–6, 108
new platform society, 91, 93–95
public sphere, 7, 94
  collective dimension of communication, 97
  dissolution of law into cognitive mechanisms, 96–97
  success of, 97–99
semantics of time
  contingent future, 108
see also digital platforms
platforms, see digital platforms
platformisation of the Internet, 88–89, 90, 97, 159n714
pluralism, see legal pluralism
Pocock, John, 32–33
political economy, xxiii–xiv, 137n408
  national and international, relationship between, 62
  platforms, 91–94
  society of organisations, 93–94
  sovereignty, 62
  statehood, 62
political obligation:
  evolution of, 30–32, 102–3
political romanticism, 51–54, 131n316
positivisation of law, 25
positivism, 43, 45, 59, 87, 129n293
power and language, 45–46
public sphere:
  bourgeois society, 95
  collective dimension of communication, 97, 98
  Habermas, Jürgen, xxiv, 95, 153n645–646
  platform society, 7, 94
    collective dimension of communication, 97
    dissolution of law into cognitive mechanisms, 96–97
    structuring of transnational public sphere, 100–1
    success of, 97–99
  political romanticism, 51
  positivity of law, 16
  society of individuals, 35, 95
  society of organisations, 94–95

collective dimension of communication, 96
knowledge generation, 95–96
nation-state regulatory regime, 96
structuring of transnational public sphere
  digital platforms, 100–1

recognition of non-European states, 50
recording media, 74–75
  see also reproduction
reproduction techniques, 72–73, 74–75
Roman law, 60, 107, 136n390, 137n406
rule of code, 107
rule of law, 107, 117n117, 118n128, 140n444, 140n451

Schmitt, Carl, 5–6, 42–44
  Eurocentric concept of culture, 45
  Forsthoff, correspondence with, 66–67
  allocation of social goods, 69
  Daseinsvorsorge concept, 68–69
  governmentality, 69
  partisan and industrial society, relationship between, 67–68
  society of organisations, rise of, 68
  technology, 68–69
  nomos and concrete order, relationship between, 48–49
  political economy, 62
sectoral standardisation, 23–24, 66
secularisation, 2
  consumption, relationship with, 53–54
  disintegration of old order, 60–61
  religious power, 53
  reoccupation of art, 53
self-evidence of a world society, 10–13, 17
self-organisation, 31–32, 66, 71, 71–72, 107
self-reference of law, 3, 24, 47–48
semantics:
  ius publicum europaeum
    civilised and uncivilised peoples, 54
  semantics of law, see semantics of law
  semantics of time, see semantics of time
  social structures, relationship with, 16–17, 104–5
semantics of law:
  law as social time binding, 34–38
  law from perspective of time, 34
  semantics of time, relationship with, 34–38
  time from perspective of law, 34, 104
    digital technologies, 105–6

semantics of time:
  contingent future, 32–34
    platform society, 108
  digital era, 83
  experience and expectation, relationship between, 32–33
  law from perspective of time, 34
  past and present, 30–32
  semantics of law, relationship with, 34–38
  time from perspective of law, 34
semantics of modern law, 16–17, 104–5
social conventions, xvi, 30–31, 38
social dynamics, xx, 47, 49, 50–51, 52, 57–58, 63–64, 88, 107
social knowledge, xxiii, 1, 11, 37–39, 41, 46, 59–60, 82–83, 84, 87, 93, 94–95, 147n558
social systems theory, 11–12, 14–15, 22–25
  semantics, relationship with, 16–17
society of organisations, 69–70
  collective dimension of communication, 96, 97
  emergence, 68
  knowledge generation, 70, 95–96
  normalisation and standardisation, 70–71
  political economy, 93–94
  political economy, 93–94
  public sphere, 94–95
    collective dimension of communication, 96
    knowledge generation, 95–96
    nation-state regulatory regime, 96
  war management, beyond, 71–72
sovereignty:
  dispersion of sovereignty, 54, 56–57, 58, 60–61, 62–63, 92
  Forsthoff, 69
  Foucault, 69
  Hobbes, 62
  ius publicum europaeum, relationship with, 60–61, 62–63, 134n360, 135n365
  Koskenniemi, 77
  Machiavelli, 137n403
  obsession with sovereignty, 59
  political economy, 62
  Schmitt, 41, 125n241
    see also Schmitt, Carl
  virtue and fortune, 92
  Vogl, 137n405
spatial boundaries, 11–12

standardisation:
  normalisation and standardisation, 70–71
  nationality and internationality compared, 71
state theory, 40–42, 135n380, 136n390
  see also personification
statehood, xxiv–xxv, 50, 61, 76, 137n403
  law and politics, 41–42
  political economy, 62
systems theory and world society:
  Luhmann, 13–18
  Teubner, 18–28
  see also individual entries

technology:
  Daseinsvorsorge concept, 68–69
  intellectual property rights, 72–74
    existing law, challenges to, 74–75
  reproduction techniques, 72–73, 74–75
  technological innovations and social relations, 72
temporal binding, xvii
  law as a form of time binding, 5, 17–18, 21, 29, 105–6, 108
  social dimension, 34–38, 123n207
territoriality, 87, 110n33
  see also boundaries
Teubner, Gunther, 17–18
  degradation, 18
  functional differentiation, xviii–xix, 17, 19, 25–26, 27, 119n146, 120n154–n55
  legal pluralism, xviii, 19–20, 27, 114n86
  reinvention of systems theory, 18–28
  systems theory and world society, 18–28
  transnational constitutional pluralism, 27–28
  validity/legitimacy of law, 21–26
time-binding, *see* temporal binding
transition to modern society, 29
  coevolution of national and transnational, 62–63
transnational constitutional pluralism, 25, 27–28, 117n120, 117n122
transnational law concept, 13, 111n50, 124n230
  law and politics, 40–41
  see also cross-border effects of law; international law
treaty law, 57–58
trust in global society:
  transformation, 60–61

uninfluenceability of simultaneous events, 82, 84
United States:
    Communications Decency Act, *see* Communications Decency Act s.230
unity crisis:
    social fragmentation, relationship with, 86–87

validity of law, xvii, 20–22, 25, 35, 117n117, 127n264
Versailles Peace Treaty, 49
virtus and *ius*, relationship between, 60, 136n385
volonté générale, 1

Westphalia:
    myth of Westphalia, 43–44, 47–48
    Peace of Westphalia, xx, 126n259

will of the sovereign, 1
World Intellectual Property Organization (WIPO), 79–80
world society, xvii–xviii, xxi, 10–11
    growth, 12–13
    linguistic dimension, 44–47
    Luhmann, 13–18
    national systems, relationship with, 11, 12–13
    post-colonial lens, 46–47
    spatial boundaries, 11–12
    systems theory, 13–17
    Teubner, 18–28
    see also individual entries
World War II, 49–50, 67, 109n18, 147n557, 159n721

Zollverein, 63, 137n407–409, 138n414